GRISTHORPE MAN

A LIFE AND DEATH IN THE BRONZE AGE

Gristhorpe Man on display in the Rotunda Museum, Scarborough (William Smith Museum of Geology). Photo: Tony Bartholomew/ Scarborough Museums Trust.

GRISTHORPE MAN

A LIFE AND DEATH IN THE BRONZE AGE

edited by

Nigel D. Melton, Janet Montgomery
and Christopher J. Knüsel

OXBOW BOOKS
Oxford and Oakville

Published by
Oxbow Books, Oxford, UK

© Oxbow Books and the authors 2013

ISBN 978-1-78297-207-5

This book is available direct from

Oxbow Books, Oxford, UK
(Phone: 01865-241249; Fax: 01865-794449)

and

The David Brown Book Company
PO Box 511, Oakville, CT 06779, USA
(Phone: 860-945-9329; Fax: 860-945-9468)

or from our website
www.oxbowbooks.com

A CIP record for this book is available from the British Library

Library of Congress Cataloging-in-Publication Data

Gristhorpe man : a life and death in the Bronze age / edited by Nigel D. Melton, Janet Montgomery and Christopher J. Knüsel.
    pages cm.
    Includes bibliographical references.
    ISBN 978-1-78297-207-5
    1. Bronze age--England--Scarborough. 2. Tombs--England--Scarborough. 3. Human remains (Archaeology)--England--Scarborough. 4. Grave goods--England--Scarborough. 5. Excavations (Archaeology)--England--Scarborough. 6. Scarborough (England)--Antiquities. I. Melton, Nigel D.
    GN778.22.G7G75 2013
    936.28'47--dc23
                    2013038875

Printed in Great Britain by
Berforts Information Press, Eynsham, Oxfordshire

CONTENTS

The grave goods

CONTRIBUTORS

CATHY M. BATT
Archaeological Sciences, School of Life Sciences,
University of Bradford, Bradford,
West Yorkshire, BD7 1DP, UK.
C.M.Batt@bradford.ac.uk

MICHAEL BUCKLEY
Faculty of Life Sciences, University of Manchester,
Manchester Interdisciplinary Biocentre, 131 Princess Street,
Manchester, M1 7DN, UK.
M.Buckley@manchester.ac.uk

ESTHER CAMERON
Oxford University, Institute of Archaeology,
36, Beaumont Street, Oxford, OX1 2PG, UK.
esther.cameron@ox.ac.uk

HOWELL G. M. EDWARDS
School of Applied Sciences,
University of Bradford, Bradford,
West Yorkshire, BD7 1DP, UK.
h.g.m.edwards@bradford.ac.uk

ADRIAN A. EVANS
Archaeological Sciences, School of Life Sciences,
University of Bradford, Bradford,
West Yorkshire, BD7 1DP, UK.
A.A.Evans@bradford.ac.uk

CHRIS GAFFNEY
Archaeological Sciences, School of Life Sciences,
University of Bradford, Bradford,
West Yorkshire, BD7 1DP, UK.
C.Gaffney@bradford.ac.uk

ANDREW R. GLEDHILL
Archaeological Sciences, School of Life Sciences,
University of Bradford, Bradford,
West Yorkshire, BD7 1DP, UK.
A.R.Gledhill@bradford.ac.uk

SAMANTHA HODGSON
c/o Archaeological Sciences, School of Life Sciences,
University of Bradford, Bradford,
West Yorkshire, BD7 1DP, UK.
samjhodgson@hotmail.com

TIMOTHY HORSLEY
Department of Anthropology, Yale University, New Haven,
Connecticut, 06511, USA.
Department of Anthropology, Northern Illinois University,
DeKalb, IL, 60115, USA.
Horsley Archaeological Prospection, LLC.
timhorsley@gmail.com

ROBERT C. JANAWAY
Archaeological Sciences, School of Life Sciences,
University of Bradford, Bradford,
West Yorkshire, BD7 1DP, UK.
R.C.Janaway@bradford.ac.uk

CHRISTOPHER J. KNÜSEL
Department of Archaeology, University of Exeter, Laver
Building, North Park Road, Exeter, Devon, EX4 4QE, UK.
c.j.knusel@exeter.ac.uk

NIELS LYNNERUP
Department of Forensic Medicine, University of Copenhagen,
Frederik V's Vej 11, 2100 Kobenhavn Ø, Denmark.
nly@sund.ku.dk

NIGEL D. MELTON
Department of Archaeology, Durham University,
South Road, Durham, DH1 3LE, UK.
nigeldmelton@gmail.com

JANET MONTGOMERY
Department of Archaeology, Durham University,
South Road, Durham, DH1 3LE, UK.
janet.montgomery@durham.ac.uk

STUART NEEDHAM
Langton Fold, North Lane, South Harting,
West Sussex, GU31 5NW, UK.
s.bowman1@waitrose.com

PETER NORTHOVER
Oxford Materials Characterisation Service, Oxford University,
Begbroke Science Park, Begbroke Hill, Yarnton,
Oxford, OX5 1PF, UK.
peter.northover@materials.ox.ac

SONIA O'CONNOR
Archaeological Sciences, School of Life Sciences,
University of Bradford, Bradford,
West Yorkshire, BD7 1DP, UK.
S.OConnor@bradford.ac.uk

ALAN R. OGDEN
Archaeological Sciences, School of Life Sciences,
University of Bradford, Bradford,
West Yorkshire, BD7 1DP, UK.
A.R.Ogden@bradford.ac.uk

MICHAEL PARKER PEARSON
UCL Institute of Archaeology, 31-34, Gordon Square,
London, WC1H 0PY, UK.
m.parker-pearson@ucl.ac.uk

PETER ROWLEY-CONWY
Department of Archaeology, Durham University,
South Road, Durham, DH1 3LE, UK.
p.a.rowley-conwy@durham.ac.uk

HANNAH RUSS
Oxford Brookes Archaeology and Heritage (OBAH),
Oxford Brookes University, Headington,
Oxford, OX3 0BP, UK.
hruss@brookes.ac.uk

ARMIN SCHMIDT
Archaeological Sciences, School of Life Sciences,
University of Bradford, Bradford,
West Yorkshire, BD7 1DP, UK.
GeodataWIZ Ltd.
A.Schmidt@bradford.ac.uk

ALISON SHERIDAN
National Museums Scotland, Chambers Street,
Edinburgh, EH1 1JF, UK.
a.sheridan@nms.ac.uk

KAREN SNOWDEN
Scarborough Museums Trust, 11, The Crescent,
Scarborough, North Yorkshire, YO11 2PW, UK.
karen.snowden@smtrust.uk.com

VAUGHAN WASTLING
Stoney Garth, Newlands Road, Cloughton, Scarborough,
North Yorkshire, YO13 0AR, UK.
Freelance Archaeologist/Osteologist
vaughanwastling@hotmail.com

ANDREW S. WILSON
Archaeological Sciences, School of Life Sciences,
University of Bradford, Bradford,
West Yorkshire, BD7 1DP, UK.
A.S.Wilson2@bradford.ac.uk.

INTRODUCTION:
THE GRISTHORPE MAN PROJECT 2005–2008

Nigel D. Melton, Janet Montgomery and Christopher J. Knüsel

The original discovery at Gristhorpe

On the 10th July in 1834, William Beswick the landowner, accompanied by his friend Mr Edward Alexander F.A.S. of Halifax and a number of workmen, walked up onto the cliff-top at Gristhorpe a few miles south of Scarborough to excavate the burial mound of an ancient Briton. The barrow in question was the central and most prominent of a group of three, the other two of which had been investigated by Beswick a decade previously. Beswick had attempted to excavate the central barrow the previous year but had abandoned that attempt '*after sinking to some depth, fruitlessly*' (Williamson 1834, 5). On this occasion, though, his investigations were spectacular and he returned the following day, accompanied by a group of gentleman from the Scarborough Philosophical Society to retrieve his discovery.

What Beswick and the others recovered that day quickly became a national sensation – an intact coffin, fashioned from the hollowed-out trunk of an oak tree, which had become waterlogged in its deep grave cut into clay. It contained a perfectly preserved skeleton that had been wrapped in an animal skin and buried with a range of grave goods that included flints, a bronze dagger and its whalebone pommel, and a bark vessel containing what was thought to be food residue.

The group of friends that accompanied William Beswick included John Williamson, the first curator of the Scarborough Philosophical Society's museum (now the Rotunda Museum), which had opened in 1829, and the Society Minute Books record that William Beswick donated the finds from the barrow to the museum the following day. Great care was taken in the removal of the skeleton and, uniquely for the time, it was treated by boiling it in a thin solution of glue for about eight hours under the watchful eye of John Williamson's son, the young William

Crawford Williamson (Williamson 1896, 45). Following this novel treatment, it was articulated by local doctors William Harland and Thomas Weddell, both members of the Philosophical Society, thus ensuring that it was preserved for future generations. The Gristhorpe finds, apart from the coffin base which suffered from being initially displayed outdoors, have, except from a brief period during WWII when they were removed for safety, formed a notable attraction in the museum's display ever since.

How the Gristhorpe finds achieved national and international fame

William Crawford Williamson was just 17 years old when he published, within a few weeks of the discovery, a beautifully written and illustrated report on the skeleton, coffin and other finds (Williamson 1834). This precocious achievement was made even more remarkable by the report's scientific rigour and analysis which was advanced for its time. It was published by a local Scarborough printer and came to the attention of the eminent geologist and palaeontologist Dr William Buckland - one of the many distinguished academics attracted to Scarborough by its emerging geological wonders - during a visit in 1834. Buckland recommended the young Williamson's account to the editor of the *Literary Gazette* who published it on 18th October 1834. Williamson's account was also reproduced in the *Gentleman's Magazine,* thus ensuring its widespread dissemination and leading to heated discussions over Williamson's deductions of the date of the burial. The account of the find spread quickly and came to the attention of C. J. Thomsen at the Museum of Northern Antiquities in Copenhagen. Similar finds of log coffins were being discovered and arousing interest in Denmark around this time and Thomsen published a paper on the Gristhorpe find in 1836, including an illustration of the log coffin, and comparing it to a recent Danish find. Thomsen correctly identified it as 'Bronze Age' in his recently published 'Three Age System' – probably the first British find to be so classified (Rowley-Conwy, this volume). The Gristhorpe log coffin burial also featured prominently in William Thom's introduction to his 1849 translation of J. J. A. Worsaae's *Primeval Antiquities of Denmark*, a book which helped introduce Thomsen's 'Three Age System' into the developing discipline of archaeology in Britain. This major shift in archaeological thought continued, with the Gristhorpe find at its heart, to be a point of much argument and debate over the following decades, but that the point had been won is clearly apparent in 1872 when William Crawford Williamson, by then Professor of Natural History at Owen's College, Manchester, was persuaded to produce a revised edition of his report on the Gristhorpe discovery (Williamson 1872) in which he was able to assign the find to the Bronze Age (Rowley-Conwy, this volume).

How the Gristhorpe Man project came about

During a meeting at the Rotunda Museum in 2004 attended by Nigel Melton and Janet Montgomery, curator Karen Snowden raised the question of the possibility of storage of the Gristhorpe skeleton, coffin and grave goods in the controlled environment of the conservation laboratory in the Department of Archaeological Sciences at the University of Bradford for a period between 2006 and 2008 when the Rotunda Museum was to be closed for a National Lottery-funded refurbishment. It was subsequently agreed that this should go ahead and, furthermore, that this would present an unique opportunity for a thorough scientific re-investigation of the finds which, in terms of preservation of the skeletal material and organic grave goods, remain unparalleled in the British archaeological record. This would be the first detailed study of the assemblage since its discovery in 1834, so such a project had the potential to make a significant contribution to current understanding of Bronze Age Britain. The aim was that the results of the investigation would be incorporated into the new display of the material when the museum re-opened in spring 2008.

The aims of the 2005–2008 project

The Gristhorpe skeleton, coffin lid and grave goods were packed and transported to the University of Bradford in November 2005. It was clear that the modern scientific study of this material had the potential to add substantially to knowledge of life and death in the British Bronze Age,

and the programme of research carried out in the 2005–2008 period involved a large number of collaborators at the University of Bradford and other institutions.

The project aims were:

a) To examine the skeletal remains. Tree-trunk coffin burials are a relatively rare form of burial in Bronze Age Britain and the person buried at Gristhorpe with a range of grave goods was likely to have held a special role in society. The modern analysis of the skeleton was to include an examination of its skeletal morphology and palaeopathological conditions and combine these with isotopic analyses of the bones and teeth in order to investigate mobility, diet, and status of the individual. One of the first objectives was to address doubts expressed by some colleagues as to the authenticity of the skeleton. Their concerns centred on the combination of its remarkable preservation, completeness, large stature, unusual dentition, and the evidence for it having been 'touched up' with a black substance (which Raman spectroscopy by Janet Ambers at the British Museum identified as Indian ink). It was clear, from Williamson's 1834 and 1872 reports and the detailed illustration of the skull in Davis and Thurnam's *Crania Britannica* published in 1865, that all are describing the skeleton that had been on display in Scarborough since 1834 but, it was argued, why and how had the novel conservation of what was described as a 'rotten' skeleton produced such outstanding results? Clearly the skeleton is in exceptional condition, could the conservation and subsequent wiring by local doctors Harland and Weddell have gone wrong, necessitating a replacement for display?

b) To examine the surviving coffin lid, including the unique 'face' carved onto one end of it, and the grave goods. The latter would be analysed by a range of scientific techniques in order to determine what they could reveal about the individual buried with them, his social position, inter-regional contacts and the burial rite, and to examine the relationship of the Gristhorpe burial with other British examples of Bronze Age monoxylous coffins.

c) To obtain an accurate date for the burial, if possible, by dendrochronological dating of the surviving coffin lid and by modern AMS radiocarbon dating of the skeleton.

d) To investigate the site of the original discovery by topographic and geophysical surveys and by excavation in order to confirm the location of the original excavation, to evaluate the state of *in situ* survival of the archaeological stratigraphy, and to investigate details of barrow construction which had not been noted in 1834.

e) To investigate the taphonomic conditions that prevailed within the coffin that had resulted in the unusual survival of both organic and inorganic materials, and to determine the effect of the conservation processes used in the 1830s on modern analytical methods.

f) To study the Gristhorpe discovery's role in developments in British archaeology over the middle decades of the 19th century, using, in particular, the reports produced by Williamson in 1834, 1836 and 1872.

g) To carry out a facial reconstruction for the revised display of the finds, thus updating what Williamson in his 1872 edition of the report of the discovery had referred to as *the reappearance of an old friend but emphatically with a new face* (he was commenting on the illustrations of the skull prepared for *Crania Britannica* (Davis and Thurnam 1865) that he had included in the 1872 edition). An animated facial reconstruction was to be prepared for use in the display of the finds when the museum re-opened in 2008.

Scientific analytical methods to be employed for achieving these aims included the use of lead, strontium, and oxygen isotope analysis of tooth enamel; carbon and nitrogen isotope analysis of dentine/bone and brain material (found and removed from the cranial vault after its discovery and retained in a glass vial with the grave inclusions); Raman spectroscopy of the 'mistletoe berries' and apparent areas of artificial blackening on the skeleton; an investigation by gas chromatography-mass spectrometry (GC-MS) of the contents of the bark container and brain material; proteomics analysis of the skeleton and animal skin; metallurgical, isotopic laser ablation multi-collector inductively coupled plasma mass spectrometry (LA-MC-ICP-MS) and x-ray fluorescence (XRF) analyses of the bronze dagger blade; scanning electron microscope (SEM) examination of artefacts including the animal hide and flint knife, and full body computerised tomography (CT) scanning and reconstruction of the cranial vault using the Mimics software package.

Project outcomes

In addition to this volume, the project findings have featured widely in the local and national press and on television in Eric Robson's 'Out of Town' and Michael Portillo's 'Great British Railway Journeys' series. They have formed the subject of papers in the international archaeological journal *Antiquity* (Melton *et al.* 2010), in the *Journal of Raman Spectroscopy* (Edwards *et al.* 2010) and in *Rapid Communications in Mass Spectrometry* (Buckley *et al.*, 2013), and in the popular archaeological magazine *Current Archaeology* (Melton and Montgomery, 2011).

'Gristhorpe Man' was the subject of the Archaeology and Anthropology Section Presidential Session at the British

Association Festival of Science held at Norwich in 2006 and of a day school, funded by the Royal Archaeological Institute, at the University of Bradford, also in 2006. The project was runner-up in the Awards for the Presentation of Heritage Research in the British Association Festival of Science held at Liverpool in 2008 and the findings were presented to members of the Royal Archaeological Institute at Burlington House, London in 2010.

It has proved a popular subject for local archaeological and historical societies and numerous presentations have been made to societies in Scarborough and elsewhere in Yorkshire. The project findings have been presented to the Yorkshire Archaeological Society in 2011 and the Architectural & Archaeological Society of Durham & Northumberland in 2012, as well as at archaeological conferences that include the British Association for Biological Anthropology and Osteoarchaeology (BABAO) in 2007 and 2009, and the 36th Annual Meeting of the Paleopathology Association in Chicago, Illinois, U.S.A. in 2009. They have also been presented in archaeology seminar series at the Universities of Bradford in 2006, Cardiff in 2009 and Bristol in 2010, and at the Bronze Age Forum at the University of Sheffield in 2008. The project has also formed part of the Scarborough Museums Trust's contributions to National Archaeology Week in 2007 and 2008, and to the CBA Festival of Archaeology weekend in 2010.

Special thanks to:

This project could not have taken place without the expertise, support and assistance of the staff and students in the Department of Archaeological Sciences at the University of Bradford. A significant aspect of the project has been the research undertaken in Masters dissertations by Vaughan Wastling, Joanne Hawkins, David Maron, and Samantha Hodgson, to all of whom we are particularly grateful.

Thanks are due to Mr D. Kaye and Mr N. Ankers, Blue Dolphin Holiday Park (Haven Holidays), for giving permission to carry out the geophysical surveys and excavation, and to the late Mrs D. Beswick for providing information from her family history research on William Beswick. The editors are indebted to staff at the Scarborough Museums Trust: David Buchanan for providing photographs of the display over the decades, Jim Middleton for suggesting references, Will Watts for assistance in the packing and transport of the skeleton and, especially, Karen Snowden for her unstinting assistance and advice. We are also grateful to Tony Bartholomew for giving permission to use his photograph of 'Gristhorpe Man' as the frontispiece for the volume.

Organisations that have provided funding for the project:

- Scarborough Museums Trust
- University of Bradford
- Royal Archaeological Institute
- Natural Environment Research Council
- British Academy
- British Association for the Advancement of Science
- The Leverhulme Trust Research Fellowship (RF/6/RFG/2008/0253)
- Arts and Humanities Research Council

The Gristhorpe Man Project: Collaborators

Project Directors: Nigel Melton (University of Bradford, Durham University) & Janet Montgomery (Durham University)

Janet Ambers (British Museum); Cathy Batt (University of Bradford); Julia Beaumont (University of Bradford); Esther Cameron (Institute of Archaeology, Oxford University); Elizabeth Carter (University of Sydney); Howell Edwards (University of Bradford); Adrian Evans (University of Bradford); Chris Gaffney (University of Bradford); Andrew Gledhill (University of Bradford); Michael Hargreaves (University of Bradford); Carl Heron (University of Bradford); Tim Horsley (Yale University; Northern Illinois University; Horsley Archaeological Prospection, LLC); Rob Janaway (University of Bradford); Christopher Knüsel (University of Exeter); Niels Lynnerup (University of Copenhagen); Stuart Needham (Independent Researcher); Peter Northover (Oxford University); Sonia O'Connor (University of Bradford); Terry O'Connor (York University); Alan Ogden (University of Bradford); Mike Parker Pearson (UCL, Institute of Archaeology); Peter Rowley-Conwy (Durham University); Hannah Russ (Oxford Brookes University); Armin Schmidt (University of Bradford; GeodataWIZ Ltd.); Alison Sheridan (National Museums Scotland); Karen Snowden (Scarborough Museums Trust); Ian Tyers (Dendrochronological Consultancy Ltd.); Andrew Wilson (University of Bradford).

References

Buckley, M., Melton, N. D. and Montgomery, J. (2013) Protoeomics analysis of ancient food vessel stitching reveals >4,000 year old milk proteins. *Rapid Communications in Mass Spectrometry* 43, 1–8.

Davis, J. B. and Thurnam, J. (1865) *Crania Britannica. Delineations and Descriptions of the Skulls of the Aboriginal and Early Inhabitants of the British Islands: with Notices of their Other Remains* (2 vols.). London, printed for the Subscribers.

Edwards, H. G. M., Montgomery, J., Melton, N. D., Hargreaves, M. D., Wilson, A. S. and Carter, E. A. (2010) Gristhorpe Man: Raman Spectroscopic Study of 'Mistletoe berries' in a Bronze Age Log Coffin Burial. *Journal of Raman Spectroscopy*, 41, 1243–1246.

Melton, N., Montgomery, J., Knüsel, C. J., Batt, C., Needham, S., Parker Pearson, M., Sheridan, A., Heron, C., Horsley, T., Schmidt, A., Evans, A., Carter, E., Edwards, H., Hargreaves, M., Janaway, R., Lynnerup, N., Northover, P., O'Connor, S., Ogden, A., Taylor, T., Wastling, V. and Wilson, A. (2010) Gristhorpe Man: an Early Bronze Age log-coffin burial scientifically defined. *Antiquity*, 84/325, 796–815.

Melton, N. and Montgomery, J. 2011. Gristhorpe Man. *Current Archaeology*, 250, 20–27.

Williamson, W. C. (1834) *Description of the Tumulus, lately opened at Gristhorpe, near Scarborough.* Scarborough, C. R. Todd.

Williamson, W. C. (1872) *Description of the Tumulus opened at Gristhorpe, near Scarborough*, third edition. Scarborough, S. W. Theakston.

Williamson, W. C. (1896) *Reminiscences of a Yorkshire Naturalist.* London, George Redway.

Worsaae, J. J. A. (1849) *The Primeval Antiquities of Denmark.* London, John Henry Parker.

Background/General papers

1

GEORGIAN SCARBOROUGH AND THE SCARBOROUGH PHILOSOPHICAL SOCIETY

Karen Snowden

Georgian Scarborough was a prosperous place, much more so than its size and position would ordinarily merit. Scarborough owed its prosperity to the same geological forces that had shaped the coastline creating a high, narrow spit of land that became the ideal spot for a royal castle. This connection with the defence of the realm elevated Medieval Scarborough from a small fishing village to a bustling town with the longest free fair outside London. Scarborough's prosperity seemed assured, but the hold of the Guilds on trade gradually weakened, reducing the value of Scarborough Fair; the castle, neglected by its royal owners, gradually fell into decay, its demise further hastened by the battering it took during the English Civil War. By the mid-17th century Scarborough was slipping back into obscurity and would have disappeared into rural isolation if not for the chance discovery by Mrs Farrow, a local gentlewoman, of a small mineral stream in 1626.

Mrs Farrow was in the habit of taking walks along the foot of the South Cliff, and she noticed that the rocks over which a small stream flowed were stained a reddish colour, and the water itself had a strong odour '...*thereupon did try it her self, and perswaded others also that were sickly to drink of it... it became the usual Physick of the Inhabitants of Scarborough...*' (Wittie 1667, quoted in Rowntree 1931, 247).

Among other things the water contained carbonate of iron, carbonate of lime and sulphate of magnesia. It had similar effects on the body as those achieved by modern proprietary medicines such as Andrew's Liver Salts. Mrs Farrer had discovered a cure for constipation, a complaint that many of the well-to-do suffered from in the 17th century due to a rich diet. The Corporation of Scarborough lost no time in cashing in on this discovery, and by the end of the 17th century Scarborough had re-invented itself as a spa town. In 1698 a governor was appointed to look after the wells and to manage the subscriptions of those who came to drink the waters. Richard 'Dickey' Dickinson built the first spa house for the comfort of his wealthy customers. It was replaced by a more substantial building in 1739. In his *New Historical Scarboro' Guide* published in 1815, Thomas Coultas was able to boast '...*and long before Dr Russel plunged a single patient in the sea at Brighthelmstone, Scarborough had been celebrated for it's* [sic.] *waters, it's* [sic.] *air, it's* [sic.] *situation, and it's* [sic.] *cures*' (Coultas 1815, 7). Scarborough had an edge over other inland spa towns such as Tunbridge (Kent), Bath (Somerset) and Buxton (Staffordshire) as sea-bathing and the consumption of seawater were thought to have curative powers. Prosperity and expansion went hand-in-hand as the number of summer visitors continued to grow. Cards and dancing were available at the assembly rooms on Longroom Street and actors came up from London for the season to perform at the theatre on St. Thomas` Street. Elegant shops, taken by London shopkeepers for the season, catered to the wealthy spa visitors, while several booksellers ran circulating libraries such as Ainsworth's in Newborough Street which, in addition to light summer reading, offered '... *a proportion of valuable production, on the subject of history, polite arts, and other miscellaneous matter...*' (Ainsworth 1815, 25) for 5s the season. Once the unpleasant task of taking one's daily dose of spa water (Figure 1.1) was over visitors could make up a party for an outing to Scalby Mill, where tea was served in arbours of laburnum and honeysuckle, or take a walk to Carnelian Bay to hunt for carnelians and garnets before returning to their lodgings in fashionable Queen Street for dinner.

Fig. 1.1 Scarborough Spa in 1839 (engraving by H. B. Carter. Scarborough, S. W. Theakston, undated, opposite page 38).

W. Ainsworth, in his *Scarborough Guide* of 1815, advised visitors that '*Previously to any use of the Spaw waters, or even to bathing, it is not only usual, but altogether expedient to consult some gentlemen in the medical line*' (Ainsworth 1815, 12). By 1830 Scarborough could boast fifteen doctors and five medical baths, where patients could receive the benefits of hot and cold baths as well as plunge pools and douches. John Dunn and John Travis had a medical bath on the Cliff (Figure 1.2), while Dr William Harland established his medical bath in New Road, both fashionable areas in this period. All three men were founder members of the Scarborough Philosophical Society. '*There are handsome and commodious rooms for warm bathing, which were created on the cliff, in the year 1798, by Messrs. Wilson and Travis, Surgeons and Apothecaries*' (Ainsworth 1815, 14).

In addition to numerous doctors, Scarborough could boast at least one clergyman for each of the main Christian sects, in addition to having Wesleyan, Congregationalist, and Society of Friends meeting houses. Scarborough's reputation for health made it a popular place to establish a private school, and in 1827 there were four private academies for girls and seven for boys with two drawing

masters, three music masters and one female music teacher.

Some of the wealth brought into the town by the summer visitors found its way into educational institutions. In 1729 Robert North founded the Amicable Society School with the purpose of clothing and educating the poor children of Scarborough (Figure 1.3). It was followed by the Spinning School founded by a group of Scarborough ladies in 1788, which educated poor girls in the domestic arts so that they could secure employment as servants. The Lancasterian School with premises on St. Mary's Walk, was established in 1810 and the Infant Public School in 1827. Those who wished to continue their education could do so after 1830 by joining the Mechanics Institute founded in 1830 by Mr Joseph B. Baker, Dr P. Murray and the Rev. B. Evans, all members of the Scarborough Philosophical Society. The Institute provided access to books and classes and lectures, predominantly scientific, for men and boys of the labouring classes.

Success in business or the professions brought wealth and increased leisure time that could be spent pursuing the fashionable science of geology. The abundance of easily

Fig. 1.2 William Travis's Baths (S. W. Theakston, undated, opposite page 81).

Fig. 1.3 The Amicable Society School (Cole 1829a, page 3).

obtainable specimens along the coastline encouraged the collecting of fossils and fostered a desire for a museum in which to display them. Some, like Jack Hornsey and William Bean, had museums in their own homes, which they made available to visitors,

' *Mr J. Hornsey, King-street, besides being an excellent schoolmaster, teaches drawing; ... He has a museum, consisting chiefly of subjects illustrative of natural history, which he obligingly opens to the visits of the curious, on Thursday and Saturday afternoons, after three o'clock* ' (Ainsworth 1815, 48).

The widow of the Rev. J. L. Garrett, Teacher of Natural Philosophy no doubt trying to improve her income '... *has open for public inspection, at her house in Local place, at the top of Tanner street, her much admired Mineral Temples and Chromacatoptricum*' (Cole 1829b, Appendix).

In 1820 William 'Strata' Smith, lately delivered from debtors prison in London, was invited up to Scarborough to advise the Corporation on methods of improving the water supply to the town. While Smith was in Scarborough John Dunn invited him and several other prominent men to a meeting to discuss the possibility of establishing a philosophical society in Scarborough. Regretfully the meeting concluded that Scarborough was not yet ready for such an undertaking.

John Dunn had enjoyed a successful career as a physician but was keen to make his mark as a geologist. He continued to promote the idea of a philosophical society, but it was not until the idea was taken up by Sir John Johnstone, M.P. for Scarborough, in 1827 that real progress was made. A meeting held in the town hall established the Scarborough Philosophical Society and set up a Building Committee to raise funds for a museum. By August 1829 with the support of all the principal gentlemen of the area the Scarborough Museum was completed (Figure1. 4). It is described in Cole's *Scarborough Guide* of 1829,

'*This elegant building, situated near the Cliff Bridge, belongs to a society, whose object is to promote science, and to investigate the local natural history of Scarborough and its vicinity. The lower part is appropriated as a residence for the keeper, and also for a committee room and library; and the upper part occupied by a series of geological specimens, antiquities, and curiosities in general*' (Cole 1829b, Appendix).

Thomas Hinderwell, a notable collector and local historian, bequeathed his extensive collection to his nephew Thomas Duesbury who, in turn, donated it to the Scarborough Museum. The exact content of this collection is unknown, but it included geological specimens, historical artefacts and a number of ethnographic specimens. The period between the opening of the Museum and the financial troubles that beset the Society in the late 1840s was one in which the Museum acquired its most important specimens.

In 1831 the Museum took possession of a nineteen-foot-long headless plesiosaur found somewhere south of Whitby and purchased on the Society's behalf by Isaac Stickney, a local grocer and keen natural philosopher. The Society also boasted a live baboon that was transferred to the York Philosophical Society because the Scarborough winters proved too severe for it. Other items donated to the Museum during this period include a crocodile skull, a fossil starfish, many fossil plants collected by Isaac Stickney, John Williamson and John Bury, and the cast of a small plesiosaur donated by John Hawkins.

John Williamson, a self-taught geologist and 'natural philosopher', who kept a private museum at his home in Huntriss Row, was the first keeper of the Scarborough Museum. Williamson was one of the party that met on William Beswick's land at Gristhorpe, a few miles south of Scarborough, for the opening of a tumulus in 1834. When opened the tumulus revealed what at first appeared to be the trunk of an oak tree but was subsequently recognised as a coffin containing a skeleton and grave goods. Williamson's seventeen-year-old son William Crawford Williamson was given the unenviable task of watching over the bones as they simmered in a glue solution in a washing copper (Williamson 1872, 7). The skeleton and grave goods were placed on display in the Museum, which at this time consisted of the upper room in the rotunda. The coffin was placed outside in the garden on a brick plinth, but despite all efforts to preserve it, the coffin began to decay. By the middle of the century the coffin was in serious danger, so the Museum Council decided to move it inside and in doing so some damage to the large plesiosaur occurred, in consequence of which the plesiosaur was removed from display and promptly disappeared from the Museum records.

'Gristhorpe Man', as the skeleton became known, has remained in the museum at Scarborough ever since its arrival in 1834, with the exception of a brief period during the Second World War when it was removed for safety, firstly to the report centre at the Valley Bridge, Scarborough, and then, in July 1943, to heated caves on the outskirts of Huddersfield. The *Scarborough Evening News* reported on 2nd July 1943 that this latter move was necessitated by the skeleton showing signs of dampness and that it had begun 'to shiver'. This account caused one member of the Council to remark that he '*could understand a skeleton getting damp but could not imagine it shivering*'. The closure of the museum on 1st January 2006 for restoration provided an ideal opportunity for further research into the origins of this remarkable collection, so it was sent to the University of Bradford, where it remained until 2008. In 1834 William C. Williamson wrote a monograph detailing the research into the origins of the coffin, skeleton and grave goods carried out by members of the Scarborough Philosophical Society (Williamson 1834). In 2008 Museum

Fig. 1.4 The Scarborough Philosophical Society Museum in the mid-nineteenth century (Nelson & Sons, undated, after page 47).

staff used both Williamson's monograph and the reports of the 2005–8 researchers to re-display 'Gristhorpe Man' in the context of developments in archaeological science. The learned Georgian gentlemen of the Scarborough Philosophical Society would have thoroughly approved.

References

Ainsworth, W. (1815) *The Scarborough Guide.* Scarborough, W. Ainsworth.

Cole, J. (1829a) *The Scarborough Natural Historians.* Scarborough, J. Cole.

Cole, J. (1829b) *Cole's Scarborough Guide.* Scarborough, J. Cole.

Coultas, T. (1815) *A New Historical Scarbro' Guide.* Scarborough, T. Coultas.

Nelson & Sons. (n.d.) *Scarborough and its Neighbourhood.* London, T. Nelson & Sons.

Rowntree, A. (1931) *The History of Scarborough.* London, Dent & Sons.

Theakston, S. W. (n.d.) *Theakston's Guide to Scarborough (3rd Edition).* Scarborough, S. W. Theakston.

Williamson, W. C. (1834) *Description of the Tumulus, lately opened at Gristhorpe, near Scarborough.* Scarborough, C. R. Todd.

Williamson, W. C. (1872) *Description of the Tumulus opened at Gristhorpe, near Scarborough.* Scarborough, S. W. Theakston.

Wittie, R. (1667) *Tractatiumculam hanc de Aquis Scarburgensibus.* York.

2

WILLIAM BESWICK (1781–1837) AND HIS 1834 EXCAVATION AT GRISTHORPE

Nigel D. Melton and Diana Beswick[†]

The Beswick family at Gristhorpe

The Gristhorpe estate was acquired by the Beswick family, who hailed from Ravenscar, north of Scarborough (North Yorkshire, UK), in the 16th and early 17th centuries. In 1585 a George Beswick and his son John were granted rights to land and a windmill at Gristhorpe by John Cootes of Swinton (North Yorkshire, UK) and his son Edmund (YAS, DD66/39, DD66/46). George Beswick went on to acquire the title to the Manor of Gristhorpe, together with lands at Gristhorpe and Lebberston, from Edmund Cootes in 1601 (YAS, DD66/46, DD66/55, DD66/63).

William Beswick, the son of George Beswick and Jane Wilson, was christened at Filey on the 22nd July 1781. William's father George, who was born in 1756, was a magistrate and Lieutenant for the North Riding of Yorkshire. During the years when there was widespread fear of an invasion by Napoleonic forces, the Beswick family were actively involved in the local defence preparations. In 1796 George Beswick was commissioned as a Captain in the Royal Pickering Volunteers (YAS, DD66/519), and in 1803 he was commissioned as Captain in the Pickering Lythe Volunteer Infantry, and his son William was appointed a First Lieutenant in the same unit (YAS, DD66/545, DD66/546). At this time they were under the command of Lieutenant Colonel Sir George Cayley of Brompton. Lists of the volunteers in the unit during the years 1803–1805 name more than 60 individuals, mainly farmers and agricultural labourers from the parishes of Lebberston and Cayton (YAS, DD66/554(2)).

George Beswick was appointed a Major in the 5th Regiment of Local Militia of the North Riding of Yorkshire

in 1809 (YAS, DD66/556) and a Lieutenant Colonel of the regiment in 1811 (YAS, DD66/562). William Beswick was appointed a Captain in the Battalion of Militia of the East Riding of the County of York in January 1807 (YAS, DD66/551), but his military duties, like those of his father, came to an end in 1815 and he became a magistrate and a churchwarden at St Oswald's Church, Filey. William had married his cousin Mary Keld in 1809 (YAS, DD66/558(2)). Mary, who was born in 1778, was the only daughter of Thomas and Elizabeth Keld (Thomas had married George Beswick's sister Elizabeth on 5th February 1775). Thomas

Fig. 2.1 Portrait of William Beswick (Courtesy of Mrs. D. Beswick).

Keld, the son of a master mariner, was a successful apothecary and surgeon in Scarborough.

George Beswick died in 1826, and his estate was divided between his sons, William (Fig. 2.1) and George. William inherited the Lordship and Manor of Gristhorpe and his brother George lands in Muston. At the time of the 'Gristhorpe Man' discovery in 1834, William Beswick owned around one thousand acres of land, including the cliff top land at Gristhorpe from Lebberston to Newbiggin.

William and Mary Beswick had six children: Mary, born 1811; Jane, born 1812; Ann, born 1814; George, born 1815; William, born 1817; and Thomas, born 1819. William's daughter Jane died in 1821 and their mother in 1822 when the other children were all still very young. It is not known how the Beswick children were brought up or educated, but a Colonel Michelson was appointed their guardian until they came of age. William did not re-marry and died in 1837. William's third daughter Ann had died in 1833 and, on his death, his four surviving children were each left a share of his estate, which by then consisted of six farms and just over 462 acres, the whole being valued in 1839 at £25,468 (YAS, DD66/630(2)). At the time Mary was aged 26, George 22, William 20, and Thomas 18. It is, perhaps, a reflection on their father's antiquarian interests that when they inherited money from the estate Mary, George and Tom Beswick planned a 'Grand Tour' to Egypt via Paris and Malta, returning via Naples, Rome, Florence, Lyons and Paris, and Mary and Tom both wrote diaries of their journeys (Beswick and Beswick, 1997). William did not go with them, maybe he did not share their interest in antiquities, or he might have remained at home to maintain the estate.

Tom Beswick became a qualified engineer and William was a solicitor but did not practise for long. Mary Beswick was the only one of the family to marry: William Horatio Nelson Myers, a stockbroker from Leeds, became her husband at St Oswald's in 1849. When George died in 1851 aged 36, his brother William inherited the Lordship (YAS, DD66/640(6a)).

In their latter years, William and Tom Beswick remained close to home; they had a loyal manservant called Robert Bell who lived in while other help was drawn from the village. A family story relates that 'the old uncles' as they were affectionately known by the next generation, would drink a bottle of port every night and had to be put to bed by the trusty Robert. On at least one occasion, when in their cups, they opened fire on their great grandfather William's portrait – which still exhibits signs of the damage. William died in 1884 and the Lordship passed to Tom (YAS DD66/653(2)). His sister Mary, in the meantime had had two children, a son William Beswick Myers born in 1850 and a daughter Annie born in 1851. William Beswick Myers inherited the manor (Fig. 2.2) when his uncle Tom Beswick died in 1895.

Fig. 2.2 Gristhorpe Manor in the 19th century (Courtesy of Mrs. D. Beswick).

The 1834 excavation at Gristhorpe

William Beswick's antiquarian interests preceded his inheriting the estate. William Williamson's account of the 1834 excavation informs us that Beswick had investigated the two outlying barrows on the cliff top at Gristhorpe (see Melton and Russ, this volume, Fig. 6.1) a decade previously and had discovered '*urns with imperfect remains of bones and ashes*', considered at the time to be Anglo-Saxon or Roman, in both barrows (Williamson 1834, 5).

There is little further information on these earlier excavations, but what there is does not accord with Williamson's description of '*imperfect bones and ashes*' which he left in the revised 1872 edition of his report (Williamson 1872, 5). One account states that: '*In 1824, the late W. Beswick, Esq., opened an ancient British barrow here, and under some large stones, forming a rude cist vaen, found the skeleton of a man, the skull and teeth being quite perfect*' (Bulmer 1891, 945). It is not clear to which of the two outlying barrows this is referring, but the northern barrow was excavated in 1887 by Canon William Greenwell, who was unaware that it had been previously examined (Greenwell 1890, 38). Greenwell's excavation revealed a small cist containing the cremation of an adult accompanied by three pieces of flint that had not been excavated by Beswick, and the disturbed remains of the central burial cist within which there were some bones from a '*strongly-built man*' that had not been retrieved by the original excavators.

William Beswick's digging techniques were clearly of their time, using labourers from the estate and with the retrieval of crania and artefacts the prime aim. There is a clue to his excavation methods in Williamson's account of the 1834 excavation as he describes how Beswick had attempted to excavate the central barrow in 1833, but had abandoned that attempt after '*sinking to some depth, fruitlessly*' (Williamson 1834, 5). It would seem, therefore, that Beswick was adopting the then fairly standard method of barrow excavation – digging out the centre of the barrow to reveal the central, primary interment. This would explain how the later cremation burial discovered by Canon Greenwell in the northern barrow had been missed in 1824.

It would be easy to dismiss William Beswick as a typical product of what Marsden (1999, 40) has described as '*the age of the dilettante, usually of the gentleman class, whose employees plundered mounds wholesale in the search for curios to fill showcases and cabinets*'. This might, indeed, have been Beswick's motivation in the 1820s, but what sets him apart from so many of his contemporaries was the extreme care that was taken in the recovery of the log coffin and its contents in 1834, and his far-sighted decision to donate these exceptional finds to the Scarborough Philosophical Society's newly opened museum in Scarborough.

The conditions within the waterlogged coffin had led to the survival of an assemblage of organic and inorganic grave goods that remains unequalled in the archaeological record of Bronze Age Britain. The surviving inorganic grave-goods comprise a bronze dagger (Northover, this volume; Sheridan *et al.*, this volume) and a flint knife and two other flints (*ibid.*). Some of the organic grave goods have also survived; the dagger's whalebone pommel, a bone pin, a small wooden object, possibly a toggle, and a few phalanges from a small animal (*ibid.*).

Not all the organic grave goods have fared as well. The animal skin in which the body had been wrapped (Buckley, this volume, Sheridan *et al.*, this volume), and the '*kind of dish, or shallow basket of wicker work*' (Williamson 1834, 9; Sheridan *et al.*, this volume), have survived, albeit in fragmentary form. Others such as the '*very singular ornament, in the form of a double rose of a ribband, with two loose ends*', that Williamson (1834, 10) described as '*resembling thin horn.... the surface.... curiously ornamented with small elevated lines*', and the bed of '*vegetable substance... at first believed to be dried rushes*' (*ibid.*) either disintegrated completely on removal from the coffin, or, in the case of the latter, were too decomposed to curate. The bed of vegetation within the coffin was, however, the subject of investigation in 1834

Fig. 2.3 Cartoon drawn by a friend of the Beswick family in 1900 depicting the events of 1834 (Courtesy of Mrs. D. Beswick).

Harry Woolsey

prior to its final decomposition, when a '*long, lanceolate leaf, resembling that of the mistletoe*' was distinguished (*ibid.*).

Also present were organic items that have survived, and which were originally identified as grave goods, but which are now known to relate to the body interred in the coffin. These were the '*fragments of a ring*' (Williamson 1834, 9), which have now been identified as ossified tracheal rings (Knüsel *et al.*, this volume), and what had been curated and labelled as three 'mistletoe berries' from the vegetation upon which the body had been placed. One of these has now been confirmed as a renal stone (Edwards, this volume; Knüsel *et al.*, this volume), a second appears visually identical to the analysed specimen, and the third, which has a vesicular appearance, has been identified as a small sesamoid bone (Janaway *et al.*, this volume).

An account of the recovery of the coffin published in the *York Herald and General Advertiser* on 19th July 1834 provides a fascinating insight into the interest and excitement generated by this event:

> '*A barrow was opened on Friday week, in a field bordering the lofty cliffs at Gristhorpe Bay, on the estate of William Beswick Esq., about six miles south of Scarborough, which afforded a rich treat to the antiquary. After removing the earth which had been thrown up in a circular form, to no great height, layers of bouldered stones, piled up in the ordinary manner of the Ancient Britons, and then a mass of strong clay being dug through, there was presented to view, at the depth of between seven or eight feet, some roughly hewn pieces of wood, covering a portion of the trunk of an oak, seven and a half feet long, by three in diameter, lying horizontally N and S, with the representation of a human face, most coarsely carved, at the northern extremity. This oak log being struck, sounded hollow, and the expectations of the bystanders, thus greatly raised, were by the liberal and judicious arrangements of Mr Beswick, fully gratified. A windlass being put up, and cords and chains dextrously introduced, so as to ascertain the existence of a wooden sarcophagus of two pieces, excavated out of the rough trunk of a tree, a thing hitherto unprecedented, we believe, in such researches; and the lid being slowly raised, gradually disclosed a skeleton, wholly black, but with the bones entire, though disunited, as might well be expected, from the decomposition of the ligaments and cartilages.*
>
> *The scene was now really one of much singularity and interest, when we looked at the place, a lofty rugged pasture, far from almost any human habitation, and nearly overhanging the ocean, with another tumulus rearing its green and rounded summit close to hand, and the opened sepulchre surrounded by an eager group anxiously watching every movement of the lid as it separated and was hoisted up, and fearing lest it might break in pieces in the ascent, and demolish the frail relics underneath. But at last it was safely got up; and towards evening the under portion likewise, and both by the liberality of the proprietor of the ground, now deposited in the Scarborough Museum*'.

This account of the find also provides a list the group assembled to witness the recovery of the coffin: '*The following gentlemen were present at the disinterment: – Wm. Beswick, Jno. Barry, Edwd. Alexander, John Tindall, J. Gillespie,*

Esquires; Mr Travis, Scarborough; Mr Munro, of Filey; Dr P. Murray, Scarborough, Medical Gentleman; Mr Williamson, Curator of the Scarborough Museum'. Edward Alexander F.A.S., from Halifax, had also accompanied William Beswick the previous day when the log coffin was first encountered (Williamson 1834, 5) and was stated to be preparing an account of the find for the Society of Antiquaries (in fact, after the event William Crawford Williamson's 1834 account of the discovery was accessioned by the Society (Rowley-Conwy, this volume)).

Many of the names of those present for the raising and opening of the coffin appear in the Minute Books of the Scarborough Philosophical Society. William Beswick clearly had close links with the Society and may have been a member. The Minute Books of the meeting of the Council held on 12th July 1834 record:

> '*Present Jno Rowntree VP in the chair, W. Travis, Jno Dunn, W. Smith, W. Harland, F. Weddell, P. Murray, J. Bury, J. Williamson, E. F. Wellburn & I. Stickney.*
>
> '*William Beswick Esq., having in the handsomest manner, presented to the Society an ancient coffin, skeleton etc, exhumed from a tumulus in the neighbourhood of Gristhorpe.*
>
> *Resolved that the Secretary be requested to convey to him the sincere thanks of the Council and the Officers of the Institution for his liberal gift; and W. Travis, Rt. Tindall, W. Smith, F. Weddell, W. Harland and P. Murray are appointed a committee to prepare a plan for placing the coffin in a conspicuous position on the outside of the building, and also an estimate of the expense: – they are further requested to ascertain the best method of preserving the skeleton etc and to carry the whole into effect*'. (Transcribed by K. Snowden).

A month later, newspaper reports published between the 16th and 25th August confirm that the articulation of the skeleton by Drs. Weddell and Harland was completed and that a '*suitable sarcophagus*', built of brick and tufa from Forge Valley near Ayton, and equipped with folding wooden doors, had been constructed near the entrance of the museum in order to house the oak coffin.

The local interest that Gristhorpe skeleton aroused is reflected in two poems that appeared in the *Scarborough Herald* in October 1834. One of these (Appendix 2.1), composed by 'D', is likely to be the work of John Dunn, the Secretary of the Scarborough Philosophical Society (K. Snowden, pers. comm.). The other, composed by '*WB*' on '*Gristhorpe Cliff*', must surely be by William Beswick: –

> '*Lines addressed to the skeleton in the Scarbro' Museum*
> *O'er my moulder'd ashes cold*
> *Many a century hath roll'd,*
> *Many a race hath disappear'd*
> *Since my giant form I rear'd;*
> *Since my flinted arrow flew*
> *Since my battle horn I blew,*
> *Since my brazen dagger's pride*

Glitter'd on my warlike side'
Which transported o'er the wave,
Kings of distant ocean gave.
Ne'er hath glar'd the eye of day,
My death-bed secrets to betray,
Since, with mutter'd Celtic rhyme,
The white-hair'd druid-bard sublime,
Mid the stillness of the night,
Wak'd the sad and solemn rite,
The rite of death, and o'er my bones
Were pil'd the monumental stones,
Passing near the hallow'd ground,
The Roman gaz'd upon the mound,
And murmur'd with a secret sigh,
'There in the dust the mighty lie,'
E'en while his heart with conquest glow'd,
While the high-rais'd flinty road
Echoed to the prancing hoof,
And golden eagles flam'd aloof,
And flashing to the orient light,
His banner'd legions glitter'd bright;
The victor of the world confess'd
A dark awe shivering at his breast.
And shall the sons of distant days,
Unpunish'd on my relics gaze
Hence! although my grave ye spoil,
Dark oblivion mocks your toil:
Deep the clouds of ages roll,
History drops her mould'ring scroll,
And never shall reveal the name
Of him who scorns her transient fame!
- There spake from its disturbed bed
The spirit of the mighty dead.
          Gristhorpe Cliff, 25th Oct., 1834, WB'

It is interesting that William Beswick mentions a 'brazen dagger'. This stands in contrast with Williamson's (1834, 8–9) account in which the dagger blade was incorrectly identified as 'the head of a Spear of Javelin' and its pommel as 'probably ... the ornamental handle of a Javelin, of which the metal Head, has formed the opposite extremity' with the comment 'but as notice was not taken when the Coffin was opened of their relative situations, it is impossible to speak decisively as to this point'. William Beswick was present at the opening of the log coffin. It seems he may have seen the grave goods in situ, and this could explain his reference to a 'brazen dagger'.

The young William Williamson was not present when the coffin was opened, but it would be strange if he had not consulted with those who had been there before writing his report. It is possible he relied on the account of his father John Williamson, the curator of the Society's museum in Scarborough, and this, for some reason, was flawed. It may be noted that there is also a discrepancy in Williamson's account and that in the local newspaper quoted above. This concerns the recognition of the 'log' as a coffin. Williamson (1834, 5) describes how, on the second day, the assembled

guests gathered to witness the removal of the 'log' from its 'argillaceous sarcophagus' and states how surprised the onlookers were when, in the course of its removal, it split, revealing it to be a coffin. He repeated this description in his autobiography, writing the 'upper part of it came away, leaving the lower portion embedded in clay' revealing it to be a 'rude coffin' (Williamson 1896, 44). The newspaper report informs us, however, that the finders had struck the 'log' and determined that it sounded hollow, and that the raising of the coffin was undertaken with this prior knowledge.

The Gristhorpe find was widely reported in newspapers from London to Midlothian, and Williamson's report, produced within weeks of the discovery, was seen by the eminent scientist Professor William Buckland when he visited Scarborough that year with Professor Louis Agassiz (Williamson 1877, 196–7). It was Buckland, Williamson later surmised (Williamson 1896, 46–47), who caused the account to be published in the Literary Gazette in October 1834, leading to further interest and the discovery's prominent role in the development of archaeology as an academic discipline in Britain (Rowley-Conwy, this volume). The find also gripped the popular imagination: the Gristhorpe skeleton becoming known as the 'Black Prince' (Wright 1857, 116), and was referred to as such by Canon Greenwell in a lecture that he gave to the Royal Institution in 1867 (Anon. 1867).

Acknowledgements
The first part of this paper is based on the late Mrs D. Beswick's investigations into her family's history that she was kind enough to provide at the commencement of the project in 2005. It is included as a tribute to her enthusiastic support of the project and in thanks for her permission to use the family portrait of William Beswick, the cartoon drawn by a friend of the family in 1900, and the 19th-century photograph of Gristhorpe Manor.

The author is grateful to Karen Snowden, Scarborough Museums Trust, for providing transcriptions of the entries in the Scarborough Philosophical Society Minute Books and for drawing to his attention the poems published in the local newspaper. Thanks are also due to staff at the Yorkshire Archaeological Society for assistance in researching the Gristhorpe papers in their archives collection.

References

Anon. (1867) Who were the Ancient Britons?: The Medical Times and Gazette gives the following account of the Rev. W. Greenwell's recent lecture. Anthropological Review 5, 253–6.
Beswick, T. and Beswick, M. (1997) Chronicles of a Journey, 1839–1840: The Diaries of Mary and Tom Beswick of Gristhorpe. Transcribed by Kenneth Clegg. Filey, Yorks., Kenneth Clegg.

Bulmer (1891) *History, Topography and Directory of North Yorkshire Part II, Containing the Thirsk and Malton and Whitby Divisions, and Part of the Wapentake of Claro.* Preston, Lancs., T. Bulmer and Co.

Greenwell, W. (1890) Recent researches in barrows in Yorkshire, Wiltshire, Berkshire etc., *Archaeologia* 52, 1–72.

Marsden, B. M. (1999) *The Early Barrow Diggers.* Stroud, Glos., Tempus.

Williamson, W. C. (1834) *Description of the Tumulus, lately opened at Gristhorpe, near Scarborough.* Scarborough, Yorks., C. R. Todd.

Williamson, W. C. (1877) Reminiscences of a Yorkshire Naturalist. *Good Words* 18, 62–66, 133–136 and 194–197.

Williamson, W. C. (1896) *Reminiscences of a Yorkshire Naturalist.* London, George Redway.

Wright, T. (1857) On some curious forms of sepulchral interment found in East Yorkshire. *Gentleman's Magazine* 1857(II), 114–119.

Primary sources in the Yorkshire Archaeological Society Archives (YAS)

DD66/39. 1585 Mar 27. Grant by John Coottes and Edmund Coottes his son of Swynton [*sic.*] Co. York, Gentleman, to George Beswicke and John Beswicke his son of Gristhorpe, Yeomen, of land and a mill at Gristhorpe.

DD66/46. 1595 Mar 27. Copy of the Grant of this date made by John Cootes and Edmund Cootes his son of Swinton, Gentlemen, to George Beswicke and John Beswicke his son of Gristhorpe, Yeomen, of a windmill and lands at Gristhorpe.

DD66/51. 1601 July 21. Grant by Edmund Cootes of Swynton [*sic.*], Gent, to George Beswicke of Gristhorpe, Yeoman, of the manor and lands of Gristhorpe and Lebberston

DD66/63. Release of the title to the Manor of Gristhorpe by Edmund Cootes of Swynton Co. York, Gent, to George Beswicke of Gristhorpe, Yeoman.

DD66/519. 1796 Nov 17. Commission of Geo. Beswick Esq. as a Captain in the Royal Pickering Volunteers

DD66/545. 1803 Aug 28. Commission of Geo. Bewick Esq. as Captain in the Pickering Lyth [*sic.*] Volunteer Infantry.

DD66/546. 1803 Aug 28. Commission appointing Wm. Beswick, Gent, to be First Lieutenant in the Pickering Lyth [*sic.*] Volunteer Infantry (Geo. Beswick Esq. Captain)

DD66/550. 1806 Sep 19. Commission of Wm. Beswick, Gent, as a Lieutenant in the Battalion of Militia of the East Riding of the Co. of York, and town and county of Kingston-upon-Hull.

DD66/551. 1807 Jan 27. Commission of William Beswick Esq. as a Captain in the Battalion of Militia of the East Riding of the Co. of York, and town and county of Kingston-upon-Hull.

DD66/554(2). (i) The Pickering-Lythe Volunteers. Regulations dated 18 April, Brompton, signed by George Cayley Bart, Lieut. Col. Commandant. (ii) List, dated 28th November 1803, of those enrolling in the regiment of infantry.

DD66/556. 1809 Feb 28. Commission of Geo. Beswick as Major in the 5th Regiment of Local Militia of the North Riding of York.

DD66/562. 1811 Feb 9. Commission to Geo. Beswick as Lieutenant-Colonel in the 5th Regiment of Local Militia of the North Riding of York.

DD66/630(2). 1839 March. Valuation of an estate at Gristhorpe and Lebberston of Messrs. Beswick.

DD66/640(6a). 1851 June 18. (Proved) Copy of will with probate attached of George Beswick of Gristhorpe, gent, dated 5 Feb 1850. Proved at York.

DD66/653(2). 1884 Sept 28. Copy of the will with probate attached of William Beswick of Gristhorpe Esq, dated 15 Oct 1883, proved at York 28 Sept 1884.

Appendix 2.1

'Lines addressed to the skeleton in the Scarbro' Museum' published in the Scarborough Herald, 11th October 1834.

Welcome, old Druid, Warrior, or whate'er
In days of yore, thy living rank might be;
Forgive me if I feel a little queer,
As thus with wond'ring eyes I gaze on thee:
A sort of nervous, shivering sensation,
Not absolutely fear, – but trepidation;
In sooth, if such a term be not unlawful,
I must pronounce thee – most exceeding awful.

A word, old friend: – say can'st thou not unfold
Some story of the olden times, when thou
(I judge thou art some scores of centuries old,)
Wor'st the Tiara on thy sacred brow?
Methinks, to see thee in thy robes pontifical,
Had been a sight exceedingly magnifical,
And most unlike (forgive the insinuation)
Your worship's present looks and situation.

Perchance thou wast a soldier? – Is it so? –
In truth thy aspect is somewhat pugnacious; –
What – silent still, old fellow? – Yes, or no? –
I would thou wert a little more loquacious.
Come, come, believe me, I'm no tittle-tattle,
How many foemen hast thou kill'd in battle?
And entre-nous, your captives – when you'd beat them,
(Rely on my discretion) – did you eat them?

Come, tell us, what in your days was the fashion;
How did you travel then, – by air or steam?
The ladies too – were gigot sleeves the passion? –
Was scandal then, as now, their fav'rite theme?
What were their studies? – Physiology, –
Greek, – Latin, – Mathematics, – and Conchology?
Or, what is obsolete with us, poor sinners,
Was it their province then to cook your dinners?

I see you're not inclin'd for conversation,
So for the present, I shall say adieu:
But, should you wish for more communication,
I'll leave my name, and my address with you.
Somehow, I always had a curiosity,
To see each fresh (excuse the word) monstrosity
And so I hope you'll pardon my intrusion,
Which brings me happily to a conclusion.

Saturday, October 11th   D

THE GRISTHORPE BURIAL IN 19th-CENTURY ARCHAEOLOGY: AN ESSAY ON THE DEVELOPMENT OF ARCHAEOLOGICAL THOUGHT

Peter Rowley-Conwy

Introduction

The Gristhorpe burial was probably the single most quoted, discussed, illustrated and re-analysed archaeological find in Britain in the 19th century. It was central to arguments for and against a variety of archaeological chronological schemes. It was arguably the first British site where the finds were treated as a coherent *assemblage* rather than a series of individual objects; and it was certainly the first British site to be dated according to the 'Three Age System' of Stone Age, Bronze Age, and Iron Age. This level of coverage invites comparison with that of the nearby site of Star Carr over a century later.

In this contribution I will examine why Gristhorpe was so important. In the 1830s archaeology was on the brink of massive changes. Gristhorpe is an ideal case-study through which to examine these changes, and to consider the chronological ideas and conflicts of the time. I will consider how Gristhorpe was used in various chronological schemes in the 50 or so years following its initial publication. These changes in chronology saw archaeology move from a short historically-based chronology to a long empirically-based one, marking the effective origins of the discipline as we know it. Gristhorpe provides a unique window into the history of archaeology.

The Gristhorpe burial was recovered on 10–11 July 1834. It was immediately recognised as a spectacular find, with its log coffin, well preserved skeleton and associated artefacts. A long description appeared in the *York Herald* on 19 July, and several other newspapers also reported it (see Melton and Beswick, this volume). The August issue of the *Gentleman's Magazine* contained a paragraph dated 12 July, describing the find and mentioning the *"brass point of a spear"* (Anon. 1834, 195). One of those present at the excavation was John Williamson, curator of Scarborough Museum, and his son William, then just 18 years old, published the entire find in a 17 page pamphlet (Williamson 1834). This pamphlet was reproduced verbatim (but without the tables) in both the *Gentleman's Magazine* (1834 part II, 632–635) and the *Literary Gazette* (18 October 1834). It was also read by the expert audience: the pamphlet was accessioned by the Society of Antiquaries of London in 1838 (*Archaeologia* 28, 1840, p. 468). When the Archaeological Institute's annual meeting was held in York in 1846, Williamson displayed the finds to the assembled members (Archaeological Institute 1848, 1–2). Williamson republished his pamphlet twice more: slightly modified in 1836, and very differently in 1872.

William Williamson and the Phoenician chronology

British archaeology in the 1830s had effectively no means of dating finds except through historical records. No such records provided any direct help regarding Gristhorpe, but Williamson put forward a logical and coherent argument about the date of the find. The controversy in which this immediately embroiled him illustrates how British archaeologists approached chronology in the 1830s.

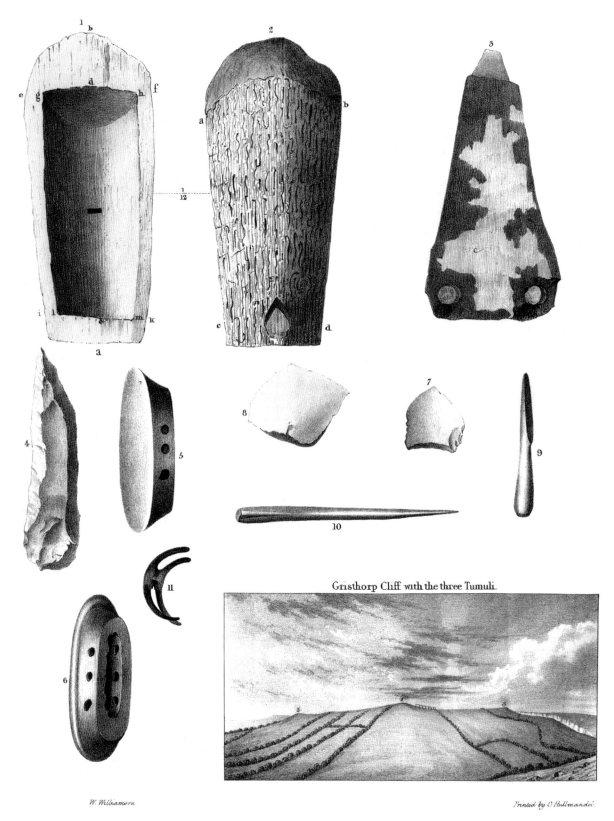

W. Williamson.   Printed by C. Hullmandel.

Figure 3.1 The finds from Gristhorpe, as illustrated by Williamson (1834, 1836).

Crucial to Williamson's dating was his understanding that, because the objects were found inside the coffin, they belonged to the individual who had been buried, *i.e.* that they formed what would now be called a single assemblage. He illustrated the coffin and finds (Fig. 3.1), which included "*the head of a spear or javelin*" made of brass or copper, which had lost part of its point (1834, 8; Fig. 3.1 no. 3), some flint objects interpreted as javelin points and arrowheads (Fig. 3.1 nos. 4, 7, 8), and a perforated object made of horn or whalebone (Fig. 3.1 nos. 5, 6) which Williamson thought might be "*the ornamental handle of a javelin*" (1834, 9).

How could Williamson date the Gristhorpe find? He had virtually no archaeological information from which to start. He mentioned a similar log coffin found by Sir Richard Colt Hoare, and also a comment by Fosbroke to the effect that the presence of arrowheads indicated that the burial was that of a hunter (1834, 14). Neither of these provided any help with regard to date – Colt Hoare hardly discussed such matters, simply referring to his barrows as 'Celtic' or 'British' (*e.g.* Colt Hoare 1810), and Thomas Fosbroke's *Encyclopædia of Antiquities* (1825) was not helpful because it mentioned very few pre-Roman finds. Not surprisingly, Williamson turned to a historian for inspiration.

Williamson's dating rested on Robert Henry's 12–volume *History of Great Britain* (Henry 1800). Like most of his contemporaries, Henry regarded the Europeans as descendants of Japhet the son of Noah (1800, I, 136). He used the few available historical references to discuss Britain before the Roman invasion, cautioning that they were all problematic (1800, I, 1–2). Crucially for Williamson's dating of Gristhorpe, Henry argued that bronze had been introduced to Britain by the Phoenicians, who came in search of tin.

In invoking the Phoenicians, Henry was following an academic tradition already more than two centuries old. Classical authors including Strabo had described Phoenician voyages to the mysterious Cassiterides, or 'tin islands', situated somewhere in the Atlantic. William Camden, whose *Britannia* appeared in Latin first in 1586, suggested that these were the Scilly Isles: Cornish tin was well known, and although the classical descriptions were very vague, he doubted whether any better candidates for the islands could be found. As the 1695 English translation of *Britannia* put it:

> "*If any deny these* [the Scilly Isles] *to be the* Cassiterides..., *let him inquire somewhere else than where they are already supposed to be, and I believe he'll hardly find them, by going this way to work. For the truth on't is, the Ancient writers knew nothing certain of these remote parts and Islands; no more than we of the Islands in the Straights of* Magellan, *and the whole tract of* New Guiney" (Camden 1695, 1112, original spelling, original italics underlined).

Over time, the Phoenician connection became more firmly accepted. For example, the Cornish archaeologist William Borlase, in his *Antiquities Historical and Monumental of the County of Cornwall* (1769), stated that the Phoenicians arrived in Britain in *c.* 600 BC, bringing with them ceramics and "*brazen ware*" (1769, 28). The Scillies were definitely the Cassiterides, and their tin was exported as far afield as India (1769, 29). Evidence of Phoenician presence was available in the "*many rude obelisks*" in Cornwall, which were symbols of Phoenician deities (1769, 31).

This was the chronological perspective within which Robert Henry operated. He believed that the British people whom the Phoenicians encountered had little knowledge of agriculture (1800, II, 99–100); they went naked, but adopted clothing after seeing well-clothed Phoenicians, animal skins being the first type they used (1800, II, 125); and they probably began using metals (1800, II, 135–8) and ceramics (1800, II, 205) for same reason. Like Borlase, Henry dated the Phoenician arrival to *c.* 600 BC, although the date was uncertain (1800, II, 201).

Williamson adopted this chronology, and he used various clues to date Gristhorpe within it. There was only one metal weapon, but three flint items. This suggested a date soon after Phoenician contact, because a high status individual (as the man buried at Gristhorpe evidently was) would not have continued to use flint tools for long after metal ones became available (1834, 12). The animal hide in the coffin also suggested a date shortly after the adoption of clothing (1834: 11). Thus an age of at least 2200 years was likely (1834, 16), which to a writer in the early 19th century would be 400 BC or earlier. Since the Phoenicians had arrived in 600 BC, the period 600–400 BC was the likely date.

Williamson deduced various things about the individual buried. The skeleton was of a large, robust man, at least 6 feet 3 inches in height (1834, 15). The sheer scale and wealth of the burial suggested high status (1834, 12). Williamson used the then-accepted science of phrenology, the use of external skull features to infer personality, to demonstrate that the Gristhorpe man was a combative and destructive individual with high self-esteem and a very large sex drive (the latter discreetly termed 'philoprogenitiveness'), thanking a Dr. Harland for this study (1834, 7–8). These personality traits, and the fact that the man was likely to belong to the Brigantes, the tribe resident in Yorkshire when the Romans arrived, led to the overall conclusion that "*this man is elevated to the high rank of a Brigantian chief*" (Williamson 1834, 16).

Williamson's chronology was challenged almost immediately – but it was his *relative*, not his *absolute*, chronology that was contested. This happened because of the excavation of another Yorkshire barrow, this one near Scarborough. The excavator was John Gage, an important archaeologist, being the Director of the Society of Antiquaries of London. A short note appeared in the *Gentleman's Magazine* (Anon. 1835, 540), and a pamphlet on it was published the next year by Dr. William Travis (1836). Travis stated that because of the absence of metal in the barrow, Mr. Gage *"even conjectures it to be of more ancient date that the celebrated barrow at Gristhorp [sic], in this neighbourhood, opened in 1834"* (Travis 1836, 8, added emphasis in original underlined).

The same year saw the publication of the second edition of Williamson's pamphlet on Gristhorpe (Williamson 1836). This contained a few amendments from the 1834 version: the bronze spear or javelin became a *"spear or dagger"* and two parallels were cited (1836, 8); a similar log coffin, excavated in 1767, was mentioned (1836, 14); bones previously identified as small dog had been identified by Professor Buckland as those of a weasel (1836, 14); and finally, Williamson mentioned the newly excavated barrow near Scarborough. Stressing that he had not been present at the excavation, he gave it as his opinion that the primary interment was *"no doubt British, but of rather more modern date than the one at Gristhorpe"* (1836, 18, added emphasis in original underlined).

Then as now, arguments about 'whose site is older' were keenly fought out. The *Gentleman's Magazine* presented both sides of the ensuing debate (Anon. 1836). This started with a description of the Scarborough burial by Travis. Gage's excavation had evidently been well conducted, for in a remarkably early example of stratigraphic observation, Travis described two separate phases of burial, first a skeleton in a cistvaen (stone cist), and later an urn cremation:

> *"The urn being found nearer to the surface than the apex of the cistvaen, furnishes a decided proof of its having been a secondary or subsequent deposit; and it is evident that the contents of the urn, where the subject (the corpse) had undergone cremation, were distinct from those of the cistvaen, in which the deposit was found entire"* (op. cit. 416, original emphasis underlined).

The primary inhumation contained no metal artefacts. Travis reiterated that because of this, John Gage believed the Scarborough interment to be *older* than that from Gristhorpe.

Opposition from someone so senior as the Director of the Society of Antiquaries might have daunted a young man of 20 – but Williamson counterattacked him in the same section of the *Gentleman's Magazine*. The absence of metal at Scarborough, he argued, proved nothing: the Scarborough burial was of a much lower status individual – the skeleton was crammed into a stone cist measuring only 3 ft 8 in (112 cm) in length, and the man buried there had been of too low status to obtain any metal. There was no sign that he had been either a warrior or a hunter, the only two

professions that would require metals. Furthermore, the primary interment at Scarborough had been accompanied by a pot. Henry (1800, II, 205) had stated that pottery had been introduced by the Phoenicians, so the Scarborough burial could not be pre-Phoenician. Crucially, Gristhorpe did not have any pottery; there was a dish, but:

> *"the dish was not of earthenware, but (what I think proves a far lower state of an acquaintance with domestic comfort) of slips of bark stitched together with sinews of animals, a utensil which would never have been used for such a purpose by a people acquainted with the art of ornamental pottery, which evidently was known at the time the Scarborough tumulus was formed (op. cit. 418, original emphasis underlined)."*

For these reasons Williamson concluded that, despite Gage's views, the Gristhorpe burial really was earlier than that from Scarborough.

This debate encapsulated what was to become a major issue in the next decades: whether grave contents reflected time, or status, or a combination of both. But before we consider how Gristhorpe was used in this debate, we will examine how the site was employed by another archaeologist from a completely different chronological tradition: none other than the renowned developer of the Three Age System, C. J. Thomsen himself.

C. J. Thomsen and the archaeological chronology

Thomsen approached Gristhorpe from a completely different perspective. In 1836 he published a paper on the site, in Danish, in the periodical *Nordisk Tidskrift for Oldkyndighed* ('Scandinavian Journal of Archaeology'). The paper is technically anonymous, but in volume 1 of the journal (1832, p. 370) it is stated that reports on antiquities would be written by a triumvirate comprising Finn Magnusen, C. C. Rafn and C. J. Thomsen. Magnusen and Rafn were specialists in early literary sources and runes, so the sections on artefacts can confidently be assumed to have been written by Thomsen (Petersen 1938), much of whose output is thus not credited to him by name. This goes for his major publication of the Three Age System itself (Thomsen 1836a), as well as for his paper on Gristhorpe (Thomsen 1836b).

By 1836 Thomsen was an archaeologist of vast experience. For 20 years he had been secretary to the Danish government's Royal Commission for the Preservation of Antiquities. In that time many thousands of artefacts had been received, and Thomsen had devised a recording system that treated them as assemblages rather than individual objects (Street-Jensen 1988). From this assemblage-based perspective, Thomsen realised that the chambers of megalithic graves routinely contained stone artefacts, amber jewellery and uncremated skeletons; if bronze artefacts were found at such sites, they were in cremation urns dug into the surface of these mounds, and thus clearly of a later date. Inside one megalithic grave, Thomsen found iron objects – but they lay well above the primary inhumations in the chamber, separated from them by a layer of sterile sand; the iron was thus likely to be a later insertion (Thomsen 1836c, 301). Most excavators were not careful enough to observe this sort of stratigraphy; Thomsen would no doubt have approved of John Gage's careful excavation of the Scarborough tumulus.

Thomsen read Williamson's 1834 pamphlet with great interest, because he had precisely the detailed comparison that Williamson lacked: the log coffin burial from Bjolderup in Jutland recovered in 1827. Thomsen's paper stressed the similarities between the two. He presented an illustration of the Gristhorpe coffin (Fig. 3.2), evidently redrawn in Copenhagen after Williamson's original but to show a different angle of view, because he stated that it depicted "the approximate appearance of this coffin" (1836b, 280, my translation). The coffin and artefacts from Bjolderup were also illustrated (Fig. 3.2). Thomsen's experience allowed him to correct a couple of errors made by Williamson. He correctly identified the bronze item as a dagger – *"the English antiquarians took this item to be a spearhead, a mistake*

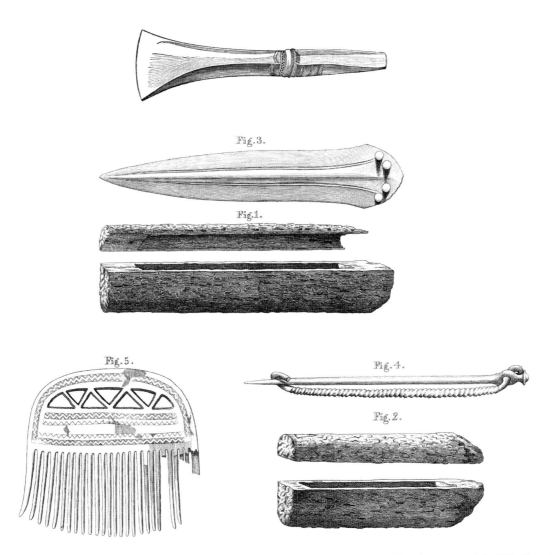

Figure 3.2 Thomsen's illustrations of Bjolderup and Gristhorpe. Top: palstave from Bjolderup (after Thomsen 1836b, 285). The others are from Thomsen's tab. I. 'Fig. 2' is his redrawn version of the Gristhorpe log coffin, 'Fig. 1' the one from Bjolderup. The rest show artefacts from Bjolderup.

which is often made; but both the complete item of the same type from Bjolderup..., and many more in the possession of our museum, reveal the correct identification" (Thomsen 1836b, 281, my translation). He also correctly identified the curious bone item, nos. 5 and 6 in Fig. 3.1, as the dagger's pommel. Bjolderup contained a woollen cloak, which was rare, but Thomsen stressed that the other items were well-known: a sword (not illustrated) "*is of the usual shape and length*"; the bronze fibula (4, in Fig. 3.2) is "*of a type of which several have been found in heathen burial mounds*"; the comb "*is similar in shape to those often found in Scandinavian burial mounds*" (all quotes from Thomsen 1836b, 285–6, my translation).

Thomsen was thus placing Bjolderup and Gristhorpe into an *archaeological* context that he already knew well, in a way that Williamson had not been able to do. This was explicitly the *Bronze Age*, which he defined in 1836 as the period when bronze was used for weapons and cutting tools. When iron became available it replaced bronze for these purposes, although bronze continued to be used for decorative items and jewellery (Thomsen 1836a, 58–60). Thomsen's ascription of Bjolderup and Gristhorpe to the Bronze Age means that Gristhorpe is apparently the first British archaeological site ever dated with respect to the Three Age System.

But what absolute date did Thomsen ascribe to the Bronze Age? He believed that iron had been brought to Denmark in the first century BC by immigrants (Thomsen 1836a, 60). He did not speculate about how far back the Bronze Age extended. But it is likely that he would have found Williamson's date of 600–400 BC to be perfectly plausible – even though arrived at by a completely different method of chronological deduction.

Thomsen's achievement was to outline a scheme based on the artefact assemblages themselves, not upon shaky quasi-historical foundations. There were no Phoenicians in Thomsen's discussion. The only Scandinavian who argued for Phoenician visits was Sven Nilsson, who thought that amber tempted them to the Baltic, not a huge step further than the Scilly Isles, which he accepted were the Cassiterides (Nilsson 1862–64). Most Scandinavian archaeologists did not agree. Hans Hildebrand pointed out that Strabo's description of the Cassiterides was unlikely to apply to the Scillies, because the Scillies themselves have no tin: this comes from adjacent Cornwall. There was no historical reason to suppose the Phoenicians had ventured as far even as Britain, never mind Scandinavia. Nor was there any archaeological trace of them, apart from one undated tin ingot from England (Hildebrand 1895). Sophus Müller, the leading Danish archaeologist at the turn of the 20th century, dismissed Phoenician visits to Scandinavia: "*this hypothesis has never gained acceptance and for a long time has been recognised as completely erroneous*" (Müller 1897, 207, my translation).

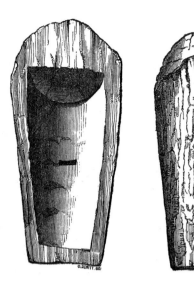

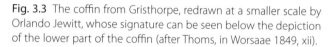

Fig. 3.3 The coffin from Gristhorpe, redrawn at a smaller scale by Orlando Jewitt, whose signature can be seen below the depiction of the lower part of the coffin (after Thoms, in Worsaae 1849, xii).

The first English mention of Gristhorpe as a Bronze Age find came in 1849. The youthful J. J. A. Worsaae had published a book in Danish in 1843, which mentioned Bjolderup but not Gristhorpe (Worsaae 1843). This book was translated into English by W. J. Thoms, who added a long preface of his own. Thoms knew of Thomsen's paper, and included a lengthy comparison between Gristhorpe and Bjolderup (in Worsaae 1849, xi–xix). This included a woodcut of the Gristhorpe coffin, redrawn for publication in a smaller format by Orlando Jewitt, brother of the archaeologist Llewellynn Jewitt (Fig. 3.3). However, when Thoms discussed the Gristhorpe artefacts, he mentioned "*the head of a spear or javelin*," and a "*beautifully formed ornament of either horn or the bone of some of the larger cetaceous tribe of fishes*" (in Worsaae 1849, xiv, xv) – apparently not grasping Thomsen's identification of these as dagger and pommel respectively.

But the idea of Gristhorpe as a Bronze Age site was not to take root in England for nearly twenty years. The Danish system of archaeological periods fell on the stony ground of Thomas Wright's short chronology.

Thomas Wright and the short chronology

Thomas Wright's approach to Gristhorpe was completely different from either of those described above. Wright was one of the most influential British archaeologists in the mid-19th century, and was typical of a group of men who stressed observation and facts, and eschewed all theory – and it mattered little whether the theory involved druid temples, Phoenician visits, or the existence of a Bronze Age. In one way the stress on facts was beneficial: it led to a huge increase in published data. But the eschewing of theory also meant that finds were sometimes treated uncritically, leading to incorrect associations being made between artefact categories.

Champion (2001) has shown that the Phoenicians retained a high profile in popular culture, and he argues persuasively that this was because they were seen as maritime colonists, bringing the benefits of commerce and civilisation to primitive island inhabitants – precisely the role that the British Empire saw itself fulfilling at the time. This continued throughout the 19th century; Champion mentions a painting executed in 1894–5 by Lord Leighton, entitled 'Phoenicians trading with early Britons', in which *"the richly clad Phoenicians are presented as the bringers of civilisation, learning and technical skill to the mostly fur-clad Britons, with whom they traded textiles and high-quality manufactured goods in exchange for furs and metal"* (Champion 2001, 452).

The Phoenicians, however, largely disappeared from archaeological writings in the mid-19th century, because the physical evidence for Phoenician contact was non-existent. A 158 lb H-shaped tin ingot (mentioned by Hildebrand: see above) dredged from the River Fal was thought by some to be Phoenician – two such ingots are visible in Lord Leighton's painting – but it is probably late medieval (Champion 2001, 454). Wright knew that standing stones – Borlase's Cornish symbols of Phoenician deities (see above) – were found all over Britain, and were erected at many different times (Wright 1852, 61).

Thomas Wright and his colleagues believed that the first occupation of Britain was unlikely to date as far back as any putative Phoenician visits. This very short chronology was derived from the ethnological writings mainly of James Cowles Prichard (Rowley-Conwy 2007, 89–99). Both Wright and Prichard believed (like Robert Henry – see above) that Europeans were descended from Japhet the son of Noah. The Celts, inhabitants of western Europe when Roman historians were writing, were descended from Japhet's son Gomer. But was western Europe already occupied when the Celts arrived in the last centuries BC? Prichard thought it likely (1841, 8–9), although all the skulls he had so far seen were of Celtic type (Prichard 1848, 191–2). Wright doubted that the pre-Celts had left any material traces of their existence, and thought the Celtic period filled *"a few generations, at most"* before the arrival of the Romans (Wright 1866, 176). In this short time, there was no space for successive ages of stone, bronze and iron, a theory that Wright regarded as the result of *"a spirit of too hasty generalising"* (1866, 176) by Thomsen and his colleagues.

This led Wright to accept problematic artefactual associations. He cited Thomas Bateman's excavation of a megalith at Minninglowe Hill, in which were found six Roman coins; this demonstrated that megaliths were of Roman date (Wright 1852, 81–2). Thomsen would surely have questioned this association; but Wright did not. Echoing Williamson's reply to Gage (above), Wright regarded variations between barrow contents as reflecting the status of the interred person, not the date of the burial (Wright 1852, 81). He considered most or all bronze items as of Roman manufacture (1852, 74–77), and most of his contemporaries agreed. In a catalogue of antiquities in the Museum of London, Charles Roach Smith (1854, 80) argued that all the bronze items were Roman or Romano-British. Albert Way (1849) dated a barrow on Anglesey containing a cremation urn and a fragment of bronze to the early Roman period, because of a legendary association of the site with a British princess of the first century AD.

It was from this perspective that Thomas Wright undertook his major review of Gristhorpe. The site was already prominent in the archaeological literature. For example, Thomas Bateman, the excavator of hundreds of Derbyshire barrows, regularly compared his finds to Gristhorpe. In one barrow he found *"a small article of ivory, perforated with six holes"* which he stated was similar to that from Gristhorpe, though he did not know its purpose (Bateman 1848, 39); he was unaware that Thomsen had already identified the Gristhorpe example as the dagger pommel. Several years later, still mystified as to its purpose, Bateman mentioned another which he compared to *"that found with the celebrated skeleton of the Ancient British Chieftain discovered at Gristhorpe"* (Bateman 1855, 25).

Wright contested the pre-Roman dates put forward by Williamson and Bateman. He clearly regarded his contribution as important, because he published it twice: once for the general public in the *Gentleman's Magazine* in 1857, and verbatim for the academic readership in a volume of archaeological essays four years later (Wright 1857, 1861). He described the find, including the skeleton, *"which has been unadvisedly called that of a 'British chief'"* (1861, 41). He too was unaware of the function of the bone dagger pommel, referring to it as *"a large stud or button"* (1861, 39).

Wright published an illustration of the Gristhorpe artefacts (Fig. 3.4), redrawn from Williamson's original presumably by himself, along with Orlando Jewitt's depiction of the coffin (Fig. 3.3). Few of the Gristhorpe artefacts were easy to date. Stone tools were not helpful: Wright stated that he had found flint artefacts in both Roman and Saxon graves (1861, 40), and elsewhere claimed that some Anglo-Saxons fought with stone tools at the Battle of Hastings (1852, 72). The bronze dagger, however, was datable. It:

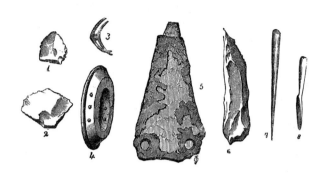

Fig. 3.4 The Gristhorpe artefacts, redrawn probably by Thomas Wright (after Wright 1861, 39).

"belongs to a type of which several examples have been found in the Wiltshire barrows, as well as in similar circumstances in other parts of England, which, from all the circumstances connected with them, we should be led to ascribe to a remote date, perhaps to the earlier period of the Roman occupation of the island" (1861, 40).

Wright cited two recent similar finds from Yorkshire, which he thought were also Roman (1861, 44). This dating was strongly supported by another find of no fewer than 14 coffins made of hollowed oak trunks. Crucially, these were Christian, from the site of a former churchyard. Wright believed them to be Anglo-Saxon, the log coffins continuing the Gristhorpe tradition from the Roman age into this period.

In the 1860s many continued to accept the short chronology. John Thurnam included a major entry on Gristhorpe in *Crania Britannica*, his massive collaborative work with Joseph Barnard Davis (Davis and Thurnam 1865, vol. II entry 10). He reproduced both Jewitt's illustration of the coffin (Fig. 3.3), and Wright's one of the finds (Fig. 3.4). Thurnam and Davis may have been the first British

archaeologists to realise that the bone object was in fact the dagger's pommel (Davis and Thurnam 1865, unpaginated; Davis 1865, 4). Thurnam thought the burial was pre-Roman, but no earlier than the last two or three centuries BC (Davis and Thurnam 1865, unpaginated). Wright however stuck to his Roman date. In a paper in 1866 he presented proof that bronze daggers were Roman: similar ones were depicted on Roman coins. He illustrated one struck by Brutus celebrating the death of Julius Caesar (Fig. 3.5):

> *"We see at a glance that the dagger with which Cæsar was slain was identical in every particular with those found in the tumuli of Britain which some antiquaries are now ascribing to the remote age of Phœnician colonies! Thus we see that the bronze swords, the bronze shields, the bronze spears, the bronze daggers, which have been found in Britain, are all Roman in character... It is my firm conviction that not a bit of bronze which has been found in the British islands belongs to an older date than that at which Cæsar wrote that the Britons obtained their bronze from abroad, meaning, of course, Gaul..."* (Wright 1866, 189).

Wright went to his grave in 1877 still committed to this view, having reprinted the 1866 paper quoted here as the first chapter of the updated third edition of his 1852 book (Wright 1875). In the 1870s some still followed his interpretation of Gristhorpe. Thomas Snagge (1873) described oak coffins recently found in Northumberland, citing precedents of which Gristhorpe was the most famous. Tellingly, he stated that *"a full account of this discovery* [Gristhorpe] *illustrated by woodcuts was given by Thomas Wright, Esq. F. S. A. in the Gentleman's Magazine."* He mentioned Williamson's original publication only in a footnote (Snagge 1873, 13). Others admitted that the site was pre-Roman, but adhered to the short chronology. Llewellynn Jewitt wrote an entire book on barrows, referring to pre-Roman examples only as 'Celtic' and making no mention whatsoever of the Three Age System. He presented a lengthy description of Gristhorpe – reusing his brother Orlando's illustration of the coffin and Wright's of the finds (cf. Figs. 3.3 and 3.4) (Jewitt 1870, 44–49).

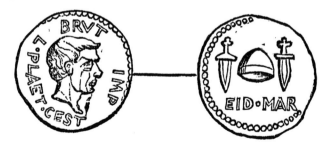

No. 7. Coin of Brutus.

Fig. 3.5. Wright's illustration of a Roman coin on which are depicted daggers like the bronze ones found in British barrows (after Wright 1866, fig. 7).

Anders Retzius, John Thurnam, and the racial chronology

Gristhorpe played a major part in the debate about possible pre-Celtic inhabitants of Britain. As stated above, James Cowles Prichard regarded all Europeans, and all Asians not of Semitic ancestry, as the descendants of Japhet. Those speaking Indo-European languages descended from Japhet's son Gomer. This lineage he termed 'Iranian' (Prichard 1841), soon amended to 'Arian' (Prichard 1843). Northern Eurasian descendants of Japhet's other sons, not of Indo-European stock, were collectively termed

'Allophylian' (Greek for 'other lineage') by Prichard (1841, 8; 1843, 185); other terms for these people were 'Turanian' or 'Scythian'. Allophylians must once have occupied Europe; non-Indo-European languages like Basque and Finnish were residual islands of Allophylians in a sea of immigrant Indo-Europeans.

Casts of interesting skulls were routinely exchanged between the specialists in various European countries. Prichard examined the cast of a skull from Denmark originally published by Daniel Eschricht (1837). Was it Arian, or Allophylian? Although it had some primitive features, Prichard (1843, 192–3) concluded that it was likely to be Arian, possibly a Celt. His identification became more certain a year later, when he examined four skulls from modern Allophylians, two Finns and two Lapps. He concluded that they were clearly different from those of Indo-Europeans (Prichard 1844).

This caused a problem in Scandinavian circles, because Eschricht's skull came from a Stone Age grave, and was thus one of the earliest inhabitants. Sven Nilsson (1838–43) examined several more Stone Age skulls; they were all similar, being quite round in shape ('brachycephalic'). After comparing them to modern Lapps, Nilsson was certain that his Stone Age skulls were ancestral Lapps, *i.e.* Allophylians, not ancestral Danes or Swedes. He tentatively identified some long-skulled ('dolichocephalic') Bronze Age individuals as Celts, immigrants who drove the Allophylian peoples into the far north. Eschricht's Stone Age skull therefore had to be Allophylian, not Celtic.

The Swedish anatomist Anders Retzius then received a cast of the Gristhorpe skull, sent to him by Prichard himself. Retzius (1849) published his analysis of the skull, misspelling the site 'Gristorph', along with a rather poor drawing of it (Fig. 3.6 top), and a detailed description of the whole find – Prichard had also sent a copy of Williamson's (1836) pamphlet. He quoted Prichard's accompanying letter identifying it as the "*skul* [*sic*] *of ancient British Chief of the Brigantian tribe*" (1849, 123). But Retzius did not agree. The Gristhorpe skull was clearly brachycephalic, like the very earliest Scandinavian skulls, and could not therefore be Celtic. Furthermore, Prichard had sent Retzius the cast of another skull from a burial ground near York (Fig. 3.6 bottom), and Retzius identified this one as Celtic because of its similarity to those of living Celts he had examined (1849, 131–33). Retzius' conclusion was that:

"*the skull in question* [*i.e.* Gristhorpe], *although presumably one of the earliest inhabitants of the country, is however not Celtic; that the Celts were not the earliest inhabitants of England, but these aborigines belonged to a different people*" (Retzius 1849, 124, my translation).

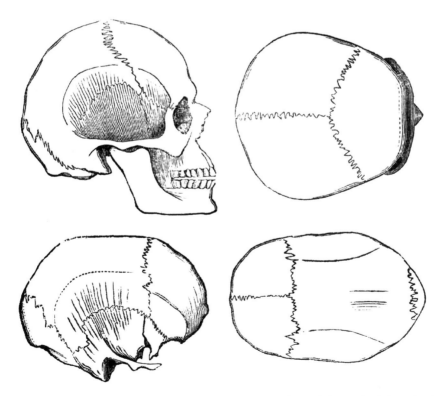

Fig. 3.6 Retzius' drawing of the brachycephalic Gristhorpe skull (top), and the dolichocephalic one he believed to be Celtic (bottom) (from Retzius 1849, 121 and 132).

The Gristhorpe man must therefore be Turanian (=Allophylian), and his people were later displaced by bronze-using Celts (1849, 127). This of course overlooked the fact that the Gristhorpe assemblage included a bronze dagger, as Retzius knew perfectly well because he had mentioned the dagger earlier in his article (he also correctly identified the bone object as the pommel; perhaps he had read Thomsen's 1836 paper) (1849, 119).

In England, John Thurnam published a paper in the same year (1849). He knew about the chronological sequence of Scandinavian skulls established by Eschricht, Nilsson and Retzius, but he had not yet heard of Retzius' diagnosis of the Gristhorpe skeleton as Allophylian (1849, 128). He lamented that there were too few dated British skulls for any sequence to be established, but did agree with Prichard that the available ancient British skulls were Celtic. Gristhorpe was central to his argument:

> "The few crania which I have myself seen from early British tumuli correspond very much with Dr. Prichard's description. They had, for the most part, a shortened oval form; ample behind, and somewhat narrow and receding in the forehead. The cranium from the undoubtedly British tumulus at Gristhorpe, near Scarborough, has this general form; it is, however, unusually large, and not deficient in frontal development; its form, too, is in some respects fine, particularly as regards the full <u>supra-orbital</u> region, and the high and fully developed middle head" (Thurnam 1849, 129, original italics underlined).

In 1854, Thurnam excavated a megalithic burial at Uley. The skulls were remarkably long (Thurnam 1854, 323), but he drew no chronological conclusion from this. Like Thomas Wright, he believed that differences between megaliths and round barrows reflected social status not date: the Uley burial "appears to bear the same relation to a simple barrow of the same age, as the mausoleum of a noble of the present day does to the turf-grave of a village churchyard" (Thurnam 1854, 324).

Gristhorpe made a published appearance in the USA, in a paper by Joseph Barnard Davis, the other leading British craniologist of the time. He concurred with Thurnam that the Uley skulls were indeed long; however, skull form would be variable in any population, and there was no reason to assume that a pre-Celtic population was involved (Davis 1857, 42–3). People varied in all sorts of ways, for example height – and here the tall man from Gristhorpe provided an excellent example:

> "In <u>stature</u> we have reason to know the ancient Britons varied a good deal. A famous skeleton of a British chieftain, discovered in a coffin made out of the trunk of a tree, in 1834, at Gristhorpe, near Scarborough, and now preserved in the museum of that town, measured 6 feet 2 inches in height" (Davis 1857, 44, original italics underlined).

This refusal to admit the existence of a pre-Celtic population allowed Thurnam and Davis to accept the very short chronology of Thomas Wright (above). By the 1860s their views had diverged somewhat. Davis continued to argue that populations displayed a lot of variability in skull shape, so long and round skulls did not form a chronological sequence (in Davis and Thurnam 1865). Thurnam was however a prolific excavator and had recovered many more skulls both from long and round barrows. Long barrows consistently produced stone tools and long skulls: "a sort of axiom has, I think, now been established to this effect: <u>Long barrows, long skulls; Round barrows, round or short skulls</u>" (Thurnam 1865, 158, original emphasis underlined). This was, of course, the opposite sequence from Scandinavia, where the round skulls came first. Thurnam, however, still espoused a very short chronology, because he refused to accept the evidence for human antiquity which had been recently published (e.g. Evans 1860). He did not therefore need to stretch Britain's pre-Roman occupation back to link up with earlier epochs. He thus achieved the unique feat of fitting the entire Stone Age and the Bronze Age into just a century or two, regarding the Romans as the bringers of iron.

But were there any Allophylian skulls in Britain? Davis continued to deny it, stressing variability. He published a new find of a log coffin from Scale House in Yorkshire, excavated by Greenwell in 1864 (Davis 1865). There were no finds apart from fragments of a woollen garment, and the skeleton had decayed. Davis therefore used Gristhorpe as his principal example, reproducing (yet again) the illustrations of the coffin by Jewitt, and the finds by Wright (Figs. 3.3 and 3.4). He accepted that Gristhorpe was Bronze Age – though he did not venture any absolute date. But Gristhorpe was certainly not Allophylian: he emphasised in several places that he was an "ancient Briton" (Davis 1865, 3, 4, 11). Two years later he reiterated that the man was "an ancient British chieftain" (Davis 1867, 3–4).

Thurnam was ambivalent about possible Allophylians in Britain because of the reversed skull sequence compared to that found in Denmark; but for Thurnam, too, the brachycephalic Gristhorpe skull was undoubtedly an ancient British Celt. He wrote the entry on Gristhorpe in Crania Britannica, illustrating the skull in a beautiful photogravure (Fig. 3.7); Thurnam wrote that "this magnificent skull is almost the largest we have had to figure" (in Davis and Thurnam 1865, not paginated). Thurnam had by now encountered Retzius' claim that Gristhorpe was Allophylian (see above). But since Thurnam believed that iron was introduced by the Romans, bronze users like the Gristhorpe man were immediately pre-Roman and thus had to be the Celts whom the Romans encountered. He took this opportunity to attack the Swede:

> "Professor Retzius enters into an elaborate argument to show that [the Gristhorpe skull], like other brachycephalic skulls..., must be referred to an aboriginal pre-Celtic population of "Turanian" race. The Celtic skull was believed by Retzius to be narrow and rather long. This

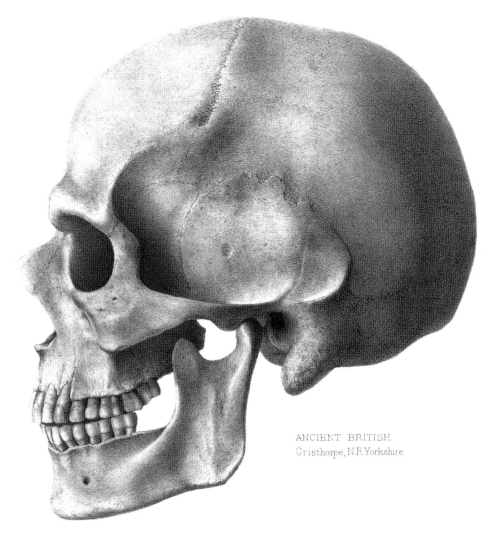

ANCIENT BRITISH.
Gristhorpe, N.R.Yorkshire

Fig. 3.7 Thurnam's high-quality photogravure of the Gristhorpe skull, from Crania Britannica (from Davis and Thurnam 1865, not paginated).

is altogether at variance with the results obtained by the authors of the "Crania Britannica," whose researches show that the usual form of the ancient British male skull is, or more or less approaches to, the brachycephalic. We suspect that the view of Professor Retzius was founded on too much examination of female heads and crania" (in Davis and Thurnam 1865, not paginated).

But the problems of craniology are illustrated by Thurnam's other drawings of Gristhorpe. Some appeared under the heading in *Crania Britannica* (Fig. 3.8). Two other views appear in another paper by Thurnam published in the very same year (Fig. 3.9). Both of these contain vertical views of the top of the skull – but the *Crania Britannica* drawing is viewed from slightly further forward because the projecting nasal bones are shown. This minor difference is sufficient completely to alter the skull's shape when viewed from above (cf. Figs. 3.8 and 3.9).

The 1860s saw some doubts raised with Thurnam's views in connection with the long chronology discussed in the next section. William Greenwell was uncertain whether a Celtic skull type could be defined, but since he was sure that the Celts encountered by the Romans had long used iron, brachycephalic Bronze Age people were not necessarily Celtic at all:

"What is the keltic type? Now many difficulties, at present, stand in the way of an answer to this, which, until they are solved, make vain, it seems to me, all attempts at a solution of the secondary question. Merely to allude, in conclusion, to one difficulty. The skull, from the round barrows, is eminently brachycephalic; the skull of the modern Irishman or Scotch highlander, whom we commonly term "Celts," is not brachycephalic..." (1865a, 205, original emphasis underlined).

William Greenwell and the long chronology

Williamson's third pamphlet of 1872 was considerably different from the first two. It reflected many of the changes that contemporary archaeology was going through. Williamson used not the short chronology described above, but the long chronology that was replacing it – and there was not a Phoenician in sight. Specifically, he concluded *"that the Gristhorpe interment took place early in the Bronze age"* (Williamson 1872, 19). Two archaeologists were, to judge

from the frequency with which Williamson quoted them, particularly influential in forming his views.

John Thurnam was mentioned several times. Williamson borrowed the description of the skull from *Crania Britannica* for his new discussion of the skeleton, and reproduced the drawings (Fig. 3.8) in his pamphlet, thanking Joseph Barnard Davis for the loan of the wood block (1872, 4). Thurnam accepted the existence of the Bronze Age – but the dates Williamson gave were much older than Thurnam accepted. Williamson stated that the Bronze Age ended in the 5th century BC (1872, 19), later adding that the man

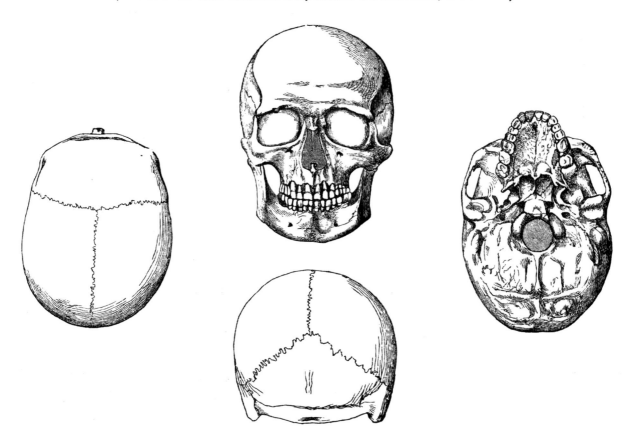

ANCIENT BRITISH SKULL.

FROM BARROW AT GRISTHORPE, NORTH RIDING, YORKSHIRE.

(REGION OF THE BRIGANTES, TEMP. PTOLEMÆI, A.D. 120.)

Cranium from Barrow at Gristhorpe.—Quarter-size.

Fig. 3.8 Thurnam's chapter heading for his entry on Gristhorpe, with his other drawings of the Gristhorpe skull. From *Crania Britannica* (from Davis and Thurnam 1865, not paginated).

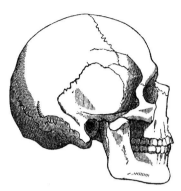

Fig. 10. Brachycephalic skull from a Round Barrow, of the Bronze period, at Gristhorpe, Yorkshire.

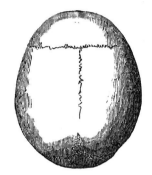

*Fig. 11. Vertical view of the same skull.—Quarter diameter.**

* (*Figs.* 10, 11.) There are many brachycephalous British skulls in collections obtained from round barrows, which may be shown to be of the bronze period; but very few, indeed, with which bronze objects have actually been found. The very perfect skull here figured, from the celebrated tumulus at Gristhorpe, Yorkshire, has therefore a peculiar interest. With it was a bronze dagger-blade, and two or three arrow-heads and flakes of flint. It has been lithographed, and fully described by myself in *Crania Britannica*, plate 52; and has been figured by Professor Retzius, and also by Professor Von Baer. It is here given as a typical instance of the brachycephalous British skull of the bronze period.

Fig. 3.9. Further drawings by Thurnam of the Gristhorpe skull (from Thurnam 1865, figs. 10 and 11).

"lived about five centuries before the Christian era" (1872, 23). These statements somewhat contradict his statement that the burial dated to the *early* Bronze Age (1872, 19), but the dates are certainly older than Thurnam would have countenanced.

Williamson's early dates were clearly derived from William Greenwell, the leading barrow digger in northern England in these years. Greenwell was quoted six times by Williamson, being the first person thanked in the preface: *"I have to acknowledge the friendly assistance which I have received from the Rev. Canon Greenwell, of Durham"* (1872, 4). Greenwell's influence was substantial. The bronze object became *"a dagger or knife"* (1872, 13), and *"Canon Greenwell informs me he has met with five such"* (1872, 14). The bone object was now correctly identified as the dagger pommel, and again Greenwell was credited with having a similar one (1872, 14). Greenwell also provided various comparanda for

the burial itself (1872, 8n, 12, 17). Greenwell's scholarship was broad, and it is probable that he drew Williamson's attention to a Danish volume dealing in part with the now substantial number of oak coffins from Denmark (Madsen 1868, cited in Williamson 1872, 18–19).

Greenwell was the first English excavator to espouse the long chronology. Iron had been in use for a long time when the Romans invaded. How far back before this might the Bronze Age extend? He felt that 1000 BC was not too early (1865a, 204). Two factors probably influenced him. First, unlike Thurnam, he accepted human evolution and antiquity (1865b, 107 n5), and so had no theoretical problems with stretching the later prehistoric periods back to connect with the pre-modern humans. He discussed dating at length, mentioning various sites including the *"well-known burial at Gristhorp [sic]"* (1865b, 254 n1). Second, Greenwell's northern base in Durham placed him physically closer to Edinburgh than to London. He dug barrows in Scotland, and in 1879 was made an Honorary Fellow of the Society of Antiquaries of Scotland (Hodgson 1918, 14). These factors may have made him more open to the work of the Scottish archaeologist Daniel Wilson.

Daniel Wilson's epoch-making book *The Archaeology and Prehistoric Annals of Scotland* appeared in 1851. Wilson was considerably influenced by Scandinavian archaeologists, in particular the Norwegian Peter Andreas Munch (Rowley-Conwy 2006). Human antiquity had yet to be established, but Wilson adopted a long chronology because he had to fit *two different Allophylian races* into his sequence before the arrival of the Celts. Wilson established a craniological sequence for Scotland at a time when Thurnam and Davis had too few skulls to create one for England (see above). He accepted Nilsson's and Retzius' definition of the Celtic skull as relatively long, and his Iron Age ones matched this. Before that, Bronze Age skulls were round (brachycephalic), and before them again his Stone Age examples were long (primitive dolichocephalic, or 'kumbecephalic') (Wilson 1851). He tentatively dated the start of the Bronze Age to around 1000 BC (1851, 196), the end to before 100 BC (1851, 351).

Wilson discussed the date of Gristhorpe from this perspective. For Thomsen, the Bronze Age ended in the first century BC (see above), but his energetic follower J. J. A. Worsaae argued that it continued much later, ending around AD 800 (Worsaae 1841). If correct, this would pull the Bjolderup oak coffin into the first millennium AD, a date Wilson could not accept for Gristhorpe: *"so far as this single example goes, it rather tends to connect the remarkable deposit to a much earlier period"* (1851, 462). He mentioned two other oak coffin burials from Castlehill in Edinburgh that were stratigraphically probably pre-Roman (1851, 463–4). Before Greenwell, English archaeologists resisted Wilson's chronological views. The sole exception was the

Derbyshire barrow digger Thomas Bateman, who briefly adopted Wilson's ideas in one paper (Bateman 1852) – but he dropped them quickly, apparently under pressure from John Thurnam (Harlan in prep).

Greenwell had certainly read Wilson's chronological scheme (Greenwell 1866, 347). Direct connections between Wilson and Greenwell are however not usually considered by historians of archaeology, because Wilson left for Canada in 1853, and Greenwell's published writings started to appear only in the mid-1860s. It is, however, likely that the two men did actually meet. Wilson came south for the 1852 meeting of the Archaeological Institute at Newcastle upon Tyne, and presented a major paper (Wilson 1858). Greenwell was at this meeting, and gave a paper on the rock art of Northumberland (mentioned in Greenwell 1865b, 99 n7), but his paper suffered a fate not unknown in the days before photocopiers and electronic back-ups: the manuscript and illustrations were lost prior to publication (Fowler 1904, 152). Consequently, his name appeared nowhere in the publication of the meeting, and his presence there is usually overlooked. There is no proof that Wilson and Greenwell met and discussed chronological matters, but it is hard to imagine that Greenwell was not present when Wilson stood up and lambasted the English archaeologists and their short chronology:

"There are indeed those among us, I am well aware, who ridicule all attempts to peer into that dim and remote era of our island's and our race's story which lies beyond the epoch of the Roman invasion, and who smile at the believers in the existence of such Stone and Bronze periods for Britain as we know to have existed for Polynesia and Mexico. We are well content to be regarded by such as fond and credulous enthusiasts. For them assuredly, beginning their researches as they do amid the fully developed Iron age of Roman Britain, a Stone or Bronze period is as meaningless as a carboniferous or cretaceous system to the geologist who persists in tracing all terrestrial phenomena to the Noahic Deluge. Perhaps it may yet be found that the spirit in which the systematic classification of archæological periods has been pronounced to be a mere rude and specious fancy is just about as profoundly sagacious as the orthodox creed of those Mosaic geologists, who denounce the intelligent deductions of science as rash scepticism or impious profanity" (Wilson 1858, 11).

At all events, Greenwell's work was instrumental in pushing the Bronze Age, and Gristhorpe with it, well back into the 1st millennium BC, and so the site took an honoured place in the new chronology. By 1873, Greenwell understood that inhumations with simple bronze daggers were the *earliest* form of Bronze Age burial (in Evans 1873, 414), which would place Gristhorpe at the start of this period. It is likely that he had previously discussed this with Williamson – hence the latter's statement (above) that Gristhorpe was *early* Bronze Age. Greenwell mentioned "*the well-known Gristhorpe burial*" in his monumental *British Barrows* (1877, 13). John Evans discussed the site in his *Ancient Bronze Implements*

(1881, 228), and the site made a belated first appearance in Sir John Lubbock's *Pre-Historic Times* in the fifth edition (1890, 136). These publications cemented the long chronology in place, and fixed Gristhorpe's position in it.

Conclusion

The importance of Gristhorpe in the chronological discussions of the 19th century will by now be clear. The association of the brachycephalic skull, the bronze dagger, and the other items gave it an importance as an assemblage that was far greater than the individual items would have had. Gristhorpe played its part in all the chronological schemes discussed here, and may justly be described as one of a very few key sites of 19th century archaeology. The claim put forward at the start of this contribution, that Gristhorpe may be the most widely quoted British archaeological site of the 19th century, is no exaggeration; the parallel with Star Carr is appropriate.

The current re-examination of the find puts Gristhorpe once more at centre stage. If any of those who discussed the site in the 19th century could read this volume and see how far archaeological methods have progressed, they would surely be amazed – as we would be if we could see the results of future re-re-examinations a century hence.

Acknowledgements
I would like to thank Nigel Melton for asking me to write this contribution, and for providing copies of the 1834 and 1872 versions of Williamson's pamphlet as well as the pamphlet by Travis, and also for providing information about the early newspaper reports. I thank Leif Fredensborg Nielsen for help with a point of Danish translation, and Jeff Veitch for scanning Figures 3.1, 3.2, 3.3, 3.4, 3.5 and 3.9 and producing such excellent results. I also thank Newcastle University Library (the Robinson Library) for permitting me to scan the skulls in figure 3.6 from their copy of Retzius' article, and Denis Peel and the Society of Antiquaries of Newcastle upon Tyne for permitting me to scan figures 3.7 and 3.8 from their copy of *Crania Britannica*, and once again Jeff Veitch for turning my scans into passable figures.

References

Anon. 1834. Gristhorpe, Yorkshire. *Gentleman's Magazine* 1834, II, 195.
Anon. 1835. Scarborough. *Gentleman's Magazine* 1835, II, 540.
Anon. 1836. Scarborough. *Gentleman's Magazine* 1836, II, 416–418.
Archaeological Institute (1848) *Memoirs illustrative of the History and Antiquities of the County and City of York, communicated at the*

Annual Meeting of the Archaeological Institute of Great Britain and Ireland, held at York, July, 1846. London, Archaeological Institute.

Bateman, T. (1848) *Vestiges of the Antiquities of Derbyshire, and the Sepulchral Usages of its Inhabitants, from the most remote Ages to the Reformation.* London, John Russell Smith.

Bateman, T. (1852) Remarks upon a few of the barrows opened at various times in the more hilly districts near Bakewell. *Journal of the British Archaeological Association* 7, 210–220.

Bateman, T. (1855) *A Descriptive Catalogue of the Antiquities and Various Objects preserved in the Museum of Thomas Bateman at Lomberdale House, Derbyshire.* Bakewell, Privately published.

Borlase, W. (1769) *Antiquities Historical and Monumental of the County of Cornwall.* London, W. Bowyer and J. Nichols.

Camden, W. (1695) *Camden's Britannia, newly translated into English; with large additions and improvements. Published by Edmund Gibson, of Queens-College in Oxford.* London, A. Swalle.

Champion, T. (2001) The appropriation of the Phoenicians in British imperial ideology. *Nations and Nationalism* 7, 451–465.

Colt Hoare, Sir Richard, (1810) *The History of Ancient Wiltshire* (2 vols). London, William Miller.

Davis, J. B. (1857) On the crania of the Ancient Britons, with remarks on the people themselves. *Proceedings of the Academy of Natural Sciences of Philadelphia* 1857, 40–48.

Davis, J. B. (1865) Notice of the opening of a barrow at Scale House, in the West Riding of Yorkshire,; and a comparison of the barrow with certain others in Jutland. *The Reliquary* 6, 1–11.

Davis, J. B. (1867) *Thesaurus Craniorum. Catalogue of the Skulls of the various Races of Man.* London, printed for the subscribers.

Davis, J. B. and Thurnam, J. (1865) *Crania Britannica. Delineations and Descriptions of the Skulls of the Aboriginal and Early Inhabitants of the British Islands: with Notices of their Other Remains* (2 vols.). London, printed for the Subscribers.

Eschricht, D. F. (1837) Om hovedskallerne og beenradene i vore gamle gravhöie. *Dansk Folkeblad* 3, 28–29 (15 September), 109–116.

Evans, J. (1860) On the occurrence of flint implements in undisturbed beds of gravel, sand, and clay. *Archaeologia* 38, 280–307.

Evans, J. (1873) Address on the Bronze Period. *Proceedings of the Society of Antiquaries of London* second series, 5, 392–412.

Evans, J. (1881) *The Ancient Bronze Implements, Weapons, and Ornaments of Great Britain and Ireland.* London, Longmans, Green.

Fosbroke, T. D. (1825) *Encyclopædia of Antiquities, and Elements of Archaeology, Classical and Mediæval* (2 vols). London, John Nichols.

Fowler, J. T. (1904) *Durham University: earlier Foundations and present Colleges.* London, F. E. Robson.

Greenwell, W. (1865a) Notes of the opening of Ancient British tumuli in north Northumberland in 1863 and 1865. *History of the Berwickshire Naturalists' Club* 5, 195–205.

Greenwell, W. (1865b) Notices of the examination of ancient grave-hills in the North Riding of Yorkshire. *Archaeological Journal* 22, 97–117, 241–264.

Greenwell, W. (1866) An account of excavations in cairns near Crinan. *Proceedings of the Society of Antiquaries of Scotland* 6, 336–351.

Greenwell, W. (1877) *British Barrows. A Record of the Examination of Sepulchral Mounds in various parts of England.* Oxford, Clarendon Press.

Harlan, D. (in prep) Thomas Bateman (1821–1861) and *Crania Britannica.*

Henry, R. (1800) *The History of Great Britain, from the first Invasion of it by Julius Cæsar,* third edition (12 vols). London, A. Strahan.

Hildebrand, H. (1895) Kassideriderna och tennet i forntiden. *Antiqvarisk Tidskrift för Sverige* 5, 181–210.

Hodgson, J. C. (1918) Memoir of the Rev. William Greenwell, D. C. L., F.R.S., F.S.A, a vice-president. *Archaeologia Aeliana* 3rd series, 15, 1–21.

Jewitt, L. (1870) *Grave-Mounds and their Contents: a Manual of Archaeology.* London, Groombridge.

Lubbock, J. (1890) *Pre-Historic Times, as illustrated by Ancient Remains, and the Manners and Customs of Modern Savages,* fifth edition. London, Williams and Norgate 1890.

Madsen, A. P. (1868) *Afbildninger af Danske Oldsager og Mindesmærker: Steenalderen.* Copenhagen, Thieles Bogtrykkeri.

Müller, S. (1897) *Vor Oldtid. Danmarks forhistoriske Archæologi.* Copenhagen, Nordiske Forlag.

Nilsson, S. (1838–43) *Skandinaviska Nordens Ur-Invånare, ett Försök i Komparativa Ethnografien och ett Bidrag till Menniskoslägtets Utvecklings-Historia.* Lund, Berlingska.

Nilsson, S. (1862–64) *Skandinaviska Nordens Ur-Invånare, ett Försök i Komparativa Ethnografien och ett Bidrag till Menniskoslägtets Utvecklings-Historia 2: Bronsåldern.* Stockholm, P.A. Norstedt.

Petersen, C. S. (1938) *Stenalder – Broncealder – Jernalder. Bidrag til nordisk Archæologis Litterærhistorie 1776–1865.* Copenhagen, Levin & Munksgaard.

Prichard, J. C. (1841) *Researches in the Physical History of Mankind,* third edition vol. III. London, Sherwood, Gilbert and Piper.

Prichard, J. C. (1843) *The Natural History of Man; comprising Inquiries into the Modifying Influence of Physical and Moral Agencies in the Different Tribes of the Human Family.* London, Bailliere.

Prichard, J. C. (1844) On the crania of the Laplanders and Finlanders, with observations of the differences they presented from other European races. *Proceedings of the Zoological Society of London* 12, 129–135.

Prichard, J. C. (1848) *The Natural History of Man; comprising Inquiries into the Modifying Influence of Physical and Moral Agencies in the Different Tribes of the Human Family,* third edition. London, Bailliere.

Retzius, A. (1849) Cranier ur gamla grafvar i England. *Öfversigt af Kongliga Vetenskaps-akademiens Förhandlingar* 6, 118–142.

Roach Smith, C. (1854) *Catalogue of the Museum of London Antiquities.* Printed for subscribers.

Rowley-Conwy, P. (2006) The concept of prehistory and the invention of the terms 'prehistoric' and 'prehistorian': the Scandinavian origin, 1833–1850. *European Journal of Archaeology* 9, 103–130.

Rowley-Conwy, P. (2007) *From Genesis to Prehistory. The archaeological Three Age System and its contested reception in Denmark, Britain, and Ireland.* Oxford, Oxford University Press. (Oxford Studies in the History of Archaeology).

Snagge, T. W. (1873) Some account of ancient oaken coffins discovered on the lands adjoining Featherstone Castle, near Haltwhistle, Northumberland. *Archæologia* 44, 8–16.

Street-Jensen, J. (1988) Thomsen og tredelingen – endnu en gang. In U. L. Hansen (ed.) *Christian Jürgensen Thomsen 1788 – 29. december – 1988,* 19–28. Copenhagen, Det Kongelige Nordiske

Oldskriftselskab. (Aarbøger for Nordisk Oldkyndighed og Historie 1988).

Thomsen, C. J. (1836a) Kortfattet udsigt over mindesmærker og oldsager fra nordens oldtid. In *Ledetraad til Nordisk Oldkyndighed*, ed. C.C. Rafn, 27–90. Copenhagen, Det Kongelige Nordiske Oldskriftselskab.

Thomsen, C. J. (1836b) Sammenlignende undersøgelse om nogle oldsager fra hedenold, fundne ved Gristhorpe i Yorkshire of ved Bjolderup nær Haderslev. *Nordisk Tidskrift for Oldkyndighed* 3, 279–286.

Thomsen C. J. (1836c) Antikvariske Efterretninger, *Nordisk Tidskrift for Oldkyndighed* 3, 289–339.

Thurnam, J. (1849) Description of an ancient tumular cemetery, probably of the Anglo-Saxon period, at Lamel-Hill, near York. *Archaeological Journal* 6, 27–39, 123–136.

Thurnam, J. (1854) Description of a chambered tumulus, near Uley, Gloucestershire. *Archaeological Journal* 11, 315–327.

Thurnam, J. (1865) On the two principal forms of ancient British and Gaulish skulls. *Memoirs read before the Anthropological Society of London* 1, 120–168, 459–519, and appendix.

Travis, W. (1836). *A Letter from William Travis, M. D., Scarborough, to Sir John V. B. Johnstone, Bart., M. P., President of the Scarborough Philosophical Society, communicating Discoveries made on the recent Opening of a British Tumulus in that Neighbourhood.* Scarborough, C. R. Todd.

Way, A. (1849) Account of sepulchral deposit, with cinerary urns, found at Porth Dafarch, in Holyhead Island. Communicated by the Hon. William Owen Stanley. *Archaeological Journal* 6, 226–239.

Williamson, W. C. (1834) *Description of the Tumulus, lately opened at Gristhorpe, near Scarborough.* Scarborough, C. R. Todd.

Williamson, W. C. (1836) *Description of the Tumulus, lately opened at Gristhorpe, near Scarborough*, second edition. Scarborough, C. R. Todd.

Williamson, W. C. (1872) *Description of the Tumulus opened at Gristhorpe, near Scarborough*, third edition. Scarborough, S. W. Theakston.

Wilson, D. (1851) *The Archaeology and Prehistoric Annals of Scotland.* Edinburgh, Sutherland and Knox.

Wilson, D. (1858) On the advantages derived from archæological investigation. An address delivered at the Newcastle meeting of the Archæological Institute, August, 1852. In *Memoirs chiefly illustrative of the History and Antiquities of Northumberland, communicated to the annual meeting of the Archæological Institute of Great Britain and Ireland held at Newcastle-on-Tyne in August 1852*, volume I, 1–14. London, Bell and Daldy.

Worsaae, J. J. A. (1841) Undersögelser af gravhöie i Danmark. *Annaler for Nordisk Oldkyndighed og Historie* 1840–41, 137–163.

Worsaae, J. J. A. (1843) *Danmarks Oldtid oplyst ved Oldsager og Gravhøje.* Copenhagen, Selskabet for Trykkefrihedens rette Brug.

Worsaae, J. J. A. (1849) *The Primeval Antiquities of Denmark.* London, John Henry Parker.

Wright, T. (1852) *The Celt, the Roman, and the Saxon.* London, Arthur Hall, Virtue.

Wright, T. (1857) On some curious forms of sepulchral interment found in East Yorkshire. *Gentleman's Magazine* 1857(II), 114–119.

Wright, T. (1861) *Essays on Archaeological Subjects* vol. I. London, John Russell Smith.

Wright, T. (1866) On the true assignation of the bronze weapons, etc., supposed to indicate a bronze age in western and northern Europe. *Transactions of the Ethnological Society of London* 4, 176–195.

Wright, T. (1875) *The Celt, the Roman, and the Saxon*, third edition. London, Trubner.

4

BRONZE AGE TREE-TRUNK COFFIN GRAVES IN BRITAIN

Mike Parker Pearson, Alison Sheridan and Stuart Needham

Introduction

The Gristhorpe tree-trunk coffin grave is exceptional, not only for its remarkable state of preservation when found but also for the amount and quality of information that it has yielded. It is not unique, however. Over 60 other examples of tree-trunk coffins (also known as log coffins and monoxylous coffins) are known from Early Bronze Age Britain (Appendix 4.1), and the practice is also attested in several parts of north-west and central Europe, in contexts ranging in date between *c.* 2500 BC and *c.* 1000 BC. The best known of the Continental examples are the excellently-preserved Middle Bronze Age specimens from southern Scandinavia, mainly Denmark, of which 18 have been dated by dendrochronology to between 1396 BC and 1268 BC (Glob 1974; Kähler Holst *et al.* 2001; Jensen 2002, 164–220; Randsborg and Christensen 2006). Other Continental examples include those from barrows dating to between *c.* 2500 and *c.* 1500 BC in the Netherlands (Drenth and Lohof 2005, 439–40); those found in Unĕtice-period Early Bronze Age (2200–1600 BC) flat cemeteries in Bohemia, Moravia and Silesia (Harding 2000, 105–107); and those in Early to Late Bronze Age cemeteries in Germany (*ibid.* 2000, 105).

In Britain, the practice of burial within a hollowed-out tree trunk is not limited to the Early Bronze Age. A cemetery of fourteen such coffins orientated east-west, found in 1857 near the old parish church of Selby, North Yorkshire, is very likely to be of early Medieval date (Snagge 1873, 13), as is a single coffin from Beverley Parks, East Riding of Yorkshire, whose lid had been fixed to the base using wooden pegs (T. Wright 1857; Mowat 1996, 140; Terry Manby, pers. comm.). A coffin found in 1973 at Quernmore, Lancashire, originally assumed to be of Early Bronze Age date (Edwards 1973; McGrail 1978, 93; Mowat 1996, 141), was subsequently radiocarbon dated to 1340±110 BP (cal AD 590–850 at 62.4% probability, cal AD 430–970 at 95.4% probability: White 2001); while an example from St. Saviour's Edge in York, with two boards set into grooves, is believed to be of Anglo-Scandinavian date (Elgee and Elgee 1949, 102). An even later date, within the High Medieval period, has been ascribed to two tree-trunk coffins found on Castlehill, Edinburgh; these had recesses for the head and upper limbs '*in apparent imitation of medieval stone coffins*' and are suspected to be extempore high-status graves, one of a man, the other of a woman (Mowat 1996, 86). This chapter will not concern itself with such post-Bronze Age examples, although Appendix 4.2 presents evidence concerning a group of at least eight well-preserved tree-trunk coffins found in marshy ground at Wydon Eals, near Haltwhistle, Northumberland (Snagge 1873), since these have entered popular consciousness as being of Early Bronze Age date. As will be seen, these differ in several respects from Early Bronze Age examples, not least by their abundance, and it is strongly suspected that they significantly post-date the Bronze Age.

This chapter focuses on the Early Bronze Age British examples of burial within a tree-trunk coffin, in order to set the Gristhorpe grave within its broader context. In the following text, references to 'No. 1', 'No. 2', etc. relate to entries in the catalogue presented in Appendix 4.1.

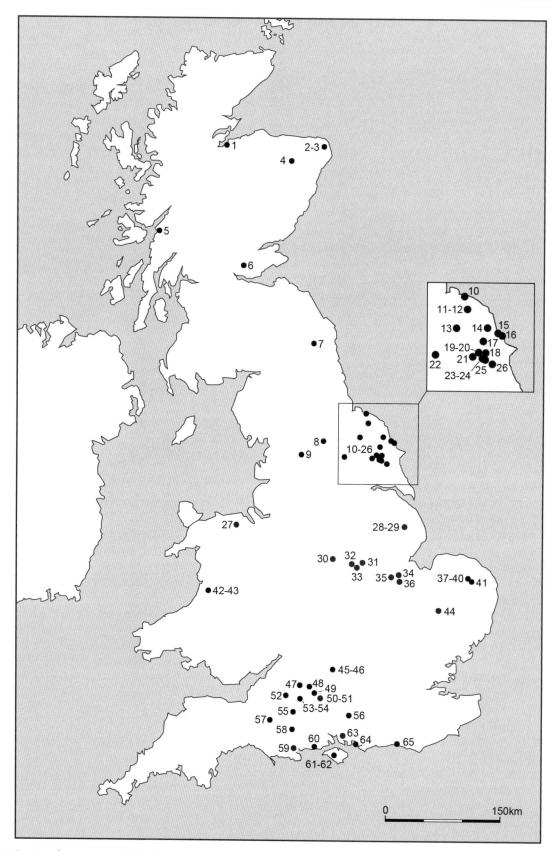

Fig. 4.1 Distribution of tree-trunk coffin finds in Britain. See also Table 4.1, *Addenda*, which include two examples from a findspot in Cornwall.

British Early Bronze Age tree-trunk coffin graves: numbers, distribution and some noteworthy examples

The earliest recorded find of a tree-trunk coffin in Britain is that found under the large, 30 metre-diameter King Barrow at Stoborough, Dorset on January 21, 1767 (No. 59; Hutchins 1767; see Ashbee 1960, 86, 88 for a full account). Here, according to John Hutchins, an unusually-long, roughly-hollowed ('*rudely excavated*') tree-trunk coffin measuring 10′ by 4′ (3 m × 1.2 m), with decayed ends, was found to contain an unburnt body wrapped in sewn deer skins, accompanied by '*gold lace*' and a '*wooden*' vessel which was probably a shale cup (Needham *et al.* 2006, 53, 103–4). Unfortunately, the present whereabouts of the finds (if they have survived at all) is unknown, and the nature of the enigmatic, and unparalleled, '*gold lace*' is open to question (*ibid.*, 104).

The 19th century saw the discovery of further tree-trunk coffin graves – including the Gristhorpe example – with the barrow-digging antiquaries John Mortimer, Canon William Greenwell and Sir Richard Colt Hoare unearthing several in Yorkshire and Wessex. Most of the early and mid-20th century finds also resulted from curiosity about the contents of barrows and cairns, the investigations being undertaken by individuals showing varying degrees of skill and attention to detail, while those found over the last few decades have mostly been discovered as a result of developer-funded excavations. Previous syntheses and discussions have included those by Wright (1857), Whiting (1937), Grinsell (1941, 365–6), Elgee and Elgee (1949, 105–6), Ashbee (1960, 86–91), Field (1985, 133–4), Mowat (1996) and Cressey and Sheridan (2003, 78–9).

Today, around 65 examples, from 57 findspots, are known (Appendix 4.1 and Fig. 4.1. Note also the *Addenda* at the end Appendix 4.1, which are not included in the statistics presented here.). Arriving at a precise total is made difficult by the fact that in some cases, as discussed below and in Appendix 4.1, it can be difficult to distinguish a tree-trunk coffin from other forms of wooden grave structure (e.g. a bier) when only a stain in the ground, or fragments of wood, charcoal or manganese oxide-replaced wood, are all that survives. Furthermore, the degree of detail provided by the published accounts varies considerably. Appendix 4.1 summarises the available evidence, offering a categorisation into 'definite', 'probable' and 'possible' examples, and listing those which may have been mentioned or included in previous discussions of this type of grave but which are excluded from the present catalogue, for various reasons. The Appendix also provides bibliographic references for each entry, so these will generally not be cited in the main text.

The geographical distribution (Fig. 4.1) shows that the practice of burial in a tree-trunk coffin was not only extensive – with examples extending from the Moray Firth to the Channel coast, and from western Wales to East Anglia – but also highly regionalised. There is a marked concentration in Yorkshire, where a quarter of all known examples (16 coffins, from 15 findspots) have been found on or around the North York Moors and Yorkshire Wolds. The Gristhorpe example lies within this concentration. There is a second, and less dense cluster, in Wessex and along the south English coast as far as Sussex. The results of rescue archaeology, especially over the last 30 years, have led to the identification of a third regional cluster, in the Welland and Lower Nene valleys of Leicestershire and Cambridgeshire and extending into northern East Anglia. Interestingly, despite large-scale excavations of Early Bronze Age cemeteries in similar environmental circumstances along the Upper Nene and Thames valleys (where traces left by decayed tree-trunk coffins should be just as easily recognisable in the gravels), no certain evidence has come to light; just one probable and one possible example are known from the Barrow Hills cemetery at Radley, Oxfordshire (Nos. 45 and 46). Elsewhere, there is a thin scatter in Scotland (including examples near the north-east and south-west ends of the Great Glen, at Seafield West (No. 1) and Dalrigh (No. 5), respectively); in northern England outside the aforementioned Yorkshire concentration; and in Wales. No example is known from Ireland.

As will be seen below, there is a chronological dimension that needs to be borne in mind when considering the geographical patterning of this practice. There may also be a degree of structural variability that can be related to time and place. Before exploring these aspects, however, a snapshot of some of the best-preserved or otherwise noteworthy examples is offered, to give some sense of the range of structures, rites and grave goods involved.

One example that may be broadly contemporary with the Stoborough grave was found in 1856 at Palmeira Avenue, Hove, Sussex, under a large round barrow (No. 65). It was described as being '*a rude oak coffin, hollowed out of a single tree-trunk, and shaped with an axe*'. It was 6′–7′ (1.8 m–2.1 m) long, and contained fragments of '*carious bone, apparently charred*' and, at its centre, an amber cup, a bronze-bladed dagger, a stone battle-axehead and a whetstone (Fig. 4.2). The coffin crumbled to pieces and nothing was recorded of its shape. Later writers have been unsure whether the fragmentary skeletal remains described were really burnt or not (Curwen and Curwen 1924, 22).

At Milton Lilbourne, Wiltshire (No. 49), an apparently unlidded rectangular coffin *c.* 0.9 × 0.3 × 0.1 m, shaped like a flattened 'U' in both longitudinal and transverse section, was found under the centre of a sizeable bell barrow, in

Fig. 4.2 The amber cup, battle axe, bronze dagger and whetstone from the Hove tree-trunk coffin (courtesy of National Museums Scotland).

a rectangular area that may well have been the location of a cremation pyre. The coffin contained the cremated remains of a tall, relatively old man aged 40–60, along with the accessory vessel that may have held the embers used to light his pyre; his remains had been laid within a boat-shaped hollow in the split log, on a sheet of bark. The top of the coffin had been burnt to wood-ash.

There have been two finds of well-preserved tree-trunk coffins from North Yorkshire besides the Gristhorpe example. That from Scale House barrow at Rylstone, Craven, North Yorkshire (No. 9) was of oak, 7′3″ (2.2 m) by 1′11″ (0.6 m), partially rounded outside and worked with a narrow-edged metal blade. The description implies that it had been lidded with the other half of the split trunk. Inside, the unburnt body, surviving as '*unctuous white adipocere*', was wrapped from head to foot in woven woollen fabric. Apart from this fabric, no artefacts were found in the grave.

The other find, from a round barrow excavated in 1937 at Loose Howe on the North York Moors, consists of a lidded coffin with both halves shaped like a logboat, with a straight 'stern' and pointed 'prow', together with a slightly smaller and unlidded but similarly-shaped object with a rounded stern, found beside it (Nos. 11–12). The excavators (Elgee and Elgee 1949), along with Paul Ashbee (Ashbee 1960, 90) regarded the latter as an actual dugout canoe but this interpretation has been challenged (McGrail 1978, 93) and it may well be that this was a second boat-shaped coffin; the question of boat-shaped tree-trunk coffins will be discussed

below. The unburnt body within the lidded coffin survived only as a '*wet, black, greasy substance*', along with one ankle bone. It had lain on a bed of rushes, reeds or straw, with a pillow of grass or straw under the head; the excavators believed that it had been laid out at full length. Together with a fragment of 'foot-wrapping' and a piece of shoe with two lace holes, there was a bronze-bladed dagger, three flints, hazelnuts and hazel branches. A fragment of what is likely to be flax fibre was considered to constitute the last remains of linen fabric, used either to clothe or to wrap the corpse; the presence of the footwear traces was regarded as evidence that the deceased had been buried fully clothed.

In 1937, at Disgwylfa (Dysgwylfa) Fawr, Ceredigion, a short, one metre-long tree-trunk coffin containing cremated human remains and a Food Vessel, covered with a piece of animal fur, was found as a secondary interment above, and to one side of, a longer tree-trunk coffin, c. 2.5 m long, in a round barrow (Nos. 42–43). Both coffins had rounded ends and neither appears to have been lidded. Well-preserved tree-trunk coffins of various shapes have been found in Scotland at Cairngall, Aberdeenshire in 1813 (Nos. 2–3); at Williamston, Aberdeenshire, in 1812 (No. 4); at Dalrigh, near Oban, Argyll & Bute, in 1879 (No. 5); and at Dumglow (or Drumglow), Perth & Kinross, in 1904 (No. 6). The Dalrigh example is believed to have been a re-used logboat, while at Williamston, six substantial pieces of a split oak trunk appear to have been assembled into a massive kind of wooden cist.

Shape, size and construction

As is clear from the examples cited above, there is considerable variability in the shape, size and method of construction of tree-trunk coffins. There are eight definite and probable examples (Nos. 7–9, 11, 16 (= Gristhope), 18, 26 and 47) and several possible examples (e.g. No. 55) where the coffin consists of two halves of a split trunk; in the case of Loose Howe, North Yorkshire (No. 11), the lid came from a different tree from the base. The lids and bases articulated without the need for fastenings. In a unique variation of this 'all-round tree-trunk' design, the coffin at Sigwells, Somerset (No. 57) is described as having been made from *'two pieces of bark... fastened together so as to leave two ends projecting freely, not wrapped around each other'* (Rolleston and Greenwell 1878, 78). The number of 'all-round tree-trunk' coffins is undoubtedly under-represented due to the vagaries of preservation, but it is clear that some coffins had other kinds of cover: the two found in a mound at Cairngall, Aberdeenshire (Nos. 2–3) are reported to have been covered by boards, while at Dalrigh, Argyll and Bute (No. 5) fragments of sewn birch bark may well have belonged to a bark cover, and at Pant-y-Dulaith, Clwyd (No. 27), the coffin had been covered with earth and sealed over with flat stones. In several cases (e.g. Nos. 15, 20, 23, 24, 51), the presence of traces of wood attest to some kind of wooden cover, but whether this had been the second half of a split trunk, or some other kind of lid, is impossible to determine. In many other cases there is no trace of a lid, so it is unclear whether the coffin had been buried unlidded, or covered with some organic cover that has not survived. The presence of branches above the coffin, as noted at Gristhorpe, is paralleled in two, possibly three other instances (Nos. 5, 26 and possibly also 53) with the example at Dalrigh (No. 5) also being covered by logs.

In terms of their ground plan, coffins generally have parallel or slightly tapering long edges, following the shape of the trunk, but the ends vary: out of the 47 cases where the end shapes are known, 23 (i.e. around 50%) have two straight ends; nine have two curving ends; while 11 (i.e. nearly a quarter) – including the Gristhorpe example, and the aforementioned examples from Loose Howe – have one straight end and one curving or pointed end, giving the coffin a distinctly boat-like shape. An additional, more irregularly-shaped example is No. 28 from West Ashby, Lincolnshire, and a further possible example is No. 31 from Stroxton, Lincolnshire. Furthermore, as noted above, the rectangular coffin from Milton Lilbourne (No. 49) had a boat-shaped hollow, as do several other coffins. We shall return to the question of whether any coffins had previously served as boats, and to the broader issue of boat imagery in British Early Bronze Age funerary practice, later on.

As regards their shape in cross-section, where this can clearly be discerned, they are mostly a broad U-shape in transverse section, following the natural shape of the trunk (except in cases where the exterior has been modified). The 'canoe' from Loose Howe (No. 12) has a distinctly keeled appearance (Elgee and Elgee 1949, fig. 4). In longitudinal section they may be straight, or they may have one or both ends that curve, as in the aforementioned case of Milton Lilbourne, Wiltshire (No. 49) and at Gristhorpe (No. 16), for example.

The coffins vary in size, from the reported length of 3.66 m at Stoborough (No. 59) to just 0.35 m at Sproxton, Lincolnshire (No. 33). This variability mostly relates to the funerary rite and to the age of the deceased, with the smaller examples below *c.* 1.3 m in length containing cremated remains (e.g. No. 20) or the unburnt remains of children (e.g. No. 27), and with coffins for unburnt adult bodies being over 1.6 m long. However, there are a few exceptions, where cremated remains (e.g. No. 50), or the unburnt remains of children (e.g. No. 34) have been found in coffins exceeding 1.3 m in length.

The degree to which the shape of the split trunk had been modified varies. While virtually all had been hollowed (except No. 4 – see above), and some had had their ends rounded off and/or bevelled, in many cases this was all that had been done. Bark is reported to have been left on part or all of the trunk in 15 cases (while the presence of knots and/or branches on a sixteenth suggests that this, too, had not had its surface altered) and its presence is implied in many other accounts (e.g. No. 18). However, in a few cases there had been more substantial modifications to the split trunk. The aforementioned possible reused logboat at Dalrigh (No. 5; Fig. 4.3) may have had its bark removed and, in addition to having what appears to have been its original transom-board at its stern end, it had had a second board slotted into a less well-executed groove at its other (northern) end, to create a closed-off hollow (Mapleton 1879, 337). The 'canoe' from Loose Howe (No. 12) had had its bottom carved into a keel; whether the partial ridge along the base of the lidded coffin (No. 11) had also been a carved keel was, however, uncertain. The boat-shaped coffin found at Scrubbity Coppice, Dorset (No. 58), whose form was replicated for Pitt-Rivers (Fig. 4.4; Pitt-Rivers 1888, pl. 87), seems to have been worked all over to create a smooth-surfaced, flat-based receptacle, and it may be that the coffin from Winterbourne Stoke barrow G9, Wiltshire (No. 54) that was described by Colt Hoare as being *'a shallow case of wood, of a boat-like form'* (Hoare 1812, 125) had been similarly worked. The coffin from Radley, Oxfordshire (No. 46) that has been published as a probable 'hollow alder log' (Barclay and Halpin 1998, 253) has a suspiciously flattish base, but whether this was due to trimming the outside of the log is unclear.

Fig. 4.3 Photograph of the Dalrigh logboat-coffin shortly after its discovery. From Mapleton 1879, reproduced by permission of the Society of Antiquaries of Scotland.

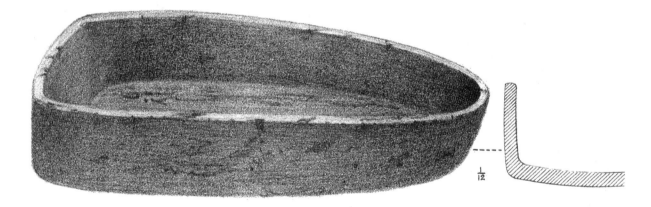

Fig. 4.4 Engraving of the replica of the coffin from Scrubbity Coppice, Dorset, made for Pitt-Rivers. From Pitt-Rivers 1888.

With the sole exception of the two coffins from Cairngall, Aberdeenshire that have clear projections at their ends (Nos. 2–3, Fig. 4.5), none of the coffins has any feature that could be construed as a handle. Other carved features are very rare: there is a teardrop- (or face-) shaped carving on the lid of the Gristhorpe coffin (No. 16; Fig. 12.1 and see Sheridan *et al.*, this volume), and an enigmatic triangular hollow, 25 mm deep and with sides 45 cm long, on the underside of the Loose Howe 'canoe' (No. 12; Elgee and Elgee 1949, 92 and fig. 4). The 'canoe' also has a T-shaped recess on its underside, as does the Loose Howe coffin cover (No. 11); the significance of these

recesses is unknown, unless they were used to help in the uphill transportation of the objects to their final resting place. A hole carved in one corner of the Cartington coffin (No. 7) is thought to have been drilled to facilitate haulage, while the small hole through the bottom of the Gristhorpe coffin (No. 16) is more likely to have served as a way for the liquid products of decomposition to escape.

The presence of tool-marks has been recorded in three examples (Nos. 7, 9 and 16) and is implied in others. The evidence from Gristhorpe (No. 16) suggests that a stone-bladed axe had been used to shape the exterior (and probably also fell the tree), while the interior had been hollowed

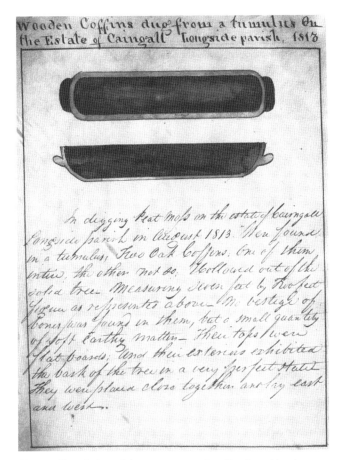

Fig. 4.5 Description of the two tree-trunk coffins found in a barrow at Cairngall, Longside parish, Aberdeenshire. The text reads: '*Wooden coffins dug from a tumulus on the Estate of Caingall* [sic.] *Longside parish, 1813. In digging peat moss on the estate of Cairngall Longside parish in August 1813. Were found in a tumulus, two oak coffins, one of them intire, the other not so. Hollowed out of the solid tree measuring seven feet by two feet figure as represented above. No vestige of bones was found in them, but a small quantity of soft earthy matter. Their tops were flat boards; and their exteriors exhibited the bark of the tree in a very perfect state. They were placed close together and lay east and west.*' Aberdeenshire Museums Service collections: reproduced by permission of Aberdeenshire Council.

using a metal-bladed adze (as discussed and illustrated in Sheridan *et al.*, this volume); the Rylstone coffin (No. 9) also seems to have been hollowed using a tool (probably an adze) with a narrow metal blade. Deliberate scorching or burning – perhaps as a way of creating the hollow, perhaps for other reasons – is suggested in nine cases (e.g. No. 41) where charcoal is reported to have been present as part of the coffin. Indeed, in some instances, this constitutes the only surviving trace of the coffin. The same is true for some plank-built coffins, as at Etton barrow 1, Cambridgeshire, for example (French and Pryor 2005, 106), and also for the plank or bier found at Barnack, Cambridgeshire (Donaldson 1977). It should be noted, however, that highly degraded

wood, and wood whose structure has been replaced by manganese oxide (e.g. No. 22), can resemble charcoal and so, unless the material has been positively identified as charcoal, it should not be assumed that deliberate scorching or burning has taken place.

The raw material: tree species and availability

In the 28 cases where the species of the wood used for the coffin has been identifiable, it has almost invariably been oak (25 examples, or 89%). The exceptions, all from southern England, are of alder (at Radley, Oxfordshire, No. 46), elm (Winterbourne Stoke, Wiltshire, No. 53) and wych elm (at Sigwells, Somerset, No. 57 – although the same account also refers to oak, possibly accidentally). It may be no coincidence that these non-oak examples have all been from southern England, as current and recent environmental analyses from the chalklands of Wessex (French 2003; French *et al.* 2007; Cleal *et al.* 2004) and from the Cambridgeshire and Lincolnshire Fenland and its margins (French 2003; French and Pryor 2005) indicate that large stretches of these landscapes were actually devoid of mature woodland by the Early Bronze Age. Obtaining an oak tree trunk of the desired girth and height might therefore have been problematic; mourners may have had to travel 10 km or more to find a tree suitable for conversion into a log coffin. This makes a large oak tree-trunk coffin, such as the examples from Stoborough, Dorset (No. 59) and Hove, Sussex (No. 65), all the more impressive when one considers the effort that must have been expended in procuring the appropriate tree. (See also Ashbee 1986, 87 on the conspicuous consumption of wood in Early Bronze Age funeral pyres in Wiltshire.)

Context, grave construction, orientation

With but one exception (namely No. 45, the 'flat' grave 950 from Radley, Oxfordshire, which is not certainly a tree-trunk coffin), every Early Bronze Age tree-trunk coffin in Britain has been associated with a barrow or cairn, and often as the first (and sometimes the only) grave to be created. A frequent feature is the large size (over 20 metres in its diameter) and/or prominent location of the barrow or cairn. Clearly, a great deal of effort had been expended in creating tree-trunk coffin graves, from the initial felling of the tree and the splitting and hollowing of the trunk segment, to the hauling of the often heavy coffin into position – sometimes up a steep slope, as has been suggested for the examples from Cartington, Northumberland (No. 7) and Loose Howe, North Yorkshire

(Nos. 11–12), for instance – and the final covering of the grave. While some coffins had been deposited on the old land surface, others were buried in pits, and at Willie Howe, East Riding of Yorkshire (No. 18), the coffin had been placed in a deep, rock-cut pit. Various means were used to secure the coffin in position, including the use of logs (at Dalrigh, Argyll and Bute, No. 5), an upright branch (at Gristhorpe, No. 16), rubble (at Willie Howe, No. 18) and 'a plaster of pounded chalk' (at Collingbourne Ducis barrow G10, Wiltshire: Lukis 1867, 96). In Yorkshire, several instances are known where coffins had been encased in clay, and at Towthorpe barrow 139 (No. 19) and Hanging Grimston (No. 21), both in North Yorkshire, the clay had been brought in from over 1.5 kilometres away (Mortimer 1905, 3–5 and 97). Not only would this have served to keep them in position; it may also have been done to keep them watertight, perhaps in a bid to confer immortality on the inhabitant. An analogous practice has been noted in the case of Danish Middle Bronze Age tree-trunk coffin graves (Breuning-Madsen and Kähler Holst 1995).

In terms of coffin orientation, there is a preference for N-S, NE-SW and E-W, although a few NW-SE examples are also known.

The occupants and the funerary rite

Our knowledge of the people who had been buried in tree-trunk coffins is limited by the facts that, in many cases, the remains have simply not survived, and with many of the older discoveries, the human remains were either re-buried or lost. Of Mortimer's finds (Mortimer 1905), only the skulls were retained. Many of the old finds were either not studied by an anatomist, or were studied to standards that are no longer deemed acceptable; and a thorough osteological re-examination, of the kind undertaken for Gristhorpe Man (Knüsel et al., this volume), is needed for the surviving remains. That said, it is possible to draw some conclusions from the evidence available to us.

In all but three cases where human remains have been found in a tree-trunk coffin, just one individual is represented. The exceptions are from Irton Moor, North Yorkshire (No. 15) where the cremated remains of two individuals were buried together; Wetwang Slack Area 16, East Riding of Yorkshire (No. 24), where the coffin seems to have been opened and its original occupant's bones re-arranged when a second person was buried in it; and Old Sunderlandwick, North Yorkshire (No. 26), where the remains of three people were found, one deposited head-to-feet with the others. At Bishop's Waltham, Hampshire (No. 63), a crouched unburnt body had been buried immediately above a tree-trunk coffin containing cremated remains of another person, and there need not have been a long

interval between the two burials. The same may be true of the deposits of cremated bone close to the coffin at Howe Hill, Brotton, North Yorkshire (No. 10). At Wetwang Slack (barrow B, No. 23), cranial fragments from a second individual are assumed to have been residual from an earlier grave.

Inhumation of an unburnt body seems to have been the dominant rite, being demonstrated or presumed (through the absence of remains) in 81% of tree-trunk coffin graves. There are only 13 definite cases where the rite had been cremation, and there is a clear regional bias to this practice, with eight of these being located in southern England south of the Severn and Thames rivers. As will be seen below, there also seems to be a chronological element, with most of the graves with cremated remains belonging to the later part of the currency of tree-trunk coffins.

While both adults and children had been buried in these coffins, there is a clear bias towards adult males: in the 16 cases where the sex has been identified, it has been male in all but one. Furthermore, 'Gristhorpe Man' is not alone in being unusually large, at a height of 1.78 m (Knüsel et al., ths volume). Unusually tall men have been noted in four other cases, at Willie Howe (No. 18; 1.76 m tall, and described as 'robust'), Towthorpe barrow 139 (No. 19, 1.8 m tall); West Overton barrow G1, Wiltshire (No. 48) and Milton Lilbourne barrow 4, Wiltshire (No. 49). Three of these tall men – from Gristhorpe (No. 16), West Overton (No. 48) and Milton Lilbourne (No. 49) – had also been relatively old for the period in question, and it may be that there are further examples of tall old men among the remains that have not been subject to osteological recording. That the practice was not exclusively linked to such individuals, however, is clear from the several examples where younger men had been interred (eg No.25, Garton Slack, aged 16–17).

The sole example where the human remains may be of a female is from Bishop's Waltham, Hampshire (No. 63), but here the sex identification of the cremated remains was tentative, and indeed the associated grave goods are those normally associated with males. The only other example where the presence of a female has been suggested is Winterbourne Stoke barrow G9 (No. 54), since Early Bronze Age necklaces of amber and jet tend to be associated with women; but in the absence of the human remains, this is impossible to check. As for the graves containing (or presumed to have contained) the remains of children and individuals under 15 years of age, there are eight examples, all involving inhumation of unburnt bodies as the rite (Nos. 14, 17, 27, 28, 32, 34, 41 and 46; two old descriptions of cremated remains as being of 'young' individuals (Nos. 51 and 57) are unhelpful as these could mean 'young adult'). In several cases, including Hutton Buscel, North Yorkshire (No. 14), Pant-y-Dulaith, Clwyd (No. 27) and Deeping St.

Nicholas, Lincolnshire (No. 34) these children's graves were the primary graves under the mound.

Where the posture of the deceased had been recorded, in 17 cases the body had been laid on its side, in a flexed or crouched position (i.e. with the legs slightly or more markedly bent); at Tallington, Lincolnshire (No. 35), the body was so tightly crouched that the excavator felt that it had been trussed, and the man's head had been tilted backwards. There are only six cases where burial in an extended, supine posture has been noted, or claimed (Nos. 9, 11, 19, 29, 32 and 53). With the flexed and crouched individuals, where the 'sidedness' had been recorded, individuals had been laid on their left side in 13 cases (Nos. 1, 7, 18, 25, 34, 35, 37, 38, 40, 44, 46, 48 and 55) and on their right in four (Nos. 10, 16, 17 and 23; the individual from Bishop's Waltham, No. 63, is excluded as the body lay above the coffin). Of the individuals laid on their left side, in the six instances where the sex of the individual had been determined, this has been male (Nos. 10, 25, 35, 44, 48 and 55); the same is true of the three sex-determined individuals laid on their right, (Nos. 10, 16 and 23), including 'Gristhorpe Man'. The significance of this finding is discussed below. As for the orientation of the body and the direction in which the deceased was 'looking' (ie facing), there is variability but a tendency for the head to lie at the E, NE or SE end of the coffin and a slight tendency for the line of sight to be orientated towards the E, SE or S.

Grave goods and other coffin contents

As noted above, there are hints (from Loose Howe, No. 11) that the deceased had been buried fully clothed, and the traces of textiles or animal hides found in several coffins may relate to the wrapping of the body in a shroud-like funerary garment. (Alternatively, some of the textiles may relate to other items of clothing.) The inclusion of other artefacts, as grave goods, varies considerably and several coffins appear to have no grave goods at all, although it is impossible to tell how many had originally contained organic items that simply have not survived. The survival of the bark and wood container, and of other organic items at Gristhorpe, is due to the exceptional conditions of preservation at that site.

As Table 4.1 demonstrates, the objects found within tree-trunk coffins vary from the mundane (i.e. flint flakes and simple flint tools, as at Willie Howe, No. 18) to the rare and precious (as with the amber cup in the Hove coffin, No. 65 and the probable shale cup, plus 'gold lace', from Stoborough, No. 59). Indeed, some coffins stand out as having an array of rare and precious grave goods (e.g. Nos. 19, 50, 53, 54, 59, 63 and 65); notably, all but one of these fall within the 'Wessex and S English coast' cluster, and are part of the so-called

'Wessex' series of rich graves (Piggott 1938; Needham 2000; Needham *et al.* 2006). Bronze-bladed daggers and knives fall into the category of 'precious' grave goods, as these would have been comparatively rare possessions during the Early Bronze Age, with ownership probably restricted by gender, age and social position (Henshall 1968; Baker *et al.* 2003, 111–12; Needham 2004; Needham forthcoming). Indeed, daggers seem to have been the archetypal male status symbol of choice over a large part of Britain, and were often embellished with 'showy' pommels in unusual materials (as at Gristhorpe, with its whalebone pommel: see Sheridan *et al.,* this volume). Some daggers, although none from a tree-trunk coffin, have had gold pommel-bands as an additional elaboration (e.g. at Forteviot, Perth and Kinross: Noble and Brophy 2011). Fifteen bronze-bladed daggers and knives have been found in 13 tree-trunk coffins; in other words, nearly a quarter (23%) of all tree-trunk coffins have held at least one bronze-bladed object. When compared with the broader picture, where the incidence of such objects in Early Bronze Age graves in general is estimated at only *c.* 1%, this is a markedly high frequency. Maces and battle axes, mostly represented by their stone or antler heads, are known from four coffins (Nos. 19, 21, 51 and 65); like daggers, these would have been male status symbols (Needham and Woodward 2008), and once more the frequency of their occurrence in tree-trunk coffins is higher than in the generality of Early Bronze Age graves. At Towthorpe barrow 139, North Yorkshire (No. 19), both types of status symbol were found together on the left of the skeleton, with the remains of a 45 cm-long ash mace haft still visible. As noted above, there is only one instance where a type of grave good normally associated with high-status women – a necklace of amber and jet or jet-like beads – has been found (No. 54, Winterbourne Stoke barrow G9, Wiltshire; see also below, regarding bronze awls). Other noteworthy prestige items are the crutch-headed bronze pin and bronze axehead from West Overton barrow G1, Wiltshire (No. 48; Needham *et al.* 2010b); the ring-headed bronze pin from the richly-furnished grave at Collingbourne Ducis barrow G4, Wiltshire (No. 50); and the unusual, five-handled biconical jar from Winterbourne Stoke barrow G5, Wiltshire (No. 53). The Continental, and especially Breton, affinities of the jar and of pin use in Wessex series graves have been discussed by Needham (Needham 2000, 178–179, 180–1). Metal awls had also, arguably, played a role in the Early Bronze Age vocabulary of esteem, since they would have been considerably rarer than their counterparts in bone; they have been found in three coffins, all in Wiltshire and Hampshire, including the aforementioned Winterbourne Stoke G5 example (Nos. 53, 54 and 60). While bronze awls tend to be a female grave good (Thomas and Ellwood 2005), and indeed the example from Winterbourne Stoke barrow G9 (No. 54) may have been associated with a woman, to judge

Table 4.1 Grave goods and other items found in British Early Bronze Age tree-trunk coffins. (See also Appendix 4.1, *Addenda*).

	Flint items						Stone items				Pottery					Items of, or containing, copper alloy						Antler and bone artefacts				Amber, jet/shale			Organics						Misc.
	Flake/blade/chip	Knife/knife or scraper	Arrowhead/s	Piercer	Scraper	Fabricator/strike-a-light	Macehead	Battle axehead	Pebbles/other	Whetstone-pendant	Beaker	Food Vessel	Prob. cinerary urn	Accessory Vessel	Armorican-style pot	Series 2 dagger	Series 3 or later dagger	Knife/knife or razor	Awl	Axehead	Pin	Antler	Antler 'macehead'	Antler pick	Bone pin	Amber cup	Shale cup	Beads, amber and jet/shale	Bark and wood container	Wooden fastener	Hide/textile	Fur/bones of furry animals	Plant material	Bark sheet	Misc.
Coffins definitely or probably dating to Needham's Period 2/early Period 3																																			
1 Seafield West, Highland																×																			
5 Dalrigh, Argyll and Bute																																		×	×
7 Cartington, Northumberland	×				×						×																						×		
8 West Tanfield, N. Yorks		×										×																			×				
9 Rylstone, N. Yorks																															×				
11 Loose Howe, N. Yorks	×															×															×		×		×
13 Pockley, N. Yorks												×																							
14 Hutton Buscel, N. Yorks																																			×
15 Irton Moor, N. Yorks			×						×																										
16 Gristhorpe, N. Yorks	×	×										×				×									×				×			×	×		×
17 West Heslerton, N. Yorks	×																													×		×			
18 Willie Howe, E.R. Yorks	×																													×					
21 Hanging Grimston barrow 90, N Yorks								×																											
23 Wetwang Slack barrow B, grave 1, E.R. Yorks												×																							
24 Wetwang Slack Area 16, WK 8, E.R. Yorks											×																								
25 Garton Slack 29 (3ii), E.R. Yorks	×										×																								
28 West Ashby F66, Lincs																															?		?		
29 West Ashby F48, Lincs												×																			×				
30 Swarkeston barrow 4, Derbs		×				×																													
31 Ponton Heath, Lincs		×										×																							
34 Deeping St Nicholas, Lincs		×																													?				
35 Tallington, Lincs	×											×																							×

Coffins definitely or probably dating to Needham's Period 3/ Period 4

- 43 Dysgwylfa (Disgwylfa) Fawr, Ceredigion
- 45 Radley, flat grave 950, Oxon
- 46 Radley, grave 4969, Oxon
- 19 Towthorpe barrow 139, N Yorks
- 47 Yatesbury barrow 3/G9, Wilts
- 48 West Overton barrow G1, Wilts
- 49 Milton Lilbourne barrow 4, Wilts
- 50 Collingbourne Ducis G4, Wilts
- 51 Collingbourne Ducis G10, Wilts
- 52 Upton Scudamore G1, Wilts
- 53 Winterbourne Stoke G5, Wilts
- 54 Winterbourne Stoke G9, Wilts
- 55 Fovant, Wilts
- 56 Weaver's Down, Hants
- 57 Sigwells, Somerset
- 59 Stoborough, Dorset
- 60 Latch Farm, Hants
- 61 Newbarn Down, Hants
- 63 Bishop's Waltham, Hants
- 65 Hove, Sussex

Coffins that could date to any time within Needham's Periods 2, 3 and 4

- 4 Williamston, Aberdeenshire
- 36 Whittlesey, Cambs
- 37 Bowthorpe central grave, Norfolk
- 40 Bowthorpe grave 75, Norfolk

Notes:

1 Coffins with no recorded grave goods: Nos. 2–3, 6, 10, 12, 20, 22, 26, 27, 32, 33, 38, 39, 41, 42, 44, 58, 62, 64. See Appendix 1 for entries where items present but not necessarily as grave goods

2 For details of 'Miscellaneous' finds, see Appendix 1

3 The Ponton Heath and Tallington Food Vessel graves are assumed to date to Needham's Period 2 or early Period 3 – the C14 date for Tallington is unreliable – but more dating needs to be undertaken on Food Vessels in this part of England

4 The Bowthorpe coffin graves are suspected to be more likely to date to Period 2/early 3 than to a later time

5 The C14 date for the Dysgwylfa Fawr coffin (No. 43) is suspected to be too late; by analogy with similar Food Vessels in Ireland, this grave should date to Period 2

6 It is impossible to tell whether the 'red hair' found at Weaver's Down, Hants was human, or from a hide, or from a pelt

7 It is likely that the Food Vessel from Newbarn Down dates to Needham's Period 3, rather than Period 2, as at least one Food Vessel of this date is known from southern England (at Long Ash Lane, Frampton, Dorset, together with a necklace of segmented faience beads; associated cremated bone dated to 3315±35 BP, GrA-24867, 1630–1530 cal BC at 68.2% probability, 1690–1510 cal BC at 95.4% probability)

from the associated necklace, the inclusion of one such awl in the Winterbourne Stoke G5 coffin does not mean that the individual buried there had not been a man.

As regards other grave goods, pottery has been found in 18 tree-trunk coffins (including the aforementioned Winterbourne Stoke G5 coffin), in various capacities. In 14 instances the pot had probably contained food or drink for the deceased's journey into the Otherworld, and in this respect it would have played the same role as the bark and wood container in the Gristhorpe coffin. Nine of those pots have belonged to the Food Vessel tradition (Nos. 8, 13, 17, 23, 28, 31, 35, 43 and 61), while four (Nos. 7, 24, 25 and 45) belong to the Beaker tradition, including a probable example of an All-Over-Cord decorated Beaker at Cartington, Northumberland (No. 7). (See also Appendix 4.1 Addenda.) The Breton-like jar from Winterbourne Stoke, found beside the head of the deceased, may also have been used in this way. Pottery in other coffins had been used in other ways. The tall, narrow-based pot from Williamston, Aberdeenshire (No. 4) is likely, from its description, to have been a cinerary urn, although the 1845 account of its discovery in 1812 makes no mention of it having contained cremated remains. The accessory vessels found with cremated bones at Milton Lilbourne, Wiltshire (No. 49) and Collingbourne Ducis G4 (No. 50) could well have been 'chafing' vessels, used to hold the glowing embers that lit the funeral pyre. Whether the 'little urn of a very neat form' from Winterbourne Stoke G9, Wiltshire (No. 54; Hoare 1812, 125) had also been an accessory vessel is unknown, as the pot is lost, but here the rite had been inhumation of an unburnt body, and so its presence is puzzling.

These were not the only items found inside tree-trunk coffins. The presence of plant material in six instances – Cartington (No. 7), Loose Howe (No. 11), Gristhorpe (No. 16), Towthorpe barrow 139 (No. 19), Milton Lilbourne (No. 49) and Bishop's Waltham (No. 63) – shows that the hollow of these coffins had been lined prior to the deposition of the body (or, in the case of No. 63, cremated remains). The sewn birch bark sheets found in the Dalrigh coffin (No. 5) could also have been used as a lining, as well as as a putative cover. A piece of fur, of indeterminate species, was found lying over cremated bones and a Food Vessel at Dysgwylfa Fawr, Ceredigion (No. 43), while at Gristhorpe (No. 16), the paw bones of fox and pine martin could either have belonged to pelts laid on the base of the hollow, or else to paws used as amulets.

The chronology of British tree-trunk coffins

There are three sources of information about the date of British tree-trunk coffins, namely radiocarbon dates on the coffins or their contents (Table 4.2); stratigraphic information from the findspots; and comparative dating of artefactual finds.

Sixteen coffins, from 15 findspots, are associated with radiocarbon dates, with eight coffins dated directly, six dated from the associated human remains (all unburnt) and five from other material in, or directly associated with, the coffin. (The Willie Howe coffin was dated both from the coffin wood and from the unburnt human bone inside it; and the Gristhorpe coffin was dated from the coffin itself, from bone and dentine, and from branches overlying it: see Batt, this volume. See also Appendix 4.1 Addenda.) The quality and reliability of these dates vary, partly because of the danger of an 'old wood' effect from the oak coffins, and partly because some dates were determined during the 1970s and 1980s, before the procedural advances of subsequent decades. The recently-obtained suite of AMS dates obtained for the Gristhorpe coffin and its contents (as discussed in Batt, this volume) is particularly valuable, as is the recently-obtained AMS date for the skeleton from West Overton barrow G1, Wiltshire (No. 48; Needham et al. 2010b), while by contrast the date of 4060±200 BP (GU-1589, 3320–2020 cal BC at 95.4% probability) for oak charcoal from the Harford Farm coffin is effectively useless and should be discounted. Similarly, the date of 3189±46 BP (BM-682, 1610–1320 cal BC at 95.4% probability) for the Hove coffin should be regarded as highly suspect: it is, suspiciously, significantly later than the estimated date of c. 1750–1550 BC for each of the grave goods – the amber cup, the dagger, the perforated whetstone and the battle-axehead – to judge from dated examples of these artefact types elsewhere (Garwood 2003, 53; Needham et al. 2006, 60–63).

Stratigraphic information (as summarised in Appendix 4.1), together with comparative dating of grave goods, provides a valuable counterpart to the radiocarbon dates. Significant advances have been made over the last decade in the dating of certain artefact types including Beaker pottery (e.g. Needham 2005, Sheridan 2007a), Food Vessel pottery (e.g. Sheridan 2004a) and daggers (Needham 2012; forthcoming; Curtis and Wilkin 2012; Sheridan 2007b). In particular, advances in our understanding of the chronology of copper alloy daggers have allowed a relatively fine-grained picture to emerge (Needham forthcoming). Together, the various sources of dating information indicate that the use of tree-trunk coffins is likely to fall between the 22nd century BC and the 17th century BC – that is, Periods 2–4 in Needham's chronological scheme for the British Chalcolithic and Early to Middle Bronze Age (Needham et al. 2010b). Bayesian modelling of the radiocarbon dates would no doubt narrow the range, but it is recommended that further radiocarbon dates are obtained (e.g. from cremated bone) before such an exercise is undertaken.

Table 4.2 Radiocarbon dates associated with Early Bronze Age tree-trunk coffins in Britain. (See also Appendix 4.1, *Addenda*).

Cat. No.	Findspot	Material dated	Lab no.	Date BP (*=AMS)	Date cal BC, 68.2% probability	Date cal BC, 95.4% probability	Comment (including statement of when date obtained, if before mid-1990s)
1	Seafield West, Inverness, Highland	Hide and wood from dagger scabbard	Weighted mean of GrA-27037 and GrA-27039	3600±30*	2020–1910	2040–1880	Reliable date. This supersedes an unsatisfactory, anomalously late date for this scabbard: see Sheridan 2004b, 176
5	Dalrigh, near Oban, Argyll and Bute	Birch bark from coffin cover or lining	OxA-6813	3555±60*	2010–1770	2020–1730	Reliable date
7	Cartington, Rothbury, Northumberland	Coffin (oak, outer rings, sub-bark)	GU-1648	3790±65	2340–2060	2460–2030	Should be reliable date. Sample from outer growth rings below bark. Date obtained early 1980s
16	Gristhorpe, North Yorkshire	i) Coffin (oak), 6 dates	OxA-17454	3669±30*	2140–1980	2140–1950	Mostly reliable dates. See Batt, this volume for details. Of the coffin dates, only the date for the outermost tree rings is cited here. The dates for the branches provide *termini ante quos* for the coffin. The HAR-4424 date was obtained during the 1980s and is of negligible value due to its large standard deviation. Further dating of the branches is recommended to check whether OxA-16812 is a suspect date
		ii) Unburnt human bone	OxA-19219	3743±32*	2210–2050	2280–2030	
		iii) dentine	OxA-16844	3671±32*	2140–1980	2150–1950	
		iv) oak branches overlying coffin	OxA-16812	3375±31*	1740–1620	1750–1540	
			HAR-4424	3590±100	2130–1770	2280–1680	
18	Willie Howe, Cowlam, East Riding of Yorkshire	i) Unburnt human bone	HAR-4995	3358±70	1740–1530	1880–1490	Dates obtained early 1980s. The HAR-4424 date is referred to in Powlesland *et al.* 1986,122 and Dent 2010, 100, but not in Brewster (unpublished). The bone date may well be too young; it is known that there were sometimes problems in obtaining enough collagen. Position of oak sample not known, so potential for an 'old wood' effect, although is closer to expected date of coffin than the bone date
		ii) Coffin, oak	HAR-4424	3590±46	2020–1880	2130–1770	
24	Wetwang Slack (Area 16, WK 8), East Riding of Yorkshire	Coffin, oak; charcoal from probable lid, side and base dated	Weighted mean of HAR-9244, 9245, 9247	3710±49	2200–2030	2280–1950	Dates obtained 1988–1989. See Dent 2010, 100 for details of the three dates. Possibility of 'old wood' effect, although date in line with expectations
33	Sproxton (Saltby Heath, barrow C, F46), Leicestershire	Charcoal, prob. pyre wood, mature ash	HAR-3129	3500±70	1920–1740	2030–1640	Date obtained late 1970s. Possibility of old wood effect although date in line with expectations
34	Deeping St Nicholas (barrow 28), Lincolnshire	Unburnt human bone	GU-5358 (Weighted mean of 2)	3558±38	1960–1780	2030–1770	Dates determined 1993 or 1994. In line with expectations
35	Tallington, Lincolnshire (site 16, grave 1)	Unburnt human bone	UB-450	3410±165	1920–1510	2200–1320	Date of negligible value due to very large standard deviation. Determined during 1970s
41	Harford Farm (grave 1469, ring-ditch 1022), Caistor St. Edmund, Norfolk	Coffin charcoal, oak	GU-1589	4060±200	2890–2340	3320–2020	Date of negligible value due to very large standard deviation and high probability of 'old wood' effect. Date obtained early 1990s
42	Dysgwylfa (Disgwylfa) Fawr, Ceredigion	Coffin, oak	HAR-2187	3860±70	2460–2210	2570–2130	Sample spanned 20 tree rings and taken from at least 10 rings in from outermost surviving ring. Pre-treated specially as coffin may previously have been coated with paraffin wax. Dated during 1980s. Older than expected date
43	Dysgwylfa (Disgwylfa) Fawr, Ceredigion	Coffin, species not stated	HAR-2677	3300±80	1690–1490	1770–1410	Sample lay immediately under bark. Pre-treated as per No. 42. Dated during 1980s. Slightly younger than expected date
45	Radley, Barrow Hills ('flat' grave 950), Oxfordshire	Unburnt human bone	BM-2703	3720±50	2200–2030	2290–1960	Date determined 1990. May well be reliable
46	Radley, Barrow Hills (grave 4969, pond barrow 4866), Oxfordshire	Antler	OxA-1880	3490±80*	1920–1690	2030–1620	Date determined 1988. Should be reliable
48	West Overton (barrow G1), Wiltshire	Unburnt human bone	SUERC-26203 (GU-19959)	3550±35*	1950–1780	2020–1770	Reliable date
65	Hove, Sussex	Coffin, oak	BM-682	3189±46	1510–1420	1610–1320	Dated early 1970s; seems anomalously late and its reliability is questionable

Notes:

1 Dates calibrated using OxCal 4.1.7, with INTCAL09 atmospheric data; results rounded out to nearest decade.

2 There may be issues of reliability with some of the dates determined before the mid-1990s (as indeed there may be with some more recently-obtained dates). For a useful discussion of the reliability of dates determined at the Harwell laboratory, see D. Jordan, D Haddon-Reece and A. Bayliss (1994) *Radiocarbon Dates from Samples Funded by English Heritage and dated before 1981*. London, English Heritage; and A. Bayliss, R. Hedges, R. Otlet, R. Switsur and J. Walker (2012) *Radiocarbon Dates from Samples Funded by English Heritage between 1981 and 1988*. London, English Heritage http://www.english-heritage.org.uk/publications/radiocarbon-dates-1981-88/radiocarbon-dates-1981-88.pdf (accessed February 2013). This concluded that HAR- dates on bone and antler may be inaccurate, while dates on wood – if from single-species samples , from short-lived species or from the outermost part of a long-lived tree, can be accurate.

3 Eaton F10, Leicestershire (No. 32) has a *terminus ante quem* of 3450±70 BP (HAR-3941) for charcoal from ring ditch, dated to 3430±80 BP (HAR-3942). Both dates obtained before 1981.

There is no unequivocal evidence for the use of tree-trunk coffins in Britain prior to the beginning of the Bronze Age in the 22nd century BC. While the use of Beaker pottery appears to have commenced some two to three centuries earlier (Needham 2012), and while All-Over-Cord (AOC) decorated Beakers are among the earliest type found in Britain, this does not mean that the coffins containing Beakers pre-date the 22nd century BC. The oak coffin from Cartington, Northumberland (No. 7), which contained a probable AOC Beaker, produced a date – from outer, sub-bark rings (Jobey 1984) – of 3790±65 BP (GU-1648, 2460–2030 cal BC at 95.4% probability). This does not demonstrate, however, that it pre-dates the Early Bronze Age, nor does the presence of the AOC Beaker, since the currency of this particular Beaker type seems to have extended into, and possibly beyond, the 22nd century (Sheridan 2012a; see also Needham 2012, 9). Similarly, the fact that bone from the Beaker-associated flat grave 950 at Barrow Hills, Radley (No. 45) produced a date of 3720±50 BP (BM-2703, 2290–1960 cal BC at 95.4% probability) does not make this a pre-Early Bronze Age example. (The identification of this grave as a tree-trunk coffin must remain tentative, as it survived only as a stain in the gravel.) As for the other Beaker-associated tree-trunk coffins, a date in or after the 22nd century BC is quite plausible, given our understanding of the currency of the Beaker tradition (cf. Needham 2005).

The evidence for the use of tree-trunk coffins within Needham's Period 2 (2200/2150–1950 BC) is strong, particularly in northern Britain, and it appears that most of the coffins containing Food Vessels (at least in northern Britain) and Series 2 bronze daggers and knives (Needham forthcoming) belong to this period, or the early part of Period 3 at the latest. The Gristhorpe tree-trunk coffin is part of this grouping.

By contrast, most of the examples from southern England appear to belong to Needham's Period 3 (1950–1750/1700 BC) or Period 4 (1750/1700–1550/1500 BC). This is clear not only from the radiocarbon dates, but also from the style of the daggers and the nature of the other artefacts. The richest graves (as listed above) fall within these periods, and have been described elsewhere as belonging to the 'Wessex 1' and 'Wessex 2' series of rich graves (Needham 2000; Needham et al. 2006, 2010a, 2010b and see also Needham and Woodward 2008 on variability among these graves). Outside southern England, tree-trunk coffins of Period 3 or 4 date appear to be very rare: the rich grave in Towthorpe barrow 139, North Yorkshire (No. 19), is the most obvious example.

There therefore appears to be a southwards shift in the use of tree-trunk coffins over time, as though a predominantly northern practice subsequently became popular in the south during the first quarter of the second millennium BC. During its southern English floruit, we see the increasing use of cremation as a rite, and also a greater ostentation in the grave goods, in some coffins, than that shown in the earlier examples. It is also to this later period that the extensively-worked, bark-free coffin from Scrubbity Coppice (No. 58) and the 'shallow case of wood' from Winterbourne Stoke G9 (No. 54) are likely to belong. This adoption of a northern British fashion and its elaboration (here, in the choice of grave goods) accords with a broader pattern seen in southern English elite graves during the first half of the second millennium BC (as discussed, for example, in Needham et al. 2010a).

Discussion

Having described the class of funerary structure to which the Gristhorpe coffin belongs, several questions remain to be addressed. Was burial in a tree-trunk coffin a privilege restricted to the elite, and how does it relate to the broader range of Early Bronze Age funerary practices? Why did people adopt the practice? Was there a particular symbolic significance attaching to the use of a split tree-trunk? And how should we interpret the apparent boat symbolism of some tree-trunk coffins (and indeed, in the case of the Dalrigh example, the possible use of an actual logboat)?

An elite burial mode?

Various lines of evidence presented above – the effort involved in finding an appropriate tree and creating the coffin, the often primary position of the grave, the frequent association with large and/or prominently-located mounds and the relatively high incidence of rare, precious grave goods – make it clear that burial in a tree-trunk coffin marked out the deceased as having been accorded special significance in Early Bronze Age society. This impression is reinforced when one bears in mind the rarity of the practice of tree-trunk coffin burial in comparison with other Early Bronze Age funerary practices, as explored below. Furthermore, the fact that most of the occupants seem to have been adult males, in some cases distinguished by their considerable age and stature, encourages the view that most of these are indeed likely to be the graves of high-ranking men. These individuals represent a tiny percentage of the male population that was buried at this time, and an even tinier proportion of those that died in this period, suggesting that only certain men from specific lineages and kinship groups were singled out for this form of funerary treatment. It is tempting to regard these men as community leaders – with the cases where more than one tree-trunk coffin has been found under/in a mound, as at Bowthorpe, Norfolk (Nos. 37–40) and Cairngall, Aberdeenshire (Nos. 2–3), suggesting a possible 'dynastic' element – but other interpretations are possible. As noted above, there also seems to be a strong regional element to the practice, and a chronological trend. We can therefore suggest that we are dealing with a specific style of high-status male burial – a veritable fashion – that had its initial *floruit* in northern Britain, especially in Yorkshire, and then gained in popularity in southern England, especially Wessex and parts of the south coast, where some individuals were buried with a particularly ostentatious array of grave goods, in line with elite funerary norms in that region.

The fact that some children had been accorded burial in a tree-trunk coffin could indicate that high social status could be inherited. One such child, whose grave was the initial and central grave under a round barrow at Deeping St. Nicholas, Lincolnshire (No. 34), had been only 3–5 years old. This idea of status being ascribed accords with the observation that Gristhorpe Man had probably enjoyed a rich diet throughout his life; so rich, in fact, that it had resulted in kidney stones and decayed teeth, as well as in a tall and robust body (Knüsel *et al.*, this volume; Montgomery and Gledhill, this volume; Edwards, this volume).

The variability in the number and range of grave goods found in tree-trunk coffins need not imply variation in the status of the coffins' occupants, although it is a moot point whether the individuals buried in the most richly-furnished graves in southern England had controlled a larger area, and/or more people, than the dagger-owning 'big men' of Yorkshire. As argued in Needham *et al.* (2006), the south coast elite and their counterparts in inland Wessex were participating in a process of competitive conspicuous consumption that extended across the Channel to northern France. In contrast, their slightly earlier counterparts in Yorkshire were arguably mainly competing among themselves and mostly (but by no means exclusively) interacting along the North Sea coast (Needham 2009).

Tree-trunk coffin burial compared with other Early Bronze Age funerary practices

Space does not permit a detailed review of all the funerary practices in use during the Early Bronze Age; the reader is directed to other publications for parts of this fascinating story (e.g. Mortimer 1905, M. J. B. Smith 1994 and Petersen 1970, for Yorkshire). Suffice it to note that, against the background of a shift from inhumation (i.e. burial of unburnt bodies) as the predominant rite to cremation as the predominant rite by around the 19th century BC, there was considerable variability in practice, both within and between regions. Thus, for example, unburnt bodies may be laid in an unlined pit, or in a pit lined with planks, or on a platform or bier, or in a plank-built or monoxylous coffin, or a stone cist, or in an earlier kind of monument;

this list does not exhaust the range of grave types. There was also variability in the orientation and posture of the body. Cremated bones could be placed in a cinerary urn, or in some kind of organic container, or be deposited in other ways. Graves could be left flat, or covered by a mound; they could be isolated, or form part of a cemetery grouping. Grave goods of various kinds, and in varying quantities, could be included. Archaeologists are still some way from understanding the norms, concerns and beliefs that informed these choices, although excellent studies have been, and continue to be, undertaken (e.g. Wilkin 2010).

Within this dizzying array of practices, tree-trunk coffins are in some respects exceptional, while in other respects they accord with the overall picture. They are exceptional in their rarity: in a synthesis of prehistoric burial practices in southern England (Bristow 1998), only 25 tree-trunk and plank-built coffins are listed out of 1023 Chalcolithic and Early Bronze Age graves. When the focus is expanded to encompass the whole of Britain, it is clear that the 65 tree-trunk coffins listed in Appendix 4.1 form just a tiny proportion (say, 1–2%) of the several thousand graves that are known from this period. Naturally, post-depositional processes exert a profound effect on any statistics of recoverability, and so tree-trunk coffins (and other wooden funerary structures) are bound to be under-represented in the record. Wood is preserved only in extremely fortuitous anaerobic circumstances, and it is clear from Appendix 4.1 that the preservation of tree-trunk coffins has been very variable. Within the pre-modern era, monoxylous coffins were generally recorded only when the wood survived within anaerobic environments under barrows, and when the barrow was being investigated by an observant antiquary such as Colt Hoare, Mortimer or Greenwell. By the 1950s archaeologists were capable of recognising the soil stains left after the wood had decayed. Even so, it takes a degree of skill for coffin stains and outlines to be recognised during modern excavation; much depends on the nature of the sub-soil, ground conditions and burial environment. That said, if the current picture is in any way a representative snapshot of the funerary practices of the whole of the population at this time – and it seems unlikely that hundreds or thousands of tree-trunk coffins have been missed – then burial in a tree-trunk coffin would appear to be an exceptionally rare occurrence.

The practice is also exceptional in that inhumation appears to have continued to be the predominant rite even after cremation had become the norm. With the sole possible exception of the Williamston, Aberdeenshire site (No. 4) – a highly unusual tree-trunk 'coffin', and more like a massive cist in its construction – no tree-trunk coffin has been associated with a cinerary urn, even though the currency of tree-trunk coffin and urn use would have overlapped amost entirely. Furthermore, unlike some other

Early Bronze Age high status funerary practices, burial in a tree-trunk coffin appears to be a male-only (or male-dominated) practice.

In other respects, however, burial in a tree-trunk coffin accords with broader trends. It is one of a variety of ostentatious funerary practices to have emerged around the beginning of the Early Bronze Age (i.e. Needham's 'Period 2'), as alternatives to traditional Beaker funerary practices. This period, when bronze began to be used and when opportunities arose to benefit from the control over the movement of scarce resources, is marked by a considerable upswing in, and diversification of, expressions of social differentiation, particularly as articulated in the arena of funerary practices (Needham 2005; 2012). It is at this time that high-status women appear in the funerary record for the first time (Sheridan 2012b). The expressions of Early Bronze Age elite funerary ostentation include the construction of large cists, sometimes with massive capstones (as with the 'dagger grave' at Forteviot, Perth and Kinross, for example: Noble and Brophy 2011), and often buried under mounds that were significantly larger than those associated with Chalcolithic Beaker graves. The linear cemetery of large round cairns along the bottom of Kilmartin Glen is a good example of this phenomenon (Sheridan 2012b). The frequent inclusion of bronze-bladed daggers in tree-trunk coffins links these with other Early Bronze Age high status male 'dagger graves', many of which are also associated with the type of funerary monument outlined above (Henshall 1968; Baker et al. 2003; Cressey and Sheridan 2003; Noble and Brophy 2011). And the richest tree-trunk coffin graves in southern England are comparable with other elite graves in the same region, which share a similar array of precious grave goods, even though the format of the funerary monument is different (Needham and Woodward 2008; Needham et al. 2006, 2010a). One can therefore regard tree-trunk coffins as a regionally-specific expression of a broader phenomenon of high-status funerary practices. People adopted the practice as one of several ways in which to signal and emphasise the special standing of certain members of the community. The conspicuous consumption of effort and resources on the creation and burial of a tree-trunk coffin accords fully with the *Zeitgeist*. It is not necessary to suggest that the practice was adopted from elsewhere, even though earlier examples are known from the Netherlands, as noted above (Drenth and Lohof 2005, 439–40); Early Bronze Age society in Britain was sufficiently innovative at the time to have hit upon the concept itself.

This conformity with wider trends extends to the variability in orientation and posture of the bodies that has been noted for tree-trunk coffins. It had previously been thought that the fact that Gristhorpe Man was buried on his right, unlike many other men who had been buried

on their left, implied some ambiguity in the expression of his gender (Melton et al. 2010). However, thanks to a valuable comparative study of Chalcolithic and Early Bronze Age graves in Scotland and Yorkshire by Alexandra Shepherd (A. N. Shepherd 2012), it is now clear that this was not necessarily the case. Shepherd's study shows that there had indeed been a fairly strong pattern of gender differentiation in Chalcolithic Beaker graves, with men being buried on their left, their head to the east and looking south and women buried on their left, head to west and looking south. However, by the time that tree-trunk coffins started to be used, during the Early Bronze Age, this pattern had broken down somewhat (ibid., 263). Thus, while there are some examples of the 'left-east-south-male' arrangement among the tree-trunk coffin graves (e.g. at Garton Slack, East Riding of Yorkshire, No. 25), there are also a variety of other arrangements, including three where the male had been on his right side (Nos. 10, 16 and 23). This is characteristic of the broader picture at the time, and no gender ambiguity needs to be read into this.

Why burial in a hollowed tree-trunk?

As noted above, the tree-trunk coffin was just one form of wooden container or support that was in use during the Early Bronze Age to help embellish, display, cover and protect the corpse. Various other types of timber funerary structure were also in use. Rectangular plank-built, box-shaped coffins, which had been constructed since the beginning of the Chalcolithic period and may well represent an imported, Beaker-associated Continental tradition (e.g. at Upper Largie, Argyll and Bute: Sheridan 2012a), continued to be used during the Early Bronze Age, alongside tree-trunk coffins. Indeed, at Seafield West, Highland (No. 1), the two types of coffin were literally side by side and may have been buried at or around the same time (Fig. 4.6). Other cases where the two types of coffin have been found under/in the same barrow include Bowthorpe, Norfolk (Lawson 1986), Wetwang Slack, East Riding of Yorkshire (Dent 1979), and Eaton, Leicestershire (P. Clay 1981). The other Early Bronze Age timber funerary structures include plank-lined graves, platforms and biers; Fred Petersen has produced a useful review of such structures in Yorkshire (Petersen 1970). In each case, a tree would presumably have had to be felled to create the structure, and making a plank-built coffin may have been a time-consuming process as the trunk was split and the planks trimmed. Given this choice of structure, why then did people choose to use hollowed tree-trunks as coffins?

The answer may be, 'for several reasons'. The impact of making and installing a heavy tree-trunk coffin (and especially one lidded with the second half of the trunk) within the performance of the funeral should not be

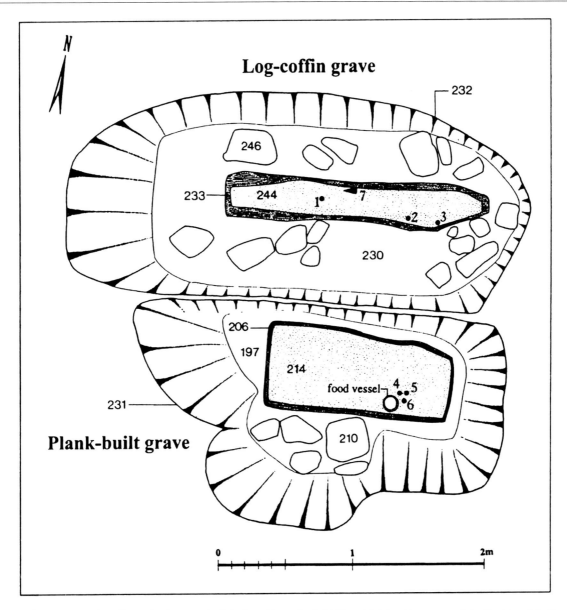

Fig. 4.6 Plan of the tree-trunk coffin and adjacent plank-built coffin at Seafield West, Highland (courtesy of the Society of Antiquaries of Scotland and Mike Cressey)

underestimated. These coffins, made using a resource that was probably scarce in some regions, would have made a powerful, visually arresting statement of the importance of their occupants, highlighting the special lengths to which the mourners were prepared to go to mark the passage of the deceased. Furthermore, manoeuvring the largest and heaviest examples into position would have demanded close co-operation among a number of people. But there could be another, additional reason, connected to Early Bronze Age beliefs and ideologies.

Because wooden coffins are familiar and practical necessities in the traditional British funeral today, it can be difficult to conceive of the coffin as an unusual and

relatively rare apparatus for enclosing the deceased's corpse or ashes. To consider coffins as merely a practical means of enclosing the dead prior to and during burial in the Bronze Age would be naïve in the extreme. As outlined above, there is good evidence that they were employed as markers of gender and some kind of social status. In addition, they may have tapped into a rich vein of symbolism.

The felling of a mighty oak has obvious connotations in relation to a life cut short, in which the tree is employed as a metaphor of history, both human and natural. '*Trees are alive, although their lifespans are considerably longer than ours. Their growth, regeneration and death may be integral to*

Fig. 4.7 Carving a wooden coffin in Androy, southern Madagascar (photo by Mike Parker Pearson). Despite this being a forested region, trees of this size for making coffins are rare and coffins may be fetched from long distances for funerals of the wealthier lineages. The coffins have no symbolic associations with boats or other artefacts made from logs; however, the coffin and cover are traditionally associated with the male on top and the female underneath, with the two joined in 'marriage' when the coffin is finally closed

conceptions of the past, the perceived world and the landscape' (Brennand and Taylor 2003). It is interesting that many British tree-trunk coffins retained their bark, in contrast to practices in other parts of the world (Fig. 4.7). This may indicate that, unlike log boats, they were intended to look as close to the original appearance of the tree as possible. While some may have stood for boats (as discussed below), others retained their appearance as tree-trunks.

Anthony Harding has pointed out that the notion of being buried within a tree might also have had metaphorical significance: *'Burial in a tree-trunk coffin, as it were inside a tree, carries with it obvious connotations of the return to the source of life, a re-enclosing within the womb from which all humans sprang'* (Harding 2000, 109). Trees, with their long lifespans, might also be significant in expressing notions of transcendence from life to death and from one generation to the next.

At the time of the tree-trunk coffins, trees were certainly still sought for construction projects. The enormous undertaking of erecting a palisade just inside the ditch of the large henge at Mount Pleasant, Dorset, took place close to the turn of the third and second millennia BC (Wainwright 1979). It must have required a colossal number of trees. But they were also sometimes used to form smaller enclosures as part of the mortuary process.

One of the most remarkable pieces of evidence for the special regard in which the unshaped tree was held, though, comes from the small timber circle at Holme-next-the-Sea, Norfolk, constructed with trees felled in 2050 and 2049 BC. This enclosed the up-turned stump of a large tree, which clearly played a major metaphorical role for the erectors (Brennand and Taylor 2003). Nearby, the two horizontal timbers at the centre of Holme II timber circle, dating to 2400–2030 cal BC (*ibid.*), have shallow indentations on their surfaces suggesting that they might once, perhaps, have supported a wooden coffin.

It is worth returning to the possible specific connotations of employing a tree-trunk coffin – that is, specific to the person interred. In landscapes poor in woodland, the remaining woods become ever more significant for certain economic and spiritual activities. For much of the population their key importance may have lain in the collection of valuable foods and materials. It is well known from ethnographic situations that trees, woods and forests tend to take on a range of other special roles within the given cosmology. Spirit-healers, in particular, may have needed to requisition certain plantstuffs from the wood for medicine as well as needing to invoke the arboreal spirits at certain times. Dense woods may also have been places associated with special acts of courage or endurance –

perhaps in the course of rites of passage and the proving of 'manhood'. It is therefore easy to envisage a situation in which select members of society came to be unusually closely associated with woods and trees because of their particular experiences or their specialist (e.g. shamanistic or ritual) roles. Burial in a tree-trunk coffin links them to that special place.

Boats for the dead? The significance of logboat allusions in some tree-trunk coffins

A recurring theme in studies of British Early Bronze Age tree-trunk coffins has been the speculation that some constituted symbolic boats for the dead, for ferrying them to the Otherworld across a stretch of water (e.g. Grinsell 1941; Elgee and Elgee 1949; Ashbee 1960, 90–91; Field 1985, 134). The 'canoe'-shaped coffins from Loose Howe (Nos. 11–12) and the boat-shaped coffin from Scrubbity Coppice, Dorset (No. 58), have certainly been taken as examples of such, as has the boat-shaped coffin from Seafield West, Highland (No. 1), and the example from Dalrigh, near Oban, Argyll and Bute (No. 5). As noted above, nearly a quarter of tree-trunk coffins whose end shapes are known, including the Gristhorpe coffin (No. 16), have one straight end and one rounded end, like a boat.

With the exception of the Dalrigh example, which may have started its life as an actual logboat before being re-fashioned into a coffin, none of these boat-shaped coffins is likely to have been an actual logboat (*pace* Elgee and Elgee 1949 and Ashbee 1960, 90). This is clear from the fact that they often retain their bark and have thicker walls than real logboats; compare, for example, the finely-worked Early Bronze Age logboat from Catherinefield, Dumfries & Galloway (Mowat 1996, 18, 20) and the even finer, nine metre-long Late Bronze Age logboat from Carpow, Perth & Kinross (Strachan 2010). As Robert Mowat has remarked, in his review of the logboats of Scotland: [the log coffin is] '*a simple piece of woodworking without any of the considerations of stability or volumetric efficiency that are necessarily involved in the construction of a true logboat, and which are generally indicated by the presence of thickness-gauge holes, thinner walls and a higher standard of workmanship*' (Mowat 1996, 139). Nevertheless, log coffins may indeed constitute symbolic versions of boats.

The use of an actual Early Bronze Age vessel in a funerary context is attested at Barns Farm, Dalgety Bay, on the coast of Fife, where an unburnt individual and the cremated remains of another had been buried in what appeared to be a coracle (grave 2: Watkins 1982, 74–77, 118–119). The presence of fish bones at a higher level in the fill of that grave underlined the maritime imagery (*ibid.*, 51), and the possibility remains that two other graves (nos. 1 and 3) in that cemetery had also been in coracles. In his

discussion of Barns Farm grave 2, Trevor Watkins drew attention to two other possible coracle-coffins of Early Bronze Age date, one from Corbridge, Northumberland, found with a Food Vessel, and the other in the Ancholme estuary near Ferriby, Lincolnshire (*ibid.*, 119).

At Gristhorpe, the 'watery' allusion of the boat-shaped coffin is reinforced by the fact that the barrow in which the coffin has been buried is near a cliff, with a commanding view of the North Sea, and also by the use of bone from a whale's jaw for the pommel of the man's dagger. (See Sheridan *et al.*, this volume, for details.) While the easterly direction of Gristhorpe Man's gaze may have been towards the rising sun, rather than directly out to sea, and while a logboat may not have been the ideal vessel for sea travel (other than near-shore navigation), nevertheless the 'watery' allusion in his grave is clear.

Why did so many tree-trunk coffin graves contain this allusion to water travel? The answer is likely to lie in the patterns of elite mobility, and in the importance of interaction at the time as a way of underpinning the power and authority of the elite. There can be no doubt that travel by water, both along inland waterways and by sea, was of crucial significance to the functioning of Early Bronze Age society, not least because it permitted the movement of valuable objects and materials, and also control over that movement. Indeed, it has been argued elsewhere (Needham 2009) that specialised maritime elite interaction networks – *maritories* – may have been operating during the Early Bronze Age, with their own particular codes of conduct and ritual. One of these maritories can be argued to have focussed on the eastern seaboard of Britain, and to have operated during the first peak of tree-trunk coffin use while another, linking communities across the Channel, would have flourished during the main period of tree-trunk coffin use in southern England (*ibid.*; Needham *et al.* 2006). As for the actual vessels that would have been used in these maritime networks, in addition to the hide-covered coracle-type boats as mentioned above, there is evidence for substantial and complex plank-constructed boats, in the remarkable series of Early Bronze Age finds from North Ferriby, on the Humber estuary, plus a plank fragment from Kilnsea, on the tip of Hornsea, East Yorkshire (E. V. Wright 1990; E. V. Wright *et al.* 2001; Van de Noort 2004). These boats – of which the earliest would have been pene-contemporaneous with the Gristhorpe coffin – could have been used for estuarine and river passage, as well as sea travel. (The famous sewn-plank Dover Boat will not be considered here, as it slightly post-dates the currency of tree-trunk coffin use.) As noted above, logboats operate best in inland and inshore contexts, although the addition of an outrigger would permit offshore maritime sailing.

Evidence for the operation of these wide-ranging networks of interaction is easy to see. The wealth of the elite in Kilmartin Glen, in the west of Scotland, seems to have been based on their ability to control the flow of metal from Ireland, up the Great Glen, to north-east Scotland (Sheridan 2012b). At the other end of the Great Glen, the logboat-like tree-trunk coffin at Seafield West, Highland, together with the Irish-style Bowl Food Vessel in the adjacent plank-built coffin, both evoke and attest to that movement. A logboat would have been an ideal type of boat to navigate along Loch Ness. Furthermore, the fact that strontium and oxygen isotope evidence from dental enamel has revealed that a high-status, Beaker-associated male at Culduthel, close to Seafield West, had originated in north-east Ireland (Sheridan 2012a) only goes to underline the mobility of certain elements of Early Bronze Age society around this time. The nature and extent of this mobility has been investigated further through the Beaker People Project (Jay *et al.* 2012).

If we look at the contemporary economy of Gristhorpe Man's region, it is clear that Yorkshire was fully articulated within a wider world. Gristhorpe Man was buried just over 30 km down the coast from the famous sources of jet in the Whitby area. The period between the 22nd century and the 20th/19th century BC saw the emergence and *floruit* of specialist jet-working in this area, producing precious and no doubt symbolically-charged elite jewellery and dress accessories, such as spacer-plate necklaces and buttons (Sheridan and Davis 1998; I. A. G. Shepherd 2009). This finery was distributed widely, not only across northern Britain (including the Kilmartin Glen), but also as far south as East Anglia, into eastern Ireland and, in more limited quantity, into Wessex. Although the mechanisms of distribution were undoubtedly varied, it is hard to escape the conclusion that coasting along the eastern seaboard of Britain was a key element of the network. In this context a profound interest in the sea on the part of coastal communities in north-east Yorkshire is hardly surprising. That transport along inland waterways would have been equally important to the operation of the Yorkshire-based network is suggested by the inland location of the Loose Howe boat-shaped coffins: these were found 20 km inland, on one of the highest peaks in the North York Moors (thus commanding considerable views), above one of the tributaries of the River Derwent (Elgee and Elgee 1949).

Conclusions

The Gristhorpe tree-trunk coffin can be understood as part of a widespread phenomenon in Early Bronze Age Britain that seems to have begun during the final two centuries of the third millennium and lasted until *c.* 1600 BC, when all ostentatious burial rites were waning. While there are

parallels (and chronological overlap) with Dutch tree-trunk coffin use, there is no reason to seek an external source for the adoption of the practice; instead, it can be seen as one of several ways in which conspicuous consumption was used to signal status from the time that bronze began to be used widely in Britain. The earliest Bronze Age saw a diversification and elaboration of funerary practices, as well as novelties in ceramic design and in other aspects of material culture. Tree-trunk coffins seem to be associated in particular with men, and the bronze daggers that are found in several of the graves were an archetypal male status symbol during the Early Bronze Age. The use of tree-trunk coffins in some areas where large trees would have been scarce underlines the investment of effort involved in creating these impressive coffins.

The boat imagery as seen at Gristhorpe and in several other examples can be understood as having a dual reference: to a vehicle for supernatural travel to the Otherworld, and to a vehicle that would have played a key role in the movement of people, objects and ideas in Early Bronze Age society.

From the foregoing it is clear that we have a reasonable understanding of the construction, date, use and symbolism of tree-trunk coffins, despite all the problems of taphonomy and recognition, and all the issues involved with old finds. There is more that could be learned from the existing body of data, with scope for the re-investigation of human remains to the standard achieved with Gristhorpe Man, and scope for the radiocarbon dating (and re-dating, in some cases) of a number of finds, especially since dating of cremated bone is now a routine practice. This, and the Bayesian modelling of the resulting dataset, should allow us to develop a more refined chronology for this fascinating funerary practice.

Note added in press: A few additional examples of tree-trunk coffins were brought to the authors' attention after the typescript was submitted for publication. These are listed in Appendix 4.1 as '*Addenda*', but do not feature in the statistics cited in the main text.

Acknowledgements
The authors wish to thank Terry Manby, John Dent, David Clarke and Adam Gwilt for providing invaluable information; Jenny Ruthven of Southampton University Library, for help in accessing Hampshire literature; David Bertie and Aberdeenshire Council, for permission to reproduce the Cairngall manuscript; and the Society of Antiquaries of Scotland for permission to reproduce the photograph of the Dalrigh coffin and the plan of Seafield West. Mike Cressey is also thanked for the Seafield West plan.

References

Abercromby, J. (1905) Report on excavations at Fethaland and Trowie Knowe, Shetland; and of the exploration of a cairn on Dumglow, one of the Cleish Hills. *Proceedings of the Society of Antiquaries of Scotland* 39 (1904–1905), 173–184.

Ashbee, P. (1957) The great barrow at Bishop's Waltham, Hampshire. *Proceedings of the Prehistoric Society* 23, 137–166.

Ashbee, P. (1960) *The Bronze Age Round Barrow in Britain*. London, Phoenix House.

Ashbee, P. (1986) The excavation of Milton Lilbourne barrows 1–5. *Wiltshire Archaeological and Natural History Magazine* 80, 23–96.

Ashwin, T. and Bates, W. (2000) *Norwich Southern Bypass, Part I: Excavations at Bixley, Caistor St Edmund, Trowse.* Gressenhall, East Anglian Archaeology (Report 91).

Baker, L., Sheridan, J. A. and Cowie, T. G. (2003) An Early Bronze Age 'dagger grave' from Rameldry Farm, near Kingskettle, Fife. *Proceedings of the Society of Antiquaries of Scotland* 133, 85–123.

Barclay, A. and Halpin, C. (1998) *Excavations at Barrow Hills, Radley, Oxfordshire. Volume I: the Neolithic and Bronze Age Monument Complex.* Oxford, Oxbow.

Bateman, T. (1861) *Ten Years' Diggings in Celtic and Saxon Grave Hills in the Counties of Derby, Stafford and York, from 1848 to 1858.* London, George Allen and Sons.

Brassil, K. S., Owen, W. G. and Britwell, W. J. (1991) Prehistoric and Early Medieval cemeteries at Tandderwen, near Denbigh, Clwyd. *Archaeological Journal* 148, 46–97.

Brennand, M. and Taylor, M. (2003) The survey and excavation of a Bronze Age timber circle at Holme-next-the-Sea, Norfolk, 1998–9. *Proceedings of the Prehistoric Society* 69, 1–84.

Breuning-Madsen, H. and Kähler Holst, M. (1995) Genesis of iron pans in Bronze Age mounds in Denmark. *Journal of Danish Archaeology* 11, 80–86.

Brewster, T. C. M. (1973) Two Bronze Age barrows in the North Riding of Yorkshire. *Yorkshire Archaeological Journal* 45, 55–94.

Brewster, T. C. M. (unpublished) *Willie Howe, Cowlam. An Early Bronze Age Barrow in East Yorkshire.* Copyright East Riding Archaeological Research Trust.

Brewster, T. C. M. and Finney, A. E. (1995) *The Excavation of Seven Bronze Age Barrows on the Moorlands of North-East Yorkshire.* Leeds, Yorkshire Archaeological Society: Prehistory Research Section (Yorkshire Archaeological Report no. 1).

Bristow, P. H. W. (1998) *Attitudes to Disposal of the Dead in Southern Britain 3500 BC–AD43.* Oxford, British Archaeological Reports (British Series 274).

Clay, P. (1981) *Two Multi-phase Barrow Sites at Sproxton and Eaton, Leicestershire.* Leicester, Leicestershire Museums, Art Galleries and Records Service (Archaeological Report 2).

Clay, R. C. C. (1929) Pre-Roman coffin burials with particular reference to one from a barrow at Fovant. *Wiltshire Archaeological and Natural History Magazine* 44 (1927–1929), 101–105.

Cleal, R. M. J., Allen, M. and Newman, C. (2004) An archaeological and environmental study of the Neolithic and later prehistoric landscape of the Avon valley and Durrington Walls environs. *Wiltshire Archaeological and Natural History Magazine* 97, 218–248.

Cowie, T. G., Pickin, J. and Wallace, C. (2011) Bog bodies from Scotland: old finds, new records. *Journal of Wetland Archaeology* 10, 1–45.

Cressey, M. and Sheridan, J. A. (2003) The excavation of a Bronze Age cemetery at Seafield West, near Inverness, Highland. *Proceedings of the Society of Antiquaries of Scotland* 133, 47–84.

Curwen, E. and Curwen, E. C. (1924) The Hove Tumulus. *Brighton and Hove Archaeologist* 2, 20–28.

Curtis, N. and Wilkin, N. (2012) The regionality of Beakers and Bodies in the Chalcolithic of North-east Scotland. In M. J. Allen, J. P. Gardiner and J. A. Sheridan (eds.) *Is There a British Chalcolithic? People, Place and Polity in the Late 3rd Millennium,* 237–256. Oxford, Oxbow/Prehistoric Society (Prehistoric Society Research Paper 4).

Dent, J. S. (1979) Bronze Age burials from Wetwang Slack. *Yorkshire Archaeological Journal* 51, 23–39.

Dent, J. S. (1983) A summary of the excavations carried out in Garton Slack and Wetwang Slack 1964–1980. *East Riding Archaeologist* 7, 1–14.

Dent, J. S. (2010) *The Iron Age in East Yorkshire: an Analysis of the Later Prehistoric Monuments of the Yorkshire Wolds and the Culture which Marked their Final Phase.* Oxford, British Archaeological Reports (British Series 508).

Dixon, D. D. (1913) Cartington oak coffin, &c. *Proceedings of the Society of Antiquaries of Newcastle* (3rd Series) 6, 79–84.

Donald, W. (1840) Peterhead Parish. *New Statistical Account of Scotland* 12, 344–396. http://www.electricscotland.com/history/statistical/peterhead.htm

Donaldson, P. (1977) The excavation of a multiple round barrow at Barnack, Cambridgeshire. *Antiquaries Journal* 57, 197–231.

Drenth, E. and Lohof, E. (2005) Mounds for the dead: funerary and burial ritual in Beaker period, Early and Middle Bronze Age. In L. P. Louwe Kooijmans, P. W. van den Broeke, H. Fokkens and A. L. van Gijn (eds.) *The Prehistory of the Netherlands. Volume 1,* 433–454. Amsterdam, Amsterdam University Press.

Edwards, B. J. N. (1973) Canoe burial near Lancaster. *Antiquity* 47, 298–301.

Elgee, F. (1930) *Early Man in North-East Yorkshire.* Gloucester, John Bellows.

Elgee, H. W. and Elgee F. (1949) An Early Bronze Age burial in a boat-shaped wooden coffin from north-east Yorkshire. *Proceedings of the Prehistoric Society* 15, 87–106.

Ellis, F. (1845) Culsalmond Parish. *New Statistical Account of Scotland* 12, 732–733. http://www.electricscotland.com/history/statistical/culsalmond.htm

Fenton-Thomas, C. (2011) *Where Sky and Yorkshire and Water Meet. The Story of the Melton Landscape from Prehistory to the Present.* York, On Site Archaeology (Monography No. 2).

Field, N. (1985) A multi-phased barrow and possible henge monument at West Ashby, Lincolnshire. *Proceedings of the Prehistoric Society* 51, 103–136.

Forde, D. (1939) Dysgwylfa Fawr barrow, Cardiganshire: a food-vessel and dug-out trunk cremation burial. *Antiquaries Journal* 19, 90–92.

French, C. A. I. (1994) *Excavation of the Deeping St Nicholas Barrow Complex, South Lincolnshire.* Heckington, Lincolnshire Archaeology and Heritage (Lincolnshire Archaeology and Heritage Series 1).

French, C. A. I. (2003) *Geoarchaeology in Action: Studies in Soil Micromorphology and Landscape Evolution.* London, Routledge.

French, C. A. I. and Pryor, F. M. (2005) *Archaeology and Environment of the Etton Landscape.* Peterborough, Fenland Archaeological Trust.

French, C. A. I., Lewis, H., Allen, M. J., Green, M., Scaife, R. and Gardiner, J. (2007) *Prehistoric Landscape Development and Human Impact in the Upper Allen Valley, Cranborne Chase, Dorset.* Cambridge, McDonald Institute.

Garwood, P. (2003) Round barrows and funerary traditions in Late Neolithic and Bronze Age Sussex. In D. Rudling (ed.) *The Archaeology of Sussex to AD 2000,* 47–68. Brighton, University of Sussex.

Gerloff, S. (1975) *The Early Bronze Age Daggers in Great Britain and a Reconsideration of the Wessex Culture.* Munich, C.H. Beck'sche (Prähistorische Bronzefunde Series 6(2)).

Glob, P. V. (1974) *The Mound People: Danish Bronze-Age Man Preserved.* London, Faber and Faber.

Greenfield, E. (1960) The excavation of Barrow 4 at Swarkestone, Derbyshire. *Derbyshire Archaeological Journal* 80, 1–48.

Greenfield, E. (1985) Five Bronze Age round barrows at Ponton Heath, Stroxton, Lincolnshire. *Lincolnshire History and Archaeology* 20, 35–44.

Greenwell, W. (1877) *British Barrows.* Oxford, Clarendon Press.

Greenwell, W. (1890) Recent researches in barrows in Yorkshire, Wiltshire, Berkshire, etc. *Archaeologia* 52, 1–72.

Grinsell, L. V. (1940) Hampshire barrows (Parts I, II and III). *Proceedings of the Hampshire Field Club and Archaeological Society* 14 (1938–1940), 9–40, 195–229, 346–365.

Grinsell, L. V. (1941) The boat of the dead in the Bronze Age. *Antiquity* 15, 360–370.

Harding, A. (2000) *European Societies in the Bronze Age.* Cambridge, Cambridge University Press.

Haughton, C. and Powlesland, D. (1999) *West Heslerton. The Anglian Cemetery. Volume 1.* Malton, Landscape Research Centre.

Hayes, P. (1958) Notes on excavations in Wales. *Proceedings of the Prehistoric Society* 24, 220.

Hayes, P. (1996) Flintshire Historical Society's Excavation of a Bronze Age barrow at Pant y Dulaith, Tremeirchion 1957. *Flintshire Historical Society Journal* 34, 15–31. http://welshjournals.llgc.org.uk/browse/viewobject/llgc-id:1219705/article/000069524 (accessed December 2012).

Henshall, A. S. (1968) Scottish dagger graves. In J. M. Coles and D. D. A. Simpson (eds.) *Studies in Ancient Europe,* 173–195. Leicester, University of Leicester.

Hoare, R. Colt (1812) *The Ancient History of Wiltshire.* Volume I (South Wiltshire). London, William Millar.

Hoare, R. Colt (1821) *The Ancient History of Wiltshire.* Volume II (North Wiltshire). London, Lackington, Hughes, Harding, Mavor and Lepard.

Hornsby, W. and Stanton, R. (1917) British barrows near Brotton. *Yorkshire Archaeological Journal* 24, 263–268.

Hutchins, J. (1767) Archaeology, Part I. *Gentleman's Magazine* 37, 94–95.

Jay, M., Parker Pearson, M., Richards, M., Nehlich, O., Montgomery, J., Chamberlain, A. and Sheridan, J. A. (2012) The Beaker People Project: an interim report on the progress of the isotopic analysis of the organic skeletal material. In M. J. Allen, J. P. Gardiner and J. A. Sheridan (eds.) *Is There a British Chalcolithic? People, Place and Polity in the Late 3rd Millennium,* 226–236. Oxford, Oxbow/Prehistoric Society (Prehistoric Society Research Paper 4).

Jensen, J. (2002) *Danmarks Oldtid: Bronzealder 2,000–500 f Kr.* Copenhagen, Gyldendal.

Jobey, G. (1984) The Cartington coffin: a radiocarbon date. *Archaeologia Aeliana* 12 (5th series), 235–237.

Jones, A. M. and Quinnell, H. (2006) Redating the Watch Hill Barrow, Cornwall. *Archaeological Journal* 163, 42–66.

Kähler Holst, M., Breuning-Madsen, H. and Rasmussen, M. (2001) The south Scandinavian barrows with well-preserved oak-log coffins. *Antiquity* 75, 126–136.

Knight, M. (2000) Henge to house – post-circles in a Neolithic and Bronze Age landscape at King's Dyke West, Whittlesey, Cambridgeshire. *Past* 34, 3–4.

Lawson, A. (1986) *Barrow Excavations in Norfolk, 1950–82.* Gressenhall, East Anglian Archaeology (East Anglian Archaeology 29).

Lukis, W. C. (1867) Notes on barrow diggings in the parish of Collingbourne Ducis. *Wiltshire Archaeological and Natural History Magazine* 10, 85–103.

Lukis, W. C. (1870) On the flint implements and tumuli of the neighbourhood of Wath. *Yorkshire Archaeological Journal* 1, 116–121.

McGrail, S. (1978) *Logboats of England and Wales with Comparative Material from European and Other Countries.* Oxford, British Archaeological Reports (British Series no. 51) and Greenwich, National Maritime Museum (Archaeological Series no. 2).

Manby, T. G., King, A. and Vyner, B. (2003) The Neolithic and Bronze Ages: a time of early agriculture. In T. G. Manby, S. Moorhouse and P. Ottaway (eds.) *The Archaeology of Yorkshire: an Assessment at the Beginning of the 21st* century, 35–113. Leeds, Yorkshire Archaeological Society.

Mapleton, R. J. (1879) Notice of the discovery of an old canoe in a peat-bog at Oban. *Proceedings of the Society of Antiquaries of Scotland* 13, 336–338.

Melton, N., Montgomery, J., Knüsel, C. J., Batt, C., Needham, S. P., Parker Pearson, M., Sheridan, J. A., Heron, C., Horsley, T., Schmidt, A., Evans, A., Carter, E., Edwards, H., Hargreaves, M., Janaway, R., Lynnerup, N., Northover, P., O'Connor, S., Ogden, A., Taylor, T., Wastling, V. and Wilson, A. (2010) Gristhorpe Man: an Early Bronze Age log-coffin burial scientifically dated. *Antiquity* 84, 796–815.

Miles, H. (1975) Barrows on the St Austell Granite, Cornwall. *Cornish Archaeology* 14, 5–82.

Mortimer, J. R. (1905) *Forty Years' Researches in British and Saxon Burial Mounds of East Yorkshire.* London, Brown and Sons.

Mowat, R. (1996) *The Log-Boats of Scotland.* Oxford, Oxbow.

Needham, S. P. (2000) Power pulses across a cultural divide: cosmologically-driven acquisition between Armorica and Wessex. *Proceedings of the Prehistoric Society* 66, 151–207.

Needham, S. P. (2004) Migdale-Marnoch: sunburst of Scottish metallurgy. In I. A. G. Shepherd and G. J. Barclay (eds.) *Scotland in Ancient Europe: The Neolithic and Early Bronze Age of Scotland in their European Context,* 217–45. Edinburgh, Society of Antiquaries of Scotland.

Needham, S. P. (2005) Transforming Beaker culture in north-west Europe; processes of fusion and fission. *Proceedings of the Prehistoric Society* 71, 171–217.

Needham, S. P. (2009) Encompassing the sea: 'Maritories' and

Bronze Age maritime interactions. In P. Clark (ed.) *Bronze Age Connections: Cultural Contact in Prehistoric Europe*, 12–37. Oxford, Oxbow.

Needham, S. P. (2012) Case and place for the British Chalcolithic. In M. J. Allen, J. P. Gardiner and J. A. Sheridan (eds.) *Is There a British Chalcolithic? People, Place and Polity in the Late 3rd Millennium*, 1–26. Oxford, Oxbow/Prehistoric Society (Prehistoric Society Research Paper 4).

Needham, S. P. (forthcoming) A revised classification and chronology for daggers and knives. Appendix 1 in In A. Woodward, J. R. Hunter and D. Bukach, *Ritual and Dress in the Early Bronze Age*. Oxford, Oxbow.

Needham, S. P. and Woodward, A. (2008) The Clandon barrow finery: a synopsis of success in an Early Bronze Age world. *Proceedings of the Prehistoric Society* 74, 1–52.

Needham, S. P., Lawson, A. J. and Woodward, A. (2010a) 'A noble group of barrows': Bush Barrow and the Normanton group of barrows two centuries on. *The Antiquaries Journal* 90, 1–39.

Needham, S. P., Parfitt, K. and Varndell, G. (2006) *The Ringlemere Cup: Precious Cups and the Beginning of the Channel Bronze Age*. London, The British Museum (British Museum Research Publication 163).

Needham, S. P., Parker Pearson, M., Tyler, A., Richards, M. and Jay, M. (2010b) A first 'Wessex 1' date from Wessex. *Antiquity* 84, 363–373.

Noble, G. and Brophy, K. (2011) Ritual and remembrance at a prehistoric ceremonial complex in central Scotland: excavations at Forteviot, Perth and Kinross. *Antiquity* 85, 787–804.

Petersen, F. (1970) Early Bronze Age timber graves and coffin burials on the Yorkshire Wolds. *Yorkshire Archaeological Journal* 42 (1967–70), 262–267.

Phillips, B. (1856) Untitled communication. *Archaeological Journal* 13, 183–184.

Phillips, B. (1857) Discovery of a tumulus at Hove, near Brighton, containing an amber cup etc. *Sussex Archaeological Collections* 9, 119–124.

Piggott, C. M. (1938) A Middle Bronze Age barrow and Deverel-Rimbury urnfield at Latch Farm, Christchurch, Hampshire. *Proceedings of the Prehistoric Society* 4, 169–187.

Piggott, S. (1938) The Early Bronze Age in Wessex. *Proceedings of the Prehistoric Society* 4, 52–106.

Pitt-Rivers, A. L. F. (1888) *Excavations in Cranbourne Chase. Volume II*. Privately printed.

Powlesland, D., with Haughton, C. and Hanson, J. (1986) Excavations at Heslerton, North Yorkshire 1978–82. *Archaeological Journal* 143, 53–173.

Rahtz, P. (1989) *Little Ouseburn Barrow 1958: Round Hill, an Early Bronze Age barrow at Little Ouseburn, North Yorkshire, England*. York, Department of Archaeology, York University.

Randsborg, K. and Christensen, K. (2006) *Bronze Age Oak-coffin Graves: Archaeology and Dendro-dating*. Copenhagen, Blackwell Munksgaard (*Acta Archaeologica* 77, Supplementa VII).

Roe, F. E. S. (1966) The battle-axe series in Britain. *Proceedings of the Prehistoric Society* 32, 199–245.

Roe, F. E. S. (1979) Typology of stone implements with shaftholes. In T. H. McK. Clough and W. A. Cummins (eds.) *Stone Axe Studies*,

23–46. London, Council for British Archaeology (Research Report 23).

Rolleston, G. and Fox, A. L. (1878) Report of excavation of a twin barrow and a single round barrow at Sigwell, parish of Charlton Horethorne, Somerset. *Proceedings of the Somersetshire Archaeologicaland Natural History Society* 24, 75–83.

Savory, H. N. (1961) Bronze Age burials near Bedd Emlyn, Clocaenog. *Transactions of the Denbighshire Historical Society* 10, 7–22.

Savory, H. N. (1980) *Guide Catalogue of the Bronze Age Collections*. Cardiff, National Museum of Wales.

Shepherd, A. N. (2012) Stepping out together: men, women and their Beakers in time and space. In M. J. Allen, J. P. Gardiner and J. A. Sheridan (eds.) *Is There a British Chalcolithic? People, Place and Polity in the Late 3rd Millennium*, 257–280. Oxford, Oxbow/ Prehistoric Society (Prehistoric Society Research Paper 4).

Shepherd, I. A. G. (2009) The V-bored buttons of Great Britain and Ireland. *Proceedings of the Prehistoric Society* 75, 335–369.

Sheridan, J. A. (2004a) Scottish Food Vessel chronology revisited. In A. M. Gibson and J. A. Sheridan (eds.) *From Sickles to Circles: Britain and Ireland at the Time of Stonehenge*, 243–267. Stroud, Tempus.

Sheridan, J. A. (2004b) The National Museums' of Scotland radiocarbon dating programmes: results obtained 2003/4. *Discovery and Excavation in Scotland* 5, 174–176.

Sheridan, J. A. (2007a) Scottish Beaker dates: the good, the bad and the ugly. In M. Larsson and M. Parker Pearson (eds.) *From Stonehenge to the Baltic: Living with Cultural Diversity in the Third Millennium BC*, 91–123. Oxford, British Archaeological Reports (International Series S1692).

Sheridan, J. A. (2007b) Dating the Scottish Bronze Age: "There is clearly much that the material can still tell us". In C. Burgess, P. Topping and F. Lynch (eds.) *Beyond Stonehenge: Essays on the Bronze Age in Honour of Colin Burgess*, 162–185. Oxford, Oxbow.

Sheridan, J. A. (2012a) A Rumsfeld Reality Check: what we know, what we don't know and what we don't know we don't know about the Chalcolithic in Britain and Ireland. In M. J. Allen, J. P. Gardiner and J. A. Sheridan (eds.) *Is There a British Chalcolithic? People, Place and Polity in the Late 3rd Millennium*, 40–55. Oxford, Oxbow/Prehistoric Society (Prehistoric Society Research Paper 4).

Sheridan, J. A. (2012b) Contextualising Kilmartin: building a narrative for developments in western Scotland and beyond, from the Early Neolithic to the Late Bronze Age. In A. M. Jones, J. Pollard, M. J. Allen & J. Gardiner (eds.) *Image, Memory and Monumentality; archaeological engagements with the material world*, 163–183. Oxford, Oxbow/Prehistoric Society (Prehistoric Society Research Paper 5).

Sheridan, J. A. and Davis, M. (1998) The Welsh 'jet set' in prehistory: a case of keeping up with the Joneses? In A. M. Gibson and D. D. A. Simpson (eds.) *Prehistoric Ritual and Religion: Essays in Honour of Aubrey Burl*, 148–162. Stroud, Sutton.

Simpson, W. G. (1976) A barrow cemetery of the second millennium BC at Tallington, Lincolnshire. *Proceedings of the Prehistoric Society* 42, 215–239.

Smith, A. C. (1879) A sketch of the parish of Yatesbury. *Wiltshire Archaeological and Natural History Magazine* 18, 329–334.

Smith, M. J. B. (1994) *The Excavated Bronze Age Barrows of North-East*

Yorkshire. Durham, Architectural and Archaeological Society of Durham and Northumberland.

Snagge, T. W. (1873) Some account of ancient oaken coffins discovered on the lands adjoining Featherstone Castle, near Haltwhistle, Northumberland. *Archaeologia* 44, 8–16.

Strachan, D. (2010) *Carpow in Context. A Late Bronze Age Logboat from the Tay.* Edinburgh, Society of Antiquaries of Scotland.

Thomas, N. and Ellwood, E. C. (2005) Early Bronze Age copper-alloy awls from Sites I and II, with metal analysis and classification. In N. Thomas, *Snail Down, Wiltshire: the Bronze Age Barrow Cemetery and Related Earthworks, in the Parishes of Collingbourne Ducis and Collingbourne Kingston. Excavations, 1953, 1955 and 195,* 219–222. Devizes, Wiltshire Archaeological and Natural History Society (Monograph 3).

Thomas, N. (2005) *Snail Down, Wiltshire: the Bronze Age Barrow Cemetery and Related Earthworks, in the Parishes of Collingbourne Ducis and Collingbourne Kingston. Excavations, 1953, 1955 and 1957.* Devizes, Wiltshire Archaeological and Natural History Society (Monograph 3).

Thurnam, J. (1860) Examination of barrows on the downs of North Wiltshire in 1853–57. *Wiltshire Archaeological & Natural History Magazine* 6, 317–336.

Thurnam, J. (1871) On ancient British barrows, especially those of Wiltshire and the adjoining Counties. (Part II. Round barrows). *Archaeologia* 43(2), 285–544.

Tomalin, D. J. (1979) Barrow excavation in the Isle of Wight. *Current Archaeology* 68, 273–276.

Van de Noort, R. (2004) Ancient seascapes: the social context of seafaring in the Bronze Age. *World Archaeology* 35, 404–415.

Vatcher, F. de M. and Vatcher, H. L. (1976) The excavation of a round barrow near Poor's Heath, Risby, Suffolk. *Proceedings of the Prehistoric Society* 42, 263–292.

Wainwright, G. J. (1979) *Mount Pleasant, Dorset: Excavations 1970-1971.* London, Society of Antiquaries of London.

Warrilow, W., Owen, G. and Britnell, W. (1986) Eight ring-ditches at Four Crosses, Llandysilio, Powys, 1981–85. *Proceedings of the Prehistoric Society* 52, 53–87.

Watkins, T. (1982) The excavation of an Early Bronze Age cemetery at Barns Farm, Dalgety, Fife. *Proceedings of the Society of Antiquaries of Scotland* 112, 48–141.

White, A. J. (2001) *The Quernmore Burial Mystery.* Lancaster: Lancaster City and Museums. (Pamphlet).

Whiting, C. E. (1937) Ancient log coffins in Britain. *Transactions of the Architectural and Archaeological Society of Durham and Northumberland* 8, 80–105.

Wilkin, N. (2010) A sunset song? The Beaker to Food Vessel transition in northern Britain (c 2200–1800 cal BC). In [M. Greig (ed.)] *A Lad O'Pairts: a Day Conference in Memory of Ian Shepherd,* 17–22. Aberdeen: Aberdeenshire Archaeology Service (http://www.aberdeenshire.gov.uk/archaeology/projects/ IanShepherdConferencePapers-WebVersion.pdf, accessed February 2013).

Williamson, W. C. (1834) *Description of the Tumulus, lately opened at Gristhorpe, near Scarborough.* Scarborough, C. R. Todd.

Williamson, W. C. (1872) *Description of the Tumulus, opened at Gristhorpe, near Scarborough,* third edition. Scarborough, S. W. Theakston.

Wright, E. V. (1990) *The Ferriby Boats: Seacraft of the Bronze Age.* London, Routledge.

Wright, E. V., Hedges, R. E. M., Bayliss, A., and Van de Noort, R. (2001) North Ferriby boats – a contribution to dating prehistoric seafaring in northwestern Europe. *Antiquity* 75, 726–734.

Wright, T. (1857) On some curious forms of sepulchral interment found in East Yorkshire. *Gentleman's Magazine* 3 (August–December 1857), 114–119.

Appendix 4.1. Catalogue of definite, probable and possible Early Bronze Age tree-trunk coffins in Britain

No.	Status	Findspot	Context	Shape, structure, species, dimensions	Coffin orientation	Rite	Sex, age	Side	Head end + dir'n of view	Grave goods and other contents	Comments	References
1	D	Seafield West, Inverness, Highland	Inside ring-ditch; under stone cairn covering just the pit with tree-trunk coffin and adjacent pit containing plank-built coffin. Found at 0.8 m below old ground surface; had been supported by boulders. Uncertain whether barrow had covered cairn	Boat-shaped, with slightly pointed 'prow' and squared-off 'stern'; slightly uneven sides. U-shaped in cross-section. No sign of any lid. Wholly degraded; present only as stain in gravel. 2 x 0.32 m. Side walls 2–3 cm thick, and thicker towards western 'stern' end	E-W, 'prow' to E	I, co	Pres ad; indet	Prob L	E,S	Bronze dagger in scabbard; dagger of Gerloff's 'Type Butterwick'; Needham's Series 2A.	Dagger scabbard C14-dated; initial published date superseded. See Table 4.2. Mesolithic flint flake residual; second flint flake also probably residual. Space between ends of body and ends of coffin hollow	Cressey and Sheridan 2003; Sheridan 2004b, 176
2–3	D	Cairngall, Longside parish, Aberdeenshire	'In a tumulus', under peat	One complete, other not; both of oak, and covered with a flat board. Bark present. Complete example round-ended at both ends, with projecting ledge-like handle at each end; 2.13 x 0.61 m	E-W	[I]	-	-	-	None	Found in 1813. Coffins found close together. No human remains found; just 'soft earthy matter'	Donald 1840, 354–355; Cowie et al. 2011, 5–6, 26 and fig. 2
4	D, odd	Williamston, Culsalmond, Aberdeenshire	Found where a cairn had previously existed; probably on the prominent Law Hillock. Sides of coffin (which were deeper than the base) rested on hard blue clay. Projecting parts of sides rested on hard oval patch of burnt substance, with many ashes; believed to be site of funeral pyre	'…of uncommon size…formed from the trunk of a huge oak, divided into three parts of unequal length, each of which had been split through the middle with wedges and stone axes, or perhaps separated with some red hot instrument of stone, as the inside of the different pieces had somewhat the appearance of having been charred. The whole consisted of six parts, two sides, two gavels, a bottom, and a lid. Only a small part of the lid remained… All the rest of the pieces were entire, and, when put together in their original position, had … the appearance of the body and shafts of a cart.' (Ellis 1845)	E-W	-	-	-	-	Large pot, c. 280 mm high, with narrow bottom and wide top, found in one corner of coffin. Pots of this shape and size are usually cinerary urns	Found 1812. Although description suggests that cremation had occurred on the site, no mention is made of any 'ashes' in the pot. The multi-part structure differentiates this from hollowed tree-trunk coffins, even though it was clearly made from a tree trunk	Ellis 1845, 732–733; Mowat 1996, 107
5	D	Dalrigh, near Oban, Argyll and Bute	In/under mound of stone and earth, 12.2 m in diameter and 1.22 m high, in peaty ground; 2.74 m of peat existed below the coffin	Rectangular, with end-boards close to each end; not lidded (but see 'grave goods'). Believed to have been re-used logboat, with original transom board forming the S end; a groove had been cut to take another board at the N end. Curvature of interior of base suggests that original logboat had not been much bigger. Oak. 1.76 x 0.61 x 0.48. Supported and covered by logs, kept in place by stakes and with gaps stuffed with moss; ends kept in place by vertical stakes	N-S	Pres I	-	-	-	No grave goods but fragments of sewn birch bark – one found against the side of the interior – prob. coffin cover or wrapping for body. Covered with branches of birch and prob. hazel, stuffed with moss. Many hazelnuts inside and outside the structure	No trace of body but soil inside structure was unctuous, charcoal-rich and foul-smelling. Birch bark C-14 dated: see Table 4.2	Mapleton 1879
6	D	Dumglow (Drumglow), Perth and Kinross	In pit under centre of round cairn, 15.3 m in diameter and 1.5 m high, on summit of Dumglow	Decayed remains of 'hollowed-out tree-trunk of oak' (Abercromby 1905, 180), 2.2 x up to 0.28 m; one end missing	E-W	Pres I	-	-	-	No grave goods	No trace of body found; assumed to have been unburnt body	Abercromby 1905, 179–181; Mowat 1996, 85

No.	Status	Findspot	Context	Shape, structure, species, dimensions	Coffin orientation	Rite	Sex, age	Side	Head end + dir'n of view	Grave goods and other contents	Comments	References
7	D	Cartington, Rothbury, Northumberland	Found within a cairn at a depth of 1.22 m, on the summit of an eminence c. 200 m OD (Dixon 1913). Coffin fixed in position by wooden wedges; large stones and clay. Large block of sandstone found on old ground surface along the N side of the grave	Rectangular, lidded with other half of trunk; bark present; 'dais or pillow' at right end, and hollow is wider where back and knees are assumed to have lain. Tool marks clearly visible. A series of complicated indentations' on S side of exterior, possibly from pressure of cairn stones. Hole in lower corner at one edge, thought to be to help with haulage. Oak. C. 1.7 x 0.5–0.6 m; hollowed area 1.2 x up to 0.64 m	E-W	I, co	Pres. ad	L	E,S	Fragment of stitched animal skin (thought to be from kid or calf as 'hair was not bristly') – from cloth ng or wrapping; flint thumbnail scraper and several smaller pieces of flint; at feet, sherds of a 'drink ng cup' (i.e. Beaker), possibly of All-Over-Cord type ; lost (Jobey 1984, 236). Bracken fronds, thought to be charcoal, in upper part of coffin fill	Found before 1813. Elgee and Elgee say that there is no evidence that the coffin had been covered by a barrow, but given the location of the findspot, the former presence of a mound seems likely. Bracken fronds had lined base of hollow. Sample from outer growth rings C14-dated; see Table 4.2	Dixon 1913, 81–84; Jobey 1984; Mowat 1996, 140
8	D	West Tanfield (Centre Hill barrow), near Thornborough, North Yorkshire	In pit under round barrow 18.29 m in diameter and 1.1 m high. Pit 0.46 m deep, lined with 'a coarse concrete, ten inches [0.24 m] thick in the middle…and so hard that the pickaxe pierced it with difficulty' (Lukis 1870, 119). Coffin rested on this	Described as: 'a wood coffin, probably the hollowed trunk of a tree, the remains of which, reduced to dust, were very discernible' (Lukis 1870, 119). Plate V.1 shows it as a complete hollowed trunk, i.e. lidded	NE-SW	I	-	-	-	Bipart te Vase Food Vessel and flint knife or scraper	Found 1864. 'Coarse concrete' probably gypsum (T. Manby pers. comm.)	Lukis 1870, 119 and pls. Il.1, Il.2 and V.1; Greenwell 1877, 377
9	D	Rylstone (Scale House), Craven, North Yorkshire	In shallow pit under centre of round barrow c. 9 m in diameter and c. 1.5 m high, with ring ditch. Laid on, and embedded in fine clay; above this, layer of charcoal-rich 'earthy matter', clay, and flat stones	Made from hollowed split trunk of oak tree, with bark still present; ends partially rounded. Slightly wider at S end. Description implies that it had been lidded with other half of trunk. 2.2 x 0.6 x 0.3 m; hollowed area 1.9 x 0.3 m	N-S	I, ex	-	-	-	Body, represented by 'unctuous white adipocere', wrapped in woven woollen fabric (Greenwell 1877, fig. 2) from head to toe. No grave goods	Discovered 1864. Cut-marks made by narrow-edged metal tool noted in hollowed area	Lukis 1870, 123; Greenwell 1877, 375–377 and fig. 2; Elgee and Elgee 1949, 106
10	D	Howe Hill, Kilton, Brotton (grave B), North Yorkshire	Under round barrow 16.46 m in diameter; interior of barrow was a cairn. One of two graves under clay floor of cairn. Boulder with cup and ring marks found between the graves	At least 1.52 x 0.23–0.46 x 0.24 m; oak	NE-SW	I	M, ad	R	NE, SE	No grave goods but 16 cup-marked stones in mound of barrow and deposits of cremated bone just beyond the head of the coffin and above the foot		Hornsby and Stanton 1917; Elgee and Elgee 1949, 104; Smith 1994, 65
11	D	Loose Howe, North Yorkshire	Under round barrow c. 18.3 m in diameter and 2.13 m high; primary grave. Not under centre of barrow. 'Prow' at ENE end	Boat-shaped, with pointed 'prow' and straight 'stern'; U- to V-shaped in cross-section; in longitudinal cross-section, base curves up to 'prow' and rises vertically to 'stern'. T-shaped hollow on underside. Lidded with similarly-shaped hollowed trunk from a second tree, with rectangular hollow. Oak. Dimensions of base: 2.5 x 0.625, with hollow up to 1.95 m long and c. 0.22 m deep. Lid: 2.7 x 0.775 m at 'prow'. Some bark present on lid but 'base' of lid 'had been very smoothly dressed' (Elgee and Elgee 1949, 95)	WSW-ENE	I, ex	Ad	-	WSW	Body survived only as 'wet, black, greasy substance', with ankle bone. Basal hollow lined with rushes, reeds or straw; 'pillow' of grass or straw at head. Presence of flax fibre suggests that body had been clothed or wrapped in linen cloth. Fragment of 'foot wrapping' at ankle bone, and of shoe with 2 lace holes. Bronze dagger of Gerloff's 'Type Merthyr Mawr' (Needham's Series 2F3)'3 pieces of flint; hazel branches and hazelnut shells	Presence of dagger, near the left hip, suggests sex as male. Excavators believed body had been laid at full length, head at stern end. Presence of footwear suggests that body had been fully clothed	Elgee and Elgee 1949; Gerloff 1975, 50, no. 53

No.	Status	Findspot	Context	Shape, structure, species, dimensions	Coffin orientation	Rite	Sex, age	Side	Head end + dir'n of view	Grave goods and other contents	Comments	References
12	D	Loose Howe, North Yorkshire	Found beside coffin (No. 11), with 'prow' at ENE	'Canoe', with pointed 'prow' and angular 'stern'; cross-section variable, with well-defined keel. T-shaped slot underneath 'stern', and triangular hollow on base. Not lidded. Oak, with bark on sides but not on base. 2.75 m long when found; after shrinkage, 2.65 x max 0.675, with hollow max 1.85 long and c. 0.3 m deep	WSW-ENE	-	-	-	-	None	No body found but may have held an unburnt body that had completely disintegrated in the absence of a lid. Opinions differ as to whether this had been an actual logboat	Elgee and Elgee 1949; McGrail 1975, 93
13	Pr	Pockley (Oxclose Farm barrow 1), North Yorkshire	Under round barrow 20 m in diameter and 0.55 m high. Stone and turf mound, with segments of 2 concentric post circles. Coffin in central grave, in pit	Rectangular, U-shaped in cross-section; no sign of any cover. Represented only by a stain. C. 2.0 x 0.75 x 0.15 m	-	Pres. I	-	-	-	Food Vessel	Pot found on its side, 0.6 from W end of coffin	Smith 1994, 111
14	Pr/ po	Hutton Buscel (barrow 2, grave 1), North Yorkshire	Under kerbed round barrow, 9.97 m in diameter at kerb. Primary grave, just S of centre of barrow. In pit; sealed by stone platform	Roughly rectangular, to judge from shape of pit; pit measured 3.85 x 1.54 x 0.77 m and coffin had lain within a ledge inside this. No traces of the coffin survived	ENE-WSW	I	Indet, child aged 8–9	-	Not stated	Fragments of a scallop shell. Seven flints, lying on a piece of turf – but may have been redeposited residual finds from barrow	Grave disturbed prior to excavation in 1965. Some of the kerbstones have cupmarks; one has an incised line. Interpreted by excavators as tree-trunk coffin on basis of similarities with Irton Moor barrow 1	Brewster and Finney 1995, 7, 55–56 and figs. 7 and 8)
15	D	Irton Moor (barrow 1, central grave), North Yorkshire	Under centre of round barrow c. 24.38 x 1.37 m; primary grave. In oval hollow; surrounded by large blocks of stone; coffin in trough within hollow. Rest of mound of turves and soil	One end slightly rounded, the other straight; lidded; oak. C. 1.30 x 0.30 m	NE-SW	C	Ad M aged c. 30 and young ad aged c. 18	-	-	2 burnt barbed-and-tanged flint arrowheads; 3 quartz pebbles	Impossible to tell whether arrowheads had been grave goods or lodged in bodies; had been cremated	Brewster 1973, 56–72
16	D	Gristhorpe, North Yorkshire	In pit under centre of round barrow 12.2 m in diameter, dug into natural clay, and clay used to cover oak branches above coffin	Boat-shaped, with rounded broad end, tapering sides and straight narrow end; lidded with other half of trunk, both halves being hollowed. Bark present. Carved 'face' at narrow end. Oak, with oak branches above coffin and one placed upright at one end of coffin. 2.29 x 1.17–1.45 m	N-S	I	M, ad, prob aged >50	R	S,E	Cattle hide fastened with bone pin; paws or pelts of fox and pine marten; bronze dagger of Gerloff's 'Type Merthyr Mawr, variant Parwich' type (Needham's Series 2F3), in scabbard or sheath; flint knife, 2 flint flakes; organic ornament; bark and wood container; wooden fastener; plant matter	See this volume, Ch 12 on arrangement of items in coffin	Williamson 1834;1872; this volume
17	Pr	West Heslerton (grave 157, barrow 1R), North Yorkshire	In pit under round barrow; one of several secondary graves	Sub-rectangular, U-shaped in cross-section; no sign of any lid. Wood had decayed; identified only by distinctive nature and shape of fill. C. 1.0 x 0.4 m	Appx E-W	I, fl	Indet, child aged 7–9	R	E, NNW	Undecorated Food Vessel, found on side between skull and shoulder; 1 worked flint. Fragments of bone of adult female found in grave backfill		Powlesland et al 1986, 110 and figs. 34, 40 and 41

No.	Status	Findspot	Context	Shape, structure, species, dimensions	Coffin orientation	Rite	Sex, age	Side	Head end + dir'n of view	Grave goods and other contents	Comments	References
18	D	Willie Howe, Cowlam, East Riding of Yorkshire	Under round barrow (second, enlarged phase) surrounded by ring ditch c. 27.4 m in diameter. In deep rock-cut grave, eccentric to mound; coffin 'had been securely held in place by chalk rainwash and rubble' and was covered by chalk cobbles. Secondary to a central grave containing three adult male skeletons (mostly robbed), and to a grave containing a long-necked Beaker with the contracted skeleton of an adult woman	Survived as thin, blackish, rotted remains of the trunk and as a 'hollow imprint in the compacted infill of the grave', preserving the exact shape of the coffin (Brewster unpub, 14). Rectangular; in cross section, base U-shaped. Oak; lidded. 1.9 x 0.7 m; ht of base c. 0.4 m; est. overall height c. 0.7 m	NW-SE	I, co	M, ad, prob. aged 25–30	L	SE, c. S	Laurel leaf-shaped flint blade; irregular flint blade; dark grey flint flake with edge retouch. All in dark grey flint	Excavated by T. C. M. Brewster, 1967. Man had been 'fairly robust' and tall – c. 1.76 m. Laurel-leaf blade found between feet and NW end of coffin; irregular blade in front of skull; flake beneath skull. Skeleton C14-dated. Note: this barrow is not to be confused with the massive Willie (Willy) Howe barrow in Wold Newton parish	Manby et al. 2003, 74, 75; Brewster unpub; Terry Manby pers. comm.
19	Pr	Towthorpe (barrow 139), North Yorkshire	In pit under centre of large round barrow (Mortimer 1905, fig. 5), 40.23 m in diameter and 3.81 m high. Coffin had been enclosed in clay brought from 1.6 km and 2.4 km away and supported by 'rough chalk'. Three probable post-holes outside and close to E end of grave pit, suggesting pre-barrow feature	Coffin had decayed completely but shape preserved as 'boat-shaped block of clay and soil'	E-W	I, ext	M, ad	-	W	Bronze dagger, with 4 rivets, of Gerloff's Armorico-British A (Type Winterbourne Stoke) type, Needham's Series 3A, prob. in sheath or scabbard; mace consisting of stone macehead in haft, probably of ash, c. 45 cm long; plano-convex knife of black flint, w th no signs of use. Under and over the dagger 'was a large quantity of dark matter, resembling decayed and compressed leaves' (Mortimer 1905, 5)	Male had been tall – 1.8 m – and laid on back, with head to W, with L arm bent over body and R arm bent with hand at shoulder. Dagger beside L humerus; mace to L of head, with handle extending to beside dagger	Mortimer 1905, 3–5 and figs. 5, 9, 10; Gerloff 1975, 71 (no. 111)
20	D	Towthorpe (barrow 173), North Yorkshire	In pit around centre of, and under, round barrow 18.3 m in diameter and 2.29 m high	Ends squared off; sides rounded; lidded. Survived as 'greatly decayed portions of a small coffin, made from the trunk of an oak…Impressions of the squarely-cut ends and rounded sides of the coffin were sharply defined on the soil and subsoil of the old land surface' (Mortimer 1905, 6). 1.06 x 0.44 m	SE-NW	C	Ad	-	-	None	Bones found at NW end of coffin	Mortimer 1905, 6
21	Pr	Hanging Grimston barrow 90, North Yorkshire	Under large barrow; coffin rested on thin layer of blue clay and was surrounded by core of blue clay, brought from c. 1.6 km up a steep slope. Covered by outer mound of 'soil and gritty matter', c. 25 m in diameter and c. 1.83 m high	Presumably roughly parallel-sided; north end cut obliquely (with implication that S end had been straight). Small (but dimensions not given). No species identification as survived only as small pieces of dark red decayed wood and as impression in clay	N-S	C	-	-	-	Stone battle axehead of Roe's 'Early' type (Stage IIIB), slightly burnt; gritstone	Found 1867. Cremated remains found at S end of coffin; battle axehead found among the bones, and had evidently passed through the pyre. No other graves found during Mortimer's excavation of much of the barrow	Mortimer 1905, 97; Roe 1966, 239, no.266; 1979

No.	Status	Findspot	Context	Shape, structure, species, dimensions	Coffin orientation	Rite	Sex, age	Side	Head end + dir'n of view	Grave goods and other contents	Comments	References
22	D	Little Ouseburn, North Yorkshire	In pit under centre of ovoid, stone-capped turf mound (c. 3 x 2.3 x 1 m) and eccentric to larger round barrow with ring-ditch; diameter of ring-ditch c. 34 m. Primary grave.	Roughly rectangular and broad U-shape in cross-section, with flat-based, eccentric hollowed area straight at S end and rounded at other end; no sign of any lid. Bark present. Boat-like, with S end very narrow, like stern board. C. 2.35 x 0.9–1.05 x 0.47m. Wood species not identifiable	NNW-SSE	I, poss co	-	-	-	Chert flake present but not necessarily as a grave good	Post-dates occupation activity associated with Beaker pottery. The 'charred' appearance of the coffin was found to be due to replacement of the wood by manganese oxide. Hollowed area large enough to take a 2 m-long body at full length; angle of surviving bone traces suggests that body may have been contracted	Rahtz 1989
23	D	Wetwang Slack (barrow B, grave 1), East Riding of Yorkshire	Under round barrow c. 11.89 m in diameter; slightly to SE of centre, in pit	Round-ended at both ends; lidded. C. 1.68 x 0.49 m	Appx E-W: ENE-WSW	I, tight-ly co	Ad M	R	W, N	Yorkshire Vase Food Vessel	Pot in front of body between head and knees, presumably placed upright. Fragments of skull of second individual possibly residual from a primary central grave. Barrow also known as 'Area 6' (Dent 1983)	Dent 1979, 26 and figs. 4 and 7.4; 1983, 10
24	D/ pr	Wetwang Slack (Area 16, WK 8), East Riding of Yorkshire	Central grave pit within ring ditch of presumed round barrow. Two interments; bones of earlier (i) carefully arranged over feet of secondary (ii)	Sub-rectangular; abundant charcoal from sides and over bones suggests that it had been lidded. Oak. C. 1.72 x 1.01 m	E-W	I x 2; (i) disturbed; (ii) cr	Ad x 2	-	-	Beaker, Clarke type N/NR, behind head of (ii)	Presence of charcoal suggests use of fire to create hollow. Three C14 dates from remains of coffin; see Table 4.2	Dent 2010, 100 and John Dent, pers. comm. Further details of skeletons exists but is not currently available
25	Pr	Garton Slack (Area 29, Bronze Age grave 3, coffin burial 2), East Riding of Yorkshire	In pit under presumed round barrow	Sub-rectangular, bowed towards E end and straight at W end; boat-shaped; broad 'U' in cross-section. No trace of a lid. Present only as stain, but excavator assumed it to be of oak. C. 1.83 x 0.9 m	Appx E-W	I, co	M, young ad, aged 16–17	L	E, S	Beaker, Clarke type N2 (Needham's 'short-necked' tpe) behind –and toppled over onto – pelvis; flint flake	Gap between ends of body and ends of coffin. Head at 'prow' end	Brewster 1980, 563 and figs. 403, 404, 407, pl. 109; Dent 1983, 10
26	D	Old Sunderland-wick (barrow 279a), near Great Driffield, East Riding of Yorkshire	Under round barrow, close to a stream; coffin rested on ground surface	Straight-ended, lidded (using other half of trunk); interior hollowed. Oak. C. 1.82 x 1.22 m; 'resembled a rude boat with square ends' (Mortimer 1905, 297)	E-W	I x 3	Pres ad	-	W and E	No grave goods. Two large, thick branches placed above coffin	Found August 1856. Probably hollowed using fire. Three skeletons found; one with skull towards W, others towards E	Wright 1857; Greenwell 1877, 377; Mortimer 1905, 296–297
27	D	Pant-y-Dulaith, Tre-meirchion, Clwyd	Primary grave. In pit under centre of round barrow consisting of small oval primary cairn c. 2.75 m in diameter over coffin grave, covered by turf stack and subsequently by kerbed cairn 16.75 m in diameter. Stone packing in coffin pit. Large planks, including one 3 m long, found under barrow but not necessarily related to coffin grave	Small, narrow coffin described as a hollowed tree-trunk; not lidded but earth from pit placed in coffin and sealed with several flat stones. Accounts of length are inconsistent but grave pit seems, from photographs, to be c. 1.2 x 0.3 m (Hayes 1996, 23)	NW-SE	I	Indet, child, age 6–7	-	Not stated	None	Pre-dates pit containing inverted Vase Urn containing cremated remains (Hayes 1996, 25), and later grave, in top of mound, containing cremated remains and one or two pots of Food Vessel tradition. Coffin sent to York but present location unknown	Hayes 1958; 1996

No.	Status	Findspot	Context	Shape, structure, species, dimensions	Coffin orientation	Rite	Sex, age	Side	Head end + dir'n of view	Grave goods and other contents	Comments	References
28	D	West Ashby (grave F66), Lincolnshire	In pit cut into round (actually slightly oval) barrow measuring c. 6.5 x 5 m. One of several secondary graves	Irregular trapezoid approximating to a boat shape, with cross-section mostly U-shaped but flattish-bottomed at 'stern' end; no trace of lid. No species identification as survived only as stain. 0.93 x 0.55 x 0.1 m; sides 15 mm thick	NW-SE	Prob I	Prob child	-	-	Interior coffin fill suggested former presence of organic material such as cloth, hide or small branches. Yorkshire Vase Food Vessel at S end of coffin, deposited upright	No trace of body but too small to take contracted body of adult, so argued to be a child's grave	Field 1985, 109, figs. 6, 13.4, plate 2
29	D	West Ashby (grave F48), Lincolnshire	In large oval pit dug into same round (oval) barrow as grave F66; secondary to several graves	Boat-shaped, with pointed 'prow' and slightly diagonal straight 'stern'; mostly semi-circular in cross-section. No trace of lid. No species identification as survived only as stain. 1.9 x 0.36–0.56 x 0.15 m; walls 5–10 mm thick	ESE-WNW	I, poss ex	Prob ad	-	ESE	Remains of possible cloth or hide cover; no grave goods	Body attested only from stain; head at 'prow' end of coffin. Gap between ends of body stain and ends of coffin stain	Field 1985, 111, fig. 6
30	D	Swarkeston (barrow 4), Derbyshire	In pit, eccentric to irregularly-shaped barrow c. 9.14 m in maximum width; primary grave	Slightly trapezoidal; narrow E end gently rounded; wider W end straight, with rounded corners; broad U-shape in cross-section. Slightly boat-shaped. No sign of any lid. Species not identifiable as had decayed to a stain, one fragment of wood, and traces of 'charcoal'. 2.29 x 0.7–0.91 x 0.45 m	E-W	[I]	-	-	-	Flint knife, retouched along one edge	No trace of a body; assume former presence of unburnt body, decomposed in the acid soil. Grave secondary to Neolithic and Beaker-associated occupation, latter with Food Vessel; grave pre-dates secondary grave with Collared Urn	Greenfield 1960
31	D	Ponton Heath (barrow 2), Stroxton, Lincolnshire	In pit under large round barrow c. 37 m in diameter (but probably plough-spread); not under centre, but primary grave	Plan shows it to be rectangular, but pit rounded at one end, so may have been boat-shaped – see 'Comment'; U-shaped in cross-section; no sign of a lid. Almost totally decayed to a stain, but sufficient wood survived for an identification as oak. 2.1 x 0.6–0.7 m	E-W	[I]	-	-	-	Bipartite Vase Food Vessel (in SW corner); flint fabricator or strike-a-light and flint plano-convex knife with some retouch (found close together mid-way along coffin, on N side)	Description claims that the coffin had been boat-shaped, but the published plan suggests that it had been rectangular at both ends, at least at a low level. Set into a boat-shaped pit, so upper part of the coffin could have been curved. This end damaged. Flint items could have been in a pouch. No trace of a body but presumed to be unburnt	Greenfield 1985
32	D	Eaton F10, Leicestershire	Secondary grave under round barrow c. 8m in diameter, with 4 surrounding ditches; grave just off-centre, and may be associated with ring-ditch 20 m in diameter (implying enlargement of barrow)	Very slightly trapezoidal; U-shaped in cross-section; no sign of a lid. Species indeterminable as survived only as a stain, but bark impressions survived as linear stains of manganese oxide. 1.8 x 0.45–0.6 x 0.25 m	NNE-SSW	I, poss ex	Indet, adolescent aged 12–15	-	NNE	None	All that survived of the body were two crowns of teeth, near N end of grave. Secondary to F19, a small plank-built oak coffin containing cremated remains of adult and a flint flake. Succeeded by grave containing cremated remains and Beaker sherd (with associated charcoal C14-dated), then by a possible oak coffin with contracted individual. Charcoal from ring-ditch C14-dated; see Table 4.2	P. Clay 1981

No.	Status	Findspot	Context	Shape, structure, species, dimensions	Coffin orientation	Rite	Sex, age	Side	Head end + dir'n of view	Grave goods and other contents	Comments	References
33	Po	Sproxton (Saltby Heath, barrow C, F46), Leicestershire	Primary grave under small turf mound c. 4–5 m in diameter surrounded by stake circle, off-centre to larger barrow	In oval pit: carbonised oak with traces of sides, 'suggesting the remains of a hollowed log'. 0.35 x 0.27 m; pit dimensions 0.45 x 0.35 x 0.4 m	NE-SW	C	M, ad, aged c. 30–35	-	-	None	Charcoal, probably from pyre wood (mature ash), C14-dated: see Table 4.2. Excavator thought that body had been burnt on the log, but this seems most unlikely. This grave pre-dates secondary graves with cremated remains in Collared Urns	P. Clay 1981
34	D	Deeping St Nicholas (barrow 28), Lincolnshire	Under round barrow with ring-ditch; barrow diameter c. 15 m. In pit under centre of barrow; surrounded by concentric stake-rings; primary grave	Roughly rectangular; wide U-shape in cross-section; possibly lidded; species indeterminate. 1.6 x 0.5 m.	N-S	I, co/fl	Child aged 3–5	L	N, Up-wards	Plano-convex flint knife. Black stain at head may be remains of shroud	Ends of coffin close to body. Two C14 dates from skeleton – see Table 4.2	French 1994, 24–5, figs. 14–16, 33.4
35	Pr	Tallington, Lincolnshire (site 16, grave 1)	In pit under centre of primary, bell barrow c. 6.71 m in diameter and 0.43 m high, with ring ditch. Primary grave	Parallel-sided, with slightly rounded or pointed ends; survived only as 'thin line of soft dark brown powdery soil'; no trace of any lid. Cross-section shape not specified. Species unidentifiable. C. 1.57 x 0.53 m	NW-SE	I, tightly co	M, aged c. 15	Partly L, partly on back	SE, Back-wards, NE	Small Food Vessel, fragment of cockle shell, 2 small flint flakes	Body may have been trussed. Head bent backwards. Food Vessel on side, its mouth covering occipital of skull. Bone from skeleton C14-dated; see Table 4.2. Secondary grave with adult male inserted through barrow, just above grave 1 before coffin had collapsed	Simpson 1976
36	D	Whittlesey (King's Dyke West), Cambridgeshire	In deep pit under centre of large round barrow, 28 m in diameter, surrounded by penannular ditch. Grave surrounded by post ring; deposit of cremated remains near the grave	Described as tree-trunk coffin; no further details	-	I	-	-	-	Small polished flint knife	-	Knight 2000
37	D	Bowthorpe, Norfolk (central grave, 14)	In pit under centre of primary round (actually oval) barrow surrounded by oval ring-ditch, 10–12 m across. Primary grave. Coffin found at 0.7 m below old ground surface	Boat-shaped: long, with uneven, roughly parallel sides, pointed SE end and straight NW end; semi-circular in cross-section. No obvious traces of a lid; may have been covered by a turf stack. Wood species indeterminate; attested just from a stain with charcoal flecks and replaced wood fragments. C. 2.0 x 0.6 (max.) x 0.3 m	Appx SE-NW	I, co	Indet; ad	L	SE, Appx SW	Possibly a decayed organic object beyond skull in SE: sticky light-grey deposit. A few flints and pot-boilers in grave fill; not grave goods	Space between ends of body and ends of coffin. Coffin not hollowed out by burning. Note presence of other tree-trunk coffins under this barrow (Nos. 38–40, below); two plank-built coffins were also present	Lawson 1986, 23, 43, 45–46 and figs. 14–16
38	D	Bowthorpe, Norfolk (grave 17)	In pit – a 'satellite grave' to primary, central grave, but not necessarily much later than central grave – under round (oval) barrow. Grave pit cut by ring-ditch, a grave and a pit.	Rectangular, with rounded base; no obvious traces of a lid. Wood species indeterminate; attested just from a stain with charcoal flecks and replaced wood fragments. C. 1.45 x 0.6 x 0.25 m	SE-NW	I, co	Indet; ad	L	SE, SW	No grave goods; upper fill contained flint flakes, a scraper and pot-boilers	Space between ends of body and ends of coffin. Coffin not hollowed out by burning. See note above (No. 37) regarding other coffined graves in this cemetery	Lawson 1986, 23 and figs. 19–21
39	D	Bowthorpe, Norfolk (grave 66)	In pit – a 'satellite grave' to primary, central grave, and possibly one of latest graves in the cemetery. Just outside inner ring-ditch	Rectangular, with flattish base; no obvious traces of any lid. Oak, with remains of knots and/or branches on exterior. C. 1.3 x 0.65 x 0.1 m	Appx NE-SW	-	-	-	-	No grave goods; a few flint flakes and pot-boilers in grave fill	No trace of body but remains of unburnt body could well have been obscured by the thick layer of charcoal. Coffin hollowed by burning	Lawson 1986, 29 and figs. 27–28, plXIII

No.	Status	Findspot	Context	Shape, structure, species, dimensions	Coffin orientation	Rite	Sex, age	Side	Head end + dir'n of view	Grave goods and other contents	Comments	References
40	D	Bowthorpe, Norfolk (grave 75)	In pit – a 'satellite grave' to primary, central grave; lies directly over fill of inner ditch	Roughly rectangular, with flattish base and curving sides; no obvious traces of any lid. Wood species indeterminate; attested just from a stain with charcoal flecks and replaced wood fragments. C. 1.8 x 0.75 x 0.15 m	Appx NE-SW	I, co	Indet; ad	L	NE, appx SE	Retouched flint flake inside coffin; barbed-and-tanged flint arrowhead outside SE corner of coffin	Space between ends of body and ends of coffin. Coffin not hollowed out by burning. See note above (No. 37) regarding other coffined graves in this cemetery	Lawson 1986, 29 and figs. 29 and 31
41	Pr	Harford Farm (grave 1469, ring-ditch 1022), Caistor St. Edmund, Norfolk	In sub-circular shaft extending to 2 m below old land surface, within ring-ditch c. 28 m in diameter that had probably enclosed a barrow; slightly off-centre	Occurred as concave layer of charcoal (representing upper surface), with another concave layer, of charcoal-rich soil, 0.2–0.25 m below. Slightly oval; U-shaped in cross-section, with hollowed upper surface; no sign of any lid; oak. Described by excavator as being either a coffin or a bier. C. 0.7 x 0.35 x 0.25 m	NNE-SSW	Pres I	?child	-	-	None	Absence of trace of body suggests that if one had been present, will have been unburnt. Small size of grave suggests that it may have been for a child. Charcoal C14-dated: see Table 4.2. Secondary grave above this represented by body stain of contracted individual	Ashwin and Bates 2000, 69, 132 and figs. 50, 54, and 55 and pl. XXI
42	D	Dysgwylfa (Disgwylfa) Fawr, Ceredigion	Under centre of round barrow 20 m in diameter and 1.8 m high, on an isolated hill; apparently resting on old ground surface. Primary grave	Rectangular, probably with both ends rounded (of which only one now survives); slightly rounded base. Rectangular hollowed area. No trace of any lid. Oak, with bark present. Reportedly 2.5 m long; width of surviving portion c 0.35 m. Sides along hollow up to c. 50 mm thick	NW-SE	Presumably I	-	-	-	None	No trace of body found. Coffin C14-dated; see Table 4.2	Forde 1939; Savory 1980; Green 1987
43	D	Dysgwylfa (Disgwylfa) Fawr, Ceredigion	Secondary interment, found c. 0.3 m above larger tree-trunk coffin (No. 42), in round barrow	Rectangular, with rounded ends; hollow roughly rectangular. Surviving end of hollow slopes but this may be partly due to warping. Species not stated. Just over 1 m long	NE-SW	C	-	-	-	Flint blade and bipartite Yorkshire Vase Food Vessel with Irish affinities; a piece of fur (species unidentified) lay over the cremated bones and pot	Cremated bones and flint blade lost; fur not preserved. Coffin C14-dated; see Table 4.2	Forde 1939; Savory 1980; Green 1987
44	D	Risby (near Poor's Heath, burial 3), Suffolk	Under round barrow between 18.9 m and 23.17 m in diameter; in pit off-centre, but believed to be contemporary with central grave	Rectangular, one end truncated; curved base; bark suspected to be present. Species not stated. 1.83 x 0.45–0.61 x 0.3 m	NW-SE	I, co	M, ad, 30–35?	L	SE, SW	None	Possible family connection with adult male in primary grave (sutural ossicles in skull); that individual associated with long-necked Beaker	Vatcher and Vatcher 1976, 268, 284–5, fig. 3, pl 29
45	Po	Radley, Barrow Hills (flat' grave 950), Oxfordshire	In subrectangular pit dug 0.6 m into natural gravel.	Irregular sub-rectangle in plan but clearer in section as squarish 'U' in cross-section and with one end sloping up. Species indeterminable as present just as stain. No sign of any lid. C. 2.0 x 0.7 x 0.2–0.25	NW-SE	I, disturbed	M, ad, aged poss 30-35	-	-	Beaker of Clarke's 'Wessex/ Mid-e Rhine' type (Needham's 'Mid-Carinated' type); barbed and tanged flint arrowhead; also worked flints, animal bone and pottery that was probably residual	Likely that body had been deposited articulated, then subsequently disturbed. Skeleton C14-dated; see Table 4.2	Barclay and Halpin 1998, 58–59, figs. 4.18–4.21
46	Po	Radley, Barrow Hills (grave 4969, pond barrow 4866), Oxfordshire	In pit in pond barrow	Irregular trapezoid, with one square end and one slanting end; flat-based. Present as line of charcoal along grave cut and over body; presumed to be lidded. Alder. 0.9 x 0.4–0.65 m	NE-SW	I, co	Indet, youth aged 9–10	L	SW, NE	Flint piercer. Up to 6 red deer antlers along but above the sides of the coffin, plus cattle skull and pig calcaneum	Cannot rule out possibility that this had been a plank-built coffin (especially given broad flat base of pit), although confirmation of presence of charcoal led to the conclusion that this had probably been a fire-hollowed alder log coffin. One deer antler C14-dated; see Table 4.2	Barclay and Halpin 1998, 119, 253, fig. 4.62

No.	Status	Findspot	Context	Shape, structure, species, dimensions	Coffin orientation	Rite	Sex, age	Side	Head end + dir'n of view	Grave goods and other contents	Comments	References
47	D	Yatesbury (barrow 3/G9), Cherhill, Wiltshire	In 'cist' (rock-cut pit?) under large round barrow that had formerly been c. 6.1 m high. 'Cist' was 'at the depth of eight feet, formed at the level of the adjoining land' (Smith 1879, 332)	Split and hollowed trunk of oak, lidded, with base and lid from same piece of trunk; no description of shape of ends. 1.22 x 0.76 x 0.46 m	-	C	-	-	-	Bronze knife of Gerloff's 'flat riveted knife-dagger' type	Cremated bones in heap around the mid-point of the coffin base; knife on top of the bones	Smith 1879, 331–333; R. C. C. Clay 1929, 104; Gerloff 1975, 162–163 (no. 259)
48	D	West Overton (barrow G1), Wiltshire	In large rectangular rock-cut pit under round barrow 22.86 m in diameter; bottom of pit c. 3 m below top of barrow	No details about shape, size or species, but bark reported to be present: 'The skeleton seems to have been enclosed within the trunk of a tree, as we observed several remains of wood, and some bark unconsumed by time'	E-W	I, co	M, ad, senior	L	E, S	Flat bronze axehead of Willerby type; crutch-headed bronze pin; tanged and riveted knife or razor; piece or object of antler (Needham et al. 2010b)	Grave goods found close to the head (beside which the R hand had been placed), in front of face. Skull C14 dated – see Table 4.2 and Needham et al. 2010b. Thurnam identified the individual as having been of tall stature	Hoare 1821, 90; Thurnam 1860; Needham et al. 2010b
49	D	Milton Lilbourne (barrow 4), Wiltshire	On old ground surface under centre of bell barrow c. 22 m in diameter, with ring ditch. Coffin in centre of rectangular area of burnt soil with charcoal and burnt timber bauk	Roughly rectangular, with hollow straight at one end and bowed at the other, boat-like; coffin flattened U-shape in cross-section. No sign of any lid. Wood too mineralized for species identification. C. 0.9 x 0.3 x 0.1 m. Upper edge burnt – survived as wood ash	NW-SE	C	M, mature ad aged 40–50	-	-	Accessory vessel. Coffin hollow lined with sheet of bark	The individual was reported to have been relatively tall. Heap of cremated bones placed on bark sheet within hollow; accessory vessel deposited in top of heap	Ashbee 1986, 45–46, 56, 81–83, 87, 88, 89, figs. 12, 20–23, 30, 32
50	Pr	Collingbourne Ducis barrow G4, Wiltshire	Under larger of two bell barrows enclosed by oval ditch; barrow c. 25 m in diameter and c. 2.9 m in surviving height . Coffin on old ground surface below centre	Probably rectangular, described by Colt Hoare as 'wooden chest, or perhaps the more simple trunk of a tree'; 1.83 x > 0.91 m	-	C	-	-	-	Accessory vessel (lost); bronze dagger of Gerloff's 'Type Camerton' (Needham's Series 5D) in scabbard, with textile impression; ring-headed pin, of Continental type, 'in a sheath lined with cloth, the web of which could still be distinguished'	Also known as Site XIX and Hoare 24. Presence of dagger suggests that this may well be a male's grave	Hoare 1812, 185 and pl XXIII; Gerloff 1975, 105 (no. 184), with further references; Thomas 2005, 108–109, 223–226 and figs. 33 and 57
51	D	Collingbourne Ducis barrow G10, Wiltshire	Primary grave, in rock-cut pit (cylindrical shaft) under centre of round barrow; pit lined with 'plaster of pounded chalk'	Rectangular, lidded; decayed but survived as thin layer of decayed wood and as impression in the 'plaster' – showing that it had been deposited while plaster still wet. Impression shows presence of bark. Dimensions of pit: 1.19 x 0.38 x 0.30 m. Bottom of pit 2.71 m below top of barrow	N-S	C	'Young'	-	-	Antler 'hammer': perforated object of crown antler resembling blunt battle-axehead. Unburnt	Also known as Hoare 5	Lukis 1867, 96; R. C. C. Clay 1929, 103
52	Po	Upton Scudamore (barrow G1), Wiltshire	In round barrow, c. 1.5 m below top; presumably secondary, as the base of the barrow is described as being at a depth of 3.96 m	No details other than 'At the depth of five feet we found the remains of a human skeleton, which had been deposited nearly east west in a wooden box, or trunk of a tree: but the bones were nearly decomposed, owing to the wetness of the soil...'	E-W	I	-	-	-	'...a small brass dagger [i.e. bronze dagger or, more probably, knife], but so corroded that it would not bear removing'	Secondary to a cinerary urn containing cremated remains, found upright along with 'a great quantity of wood ashes' on the old ground surface below the barrow	Hoare 1812, 52

No.	Status	Findspot	Context	Shape, structure, species, dimensions	Coffin orientation	Rite	Sex, age	Side	Head end + dir'n of view	Grave goods and other contents	Comments	References
53	D	Winterbourne Stoke (barrow G5, 'King Barrow'), Wiltshire	In rectangular 'cist' (presumably rock-cut pit) under large bell barrow, c. 34 m in diameter and 4.6 m high. Primary grave; presumably under centre of barrow. Above the grave was found 'a large and heavy piece of fossil wood, of a calcareous nature, resembling a bunch of twigs'	'...a skeleton had been deposited within the rude trunk of an elm tree... The knots and bark still adhering to the tree, we were able to ascertain with certainty its distinct species...' 'Unclear from this whether the coffin had been lidded, but this is a possibility'	NE-SW	I, ex	Pres ad	-	-	2 bronze daggers of Gerloff's 'Armorico-British A' (Type Winterbourne Stoke) type'; Needham's Series 3A; bronze awl with bone handle; five-handled biconical jar; lost object of 'ivory' (probably bone; may have been dagger pommel)	Also known as Hoare 16. From description, it appears that the body had been laid at full length, on its back, with the head at the NE end. Pot found beside head. Daggers found near chest and thigh; their presence suggests that occupant had been male. Dagger near chest described as having been 'guarded by a case of wood, part of which appeared to be highly ornamented, as we found a bit of wood near it that had indentations which had certainly been gilt. The handle seems to have been made of box wood, and rounded somewhat like that of a large knife'	Hoare 1812, 122–123 and pl 15; R. C. C. Clay 1929, 104; Gerloff 1975, 70–71 with further references; Needham 2000
54	Pr	Winterbourne Stoke (barrow G9), Wiltshire	In rectangular rock-cut pit under large bowl barrow 29.57 m in diameter and 2.9 m high	Described as 'a shallow case of wood, of a boat-like form' (Hoare 1812, 125)	N-S	I	-	-	-	'...a great variety of amber and jet beads'; a lance head' (probably a bronze knife); bronze awl, 'a little urn of a very neat form', probably an accessory vessel (lost) (Hoare 1812, 125)	Also known as Hoare 26. Grave goods suggest that the occupant of the grave may have been female. The beads were found around the neck, as a necklace. Description of the coffin suggests that it had probably been carved from a single piece of wood, with bark removed	Hoare 1812, 124–125; R. C. C. Clay 1929, 104; S. Piggott 1938, 106; Elgee and Elgee 1949, 105. Not in Gerloff 1975
55	D	Fovant, Wiltshire	In pit (presumably rock-cut 'cist') under centre of round barrow 8.5 m in diameter	Rectangular; 'pointed oval' [angular U-shape?] in cross-section. Decomposed to 'soft, powdery black material very similar to charcoal' but identified as oak. Presence above as well as below bones suggests lidded. Pit dimensions 1.67 x 0.88; pit c 1 m deep. Coffin occupied lower part of pit.	SW-NE	I	M, young ad	L	SW, pres NW	Large antler in front of skull; antler pick where hips should have been; one calcined flint object but not necessarily a grave good.	Bones found lying against southern end of grave. Incompleteness of skeleton interpreted as disturbance before or shortly after burial, but this seems unlikely	R. C. C. Clay 1929, 101; Elgee and Elgee 1949, 105
56	D/ Pr	Weaver's Down (The Wylds), Selbourne, Hampshire	Under round barrow	'In one barrow...was a portion of a hollowed tree-trunk, probably the remains of a coffin' (Grinsell 1940, 195)	-	I	-	-	-	'Some red hair...which probably belonged to an animal whose skin had been worn by the person...' (Grinsell 1940, 195)	Barrow dug c. 1883. Presumed to have been unburnt body as hair was found and there were no bones. 'The hair when found was like a hard black ball, but after some time it uncurled itself into black hair much to everyone's horror.' (Grinsell 1940, 195)	Grinsell 1940, 16–17, 195, 354; Elgee and Elgee 1949, 105

No.	Status	Findspot	Context	Shape, structure, species, dimensions	Coffin orientation	Rite	Sex, age	Side	Head end + dir'n of view	Grave goods and other contents	Comments	References
57	D	Sigwells (Sigwell) (barrow II), Charlton Horethorne, Somerset	In pit, roughly under centre of round barrow – one of a pair of barrows; unclear whether primary grave	Described as 'bark coffin', 'made of two pieces of bark... fastened together so as to leave two ends projecting freely, not wrapped around each other' (Rolleston and Greenwell 1878, 78). Probably rectangular (but S end truncated during excavation); lidded. Species tentatively thought to be wych elm, although described on another page as being of oak. C. 2.13 x max. 0.91 m. Upper section thinner than lower section (6 mm vs. 20 mm)	N–S	C	'young male'	-	-	Two or three flint chips; bronze dagger of Gerloff's 'Camerton-Snowshill' type (Needham's Series 5D), burnt	Claimed that the cremated bone was of a young male, on basis of part of occipital bone. Cremated remains found along the full length of the lower part; dagger near S end of coffin	Rolleston and Fox 1878; Gerloff 1975, 108 (no. 204)
58	D	Scrubbity Coppice (Copse) (barrow 9), Sixpenny Handley, Dorset	In rock-cut pit under centre of round barrow with ring ditch; diameter of latter c. 18.29 m. Bottom of pit c. 0.3 m below old ground surface	Boat-shaped, with one round-pointed end and one straight end; bottom slightly rounded, sides near-vertical. Oak. C. 1.28 x 0.3–0.55 x 0.23 m	NW–SE	C	-	-	-	None	Pitt-Rivers had a facsimile made as original too rotten to survive excavation. Engraving of facsimile suggests that no bark had been present	Pitt-Rivers 1888, II, 40 and pls. 83 and 87
59	D	Stoborough (King Barrow), Wareham, Dorset	Under large (30 m-diameter, 3.66 m-high) turf round barrow; coffin on ground level	Oak. 3 m x 1.2 m; internal hollow c. 1 m wide	SE–NW	I	Ad	-	-	Body wrapped several times round in sewn skins of various thicknesses, reportedly including deerskin; 'gold lace'; prob. shale cup		Hutchins 1767; Ashbee 1960, 86, 88
60	D	Latch Farm (pit 3), Christchurch, Hampshire	Under bell barrow with ring ditch, 30.48 m in diameter. In pit; one of three believed to be contemporary and primary, slightly to S of centre under the barrow	Oval in plan; gently convex base and steep sides; oak, from bole of large tree, possibly 1.22–1.8 m in diameter. Hollowed from one half of vertically-cleft trunk. Pit dimensions: 0.61 x 0.91 x 0.46 m; pit not significantly larger than coffin	NE–SW	C	Not stated	-	-	Cremated bones prob. deposited in bag, packed round with loam and gravel; bronze awl prob. used to fasten bag; found outside mass of bones		C. M. Piggott 1938
61	D	Newbarn Down (Gallibury Down), Isle of Wight	In large D-shaped pit under large round barrow – one of largest in Isle of Wight; final grave of four primary graves	Rectangular (judging from photograph in Tomalin 1979); had decomposed but survived as impression in clay and as fragments of bark. Species not stated. 2.5 x c. 0.6 m	NE–SW	Pres I		-	-	Food Vessel (with same 'maker's mark' thumb impression as found on Food Vessel above first primary grave), triangular flint knife; 'small assortment of [flint] scrapers'	Orientation of coffin derived from photo in Tomalin 1979; assumes that N is at top of image. No remains of body found but former presence of unburnt body is assumed. Earliest primary grave, containing contracted skeleton and handled Dorset-style Beaker bowl, had been in plank-built coffin	Tomalin 1979
62	D	Newbarn Down (Gallibury Down), Isle of Wight	Final phase of interments in large round barrow – see above, No. 61. In shaft dug through barrow, extending below old ground surface	'Miniature tree trunk coffin'; no further details	-	-	-	-	-	-	No details provided in publication. Other final-phase secondary interments were of cremated remains in Vase Urns	Tomalin 1979

No.	Status	Findspot	Context	Shape, structure, species, dimensions	Coffin orientation	Rite	Sex, age	Side	Head end + dir'n of view	Grave goods and other contents	Comments	References
63	D	Bishop's Waltham, Hampshire	Under bell barrow surrounded by ring-ditch, in approximately rectangular grave c. 2.44 x 1.52 x 0.46 m	Rectangular, with flattish base and bowed sides; lidded; species indeterminate. 1.52 m x just under 0.91 m; surviving thickness c. 0.3 m.	ENE-WSW	C and I, co	C: indet, ? F, ad, 20–30; I: indet, ad	I: prob R	I: ENE, prob N	Straw (grass or cereal-like plant) on base of coffin. Bronze dagger, poorly preserved (of Gerloff's 'Miscell' type; poss. Needham's Series 2 or contemporary type) plus small dagger or knife with midrib (Needham's Series 5A); Bipartite Vase Food Vessel	Coffin carbonized and, in places, of almost sand-like consistency ('Ashbee 1960, 89). Cremated bones in oval heap in centre, laid on straw and covered in sheet of bast; dagger and dagger or knife on either side, also covered by the bast. Food Vessel to side of coffin; prob. orig. upright. Silhouette of I above cremated bones	Ashbee 1957; 1960; Gerloff 1975, 64 (no. 89), 169 (no. 310)
64	Pr	Windmill Hill, Hayling East, Hampshire	Under round barrow; on pebble-paved area 1.78 m from the barrow surface and resting on a layer of 'ashes'; 3.8 cm thick	No details other than that a hollowed tree trunk had been found, 'much burnt or decayed'	-	-	-	-	-	Account is unclear	Account refers to 'Other finds...flint chippings, scrapers, a few imperfect arrowheads, broken pottery (some glazed), and iron nails', but these are likely to be finds from the barrow, not associated with the coffin	Proc Hants Field Club and Arch Soc 8 (1919), 353
65	D	Hove, Sussex	Under large round barrow; coffin on natural clay	'...a rude oak coffin, hollowed out of a single tree-trunk, and shaped with an axe...' (Ashbee 1960, 89, citing the original report). 1.8 or 2.1 m long	Appx E-W	Prob I	-	-	-	Amber cup, bronze dagger (of Gerloff's Camerton type; Needham's series 5D type), battle axehead (Roe's Snowshill type), whetstone-pendant	Bones described as 'many fragments of decayed bones, but it could not be determined with certainty whether the body had been cremated or not' (Phillips 1857). Grave goods in centre, 'as if they had rested on the breast of the body' (ibid). Coffin C14-dated	Phillips 1856; 1857; Curwen 1930, 33; Ashbee 1960, 89; Gerloff 1975, 105 (no. 183) Needham et al. 2006

Key: Status = degree of certainty of identification as tree-trunk coffin; D = definite, Pr = probable, Po = possible. See 'Comments' for cases where they may be some uncertainty over the Early Bronze Age date of the coffin . Rite : I = inhumation, C = cremation.; co = contracted, fl = flexed, ex = extended. Head end + direction of view: end of coffin at which head was found; direction in which face was pointing. Grave goods: references to Gerloff = Gerloff 1975, with specific references where dagger listed by Gerloff. References to Needham's dagger scheme = Needham forthcoming.

Note: excluded from this list are the following (in addition to the definitely or probably post-Bronze Age exampled mentioned at the beginning of the chapter):

Examples that are equally or more likely to have been plank-built coffins:

- Three further graves from **Wetwang Slack** barrow B (Dent 1979, graves 2, 4 and 5) plus a nearby isolated grave (from Area 10: Dent 1983, 10): excluded since too few traces of the coffins remained to determine whether they had been of tree-trunk or plank-built construction. Both sexes, and adults and a child, are represented. Also excluded are several graves from Wetwang Slack (including WW 9:88 and WG 12:7) with long rectangular coffin stains; these have been interpreted by John Dent as plank-built coffins.

- A flat-bottomed pit containing traces of a wooden coffin within a ring-ditch at **Four Crosses** (site 5), Powys (Warrilow *et al.* 1986, 66–67). This survived as a thin band of charcoal, and although it appeared to have a rounded corner, the absence of diagnostic features such as a concentration of wood traces at the base of the pit means that one cannot rule out the possibility that it had been a plank-built coffin.

- Graves 1 and 5, found under barrow 1 on the **Etton By-Pass, Cambridgeshire** (French and Pryor 2005, 106 and figs. 57–58). While the presence of a soil stain in grave 1, and of a line of charcoal in grave 5, strongly suggest the former presence of rectangular wooden coffins, it is impossible to tell whether these had been of tree-trunk or plank construction.

- Two graves with traces of rectangular wooden coffins at **Barnack, Cambridgeshire** (features 24 and 26. Donaldson 1977, 209, 227 and figs. 4, 6). These are very similar to those from Wetwang Slack and Etton and, like them, these could have been plank-built coffins.

- Grave 22 (in ring-ditch 112) at **Harford Farm**, *Caistor St. Edmund, Norfolk* (Ashwin and Bates 2000, 60, 66 and figs. 47 and 49): primary grave in bell or disc barrow. Described as being probably of thick plank construction' rather than being a monxylous coffin.

Example where it is impossible to tell what kind of wooden structure had been present:

- A secondary grave in **barrow 139** at **Towthorpe, North Yorkshire** (Mortimer 1905, 5), described thus: '...*a few calcined bones bones of a child* [were found] *in the midst of decayed wood. As there was no trace of an urn, probably these remains had been buried in a receptacle of wood or some other perishable substance...*.' This was secondary to a probable tree-trunk coffin grave. It is impossible to tell from the description whether this 'receptacle' had been a hollowed tree-trunk or a box-like structure; had there been signs of it having been the former, Mortimer is likely to have noted that.

- **Winterbourne Stoke barrow G4 (Hoare 15), Wiltshire** (Hoare 1812, 121–123): primary grave, on old ground surface below bell barrow, described as '*a box or coffin of wood, about three and a half feet* [1.06 m] *long, by two feet* [0.61 m] *wide*.' Contained cremated remains, together with dagger of Gerloff's 'Snowshill' type (Gerloff 1975, 101, No. 154 and pl. 47C; Needham's Series 5D); bronze knife; bone or ivory pommel from dagger or knife; bone 'tweezers' and bone pin. The reason for excluding this from the list of monoxylous coffins is that Colt Hoare mentioned the presence of '*small strips of brass* [i.e. bronze]*, which probably belonged originally to the box*' (Hoare 1812, 122; Gerloff 1975, pl 47C.2). If this is correct, it implies that the coffin had been of composite, plank construction.

Other exclusions:

- A deep, rock-cut grave under a round barrow at **Cawthorn Camps, North Yorkshire**, where two extended skeletons of adults were found '*embedded in charcoal*' at the bottom (Bateman 1861, 206–207; Thurnam 1871, 319, fig. 8; Elgee 1930, fig. 22; Smith 1994, 114–115 and fig. 78). While this could conceivably have been a double tree-trunk coffin grave, it is perhaps more likely to have been a plank-lined grave, as known from other Yorkshire barrows, e.g. Metlow Hill, East Riding of Yorkshire (Greenwell 1890, 28–29). The Cawthorn Camps grave was orientated E–W and measured 4.57 x 2.13 m; its bottom was 3.35 m below the old land surface. Beside one skeleton was found a '*coarsely-made spearhead of flint*', c. 65 mm long; beside the other, a bronze dagger of Gerloff's 'Type Butterwick' (Needham's Series 2A).

- A probable logboat (now lost) from **Blaenffos, Pembrokeshire** (*Archaeologia Cambrensis*, new series 3 (1852), 28–29; McGrail 1978, i, 160, no. 13; Mowat 1996, 137, 139) which was found in a bog, possibly a former lake, in 1851. There is confusion as to whether it had been found in a mound or had been a boat on stocks. Given that confusion, and the fact that at 3.96 m long it is significantly longer than all but one of the tree-trunk coffins listed here, it is regarded as being more probably a logboat than a coffin.

- A long, megalithic-like stone cist at **Hundleton, near Corston, Pembrokeshire**, with extended skeleton and bronze dagger, and a similar structure at **Candleston, Merthyr Mawr, Glamorgan**, with cremated bones, Food Vessel and bronze dagger; in each case, Savory (1980, 22) suggested that there may have been a tree-trunk coffin within the cist, totally decayed, but there is no proof of this and the positioning of the grave goods in the latter cist argues against the former presence of such a coffin.

- A long, rectangular stone-lined grave at **Bedd Emlyn, Clocaenog, Clwyd** (Savory 1961; 1980, 144). This was one of two primary graves under a round cairn or ring-cairn, pre-dating secondary graves containing Vase Urns with cremated remains. The area enclosed by the stone lining was 3.05 m long and 0.61 m wide. Nothing was found inside but for a '*small quantity of dark greasy earth*' (Savory 1961, 11). Savory suggested that it may have held a tree-trunk coffin with an unburnt body, destroyed by the acidic environment, but this can only remain a supposition. Given the existence of other long Early Bronze Age graves (including those at Hundleton and Merthyr Mawr, and a recently-excavated example 5.5 m long at Llanmaes: Adam Gwilt pers. comm.), it may be that this had simply been a long grave, without any tree-trunk coffin. The other primary grave contained traces of a wooden structure which Savory described as a boat-shaped '*sledge or bier*' (*ibid*, 13).

- A probable logboat from **Chatteris, Cambridgeshire**, allegedly found containing a rapier (McGrail 1978, 175) and included as a possible coffin by Mowat (1996, 175) who states that human remains were also found. No mention was made of human remains by McGrail, however.

- A stone cist at **Bishopmill, Elgin, Moray**, which Elgee and Elgee (1949, 106) had claimed to be a tree-trunk coffin; see Cressey and Sheridan 2003, 79.

Addenda: (Note: this section was added at proof stage; the information given here does not feature in the statistics or discussion in the main text.)

- **West Heslerton, North Yorkshire** (Haughton and Powlesland 1999, 41–51): two neighbouring round barrows, each covering two not-quite-central graves with tree-trunk coffins, all with squarish ends. Barrow 2BA174: both roughly N–S, in massive grave pits, each containing a skeleton of an adult male (one flexed, one contracted), on R, head to S, looking roughly E and accompanied by a Food Vessel placed near the head. One, 25–35, with unburnt bones of a juvenile and flint knife. Barrow 2BA264: graves roughly E–W; bodies represented only by stains. No grave goods. Note: there may be at least one further tree-trunk coffin at West Heslerton (in addition to No. 17, above): the deep secondary grave 1110 in barrow 1L, containing the contracted skeleton of a male aged 25–30, has a profile suggesting the former presence of a tree-trunk coffin; no traces of wood found (Powelsland *et al*. 1986, 83, 87, figs. 22, 23; T. Manby pers. comm.).

- **Melton, East Riding of Yorkshire** (Fenton-Thomas 2011, 46–52): two possible tree-trunk coffins, each with contracted skeleton of adult male, within flat Late Bronze Age cemetery. Dating is problematic. Grave 2631: deep, broad grave, E–W, containing tightly contracted skeleton of male, aged 35–45, on L, head to E, looking roughly W,' skeleton... surrounded by linear soil stains that may have been part of a wooden coffin box or even a wooden stretcher on which the body had been laid' (*ibid*., 46). Unabraded sherds of 7 Beakers in the grave; not suspected to be residual. Grave 2721, N–S, containing flexed skeleton of possible male aged 25–35, on L, head to N, facing E, cut Grave 2631 and 'also had a wooden structure surrounding the body [squared off at head end, rounded at foot end] and appeared to be broadly contemporary [with Grave 2631]' (*ibid*., 48). However, the skeleton produced a radiocarbon date of 2522±47 BP (WK-21865), consistent with dates of 780–530 cal BC for the cemetery as a whole; and the osteologists argued that the skeleton in Grave 2631 was more likely to be of Late Bronze Age date as well.

- **Tandderwen, Clwyd** (Brassil *et al*. 1991): under centre of round barrow. Earliest grave roughly N–S (NNW-SSE), pit 2.3 x 1.85 x 0.8m; poorly-preserved remains of contracted adult skeleton, head to S, with long-necked Beaker and flint knife beside skull.' Within the grave were lines of manganese staining which appeared to represent the former existence of a [lidded] wooden coffin or container of some form, 0.76m wide at its southern end.' Cut by N–S grave containing tree-trunk coffin (probably lidded) with gently-rounded ends, internal dimensions c.1.6 x 0.5m; may have contained unburnt body of which no trace survived, but also contained cremated remains of 5 individuals – 2 adult males, an adult female and 2 children, along with sheep ulna and fragment of segmented faience bead. Unreliable C14 date for coffin superseded by AMS date, from one cremated bone fragment, of 3565±40 BP (GrA-24868, 2030–1760 cal BC at 95.4% probability).

- **Watch Hill, Cornwall** (Miles 1975; Jones and Quinnell 2006): two successive lidded tree-trunk coffins, with squared ends, under centre of round barrow over ring cairn. Phosphate analysis revealed former presence of unburnt body in each. No grave goods but probably contemporary with sherds of Vase Urn (not associated with bone) scattered around ring ditch. Bracken reportedly from upper coffin C14 dated to 3532±48 BP (WK-12940, 2020–1730 cal BC at 95.4% probability).

Appendix 4.2. The tree-trunk coffins of probable post-Bronze Age date from Wydon Eals, Northumberland

Wydon Eals, near Haltwhistle, Northumberland, is the findspot of a remarkable group of well-preserved tree-trunk coffins, and since these have tended to be regarded by some as being of Early Bronze Age date, they will be described here, and the reasons given for suspecting that they are considerably more recent than that.

In 'Some account of ancient oaken coffins discovered on the lands adjoining Featherstone Castle, near Haltwhistle, Northumberland', published in *Archaeologia* in 1873, Thomas Snagge reported that in 1825, workmen had uncovered five such coffins and noticed several others, lying north-south and very close to each other, around five feet (*c.* 1.5 m) below the surface, in 'swampy' ground (Snagge 1873, 8). Three further coffins were uncovered in the same field in 1859, 1863 and 1869, with the last being illustrated in Fig. 4.8; the existence of many others was suspected, on the basis of probing with a rod. Snagge described the 1869 find as being 7'4" (2.2 m) long and 1'7" (0.5 m) wide, formed from 'the trunk or bole of an oak tree rudely split from end to end' (*ibid.*, 9). '[T]he ends were roughly dubbed to a rounded point', more for severing the trunk at that place

than for shaping the coffin, according to Snagge (*ibid.*, 10). The wood had been cut with a flat-edged tool 4" (10.2 cm) wide and with an instrument of arrowhead shape (*ibid.*, 12); it appears that the bark and sapwood had been removed. There was no attempt to 'finish' the rough surface and erase the tool marks. Snagge observed that the upper and lower portions were hollowed by different hands and were '*fastened together by means of two oaken pegs an inch and a half or so* [*c.* 38 mm] *in diameter, driven into holes which had been bored into each end for the purpose*'. Near one end, a drilled oak plate had covered over a knot-hole (*ibid.*, 12). There were no grave goods and only a femur and fragments of the pelvis survived of the skeleton. Of the previous finds, the remains of bones found in 1825 had crumbled away shortly after discovery, while a skull from the 1863 find was taken away by Canon William Greenwell, '*...but I am not aware that he has since published any particulars of his discovery*' (*ibid.*, 9). Several features of the Wydon Eals finds stand in contrast to discoveries of Early Bronze Age tree-trunk coffins. Firstly, it appears that a cemetery is represented, with numerous coffins placed close to each other; in this respect the Wydon Eals site resembles the cemetery of 14 tree-trunk coffins found near the old parish church at Selby, North Yorkshire (*ibid.*, 13), which is suspected to be of early Medieval date. Early Bronze Age tree-trunk coffins, in contrast, tend to be found singly or in small numbers. Second, while the latter are invariably found under barrows, on or above the level of the old ground surface or else buried in a shallow pit, the Wydon Eals coffins were found at some depth from the surface, in marshy ground. Thirdly, Early Bronze Age examples were often buried with their bark and sapwood intact, whereas Snagge's illustration (his fig. 1) shows the 1869 find as having had this removed, and his description suggests that all the coffins uncovered there were in a similar state. It is therefore reasonable to assume that the Wydon Eals coffins significantly post-date the Bronze Age. Whether it is possible to find any of these coffins, for testing its date through radiocarbon dating, is uncertain; George Jobey reported that they were all lost (Jobey 1984), and the present whereabouts of the skull taken by Greenwell are not known.

Fig. 4.8 The two halves of the tree-trunk coffin uncovered in 1869 at Wydon Eals, Northumberland; from Snagge 1873.

The barrow site at Gristhorpe: 2006–2008 fieldwork

5

GEOPHYSICAL INVESTIGATIONS
AT GRISTHORPE 2006–2008

Armin Schmidt, Chris Gaffney, Tim Horsley and Samantha Hodgson

Section 1: The Central Barrow

The precise location and structure of the Central Barrow, opened by Beswick in 1834, is not depicted in the original report, although the approximate location was indicated on the 1854 Ordnance Survey 1:10560 map (see Melton and Russ, this volume, Fig. 2.3). To clarify the location and possibly identify internal features, three geophysical surveys were undertaken in the vicinity. On 24 May 2006, an area of approximately 60 m × 60 m was investigated over the likely mound of the 1834 excavation using earth resistance and magnetometer surveys to obtain an overview of possible buried features. The magnetometer data clearly showed circular anomalies, which were then used to position an excavation trench in March 2007 (Melton and Russ, this volume). Subsequently, a higher resolution geophysical investigation with earth resistance, magnetometer and Ground Penetrating Radar (GPR) surveys was carried out over the central area (20 m × 20 m) on 9 May 2007. Finally, several areas were investigated in Spring and Summer 2008 to the southwest of the Central Barrow, using magnetometer and magnetic susceptibility surveys with the aim to identify the 'Southern Barrow', depicted on the 1854 Ordnance Survey map. The 'Northern Barrow' shown on that map is now mostly covered by the caravan park, although there is still a rise visible in its approximate location that might possibly be made available for geophysical surveys in the future.

Measurements and Processing
The 2006 survey was undertaken along traverses running

west to east at 1.0 m separation. For the magnetometer survey a Geoscan FM256 was used walking parallel along lines (i.e. unidirectionally) and recording measurements every 0.25 m over 20 m × 20 m data grids (20 m × 20 m @ 0.25 m × 1.0 m). The earth resistance measurements were collected with a 0.5 m twin-probe array using a Geoscan RM15 and recording data points every metre over the same data grids (20 m × 20 m @ 1.0 m × 1.0 m). The location of these data grids, laid out to cover the approximately 2 m high barrow, was measured with a Total Station and referenced to landscape features that could be identified on the Ordnance Survey Landline maps. The magnetometer data only required processing with a weak Zero Mean Traverse algorithm (Geoplot threshold of ±5 nT) and subsequent interpolation to a uniform display resolution of 0.25 m × 0.25 m. The earth resistance data only required interpolation to a display resolution of 0.5 m × 0.5 m and highpass filtering with a radius of 5 m (uniform weight). The results were integrated into a GIS, based on the Ordnance Survey Landline data, as shown in Fig. 5.1. The data acquired later with higher resolution (see below) are shown in a lighter shade to distinguish them.

As described by Melton and Russ (this volume), these results were used to locate an excavation trench that intersected the circular magnetic anomalies (see below). A subsequent geophysical survey in 2007 with higher resolution was then approximately aligned with the still visible outlines of the trench, to cover a data grid of 20 m × 20 m. The exact location of the trench was measured with tapes from two corners of the data grid. The resulting higher resolution geophysical data were exactly aligned in the GIS using the already existing geophysical results.

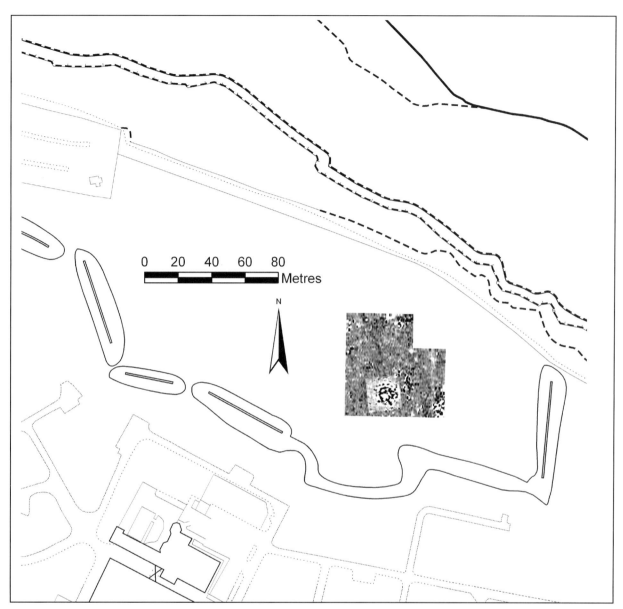

Fig. 5.1 Location of the geophysical survey areas for the Central Barrow. The data range is -2 – +4 nT (white to black) for the 60 m × 60 m area of the 2006 surveys, and -1 – +7 nT for the 20 m × 20 m data grid of the 2007 surveys. The map data are © Crown Copyright 2008. An Ordnance Survey/EDINA supplied service.

This georeferencing process thereby also determined the location of the excavation trench. The accuracy of this georeferencing is estimated to be better than 0.5 m. The second survey had a traverse separation of 0.5 m for the magnetometer survey (20 m × 20 m @ 0.25 m × 0.5 m), using a FM256 in a zig-zag survey sequence (i.e. bidirectional). The earth resistance survey had a 1.0 m traverse separation collecting three twin-probe measurements every 0.5 m (with a twin-probe separations of 1.0 m, a separation of 0.5 m measured left of centre, and a separation of 0.5 m measured right of the centre, all using a RM15 with MPX15). From these measurements two data sets were derived: a 0.5 m twin-probe survey with 0.5 m × 0.5 m resolution (i.e. in both directions twice the resolution as the previous survey) and a 1.0 m twin-probe survey with 0.5 m × 1.0 m resolution. A PulseEKKO1000 GPR was used with a 450 MHz antenna progressing parallel over the mound (i.e. unidirectionally) on traverses 1.0 m apart. Markers were recorded every metre along each traverse, resulting in an approximate in-line recording resolution of 0.03 m with 4 stacks (20 m × 20 m @ 0.03 m × 1.0 m). The magnetometer data were only processed with a weak Zero Mean Traverse algorithm (Geoplot threshold of ±10 nT) and were subsequently interpolated to a uniform display resolution of 0.25 m × 0.25 m. The only processing required for the earth resistance data was weak despiking. The GPR data were rubberbanded to 0.05 m, bandpass filtered (trapezoidal 10, 300, 500, 600 MHz), the common trace background was removed and 2D migration applied. The migration velocity was determined as 0.075 m/ns, using migration tests to minimise hyperbolic signals. Data were then converted to depth-slices of 0.1 m thickness

parallel with the ground surface, creating an onion-skin representation of the barrow's interior. This was deemed preferable over topographically corrected depth-slicing (sponge-cake slicing) due to the likely construction method of the barrow and for better comparability with the other geophysical data. To create the depth-slices the traverses of each slice were treated by first removing the median and then applying a weak in-line lowpass filter (radius 0.25 m).

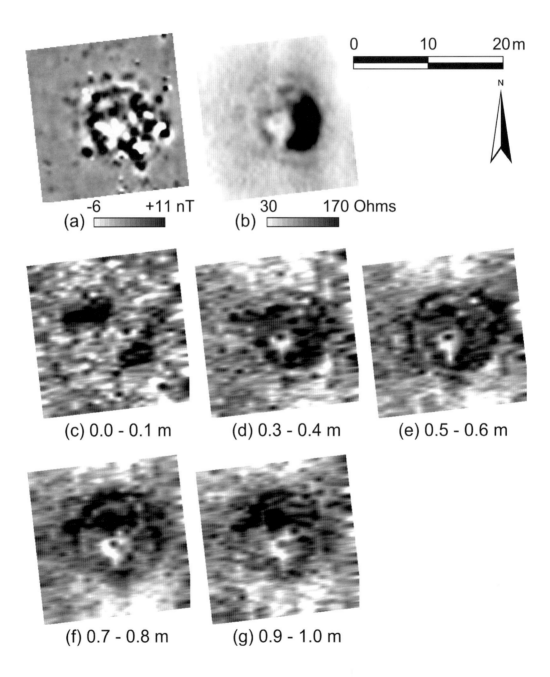

Fig. 5.2 Data from the 2007 high-resolution geophysical surveys over the Central Barrow: (a) magnetometer data; (b) earth resistance data (twin-probe 0.5 m electrode separation); (d)–(g) GPR data, strong reflections are black.

Results

The most prominent geophysical anomalies were already apparent in the initial magnetometer survey: two concentric features consisting of an outer ring of 12 m diameter and a central circular area of 8 m diameter (Fig. 5.2(a)). The centre of both features is offset from the barrow's current top by approximately 3.5 m to the southeast (Fig. 5.3). These concentric features show as anomalies in all data sets, albeit with very different characteristics for the three techniques used. The archaeological interpretation, accordingly, proved difficult and relied on results from the 2007 excavation trench that intersected both features (see Melton and Russ, this volume). The information from the excavation was essential for a better understanding of the data. In addition to the anomalies directly over the barrow, the earth resistance data also showed weak linear anomalies running north–south in the 2006 data, with separations of 7 to 9 m that are interpreted as remnants of medieval ridge-and-furrow ploughing in the area.

The outer ring ([A] in Fig. 5.3) shows in the magnetometer data as 15 mostly isolated positive anomalies of approximately 4–20 nT strength (Fig. 5.2(a)), with a typical size of less than 1 m diameter and a spacing of about 2 m. If such a 12 m diameter circle were divided equally into 15 segments, one for each isolated anomaly, it would have a segment length of 2.5 m, similar to the observed distances between the anomalies. The isolated anomalies are most regular from WSW to ENE (clockwise), where they are closest to the top of the barrow. Slightly raised earth resistance readings (with a contrast of 20 Ω above the background) are also noticeable for this feature in the high resolution data of the 0.5 m twin-probe array, and are identified because of the overall circular shape of the anomaly, despite showing only as discontinuous sections of positive contrast with several gaps. The gap from WNW to NW is exactly in the location of the excavation trench but since a similar break is indicated in the coarser resolution data from the 2006 survey (i.e. prior to the excavation) it can be assumed that the gap is not simply caused by removal of material during the excavation. The outer ring also manifests itself in the GPR data, albeit differently at different depths. The northern part shows clearly on all levels from 0.3 m down to 0.9 m. However, since pronounced disturbances from the excavation trench are visible at all levels from the ground surface down to 0.9 m, not much can be said about the outer ring within the trench. At the 0.3 m level (i.e. in the slice of 0.3–0.4 m) the ring shows only very weakly, reminiscent of the discrete magnetic anomalies, but not entirely co-located with them. At 0.5 m depth, the ring is more continuous, including the southern part, and becomes fairly substantial at 0.7 m, albeit mainly confined to the northern part. At 0.9 m depth even the northern part

of the outer ring starts to lose its definition. It is notable that the southern part only shows over a fairly narrow depth range (depth slice at 0.5m) and there only as a thin and weak anomaly. The overall interpretation of the results from all geophysical techniques for the outer ring ([A] in Fig. 5.3) is hence that it consists of a thin feature at shallow depth (approximately 0.3 to 0.5 m) that shows continuously in one or the other data set, but is discontinuous in each (especially in the magnetometer data). Deeper down it becomes a broader and more substantial feature, down to a depth level of 0.9 m, but confined to the northern part, mainly from W to ESE. This would therefore seem to correlate with the excavation results that found a kerb of stones (context [010], (see Melton and Russ, this volume) at approximately 0.4 m depth, located in direct contact with a bed of packed smaller stones (context [021]), which continued to the inside of the kerb-ring (i.e. continuing to its east in the trench). The two larger kerb stones in the excavation trench are apparently of different geological origins (a beach-boulder of fine-grained sandstone and an angular block of limestone, respectively; (see Melton and Russ, this volume) and produced together a medium-strength singular magnetic anomaly. It is hence conceivable that the kerb was deliberately constructed from different types of stone, some of which produced more prominent magnetic anomalies. The fairly regular arrangement of these magnetic anomalies over the outer ring's circumference of 38 m could indicate that they were placed deliberately to achieve a visual pattern.

The central area with a diameter of 8 m shows anomalies that have a very distinct bi-polar appearance in the earth resistance data (Fig. 5.2(b)). The eastern part is an extended kidney-shaped anomaly of approximately 4 m × 7 m [B], which shows prominently with a strong positive contrast of +400 Ω (over a background of 45 Ω). To its west, and nearly in the centre of the outer ring, lies a roughly circular negative earth resistance anomaly [C] of 3 m diameter and a contrast of -10 Ω. It has a small and weak positive anomaly in its middle (+5 Ω, [D]). To the north and west of this circular negative anomaly are further minor positive earth resistance anomalies. This pattern is very closely mirrored by the GPR data at 0.3 m depth (Fig. 5.2(d)) and even the GPR near-surface data (Fig. 5.2(c)) show a strong anomaly at the location of the kidney-shaped earth resistance anomaly [B], similar to the one produced by the 2007 excavation trench (which is the western anomaly in Fig. 5.2(c)). While the kidney-shaped anomaly disappears at 0.7 m depth in the GPR data, the nearly central negative anomaly [C] with its small inner positive anomaly [D] persists down to 0.9 m. It is possible that the central negative anomaly [C] represents an excavation shaft with fairly loose infill, potentially with a large stone thrown into its centre creating the small positive anomaly [D]. The kidney-shaped anomaly [B] could

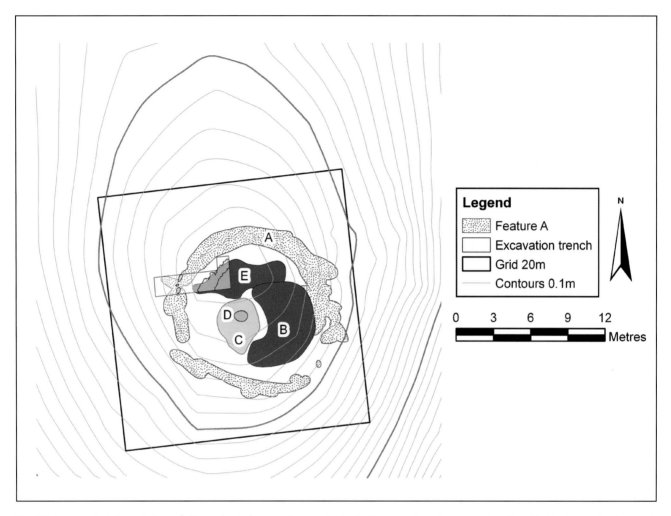

Fig. 5.3 Schematic interpretation of all geophysical anomalies, overlaid with 0.1 m contour lines, showing the offset between the barrow's peak and the centre of the outer circle [A].

then be an area of upcast from such an excavation with stones piled up to the east of the shaft with a thickness of 0.7 m. Such an interpretation of the geophysical data is clearly influenced by the report of Beswick's 1834 excavation (Williamson 1834, see also Melton and Beswick, this volume). This interpretation would also explain the magnetometer data for the central anomalies, which show various positive anomalies (Fig. 5.2(a)), most strongly and varied over the eastern extended anomaly [B], compatible with an interpretation as a stone heap (see the magnetic signals of the stones form the kerb). The central negative earth resistance anomaly [C] corresponds to a consistently negative magnetic anomaly, possibly due to the disturbed backfilled soil.

The slightly positive earth resistance anomaly [E] north of the central negative anomaly [C] shows in the GPR data more prominently from 0.7 m downwards, extending considerably in size to about 3 m × 5 m. This anomaly is most likely caused by the arc of stones that also shows in the excavation (context [004]), although the inner cut [013] and fill [007] are not apparent in the GPR data, probably due to the carefully compacted small stones [015] in that infill. At a depth of 0.9 m this anomaly nearly joins with the bed of stones that forms the broadened northern base of the outer ring (see above). It therefore appears that the bed of stones and the arc form one feature at that depth, possibly related to the central cairn (the join between the two anomalies does not have to be made entirely of stones; compacted clay could also create a similar GPR anomaly). If taken together, these two anomalies are exactly at the top of the barrow, while the outer kerb-ring is offset by approximately 3.5 m to the southeast (see above). It could hence have been laid out later to mark an off-centre burial in the southeastern flank of the barrow. Such an interpretation could explain the reason for Beswick's two excavations. In 1833 he failed to find a burial in his first attempt, in which he most likely dug directly into the very top of the barrow. Since he did not find the expected burial it is conceivable that he may have backfilled his shaft carefully with compacted stones (context [015] and lack of disturbance in the geophysics data), either already anticipating his own second attempt or possibly to thwart other antiquarians' search - we can only speculate about his reasons. On his second attempt in 1834, he may have taken note of the off-centre outer kerb-ring. Williamson (1834) described the barrow as being 40 feet (i.e. 12 m) in diameter, which suggest that he may have considered the kerb as the outline of the barrow. In this second attempt Beswick found the burial of Gristhorpe Man and may hence have been less careful when backfilling his second shaft. This would explain the clear negative earth resistance anomaly created by the possible shaft [C], accompanied by the strong eastern anomaly from the upcast of stones [B]. Based on the evidence from the geophysical data it appears that all the kerb stones of the outer ring lie at approximately the same depth below the current sloping ground surface, which indicates that the mound's topography was approximately the same as today when the ring was constructed. This raises the question why there was no burial found under the centre of the cairn, presuming that a primary burial would usually be expected to lie there.

Section 2: The Landscape Surrounding Gristhorpe Man

In addition to the investigation of the Central Barrow geophysical surveys were undertaken in Spring and Summer 2008 to study the wider landscape (Fig. 5.4) (Hodgson 2008). The burial mounds are effectively all that remains visible of the Bronze Age landscape. There is, for example, no evidence in the immediate area to suggest land use or settlement that may be linked to the barrow group. The 'entrenchments' marked on the earlier Ordnance Survey maps may be the only indications that other features had existed.

The land directly to the south and west of the Central Barrow has been modified and built upon in recent years. While the Northern Barrow appears to have been levelled considerably by recent activities, the location of the Southern Barrow is still in open farmland. Williamson (1872, 5) reported that W. Beswick, Esq., the owner of the estate opened up both the Southern and Northern Barrows retrieving 'urns' containing cremated or incomplete bones. The exact details of the excavation of the Southern Barrow remain elusive. The presumed location offers clear north-south views; to the northwest lies the band of pasture that contains the Central Barrow, while immediately

to the south the barrow is separated from a large open agricultural field by a two-metre wide boundary consisting of stones, other discarded building materials and a metal fence. The boundary is also the location of a step in the topography, caused by extensive ploughing in the large field to the south. The area of the Southern Barrow and its immediate surrounds has evidently been managed in the past and it was uncertain how much of the structure of the barrow, if any, remains *in situ*. It was hoped that geophysical investigations of the Southern Barrow and the land to its south might throw light on elements of the landscape within which the Central Barrow is situated.

The landscape element of this work consisted of two parts:

1. To examine the Southern Barrow using magnetic and electrical methods.
2. To devise and implement a strategy to investigate the potential for tracing buried archaeological remains within the field to the south of the Southern Barrow. The relatively large size of this single field meant that the whole of the approximately 6 ha of land could not be surveyed in detail and a strategy was developed to position smaller survey areas for more intensive investigations.

Measurements and Processing over the Southern Barrow

The survey over the Southern Barrow was undertaken along traverses running approximately north-south at 1.0 m separation and covered an area of 40 m × 40 m. For the magnetometer survey a Geoscan FM256 was used walking parallel along lines (i.e. unidirectionally) and recording measurements every 0.125 m over 20 m × 20 m data grids. The earth resistance measurements were collected with twin-probe arrays of 0.5 m and 1.0 m separation using a Geoscan RM15 and an MPX15 multiplexer as described for the Central Barrow. As explained above this lead to a data resolution of 0.5 m × 0.5 m for the 0.5 m separation twin-probe array and of a slightly lower resolution of 0.5 m × 1.0 m for the 1.0 m separation array. The 1.0 m separation survey maps features at greater depth than those measured using the 0.5 m separation. The location of these data grids was measured with a Total Station and referenced to landscape features that could be identified on the available Ordnance Survey Landline maps.

The magnetometer measurements required minimal processing with Zero Mean Traverse and were interpolated for a more appealing display. The processing was required due to the high level of ferrous signals that were present throughout the 40 m × 40 m survey area. The earth resistance measurements required only de-spiking and

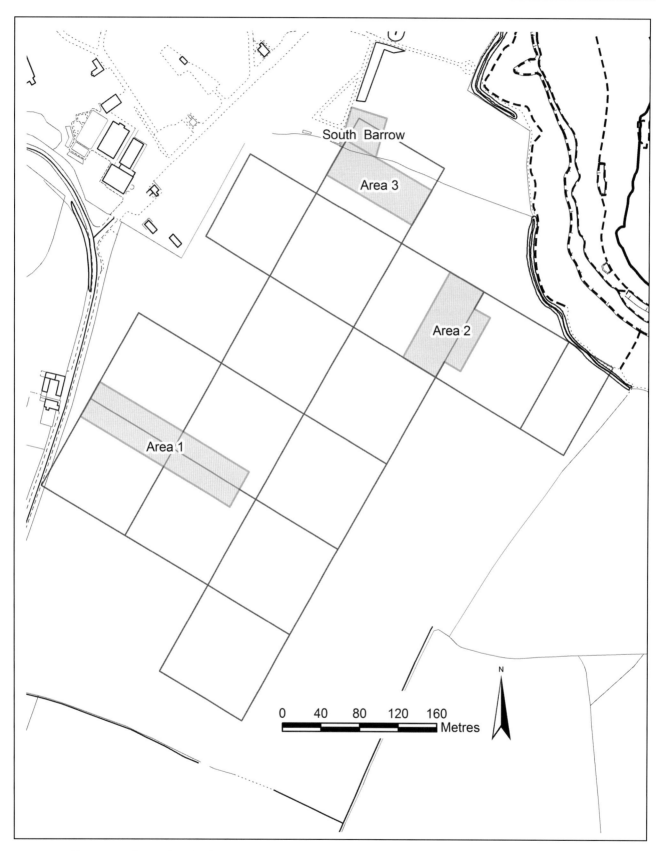

Fig. 5.4 Grid locations in the southern landscape. The map data are © Crown Copyright 2008. An Ordnance Survey/EDINA supplied service.

interpolation. However, the de-spiking that was necessary for the 1.0 m separation data was quite strong and reduced the interpretative power of this data set. All processing was undertaken within Geoplot and images were subsequently incorporated into the GIS.

Results over the Southern Barrow

The magnetometer data (Fig. 5.5(a)) clearly indicate a high level of magnetic disturbance that most likely relates to the modern management of the caravan park. It should be noted that this ferrous response does not necessarily indicate damage to subsurface remains, but does show that the magnetometer data are of little value in assessing the state of preservation of this barrow.

Given the evidence from the magnetometer data it is likely that the two earth resistance pseudo-depth slices (Fig. 5.5(b/c)) also mostly reflect modern activity. As noted above, the 1.0 m separation data showed a large number of 'spikes'. There was very heavy rain during the collection of the earth resistance data and the spikes could be a result of these weather conditions. The smaller number of spikes in the 0.5 m data may be due to the fact that they were collected after the 1.0 m data in the multiplexed switching sequence, when the electrodes had already made better contact with the ground. All strong positive anomalies in the data collected with 0.5 m separation, especially those in the northwest with nearly rectangular shapes [F] have a correspondence with weaker, more amorphous anomalies in the 1.0 m separation data. This suggests that they are

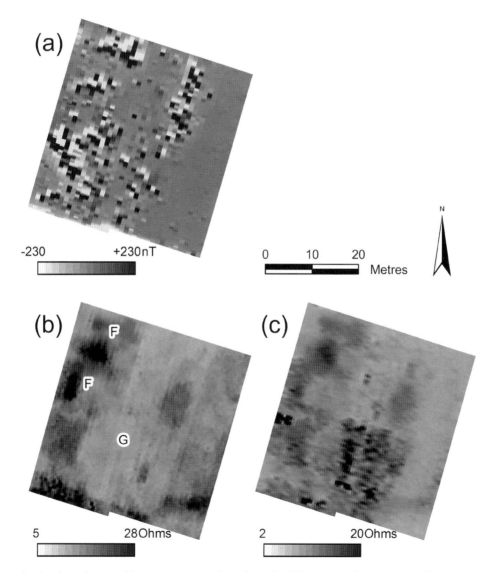

Fig. 5.5 Data over the Southern Barrow: (a) magnetometer; (b) twin-probe 0.5 m electrode separation; (c) twin-probe 1.0 m electrode separation.

caused by near-surface areas of localised high resistivity, possibly in the form of patches of stones or rubble. In between these high resistance anomalies lies a nearly circular area of lower readings, approximately 18 m in diameter [G]. It is more difficult to discern in the 1.0 m data due to the remaining spikes in this area. This anomaly is roughly located in the presumed position of the Southern Barrow but the identification has to remain tentative. A more detailed interpretation of these datasets has not been possible.

Measurements and Processing over the Southern Field

The field to the south of the Southern Barrow was 6 ha in size, and it was not possible to cover it all in detail. A modified rapid magnetic evaluation method was therefore applied instead. Different magnetic evaluation methods are currently in use by commercial contractors, including small blocks of detailed surveys, either distributed regularly or randomly, scanning with a magnetometer (Gaffney 2008) or coarsely sampled magnetic susceptibility surface measurements (Schmidt 2003). The latter approach was selected for the investigation of the Bronze Age

landscape around the barrows as magnetic susceptibility has been shown to increase over places of habitation and generally over areas of former human activity. Enhanced susceptibility can be mapped in topsoil (Clark 1996, 107–117) and areas that show higher readings can be targeted subsequently for investigation with detailed magnetometer surveys. The field was subdivided into 100 m × 100 m data grids using a total station and magnetic susceptibility readings were collected at 5 m × 5 m resolution with a Bartington Field Coil (MS2D) across the majority of the field (Fig. 5.6). The data were de-spiked, visualised as greyscale images and incorporated into the GIS. Areas of anomalous magnetic susceptibility were then identified and magnetometer surveys conducted as described for the Southern Barrow. At the time of the magnetometer surveys the crop had grown very tall and buffeted the instrument during data collection. As a result the instrument was set up and checked every two to four grids to ensure adequate data quality.

Results over the Southern Field

Figure 5.6 shows the results of the magnetic susceptibility survey alongside the 1854 Ordnance Survey map. The data

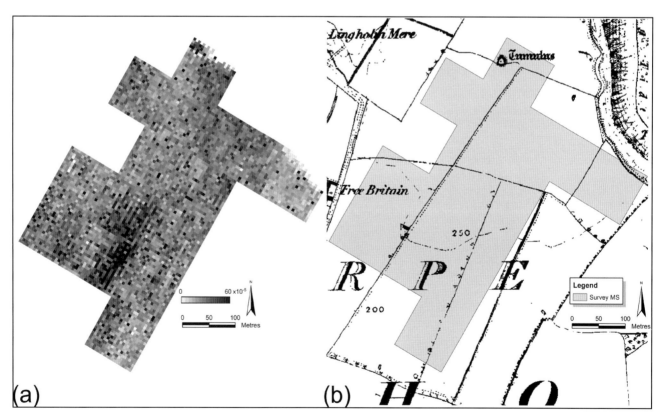

Fig. 5.6 Magnetic susceptibility survey in the south field: (a) data collected with MS2D field coil at 5 m × 5 m resolution; (b) 1854 Ordnance Survey map of the same area (© Crown Copyright and Landmark Information Group Ltd (all rights reserved 2013)).

show a distinct area of high susceptibility in the south of the field, which corresponds to a ridge in the topography and is also close to the location of a feature on the 1854 Ordnance Survey map. This forms Area 1 of the detailed magnetometer surveys and is also an area in which soil- and cropmarks show on aerial photographs from GoogleMaps and Bing, although these appear in slightly different places for the various images available. Towards the northern end of the field, just south of the Southern Barrow, the readings were also higher, although not as much as to the south, so detailed magnetometer surveys were undertaken there (Area 3), partly to investigate whether any remains of the Southern Barrow could be detected. Towards the eastern edge of the field is an area that shows lower readings of around $1 - 20 \times 10^{-5}$, compared to the average background values seen in the rest of the data of $21 - 38 \times 10^{-5}$. This part of the field was often left fallow and is marked as

a separate unit on the 1854 Ordnance Survey map. The different land use may have contributed to the lower magnetic susceptibility values. A detailed magnetometer survey was undertaken just west of this area to attempt a characterisation of the possible changes (Area 2).

The major anomalies in the magnetometer data from Area 1 (Fig. 5.7) are roughly in the location of some of the soil-marks shown on aerial photographs. These marks and most of the magnetic anomalies have broad outlines, and it is likely that they are caused by geological features, probably related to the slight ridge that runs through the field. The magnetic anomalies in the middle-south of Area 1 [H] coincide with the feature shown on the 1854 Ordnance Survey map, just west of the diagonal field boundary that is visible on that map. This small structure could be a barn and it is possible that the positive magnetic anomalies are related to it. There are some very faint anomalies [I] in the

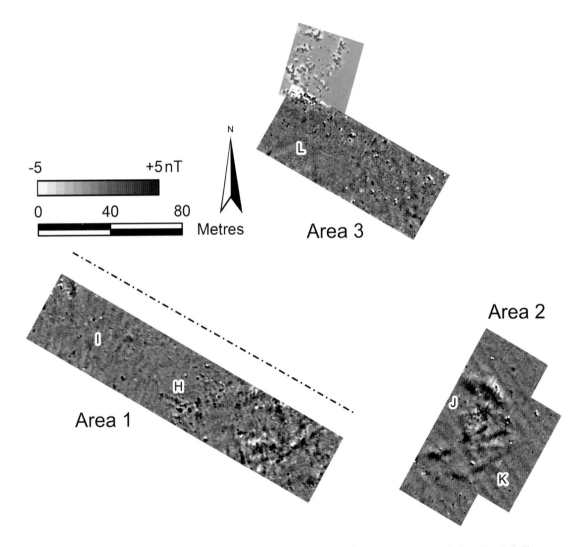

Fig. 5.7 Detailed magnetometer surveys of Areas 1 to 3. The relative position of Area 1 is not to scale (see Fig. 5.4). The magnetometer data from the Southern Barrow are shown in lighter shades north of Area 3 (see Fig. 5.5a).

western part of Area 1 (in the order of 0.5 nT) that have the same orientation as current plough lines and are possibly of agricultural origin.

Area 2 (Fig. 5.7) is dominated by several curvilinear bipolar anomalies that seem to encircle a weaker central rectilinear anomaly [J]. However, the overall appearance of these anomalies is very diffuse and an anthropogenic origin is unlikely; they are somewhat similar to the main anomalies in Area 1 and probably also related to near-surface geological features. This area shows some topographic changes, gradually rising towards the southern end, which may also be caused by the underlying geological structures. In addition, there are clear diagonal striations in Area 2 running NW to SE. They are composed of 2 m wide positive anomalies [K] of approximately 1 nT strength, located approximately 6 m apart. They are at a pronounced angle to current plough lines and are probably caused by medieval ridge-and-furrow practice.

Area 3 (Fig. 5.7) lies south of the Southern Barrow, just over the fenceline and at considerably lower ground level due to continued ploughing (see above). Similar to the survey over the Southern Barrow the data show a considerable number of small bipolar magnetic anomalies that are most likely caused by ferrous debris from modern agricultural use. Weak curvilinear anomalies (in the order of 0.5 nT) trend in different directions and create the impression of a semicircle [L], open towards the main field in the south. These may be caused by modern or medieval ploughing (as in Areas 1 and 2, respectively) towards the step in the field boundary. None of these anomalies seems to relate to the Southern Barrow.

Overall, the earth resistance and magnetometer measurements in the southeastern part of this landscape found only very few clearly interpretable anomalies. Although the layout of the Southern Barrow was not revealed in these geophysical surveys, its location seems relatively certain, based on the current topographic rise. A detailed GPR survey of this rise could be valuable. Although the magnetic anomalies are probably of geological and agricultural origin there may be an anthropogenic overprint from the Bronze Age landscape. To distinguish between the different elements would require a detailed magnetometer survey of the whole southern field, supplemented by earth resistance measurements over the soil- and cropmarks.

References

Clark, A. J. (1996) *Seeing Beneath the Soil, Prospecting Methods in Archaeology* (Revised paperback edition). London, Batsford.

Gaffney, C. (2008) Detecting trends in the prediction of the buried past: A review of geophysical techniques in archaeology. *Archaeometry* 50, 313–336.

Hodgson, S. (2008) *The Gristhorpe Man Project: Further geophysics to examine the relationship between the Bronze Age burial mounds.* MSc Thesis. Archaeological Sciences. Bradford, University of Bradford.

Schmidt, A. (2003) The lost village of Tidover – magnetic susceptibility survey as part of a sequential prospection strategy. *Archaeologia Polona* 41, 265.

Williamson, W. C. (1834) *Description of the Tumulus, lately opened at Gristhorpe, near Scarborough.* Scarborough, C. R. Todd.

Williamson, W. C. (1872) *Description of the Tumulus opened at Gristhorpe, near Scarborough.* Scarborough, S. W. Theakston.

6

ARCHAEOLOGICAL EVALUATION UNDERTAKEN IN 2007 ON THE SITE OF THE 1834 GRISTHORPE DISCOVERY

Nigel D. Melton and Hannah Russ

Introduction

The Gristhorpe log coffin burial was located under the central and most prominent of a group of three barrows on the cliff-top at Gristhorpe, approximately 6 miles (9.5 km) to the south of Scarborough (Fig. 6.1). It was found during excavations carried out in July 1834 by the local landowner, William Beswick. A report of the discovery was published the same year by William Crawford Williamson (Williamson 1834). No plans or sections were included in the report (or in the extensively revised third edition published in 1872 (Williamson 1872)), but the location of the three barrows was depicted in a vignette that was included in both reports (Fig. 6.2). This illustration, in the form of a view from inland facing out to sea, enables (given a degree of artistic license in the perspective) a number of field boundaries to be identified and the locations of the three barrows to be confirmed as those shown on the 1854 edition Ordnance Survey 1/10560 map (Fig. 6.3). A visit to the site revealed that, despite extensive landscaping in the 1950s and 1960s, a natural prominence, apparently enhanced by a barrow mound, was present at the position indicated on the Ordnance Survey plans (Fig. 6.4).

Despite the lack of plans and sections in Williamson's reports, they were advanced for the time in that they contained not only a description of the barrow – it was '*forty feet* [12.2 m] *in diameter*' and '*at its greatest height the soil raised above the original surface was not above three feet* [0.9 m] *in thickness*'– but also a list of the layers, with their approximate thicknesses, which had been dug through to reach the coffin (Williamson 1834, 10; Williamson 1872, 16). These layers comprised:

	Feet*
Vegetable Soil	1
Loose Stones	2
Clay &c	1
Loose Stones	1
Puddle, or Blue Clay	1
Oak Branches (about)	1
The Coffin	3
Solid Clay	

*1 Foot is equivalent to 30.5 cms

There were brief descriptions of some of the layers. The layers of loose stones were described as '*carelessly thrown in*', with the additional information that the lower layer consisted of '*boulders, mainly sandstone*', whilst the oak branches were stated to be '*five to eight inches* [13 to 20 cms] *in diameter*'. The branches were described as '*roughly hewn*' in an account of the find in the *The York Herald, and General Advertiser,* Saturday, July 19th, 1834 (Melton and Beswick, this volume).

There is, however, a problem with Williamson's list of the layers encountered. His 1834 report states that Beswick's dig that year was a second attempt at excavating the barrow, as he had abandoned digging the previous year '*after sinking to some depth, fruitlessly*' (Williamson 1834, 5). It is possible, therefore, that the uppermost contexts in the

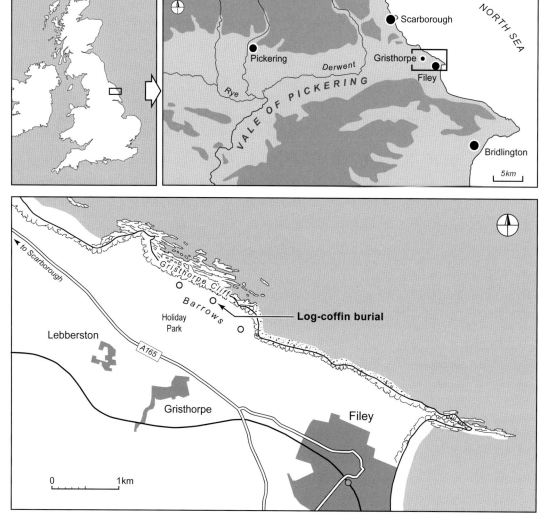

Fig. 6.1 Location of the Gristhorpe log coffin burial.

Fig. 6.2 Vignette illustrating the three barrows on the cliff-top at Gristhorpe (Source: Williamson 1834).

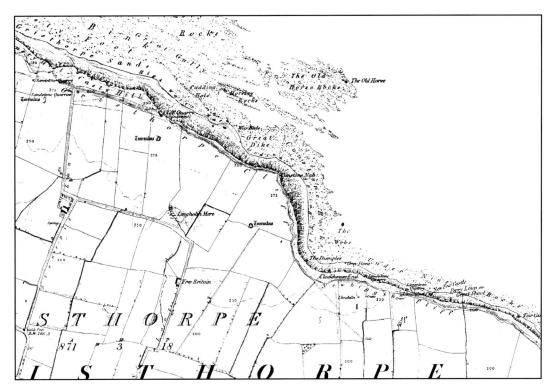

Fiigure 6.3 The barrows at Gristhorpe on the 1854 Ordnance Survey 1:10,560 map.

Fig. 6.4 The Gristhorpe log coffin barrow in 2005 (Photograph: N. D. Melton).

list are backfilled material from the unrecorded 1833 dig.

Williamson's account of William Beswick's aborted attempt on the barrow in 1833 does, however, suggest that his method of excavation was to dig out the centre of the barrow in search of the primary burial. Beswick had investigated the two outlying barrows some decade or so previously and, whilst there is no extant record by

him off these previous excavations, Williamson (1872, 5) records that he found '*Urns, with imperfect remains of bones and ashes, probably of burnt wood*' in both of these barrows. Another account (Bulmer 1891) describes how in 1824 he had found the skeleton of an adult male in a barrow at Gristhorpe. It is not clear whether this was the northern or southern barrow but the former was subsequently re-opened by Canon William Greenwell, who was unaware of Beswick's earlier excavation in 1887 (Greenwell 1890, 38). Greenwell's excavation uncovered the primary (i.e. central) burial that had been imperfectly emptied by Beswick and also revealed a second burial, a small cist containing cremated human remains, that had not been encountered in the earlier excavation (*ibid.*; Kinnes and Longworth 1985, 126, entry 266). This appears to confirm that Beswick simply dug out the centre of the barrows and provides a possible explanation for why he abandoned his 1833 attempt on the central barrow. In the northern barrow (and likely that to the south, for which no record has survived) the central, primary, burial was in a stone cist, the capstone of which was at ground level. In 1833 Beswick may have been confounded by the deep grave cut of the central barrow. An alternative explanation for his failure to locate the log coffin burial was that this was offset from the summit of the mound (Schmidt *et al.*, this volume). When he returned the following year to complete his investigation of the barrow, he did so, fortunately for posterity, with a number of members of the Scarborough Philosophical Society (Melton & Beswick, this volume).

The insight into Beswick's barrow-digging technique provided by Williamson's 1834 account and Greenwell's 1887 excavations suggested that the outer part of the central, log coffin, barrow would have been left undisturbed by Beswick. This meant that a modern investigation, even on a limited scale, had the potential to not only confirm the barrow location and find evidence relating to Beswick's excavation, but also to provide an opportunity to examine the construction of the barrow and to assess the preservation of the archaeological remains of the monument.

The 2007 evaluation trench [GRI07] (Fig. 6.6)

The archaeological evaluation of the barrow was undertaken between the 26th and 30th March 2007. The geophysical survey results (Schmidt *et al.*, this volume) and, in particular, the magnetometer survey clearly indicated two anomalies, an inner *c*.8 m diameter circular feature under the centre of the mound and an outer *c*.12 m diameter ring of discrete responses around its perimeter. The positions of these features were used to locate a 6 m by 1.5 m E-W

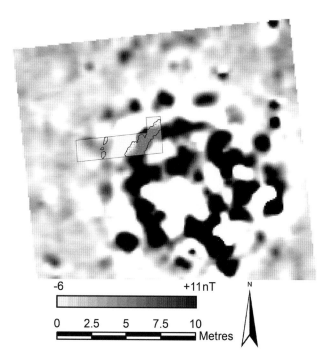

-6   +11nT

0   2.5   5   7.5   10
                              Metres

N

Fig. 6.5 Location of the 2007 evaluation trench relative to geophysical survey anomalies.

trench that would permit investigation of both of the anomalies present on the magnetometer survey (Fig. 6.5).

Excavation commenced with the removal of the turf [001] and topsoil [002]. Flint fragments and modern glass and pottery were recovered from both contexts. Removal of topsoil [002] revealed an arc of stones [004] (Fig. 6.7) in the eastern end of the trench at a position corresponding to the inner circular anomaly on the magnetometer survey. A 1m by 1m extension at right-angles to the main trench was added in order to more fully investigate the stone feature [004].

In the western end of the trench, topsoil [002] sealed a compact brown soil with clay inclusions [003]. A clayey deposit with organic layers [008] was present in the east adjacent to the stones. Context [003] contained a flint scraper and sickle fragment (GRI07 [003] /1\; GRI07 [003] /2\) and flint debitage, but no recent material. Both the brown soil [003] and the clayey deposit with thin organic bands [008] were interpreted as relating to barrow construction, the latter using turves cut from a clay-rich soil. They sealed a 0.5 m thick layer of brown organic soil [009] that contained a flint scraper (GRI07 [009] /4\) and more debitage, and which appeared to represent an earlier construction phase using turves cut from an organic topsoil. A thin black organic layer [005] at the base of [008] indicates that a ground surface had time to develop between the two phases of barrow construction (Fig.6.8).

Both contexts [008] and [009] butted the stones [004]. The latter were interpreted as the remains of a cairn that had been built over the grave cut, the bulk of which had been removed by William Beswick's 19th-century excavations. The cut for one of the latter [013] (see Schmidt *et al.*, this volume) and an upper backfill of sandy organic soil [007] were identified in the south-eastern corner of the trench. The backfilled soil [007] sealed a further backfill layer of small stones [015] which was not excavated. The stones of the central cairn [004] were also left *in situ*, so it was not possible to determine whether they sealed upcast material from the grave cut, as noted in the log coffin burial excavated at Little Ouseburn, Yorkshire (Rahtz 1989).

A sondage excavated in the north-eastern 1 m by 1 m trench extension revealed that the primary barrow turves [017] sealed the natural clay and that the stone cairn [004] had been constructed directly on the clay. No turf line representing an original ground surface was present, indicating that the site had probably been de-turfed prior to barrow construction.

In the western end of the trench, the later phase of turf barrow construction [003] sealed a kerb of large stones [010] (Fig. 6.9), the position of which corresponded to the outer circle of discrete anomalies on the magnetometer survey. The two large stones from the kerb that were exposed in the trench were a rounded beach boulder of

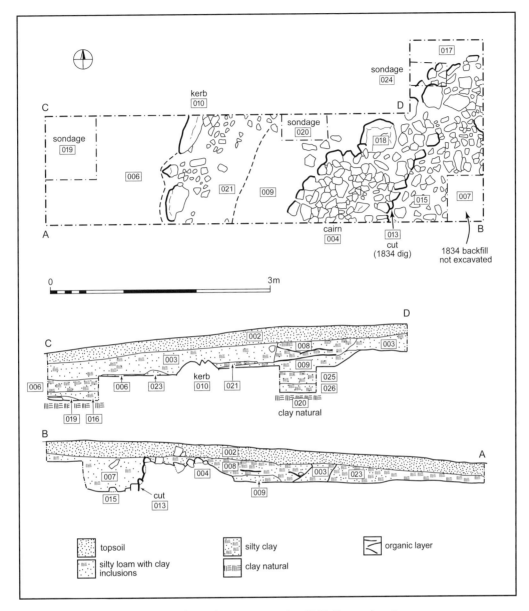

Fig. 6.6 Gristhorpe barrow excavation 2007: Plan and sections.

fine-grained sandstone and an angular block of limestone. The large stones that comprised the kerb were backed by a band of smaller stones. Of the two stone types in the kerb that were exposed in the excavation, one had produced a stronger response on the magnetometer survey, and the fairly regular spacing of the anomalies suggests that the placing of different types of stones could have been deliberate (Schmidt *et al.*, this volume), perhaps based on their colour. A thin brown silty clay layer containing thin organic bands and numerous small stones [021] was present on the inner, eastern, side of the kerb and appeared to be associated with it. This layer was interpreted as a ground

surface. It was sealed by soil turves [003] and sealed the earlier barrow turves [009].

A sondage, excavated adjacent to the northern baulk at a point approximately midway between the stone cairn [004] and kerb [010] revealed that that lower barrow turf layer [009] sealed a clay layer [025] that, in turn, sealed a silty soil layer [026]. Both of the latter contexts were interpreted as primary barrow construction layers. The silty soil [026] sealed the natural clay [020], again with no evidence of an original Bronze Age ground surface.

The clayey deposit with black organic turf lines [006] was also present to the west of kerb [010]. It was apparent,

Fig. 6.7 Stones [004] (Photograph: N. D. Melton).

Fig. 6.8 Barrow Phases II [009] and III [008] (Photograph: P. Sugden).

Fig. 6.9 Kerb [010] and stones [021] (Photograph: N. D. Melton).

Interpretation of the sequence of barrow construction

Phase I   De-turfing of the summit of the natural prominence, excavation and filling of the *ca.* 2 m deep grave and construction of the central cairn [004] over the grave.

Phase II   Construction of a turf barrow [016], [026], [025], [009]. The central stone cairn [004] appears to have been left partially exposed. This phase of construction extended beyond the western end of the evaluation trench, so its diameter was not determined.

Phase III   Construction of a smaller, approximately 14 m diameter, kerbed [010] barrow with clay turves [008] and soil turves [003] (see note below) being used to cover the stone cairn [004]. The potential ground surface [021] suggests that there was a berm between the kerb and the central barrow mound.

Phase IV   The kerbed barrow was covered with a layer of soil turves that had clayey patches [003]*, [023].

        *There was some confusion in the allocation of this context. The section of the south-facing baulk (Fig. 6.6) shows that [003] was also assigned to an earlier, Phase III, context butted by the clay turves [008]. Both of the contexts that were given this number represented barrow construction using soil turves and were visually identical despite representing different phases of activity on the site.

Given the destruction of the centre of the barrow in 1834 and the limited nature of the 2007 evaluation, it was not possible to determine whether either Phase III or Phase IV of barrow construction could be linked to the evidence for

therefore, that the barrow extended beyond the kerb, and a sondage dug in the N-W corner of the trench established that these clayey turf deposits sealed an earlier phase of construction using soil turves [016], this context being equivalent to context [026] seen in the sondage excavated to the east of the kerb.

later activity indicated by the radiocarbon date obtained from one of the layer of oak branches found over the coffin in 1834 (see Batt, this volume) although it does provide a possible explanation. Further evidence for at least two phases of barrow construction is discussed in Schmidt *et at.* (this volume).

Flint artefacts recovered at Gristhorpe

by H. Russ

Eight flint artefacts were recovered during the 2007 excavation. In addition to unstratified (GRI07 [Unstrat] /7\), topsoil (GRI07 [001] /9\), and 1834 backfill (GRI07 [007] /5\) examples, the flints were recovered from most phases of barrow construction, namely: -

GRI07 [004] /8\ from the Phase I cairn
GRI07 [009] /4\ and GRI07 [016] /6\ from the Phase II turf barrow
GRI07 [003] /1\ and GRI07 [003] /2\ from the Phase IV turf barrow

The analysis of the assemblage provides a useful insight into the use of the site and surrounding area prior to the construction of the burial mound.

Method

Each piece is described by listing the geological material of which the piece is made and the technological facet to which it belongs. Each piece is classified using current typologies. The completeness and dimensions of each piece is recorded; maximum length (L) is measured perpendicular to the striking platform, maximum width (W) parallel to the striking platform, and maximum depth (D) taken at the widest point between the dorsal and ventral surfaces. Cortex presence is recorded on a scale of 0–3, with 0 indicating an absence of cortex; 1 indicating 0.1–32.9% cortex; 2 indicating 33.0–65.9%; and 3 indicating 66.0–100% cortex. Colour is described using a Munsell soil colour chart, and patination or evidence for thermal alteration is noted.

GRI07 [003] /1 (Fig. 6.10)
Material: flint
Technology: flake
Classification: end scraper
Completeness: complete
Dimensions: L: 33.8 mm W: 26.9 mm D: 12.4 mm
Cortex: 1
Colour: 10YR 4/2 dark greyish brown
Patination: no

This artefact represents a scraper typical of the later Neolithic to Bronze Age periods. Cortex remains on the dorsal side. The scraper is narrow at the proximal end with evidence for abrasion on the lateral edges; in addition to damage to the dorsal surface at the proximal end, this may suggest that this piece was once hafted.

GRI07 [003] /2 (Fig. 6.11)
Material: flint
Technology: blade
Classification: sickle fragment
Completeness: medial
Dimensions: L: 30.7 mm W: 18.5 mm D: 10.1 mm
Cortex: 1
Colour: 10YR 3/1 very dark grey
Patination: no

Once part of a larger piece, this flint sickle fragment has evidence of thermal alteration in the form of three potlid scars on the ventral surface. Cortex on the dorsal surface appears to have been ground away to reveal the flint beneath, which had then been incised with three parallel groves, possibly to aid the hafting process. One lateral edge is bi-facially retouched, and would have been used as the cutting edge. The ventral surface bears areas of 'use-gloss', which is often observed on sickles and sickle fragments and results from their use on fibrous plant materials. Sickles during the earlier Neolithic were more often made up of several hafted flint pieces developing into single-piece sickles in the later Neolithic through to the Bronze Age. Due to the damage observed on this sickle fragment it is difficult to ascertain to which period it belongs.

GRI07 [009] /4 (Fig.6.12)
Material: flint
Technology: flake
Classification: end and side scraper
Completeness: proximal absent
Dimensions: L: 45.4 mm W: 35.1 mm D: 11.5 mm
Cortex: 1
Colour: 10YR 3/1 very dark grey
Patination: no

This artefact is a scraper typical of the later Neolithic to Bronze Age period. Cortex remains on the dorsal side and the bulb of percussion is absent. Retouch can be seen on the distal and one lateral edge, with the other lateral edge remaining un-worked. Lateral edge damage and retouch at the proximal end suggest that this piece was hafted. It appears that the modification of the piece to allow hafting weakened the proximal end, which had snapped removing the bulb of percussion and the possibility of re-hafting. In addition to distal and lateral edge retouch there is heavy use damage to the distal portion of the tool which can be seen on the ventral surface.

GRI07 [007] /5
Material: flint
Technology: fragment
Classification: core fragment
Completeness: distal
Dimensions: L: 30.8 mm W: 29.4 mm D: 25.3 mm
Cortex: 1
Colour: 10YR 6/1 grey
Patination: no

A fragment of a water-worn flint core pebble. Once the distal portion of a larger flint core, the surface of this piece bears the scars of blade and flake removal prior to it breaking from the original core. Only a single flake has been removed from the piece after it became separated from the core, perhaps because much of the piece is made up of a lower quality flint.

GRI07 [016] /6
Material: flint
Technology: flake
Classification: no retouch
Completeness: complete
Dimensions: L: 28.3 mm W: 40.1 mm D: 8.2 mm
Cortex: 1
Colour: 10YR 6/1 grey
Patination: no

This artefact is a flint flake with no evidence for retouch and possible use damage on one lateral edge. It was possibly removed from the distal portion of a core as part of core preparation processes. A small area of cortex is present and forms the striking platform.

GRI07 [unstratified] /7 (Fig. 6.13)
Material: flint
Technology: flake
Classification: end scraper
Completeness: complete
Dimensions: L: 23.7 mm W: 28.4 mm D: 4.0 mm
Cortex: 1
Colour: 10YR 6/1 grey
Patination: no

This is a small flint end scraper with cortex remaining on the proximal and lateral edges, most likely removed from a small flint pebble. It is a typical scraper of the later Neolithic to Bronze Age period. There is no evidence for hafting on this piece.

GRI07 [004] /8
Material: flint
Technology: blade
Classification: no retouch
Completeness: medial
Dimensions: L: 20.4 mm W: 10.2 mm D: 2.8 mm
Cortex: 0
Colour: 10YR 5/4 yellowish brown
Patination: no

This is a small mid-blade fragment, which had not been retouched, with lateral damage on one edge.

GRI07 [001] /9
Material: flint
Technology: blade
Classification: no retouch
Completeness: Snap to distal
Dimensions: L: 24.0 mm W: 6.2 mm D: 2.0 mm
Cortex: 1
Colour: 10YR 6/2 light brownish grey
Patination: no

This artefact represents a small flint bladelet with no re-working after its removal from the core. Cortex runs through this piece at the distal end, a possible reason why it was never worked any further.

Summary
The stone tool assemblage recovered during excavations at Gristhorpe is consistent with those recovered from sites dating between the later Neolithic and Bronze Age in Britain, with broad, relatively thin scrapers, and large flint debitage and un-worked pieces. All are made from flint, with some coming from small pebbles (as is the case for /1\, /4\ and /7\, indicated by cortex presence and morphology) most likely collected from the nearby chalk cliffs from which flint erodes onto the surrounding beaches. This is supported by the presence of a water-worn flint pebble core fragment /5\. The presence of three scrapers, a sickle fragment and other tool forms and blanks suggests that during the later Neolithic to Bronze Age period this area was used for flint tool production and working wood and/or preparing hides, crop harvesting, as well as other activities.

Acknowledgements
The 2007 excavation was undertaken by Nigel Melton, Vaughan Wastling, David Maron and Philip Sugden. Thanks are due to Mr D. Kaye and Mr N. Ankers, Blue Dolphin Holiday Park, and Haven Holidays for permission to carry out the geophysical surveys and excavation. The

Fig. 6.10 Scraper GRI07[003]/1\ (Photograph: H. Russ).

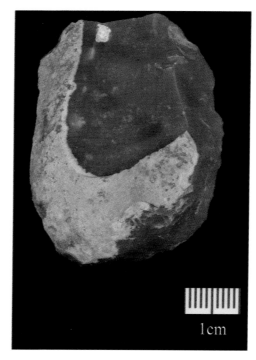

Fig. 6.12 Scraper GRI07[009]/4\ (Photograph: H. Russ).

Fig. 6.11 Sickle fragment GRI07[003]/2\ (Photograph: H. Russ).

Fig. 6.13 Scraper GRI07[Unstrat]/7\ (Photograph: H. Russ).

investigation of the barrow site was funded by a Royal Archaeological Institute research grant. Figures 6.1 and 6.6 were prepared by M. Rouillard, University of Exeter.

References

Bulmer (1891) *History, Topography and Directory of North Yorkshire, Part II, containing Thirsk & Malton, and Whitby Divisional part of the Wapentake of Claro.* Preston, T. Bulmer & Co.

Greenwell, W. (1890) Recent researches in barrows in Yorkshire, Wiltshire, Berkshire etc. *Archaeologia*, 52, 1–72.

Kinnes I. A. and Longworth, I. H. (1985) *Catalogue of the Excavated Prehistoric and Romano-British Material in the Greenwell Collection.* London, British Museum Press.

Rahtz, P. (1989) *Little Ouseburn Barrow 1958.* York University Archaeological Publications 7. York, University of York.

Williamson, W. C. (1834) *Description of the Tumulus, lately opened at Gristhorpe, near Scarborough.* Scarborough, C. R. Todd.

Williamson, W.C. (1872) *Description of the Tumulus opened at Gristhorpe, near Scarborough.* Scarborough, S.W. Theakston.

7

THE SCIENTIFIC DATING EVIDENCE

Cathy Batt

Introduction

One of the primary objectives of the Gristhorpe Man Project was to obtain accurate and precise dates for the skeleton and burial assemblage. In 1834, Williamson wrote: *'There is no possible chance of coming within a few years, or even with certainty, within two or three centuries, of the exact period of the entombing of the body;.... but the probable age of the Tumulus will be at least about 2200 years'* (Williamson 1834, 16). However, the major developments in scientific dating since then make this research area one of the most profitable for re-investigation, both to provide an insight into the sequence of events related to this burial and to allow comparison with other sites (Parker Pearson *et al.*, this volume). Previous discussion of the date of the Gristhorpe Man has focussed on the cultural tradition of the inhumation ritual, the typology of the dagger and a single radiocarbon date obtained in the 1980s, discussed below.

Dating strategy

The wealth of material available and the excellent preservation ensured that there was a wide range of possible approaches to dating the assemblage. The selection of methods was influenced by the ability of techniques to address a specific archaeological question, the precision possible in the period under consideration, the sample requirements and, inevitably, the budget. With those considerations in mind, the initial approach was to undertake a dendrochronological study of the coffin lid and radiocarbon dating of the skeleton and overlying oak branches. The dendrochronology was intended to date the felling of the tree trunk used for the coffin.

Radiocarbon dating of the individual focussed on two tissues, tooth root dentine and femoral bone. Dentine was selected as it was anticipated that this would be protected from the effects of early conservation treatments, and its dating would complement stable isotopic studies aimed at investigating evidence for diet and migration (Montgomery and Gledhill, this volume). Dating the femur allowed comparison of tissues formed at different times in the individual's life and with different rates of bone turnover as well as investigation of suggestions that the post-cranial skeleton had been replaced at some stage after excavation. The overlying branches were investigated to gain insight into the sequence of burial events and mound formation. The outcome of the dendrochronological study (discussed below) led to the decision to obtain a further six radiocarbon dates on evenly spaced tree ring samples from the coffin lid to allow detailed matching of the radiocarbon results with the calibration curve to produce a more precise date.

Whilst radiocarbon dates for the pommel of the dagger and the bone pin would have been archaeologically interesting, the materials were considered too valuable for sampling. The animal bones were not dated, and the animal skin cloak was also rejected as its preparation and conservation procedures were unknown and might have affected the quality of the date obtained.

Dendrochronology

Given the excellent preservation of the oak coffin lid, the clearly defined tree rings and the archaeological interest in the relationship between the felling of the tree and its use as a coffin, dendrochronological dating was an obvious

Fig. 7.1 Sampling the coffin lid for dendrochronological study.

approach. As the bark and sapwood were well preserved, it had the potential to provide a date to within a year for the felling of the tree (Baillie 1995). Sampling proved challenging as the wood was too hard to cut with a coring tool, but the bark was not sufficiently well attached to allow drilling. Therefore it was necessary to saw two sections from the lid, one from the foot-end, near the carving (Fig. 7.1), to include the bark and outer rings, and one from the head-end, to give the longest sequence possible. Such sampling was obtrusive, but the former was taken at a point where the coffin had had a section removed in the 1860s to enable it to be displayed in an alcove in the then newly-constructed side wings of the museum (Janaway *et al.*, this volume; Melton *et al.* 2010, Fig. 2). The section from the head-end was concealed beneath a split in the coffin

(a consequence of the waterlogged wood drying out in the 19th century) and was pegged back on for the museum display (Janaway *et al.*, this volume). Dendrochronology of the overlying branches was not possible as the period of growth represented was too short.

From the two sections, a 173–year composite ring sequence was obtained (Fig. 7.2); 126 rings from the 'head' and 108 rings from the 'foot'. The relatively small number of rings for the size of the section suggests fast growth in a favourable environment (Tyers, *pers. comm.*). Unfortunately, it proved impossible to find a match that was strong enough to date the series independent of other evidence. A number of factors contribute to this outcome: the sequence is relatively short, is taken from a single tree, the changes in ring width are not pronounced, and there

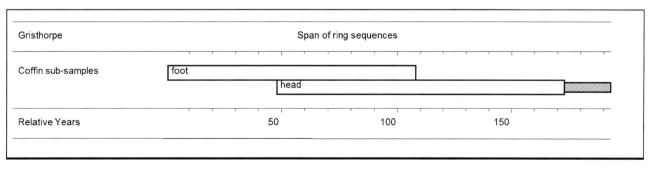

Fig. 7.2 The tree ring sequence obtained from the coffin lid. The shaded area represents the bark and sapwood (Tyers, *pers. comm.*).

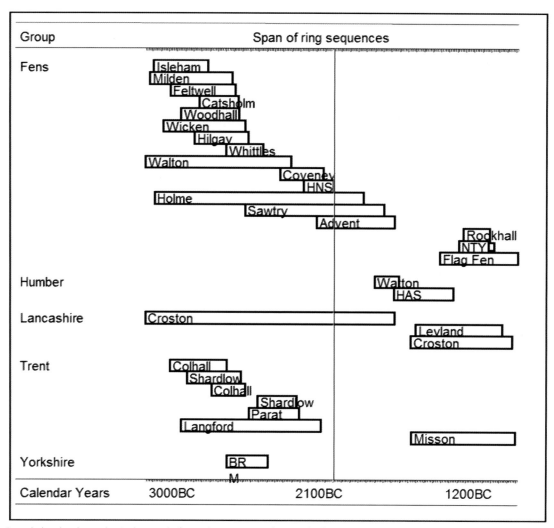

Fig. 7.3   Dated dendrochronological records from the region and period of interest (Tyers, *pers. comm.*). The red line represents the expected date of the tree ring sequence.

is a lack of dated dendrochronological records from the Early Bronze Age. Fig. 7.3 shows the existing records and the expected date for this sequence, with a clear lacuna in the period of interest. The outcome is disappointing from the perspective of the Gristhorpe Man Project; however, if the sequence can be dated independently, it can then supplement dendrochronological data in a period where such information is insubstantial, and thus contribute to the dating of other sites in future.

Radiocarbon dating

A radiocarbon date had been obtained for the branches overlying the coffin in the 1980s (Gris 0: Table 7.1). However, whilst this confirmed the material as being from the Bronze Age, the date of 2280–1680 cal BC was too broad to add much to the understanding of the burial. The improvements in

precision of dates and the reduction of sample size brought about by the development of AMS radiocarbon dating (Bronk Ramsey *et al.*, 2007a) mean that this method is likely to provide a much more precise date.

The initial AMS radiocarbon dating programme was carried out on samples from the tooth root dentine, femur and overlying oak branches, as discussed above. The second right molar was extracted from the jawbone with dental tools (Melton and Montgomery 2011, 24) and the lower half of the root removed for dating. A small plug of bone was removed, using a dental saw, from cortical bone in the mid-shaft of the right femur in an area without marks of muscle attachments. A small wood sample was obtained from one of the 'branches'. The sampled tooth was replaced with a replica and the site of the femoral sample was filled for display purposes. Radiocarbon dating was undertaken by the Oxford Radiocarbon Accelerator Unit. For details of chemical pre-treatment, target preparation and AMS

Table 7.1 Radiocarbon dates within the Gristhorpe Man Project. Radiocarbon determinations were calibrated using OxCal Version 4.1.7 (Bronk Ramsey, 2009), with the calibration data set of Reimer *et al.* (2009).

Our reference	Sample description	Material	Laboratory Number	C14 determination	Calibrated date (95% confidence)
Gris 0	Oak branch overlying coffin	Oak	HAR-4424	3590±100	2280BC–1680BC
Gris 1	Oak branch overlying coffin	Oak	OxA 16812	3375±31	1750BC–1530BC
Gris 2	Tooth root dentine	Dentine	OxA 16844	3671±32	2150BC–1940BC
Gris 3	Wiggle 1, wood from tree rings -39 to -30 (innermost)	Oak	OxA 17449	3806±30	2350BC–2130BC
Gris 4	Wiggle 2, wood from tree rings -9 to -0	Oak	OxA 17450	3697±28	2200BC–1980BC
Gris 5	Wiggle 3, wood from tree rings 21 to 30	Oak	OxA 17451	3759±29	2290BC–2040BC
Gris 6	Wiggle 4, wood from tree rings 51 to 60	Oak	OxA 17452	3674±30	2150BC–1950BC
Gris 7	Wiggle 5, wood from tree rings 81 to 90	Oak	OxA 17453	3704±31	2200BC–1980BC
Gris 8	Wiggle 6, wood from tree rings 111 to 120 (outermost)	Oak	OxA 17454	3669±30	2140BC–1950BC
Gris 9	Femur	Bone	OxA 19219	3743±32	2280BC–2030BC

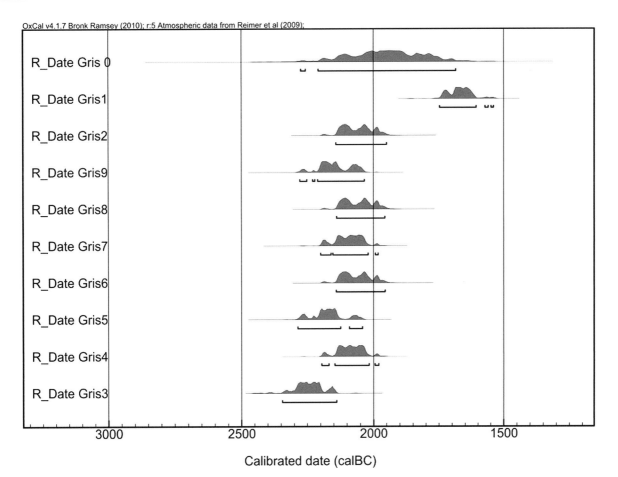

Fig. 7.4 Calibrated radiocarbon dates. See Table 7.1 for details.

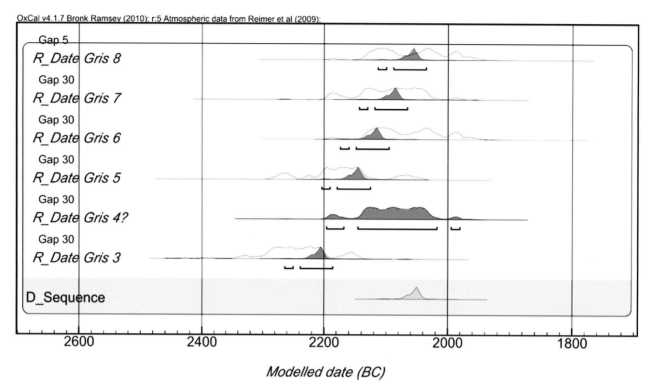

Modelled date (BC)

Fig. 7.5 Radiocarbon dates from the coffin lid following wiggle-matching as described. Gris 4 was omitted from the analysis as it showed poor agreement.

measurement see Bronk Ramsey *et al.* (2007 a and b). Radiocarbon determinations were calibrated using OxCal Version 4.1.7 (Bronk Ramsey, 2009), with the calibration data set of Reimer *et al.* (2009). Dates are quoted throughout at 95% confidence and summarised in Table 7.1.

Two complicating factors had to be borne in mind when dating the skeleton: first, whether the attempt in 1834 to consolidate the 'very rotten' bones by simmering them for eight hours in a 'thin solution of glue' (Williamson 1872, 7; Montgomery and Gledhill, this volume) had introduced animal collagen and, second, whether the skeleton is a 19th century composite, or replacement, with Indian ink (Ambers pers. comm.) used to 'touch up' substitute bones.

The dentine sample (Gris 2) dated to 2150–1940cal BC and the femoral sample (Gris 9) gave a date of 2280–2030 cal BC (Table 7.1; Fig 7.4). These clearly indicate that the skeleton is Early Bronze Age in date and refute the suggestion of later replacement, in part or in whole. In principle, the femoral date should reflect the last few decades of life (Hedges *et al.*, 2007), whereas the dentine should reflect 6 years of life between the ages of 9.5 and 15.5. (AlQahtani *et al.* 2010; Beaumont *et al.* 2013). However, the precision of the dates is insufficient to draw any detailed conclusions about the age-at-death of the individual from the radiocarbon dates. As the two

radiocarbon determinations date the same event, within the precision available, they can be combined within OxCal to give a single range of 2200–2020 cal BC for the death of Gristhorpe Man.

The oak branch overlying the coffin (Gris 1) dated to 1750–1530 cal BC, a somewhat surprising result, given the date of the skeleton. This date falls partially within the wide range obtained when these branches were first radiocarbon dated (Gris 0) but gives a much more precise, and intriguing, date.

Following the inconclusive results of the dendro-chronological study, further radiocarbon samples were taken from the sections cut for that investigation (Gris 3–8). These were obtained by carefully cutting material covering ten years of growth with an interval of 20 years between each sample, thus providing six samples from the exterior of the tree, over a known period of 170 years. The radiocarbon determinations obtained could then be 'wiggle- matched' with the radiocarbon calibration curve of Reimer *et al.* (2009), following the method of Bronk Ramsey *et al.* (2001), to obtain a much more precise calibrated date (Table 7. 1; Fig 7.5). This not only indicates that the date of felling to be 2110–2030 cal BC, but an additional benefit is that the tree-ring sequence from the coffin can now be incorporated into the dated dendrochronological records for the region.

Discussion

The combined scientific dating evidence allows a sequence of events to be proposed. The tree for the coffin was felled between 2110 and 2030 cal BC, and Gristhorpe Man died between 2200 and 2020 cal BC. The overlap between dates allows for these to be contemporary events, or for the tree to have been felled up to 90 years prior to his death. The overlying oak branches were cut between 1750 and 1530 cal BC, meaning that they cannot be contemporary with the death of Gristhorpe Man, and suggest that the branches were laid over the coffin at least 270 years after his death and possibly up to 670 years later.

The dating evidence confirms Gristhorpe Man as being of an Early Bronze Age date, with no evidence for the skeleton being a fake or of contamination resulting from the conservation treatment. The combination of dendrochronology and AMS radiocarbon dating has allowed this project to date the burial to a much earlier period and with a precision unforeseen by Williamson (or archaeologists in the 1980s!), raising intriguing questions about its parallels elsewhere (Parker Pearson *et al.*, this volume) and the construction of the monument (Melton & Russ, this volume).

Acknowledgements
The radiocarbon dates for the project were generously funded by a grant from the NERC / AHRC Oxford Accelerator Radiocarbon Dating Service. Janet Ambers (British Museum Conservation Laboratory) provided information on the possible preparation of the skeleton in the 19th century. Ian Tyers conducted the dendrochronological dating.

References

AlQahtani, S. J., Hector, M. P. and Liversidge H. M., (2010) Brief communication: The London atlas of human tooth development and eruption. *American Journal of Physical Anthropology* 142, 481–490.

Baillie, M. G. L., (1995) *A slice through time: dendrochronology and precision dating*. London.

Beaumont, J., Gledhill, A. R., Lee-Thorp, J. and Montgomery, J., (2013) Childhood diet: a closer examination of the evidence from dental tissues using stable isotope analysis of incremental human dentine. *Archaeometry* 55, 277–295.

Bronk Ramsey, C. (2009) Bayesian analysis of radiocarbon dates. *Radiocarbon 51*, 337–360.

Bronk Ramsey, C., van der Plicht, J. and Weninger, B. (2001) 'Wiggle matching' radiocarbon dates. *Radiocarbon 43*, 381–389.

Bronk Ramsey, C., Higham, T. and Leach, P. (2007a) Towards high-precision AMS; progress and limitations. *Radiocarbon 46, 17–24.*

Bronk Ramsey, C., Higham, T., Bowles, A. and Hedges, R. (2007b) Improvements to the pretreatment of bone at Oxford. *Radiocarbon 46,* 155–163.

Hedges, R. E. M., Clement, J. G., Thomas, C. D. L. and O'Connell, T. C. (2007) Collagen turnover in the adult femoral mid-shaft: modelled from anthropogenic radiocarbon tracer measurements. *American Journal of Physical Anthropology* 133, 808–816.

Melton, N., Montgomery, J., Knüsel, C. J., Batt, C., Needham, S., Parker Pearson, M., Sheridan, A., Heron, C., Horsley, T., Schmidt, A., Evans, A., Carter, E., Edwards, H., Hargreaves, M., Janaway, R., Lynnerup, N., Northover, P., O'Connor, S., Ogden, A., Taylor, T., Wastling, V. and Wilson, A. (2010) Gristhorpe Man: an Early Bronze Age log-coffin burial scientifically defined. *Antiquity*, 84/325, 796–815.

Melton, N. and Montgomery, J. (2011) Gristhorpe Man. *Current Archaeology* 250, 20–27.

Reimer, P. J., Baillie, M. G. L., Bard, E., Bayliss, A., Beck, J. W., Blackwell, P. G., Bronk Ramsey, C., Buck, C. E., Burr, G. S., Edwards, R. L., Friedrich, M., Grootes, P. M., Guilderson, T. P., Hajdas, I., Heaton, T. J., Hogg, A. G., Hughen, K. A., Kaiser, K. F., Kromer, B., McCormac, F. G., Manning, S. W., Reimer, R. W., Richards, D. A., Southon, J. R., Talamo, S., Turney, C. S. M., van der Plicht, J. and Weyhenmeyer, C. E. (2009) IntCal09 and Marine09 radiocarbon age calibration curves, 0–50,000 years cal BP. *Radiocarbon 51*, 1111–1150.

Williamson, W. C. (1834) *Description of the Tumulus, lately opened at Gristhorpe, near Scarborough*. Scarborough, C. R. Todd.

Williamson, W. C. (1872) *Description of the Tumulus opened at Gristhorpe, near Scarborough*. Scarborough, S. W. Theakston.

The Skeleton

8

THE PHYSICAL ANALYSIS OF GRISTHORPE MAN: A BRONZE AGE OSTEOBIOGRAPHY

Christopher J. Knüsel, Vaughan Wastling, Alan R. Ogden, and Niels Lynnerup

Completeness

The completeness of the skeleton is one of the most striking features of the burial. The anatomically wired individual is missing only three distal phalanges from the hands- right digit two and left digits one and two- as well as the right trapezoid. In addition to the right pedal intermediate phalanx from the third ray (although the proximal phalanx from digit three has been drilled to receive a wire, which may suggest that the intermediate phalanx has been lost since recovery of the Man in 1834) distal phalanges from rays two, three, four, and five are missing from the right foot, while the intermediate and distal phalanges from rays four and five, as well as the distal phalanges from rays two and three, are missing from the left foot. There is no hyoid bone, but ossified thyroid cartilage is present, as are ossified tracheal cartilage rings that were previously considered to be *'fragments of a ring...of horn...most probably used for fastening a light scarf over the shoulder'* (Williamson 1834, 9). Left ribs 6 and 8 were swapped in the wiring of the skeleton. Both proximal fibulae have sustained post-mortem damage, leaving gaps in their lengths, but all other bones are complete. In order to establish the social identity of the Gristhorpe remains, an analysis of them was undertaken to establish sex, age-at-death, stature, relative date, and health status.

Sex Determination
Thirty-four non-metric sex indicators of the pelvis (Fig. 8.1) and skull (cranium and mandible) (Fig. 8.2), the most

sexually dimorphic elements of the human skeleton, leave little doubt that Gristhorpe Man was male (Wastling 2006, see Appendix 8.1).

Age-at-Death Determination
In his original report of 1834, Williamson assessed the skeleton as 'advanced in years' (p. 8), based on the teeth being 'much worn and flattened by mastication' and due to the extent of cartilaginous ossification present in the sternum. These features do suggest an older age-at-death, an assessment supported using more recent methods. Because the relevant surfaces had been so tightly wired together so as to obscure the auricular surface and pubic

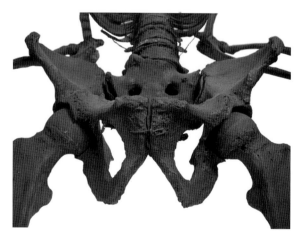

Fig. 8.1 The bony pelvis of Gristhorpe Man, indicating the v-shaped pelvic outlet and *os pubis* morphology characteristic of males.

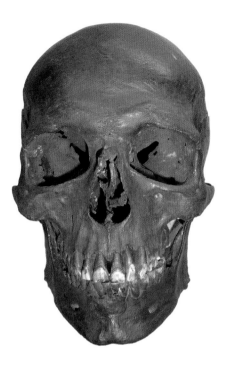

Fig. 8.2 The cranium and mandible of Gristhorpe Man, which demonstrates superciliary ridge development, rectangular orbits, and receding frontal of the cranium and gonial flare and double mental tubercle of the mandible consistent with male skeletal secondary sexual characteristics.

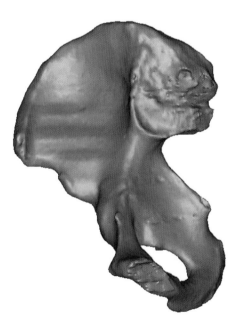

Fig. 8.3 Ct three-dimensional reconstructed image of the right *os coxae*, which shows some of the age-related detail of the *os pubis* and the auricular surface.

symphysis, age-at-death determination techniques were impossible to apply in initial assessments (see Appendix 8.2). Ct images of these surfaces were created, and these permit assessment of some age-related patterning, especially of the auricular surface (Fig. 8.3). Although these images are not as clear as the actual surfaces, they do permit observations of an irregular rim around the auricular surface that is very faint posteriorly and much more definite anteriorly, considerable retro-auricular activity, and marked apical activity. The surface has an uneven, rugose appearance that may be attributable to areas of densification. These features would suggest an older age-at-death, perhaps phase 7 or 8 of the Lovejoy *et al.* (1985) age-at-death classification system, which would equate to an age-at-death of over 50 or as much perhaps 60 plus years. This estimate is in keeping with that obtained for the pubic symphysis. Although the relative surface appearance of the face cannot be judged from the ct image (Fig. 8.3), the presence of a depressed symphyseal face and an oval, but discontinuous, crenulated and eroded symphyseal rim with evidence for ossific nodules suggests that phase 6 of the Suchey-Brooks method compares best with this appearance. This provides a range of 34–86 years of age-at-death with a mean of 61.2 (Brooks and Suchey 1990).

Three additional standard age-at-death determination methods could be employed: ectocranial suture closure (Meindl and Lovejoy 1985), sternal rib end (Işcan and Loth 1986), and tooth wear (Brothwell 1981). The cranial suture closure estimates provide a mean age of 45.2 years and 56.2 years for the vault sites and anterior-lateral methods, respectively. The sternal rib end estimate is phase 7, 59–71 years. While the tooth wear estimate, a feature so heavily relied upon by Williamson and his colleagues in the 19th century, provided a range of 25–35 years of age at death for the lower mandibular molars (Fig. 8.4), the more extreme wear of the maxillary first molars would suggest a much older age-at-death (Fig. 8.5), the left first molar of 45+ years of age, with the opposite first molar suggesting an age-at-death of 33–45 years (based on Brothwell 1981). Taken together, the three techniques place this individual in at least an 'Old Middle Adult' age category, 36 to 45 years of age-at-death and likely over 50 years of age at death. The relative lack of dental wear (but more extreme than that found in modern Western populations) may suggest the consumption of a refined diet, but the advanced degree of periodontal disease, especially indicated by porosity and recession of the alveolar margin of the distal-most molars, together with degenerative changes in the vertebral column and presence of extra-vertebral enthesophytes (see below), are suggestive of advanced age (Rogers *et al.* 1997, 85). This assessment of age-at-death is similar to that reported in the 1830's assessment, although that

Fig. 8.4 A deep carious lesion is visible on the occlusal surface of the left mandibular second molar. This lesion may have been responsible for the loss of the left third molar some time before death. The plug from the Victorian reconstruction holding the anterior incisors in place is visible beneath the roots of the anterior incisors.

was based more on anecdote than the population-based and contemporary and diachronic comparisons afforded modern researchers. Gristhorpe Man was an older adult.

Metrical Analysis

A list of cranial and infra-cranial measurements can be found in Appendix 8.3; these are discussed below.

Stature and Body Proportions

In 1834 Williamson considered that Gristhorpe Man had been 'not less than six feet and three or four inches' (Williamson 1834, 15). No calculation was applied, and this appears to have been a visual assessment only. In his revised paper of 1872, Williamson used a formula based on the femur being estimated at a 27.5 to 100 ratio of the height of an individual (Williamson 1872, 12). The Gristhorpe femora measured 19.5 inches and, using that ratio, provided a total height of 5′ 11″.

Using more recent stature regression equations (Trotter and Gleser 1952, 1958; Trotter 1970, 71–83), the combined left femur and tibia provide an estimate of 181.2 ± 2.99 cm, which accords well with Williamson's observation of 'about six feet in height'. Another method of estimating

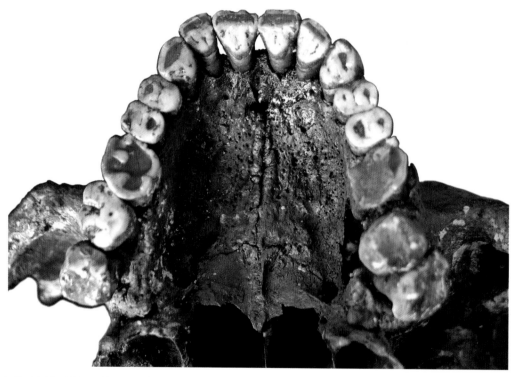

Fig. 8.5 The helicoidal (or 'ribbon-like' wear, from more extreme labial wear in the anterior dentition to greater lingual wear on the posterior dentition) wear of the maxillary dentition. The aperture indicative of a pathological process is visible in this palatal view at the posterior of the left side dentition (on the right).

Table 8.1 Reconstructed statue estimates from Bronze Age adult males buried singly in barrows or cists. Stature was reconstructed from femoral measurements (after equations in Trotter 1970, 71–83, unless otherwise stated).

Crania Britannica/ Other Reference	Location	Femoral Length		Stature		Ref.	Notes
		Inches*	mm	cm	Imperial		
V	Kinaldie, Aberdeenshire. Cist	18.5		173.25	5′8″	1	
XII	Arras, E. Yorks. Barrow	19		176.27	5′10″	1	
XIV	Wetton Hill, Staffs. Barrow	18		170.22	5′7″	1	
XVII	Ballidon Moor, Derbyshire, Barrow	18.6		173.84	5′8″	1	
XVIII	Parsley Hill, Derbyshire, Barrow	18.3		172.03	5′8″	1	
XIX	Hitter Hill, Derbyshire, Barrow	19		176.27	5′10″	1	
XX	Hay Top Derbyshire, Barrow	18.7		174.46	5′9″	1	
XXI	Green Lowe, Derbyshire	19.2		177.48	5′10″	1	
XXII	End Lowe, Derbyshire. Barrow	18.8		175.05	5′9″	1	
XXIII	Kennet Hill, N. Wilts. Barrow	20.5		185.34	6′1″	1	
XXX	Morgan's Hill, Wilts. Barrow	19.5		179.29	5′11″	1	
XXXI	Roundway Hill, Wilts. Barrow	20.5		185.34	6′1″	1	
XVI	Gratton Hill, Staffs. Barrow	19.2		177.48	5′10″	2	
XIX	Castern, Staffs. Barrow	19.2		177.48	5′10″	2	
XXI	Ramscroft, Staffs. Barrow	19.7		180.50	5′11″	2	
XXVI	Galley Lowe, Derbyshire. Barrow	19.5		179.29	5′11″	2	
XXXIII	Rolley Lowe, Derbyshire. Barrow	19.7		180.50	5′11″	2	
XXXIV	New Inns, Derbyshire. Barrow	18		170.22	5′7″	2	
XXXV	Gotham, Derbyshire. Barrow	18.5		173.25	5′8″	2	
XXXVI	Bostern, Derbyshire. Barrow	17		164.18	5′5″	2	
XXXVII	Shuttlestone, Derbyshire. Barrow	18.7		174.46	5′9″	2	
XLII	Monsal Dale, Derbyshire. Barrow	18		170.22	5′7″	2	
XLIII	Monsal Dale, Derbyshire. Barrow	18.6		173.84	5′8″	2	
XIV	Monsal Dale, Derbyshire. Barrow	17.7		168.41	5′7″	2	
XLVI	Wagon Lowe, Derbyshire. Barrow	18		170.22	5′7″	2	
XLVIII	Haddon Field, Derbyshire. Barrow	18.5		173.25	5′8″	2	
Bush Barrow	Normanton, Wilts.	20		182.30	6′	7	
Burial 1291 ('Archer')	Amesbury, Wilts.		464	174.00	5′9″	3	femur + fibula
Burial 1238 ('Companion')	Amesbury, Wilts.		485	178.00	5′10″	3	femur only
Grave 2500 (re-deposited 'Bowman')	Boscombe, Wilts.		479	176.00	5′10″	3	femur + tibia
Stonehenge Ditch	Stonehenge, Wilts.		472	175.61	5′10″	4	calculated from raw data
Chilbolton Burial	Chilbolton, Hants.		absent	170.00	5′7″	5	
Amesbury G.71 (Burial 85)	Amesbury, Wilts.		415	161.57	5′4″	6	
Amesbury G.71 (Burial 158)	Amesbury, Wilts.		468	173.53	5′8″	6	
	Mean			174.80			
	Standard Deviation			5.15			
	Maximum			185.34			
	Minimum			161.57			
	Median			174.46			

* obtained using an 'Imperial' tape measure in inches and tenths of inches, converted to cm by multiplying each measurement by 2.54
[1] Davis and Thurnam 1865, Table I, 240–241. [2] Davis and Thurnam 1865, Table II, 242–245. [3] McKinley, pers. comm. [4] Evans *et al.* 1984
[5] Russel 1988. [6] Powers and Brothwell in Christie 1967. [7] Ashbee 1960, 76.

Table 8.2 Reconstructed Bronze Age male stature estimates from Wetwang Slack, East Yorkshire, using femoral length from the left side (after Dawes n.d.), if present, and the right side, if not (after equations in Trotter 1970, 71–83).

	Wetwang Slack Bronze Age	Femoral Length		Tibial Length		Stature	
		right	left	right	left	cm	Imperial
1	VI. Gr V, TIII, Sec M (WS4)		467			172.6	5′8″
2	VII. Gr VI, Sec M + R (WS4)	503		395		181.1	5′11″
3	EJ. 201 (695/550) (WS6)	450			361	168.5	5′7″
4	WW DH WW88 (WS9)	451	454	359		169.5	5′7″
5	DH. WA77 277.5/133 (WS10)		453			169.2	5′7″
6	AJ/AR WG5 (WS12)	425	416	342	343	162.6	5′4″
7	AS WG6 (WS12)		448	381	376	168.0	5′6″
8	AS WG7 (WS12)	472	474			174.2	5′9″
9	AE WC2 (WS14)		469			173.0	5′9″
10	AB WY8 (WS14)	445	439		375	165.9	5′6″
	Mean					170.46	
	Standard Deviation					5.10	

stature, devised by Fully (1956) and considered to be the most accurate method of calculating height (Raxter *et al.* 2006, 374), is not commonly applied because it requires all of the individual bones that form the total height of an individual to be present. Due to the completeness of the Gristhorpe remains, it could be applied in this case, and this method rendered a stature of 178.27 cm (5′ 10″). Overall, then, Gristhorpe Man stood about 180 cm (6′) tall, or just a little under.

Based on a comparison with the statures of other Early Bronze Age barrow burials, whose occupants possess a mean height of 174.8 ± 5.15 cm, Gristhorpe Man is at the top end of the stature range (maximum 185.3 cm) and about a standard deviation (5.15) from the mean for the group (Table 8.1). He is also substantially taller, by over two standard deviations, when compared with a group of 10 individuals from Bronze Age Wetwang Slack, East Yorkshire, who possess a mean of 170.25 ± 5.1 cm (Table 8.2). Gristhorpe Man's surpassing height further substantiates the greater stature of males, largely interred singly, in Early Bronze Age burials (McKinley 2011).

Stature is a good measure of population and individual health and well-being from birth, with notable differences in attained adult stature in modern and historic populations due to differences in the quality of the social, economic, and political environment in which they were born and developed (Bogin 1999, 303ff., Steckel 1995, Floud *et al.* 1990, Floud 2002). Shorter stature is indicative of a poorer growth environment and lower socio-economic status, while those individuals of higher status are taller due to their environment being conducive to attaining the full genetic

potential for stature. This would indicate that Gristhorpe Man enjoyed a beneficial developmental environment. In fact, his stature is comparable to that of UK business executives, who average 177.0 cm (Eveleth and Tanner 1976, Appendix Table 5a, 285).

Body Mass

Body mass was estimated through the application of three formulae (Ruff *et al.*, 1991, McHenry, 1992, Grine *et al.*, 1995). These calculations rely on the maximum breadth of the femoral head because this load-bearing element is often preserved in archaeological contexts. Its dimensions are not influenced by activity level and muscular loading after physiological maturity has been attained (Auerbach and Ruff 2004, 331–334). These estimations, then, indicate body mass at skeletal maturity (*c.* 18 years). All three formulae produce similar results, despite the fact that the regression equation of Ruff *et al.* (1991) has been found to work best in the middle of a population's weight distribution, that of McHenry (1992) at the lighter end, while that of Grine *et al.* (1995) is better at the heavier end (Auerbach and Ruff 2004). The estimations thus include a middling weight estimate, a lighter estimation and a heavier estimation, 71.468 kg (Ruff *et al.* 1991), 69.811 kg (McHenry 1992), and 74.632 kg (Grine *et al.* 1995), respectively, which contributes a mean figure of 71.6 kg (about 168 lbs. or 11 stone). Application of the method based on stature and bi-iliac breadth (31.3 cm), which is considered to be more accurate, produced a reconstructed body mass estimate of between 78.64 and 79.57 kg (about 173 to 175 lbs). This figure is higher than those produced from femoral measurements, making Gristhorpe Man heavier, with a body mass index of 24.9. Note: the average of all the FH (femoral head) measurements (after Auerbach and Ruff's (2004) recommendations), were used in conjunction with the 178.27 stature measurement to calculate body mass, producing a figure of 24.9 (78.9/3.1684). The stature measurement of 181.2 provides a BMI of 25 (79.48/3.1684) (based on Auerbach and Ruff 2004).

Bilateral Asymmetry
Due to the human proclivity for using a preferred hand in a range of tasks- and the morphological alterations this preference makes to the bodies of those who strenuously engage in activities relying on the greater power and control of the dominant limb- limb lateralisation permits behavioural inferences (cf. Mays *et al.* 1999, Steele 2000, Blackburn and Knüsel 2006). Five measurements of the humerus and four of the clavicle were used to assess bilateral asymmetry (see Tables 8. 3 and 8.4) based on the following equation:

$$100\times \left[\frac{right - left}{(right + left) \div 2} \right]$$

The results show a right-sided asymmetry (Table 8.3). Robusticity indices (Bass 1995) calculated from computer-tomographic images used to obtain humeral length produced a figure of 19.35 for the right element and 18.18 for the left. Gristhorpe Man's right and left humeral robusticity indices exceed or are similar to the average noted for the late medieval Towton mass burial sample previously analysed by Knüsel (2000) for both right (mean= 17.8, range from 19.9–14.6) and left (mean= 18.39, range from 19.8–17.1) indices, although the values do not surpass the highest achieved in this robustly- built group. Based on the greater length and robusticity of the right humerus, Gristhorpe Man appears to have been right-handed. Based on a large sample of roughly 700 skeletonised individuals from the past, Storm (2009) reports that for measurements of elements of the humerus and pectoral girdle between 1 and 3% can be considered normal directional asymmetry. For the epicondylar breadth of the humerus the mean value is 1.0% (standard deviation 1.9%, 95% range from -2.8% to 4.7%) and for its the length, 1.0% (standard deviation 1.1%, range from -1.2% to 3.3%). Gristhorpe Man, then, with values of 6.2% and 1.8% for these measurements, respectively, is strongly lateralised (Fig. 8.6). Moreover, the population standard deviations for these measurements are, for humeral length, 1.1%, and for epicondylar breadth, 1.9%, which would indicate that Gristhorpe is not only strongly lateralised compared to this comparative population, but especially so for epicondylar breadth, being more than three standard deviations from the mean.

As can be observed in Table 8.4, the right clavicle is 4

Table 8.3 The measurements and values used to assess humeral bilateral asymmetry.

Humeral Measurement	Right (mm)	Left (mm)	% asymmetry
maximum transverse head diameter	49	48	2.62 %
maximum breadth of the greater tubercle	34	34	0 %
minimum circumference of the humeral shaft	65	60	8 %
epicondylar breadth	67	63	6.2 %
articular breadth	49	47	4.1 %
maximum length	336	330	1.8 %

Table 8.4 The measurements and values obtained to assess clavicular asymmetry.

Clavicle	Right (mm)	Left (mm)	% asymmetry
Maximum length	155	159	−2.55 %
Sagittal diameter at midshaft	14	13	7.41 %
Vertical diameter at midshaft	10	9.5	6.67%

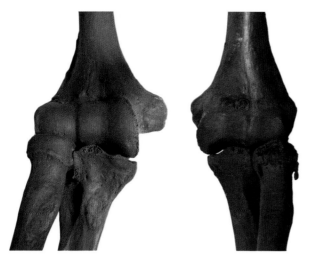

Fig. 8.6 The left and right distal humeri demonstrating strong lateralisation observed in the greater size of the right element (on the left) as opposed to that of the left side (on the right) (although not exactly to scale due to the wiring of the limbs, the difference in size is borne out by measurements).

mm shorter than the left, but with a somewhat more robust diaphysis. The right side demonstrates the restricted length known to occur on the dominant side as a result of the increased forces acting on the shoulder girdle of that side (Mays *et al.* 1999, 26). Based on measurements from over 600 individuals, Storm (2009) notes that the mean asymmetry for clavicular length is 1.2% with a standard deviation of 2.3%. Gristhorpe Man is, again, demonstrated to have been strongly lateralised, which indicates that he engaged in strenuous use of his upper limbs and preferentially the right one.

Craniometric Analysis
Previous research on cranial shape during the Neolithic period and Bronze Age suggests that the cranium changes from a dolichocranic or 'long-headed' shape that characterizes Neolithic populations to one that is more brachycranic or 'broad-headed' in the Bronze Age (Brothwell and Krzanowski 1974, Brodie 1992, Mays 2000). In light of the long-held, but incompletely understood importance of this phenomenon, cranial shape was assessed through the use of the cranial index, using the following formula from Bass (1995):

$$\frac{\text{maximum cranial breadth} \times 100}{\text{maximum cranial length}} = \frac{15.3 \times 100}{18.5} = 82.70$$

The result demonstrates Gristhorpe Man to be brachycranic, short or broad-headed, which covers the range 80.00–84.99 (Fig. 8.7). This result supports Brodie's (1992) contention that craniometric analysis separates Neolithic from Bronze Age cranial morphology, an interpretation in keeping

Fig. 8.7 The rounded (i.e. brachycranic) cranial vault of Gristhorpe Man is apparent in this *Norma verticalis* perspective. The hole suggests that the skeletal was prepared for hanging as an anatomical skeleton. The drilling of this hole may be the source of the metal inclusion visible on radiograph (inside the cranial vault) in Fig. 8.10.

with Brothwell's and Krzanowski's (1974) earlier analysis of cranial morphological change in British populations through time. Gristhorpe Man's cranial morphology is thus in keeping with his Bronze Age date. Using a series of measurements of the cranial vault, viscerocranium, and mandible, the FORDISC 3.0 (Ousley and Jantz 2005) computer package, which is used to determine the geographic affinity of an individual, identifies Gristhorpe Man to have been of European origin (posterior probability of 0.966), although he is not typical for any modern group (typicality scores are low, 0.000–0.005). Given the 4,000 years that separates this Bronze Age man from European-derived populations of more recent times, this result comes as no great surprise. It indicates that his particular constellation of morphlogical cranio-facial features is not found in the relatively more recent populations that make up the comparative database.

Palaeopathological Analysis
The dentition and dental conditions
The oblique molar cusp wear observed in Gristhorpe Man is similar to that found in other agricultural groups and differs from the uniformly flat wear observed in hunter-gatherers produced by the extensive lateral movements

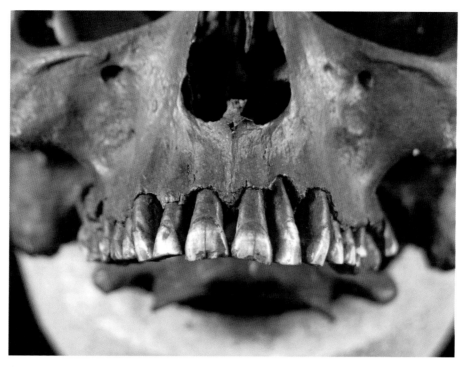

Fig. 8.8 Chipping of the central incisors. The vertical fissures visible on the labial surface are taphonomic features.

demanded by their coarse diet (Smith 1984). The type of helicoidal (or ribbon-like) wear noted is caused by the moderate side-to-side grinding movements, which is normal in humans and leads to the wear and eventual loss of the lingual cusps in the maxillary molars and the buccal cusps of the opposing mandibular molars (Richards and Brown 1986), a pattern most clearly observed in the maxillary first molars of Gristhorpe Man (Fig. 8.5). There is also chipping of the occlusal edges of the anterior maxillary incisors that may relate to the use of these teeth as tools in the manufacture of objects (cf. Wallace 1975) (Fig. 8.8). This could indicate that the teeth were used to prepare a range of materials. Wallace (1975) notes that in ethnographically recorded groups, the teeth are used to retouch stone tools, in stripping vegetable material for making ropes, and for thinning sinews. This type of activity produces the rounded wear seen in the anterior dentition of hunter-gatherers. The last of these could indicate use to produce bowstrings (cf. Webb 1991, 21–22), although there is no extant study to demonstrate the differential dental effects of these processes to date. Such wear may also be caused by grit in ingested food (Ogden pers. obs.). Bows, though, were certainly an apparently prominent component of the material culture of Bronze Age British groups, as indeed were stone tools, which are among the grave inclusions (see Sheridan *et al.*, this volume), as indeed was rope and other fibres, as attested in the later Danish Bronze Age oak coffin burials (Randsborg and Christensen 2006). Although

there is no circumstantial evidence for a bow (or for that matter sinews or rope) among the grave inclusions of Gristhorpe Man, the wear on the anterior incisors and the labial chipping may indicate that he engaged in such manufacturing activities. In addition to projectile points, there is ample evidence for bows in the Bronze Age in the form of forearm bracers, although when these are found, usually as grave inclusions, they often show no signs of wear attributable to their putative function (see Woodward *et al.* 2005, 43; 2006). Bow-use is evident as well, if anecdotally, in embedded projectile points, such as those identified in the remains of the young male found in the ditch at Stonehenge, dating to the Early Bronze Age (2170 ± 110 cal BC) (Evans *et al.* 1984).

Calculus, or mineralised plaque, was present on all teeth, and this had resulted in periodontal disease commencing around the maxillary molars, especially prominent on the right side dentition. A deep carious lesion is visible on the occlusal surface of the left mandibular second molar; a similar lesion may have been responsible for the loss of the left third molar some time before death (Fig. 8.4). Dental caries attests to the presence of cariogenic foodstuffs in the diet that could include carbohydrates from grain and fructose-bearing foods. There is also agenesis of the mandibular third molar on the right side, as confirmed from radiographic and ct-image analyses.

Abnormal destructive areas occur in the jaws indicative of dental pathologies, including a large opening in the

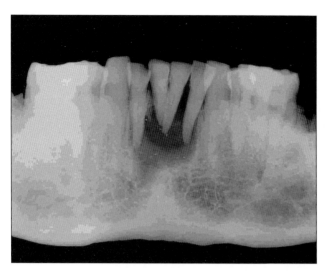

Fig. 8.9 A radiographic image of the anterior part of the mandible, showing a large radiolucent area with sclerotic margins, suggestive of granulomas that had merged and become cystic (Ogden 2008).

posterior maxilla on the left side, in the vicinity of the molars on that side (Fig. 8.5), and another in the anterior part of the mandible. All four mandibular incisors were dead but held in place by a plug of material (probably wax) that had been inserted into the opening in the mid-line of the mandible when the skeleton was prepared, presumably for display purposes (Fig. 8.4). Radiography and ct-imaging of this gap reveal a rounded sclerotic margin around

the opening indicative of bony reaction from an *in vivo* pathological process (Fig. 8.9). This probably resulted from trauma to the anterior incisors that damaged the nerve and blood supply of the roots of these teeth, leaving them held in the alveolar process by soft tissue (e.g. a granuloma) only. This would seem to indicate that these teeth were likely found loose. The posterior maxillary opening shows a well-demarcated, rounded margin that separates this area from the surrounding palatal bone on the radiograph (Fig. 8.10). The rounded margin indicates that this was an *in vivo* process, distinct from the uneven, sharp, and undulating margins of a more recent (i.e. post-mortem) break. A ct three-dimensional transverse section of the maxillary antra demonstrates that the left one is enlarged compared to the right (Figs. 8.11 and 8.12). This appearance is consistent with the presence of a large peri-apical cyst, the pressure from which caused bone resorption around the first and second molars. These two teeth appear to have been the origin of this lesion and were no longer vital through death of their pulp.

Spina bifida occulta

The neural arches of the sacrum are unfused; sacral vertebra 1 is cleft, sacral vertebra 2 is partially fused, while sacral vertebrae 3, 4, and 5 are bifurcated (Fig. 8.13). In sharp contrast, the more severe condition of *spina bifida cystica*, in which the spinal cord may protrude and sustain damage resulting in lower limb paralysis, *spina bifida occulta*

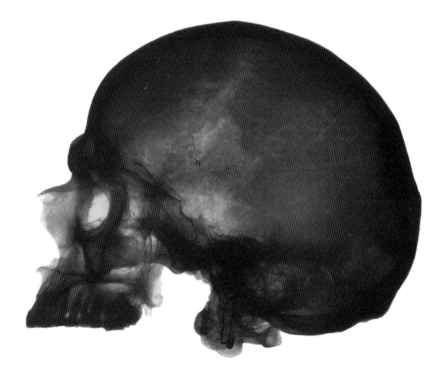

Fig. 8.10 Lateral radiographic image that shows a well-demarcated rounded lesion in the maxillary antrum. This view also shows a radiolucent patch in the parieto-temporal area where there is a radiating pattern of radiolucent streaks referred to as a 'sunray' pattern due to the presence of osseous spicules without sclerotic margins (near a U-shaped piece of metal (black on the image) from the anatomical preparation of the 19th century).

results from a neural arch defect. It would have had no obvious physical manifestations because the sacral cleft defects would have been covered and protected by strong fibrous tissue in life (Barnes 1994, 265). Gristhorpe Man would have been unaware of the condition. Today, a genetic predisposition linked to the development of such defects is triggered by an inadequate maternal diet, lacking in folic acid, selenium and, in particular, zinc (Barnes 1994, 41).

Degenerative changes
Degenerative changes are visible throughout the skeleton, the most prominent of which involve the vertebral column. Marginal osteophytic lipping (spondylosis) was present antero-laterally on the inferior and superior edges of all the vertebral bodies, from lumbar vertebra 5 to thoracic vertebra 1, being less pronounced in the more superior part of the column. A prominent syndesmophyte, 2 cm by 3cm wide, is present on the right lateral side of the first sacral vertebra (Fig. 8.14). Degeneration of the vertebral column is a common occurrence with ageing (Rogers and Waldron 1995; Knüsel *et al.* 1997) that can be exacerbated by activity-related trauma. These vertebral degenerative processes produced a slight scoliosis of the vertebral column to the left, most visible in the thoracic region of the column (Fig. 8.15). In addition to the marginal osteophytic lipping of the vertebral column (Fig. 8.15), enthesophytes are present on the *ossa coxae*, notably on the lateral rim of the left obturator foramen, an alteration of the tendon for *M. obturator internus*, a lateral rotator and abductor of the thigh in extension and flexion of the hip, respectively (Fig. 8.16). This unilateral expression stands in contrast to larger bilateral enthesophytes located in the vicinity of the attachment of the adductor muscles of the thigh, along the superior portions of the *linea aspera* of both femora (Fig. 8.17). Enthesophytes are present at the insertion of the Achilles tendons on the calcanei, and there is slight enthesophytic formation on the spinous processes of the vertebrae, the attachment of the supra-spinous ligaments. The formation of these ossified structures can be viewed as accommodating movement, the body's attempt to stabilize a joint following stress or injury, with bone formers potentially having a better outcome than non-bone formers (Rogers *et al.* 1997). They are an age-related phenomenon in that these bony changes occur in older individuals and more often in males than females (Molnar 2006, Villotte 2009). Villotte (2009) notes that they occur four times more frequently in older adults than in younger adults in an archaeological population sample and in a known-age group sample in those over 50 years of age.

The cranium
During the course of a full-body ct-scan of Gristhrope Man, scout images revealed an area of depleted cranial vault thickness on the left side. Subsequent radiographs of the vault identified a radiolucent patch, 25 to 30 mm in extent, in the anterior third of the left parieto-temporal area (Fig. 8.10). A series of small pores in this area- at first thought to be taphonomic in origin- are visible ectocranially in the same area (Fig. 8.18). The co-occurrence of these in the same area suggests that either the vault was perforated by a lesion in places or the thinning of the vault made it susceptible to post-depositional perforations, or both. Further endocranial inspection using an endoscope revealed a space-occupying, expansile lesion created by bone resorption that exposes the underlying diploïc bone. Three-dimensional ct-imaging shows this to be a space-occupying lesion with geographic (irregular) margins (Fig. 8.19). A starch-based three-dimensional anatomically accurate reconstruction made from these images permits detailed description of this lesion that aids differential diagnosis of it (Fig. 8.20). These clearly reveal that the lesion is restricted to an area of the temporal and largely affects the inner table and diploë layer. It is thus a focal, largely non-perforating, space-occupying osteolytic lesion displaying geographic (i.e. irregular), rounded margins. It disrupts the middle meningeal grooves for the middle meningeal arteries, which appear to run into the lesion. At its centre the lesion is characterised by fused, rounded, finger-like projections of bone. Taken together, these features suggest the presence of an irregularly shaped intra-cranial soft tissue mass.

The differential diagnosis of this lesion includes neoplastic conditions such as hemangioma (developed from epithelial cells that line the blood vessels in the brain), meningioma (developed from the membranous covering of the brain), glioma (developed from brain nerve cells), neuroma (developed from nerves entering the brain) or a secondary metastatic tumour (from a tumour located elsewhere in the body). In light of the lesion's close relationship to the meningeal grooves that carry the arterial supply of the brain's membranous covering (i.e. the *dura mater*) an infectious origin, either specific, as in tuberculosis, or from a non-specific source- bacteria such as staphylococcus, streptococcus, or a variety of others that cannot be distinguished from one another in the absence of soft tissue biopsy- must be considered.

Sub-dural intra-cranial abscesses, like those associated with tuberculous infection, can also spread via the bloodstream (i.e. hematogenously) from infection of the paranasal sinuses, mastoid processes, or middle ear, as well as from the skin, lungs, or dentition; some 60% of sufferers possess a pre-disposing infective condition, diabetes, or an immuno-compromised state. The most common locations of intra-cranial abscesses are the frontal and temporal lobes of the brain (Whitfield 2005), a location consistent with the location of the lesion in Gristhorpe Man. Today, such

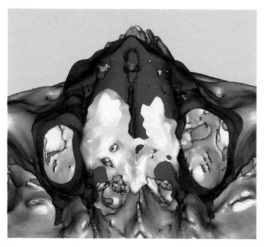

Fig. 8.11 A three-dimensional CT reconstruction showing the enlarged left maxillary antrum (on the right) indicative of an *in vivo* pathological process (inferior view).

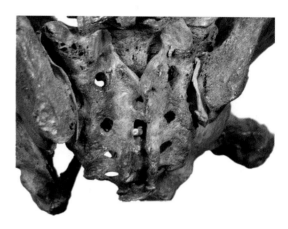

Fig. 8.13 The unfused neural arches of the sacrum; sacral vertebra 1 is cleft, sacral vertebra 2 is partially fused, while sacral vertebrae 3, 4, and 5 are bifurcated.

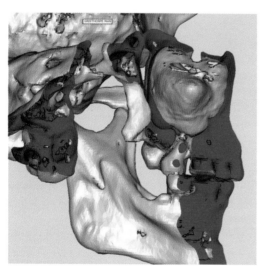

Fig. 8.12 A lateral three-dimensional CT reconstruction of the expanded left maxillary antrum.

Fig. 8.14 A prominent syndesmophyte, 2cm by 3cm wide, present on the right lateral side of the first sacral vertebra.

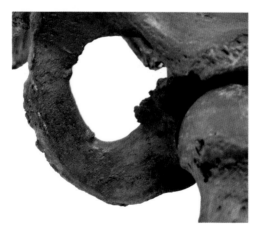

Fig. 8.16 Enthesophytes present on lateral rim of the left obturator foramen of the left *os coxae*, an alteration of the tendon for *M. obturator internus*, a lateral rotator of the thigh.

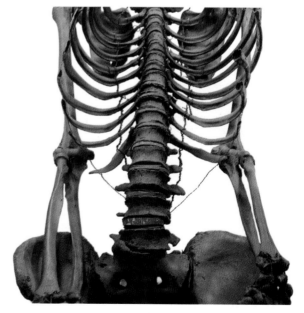

Fig. 8.15 Marginal osteophytes of the vertebral column of Gristhorpe Man. The slight scoliosis to the left is visible, most prominently in the thoracic region of the column.

Fig. 8.18 The 25 to 30 mm area of thinned bone and small pores in the anterior part of the left temporal.

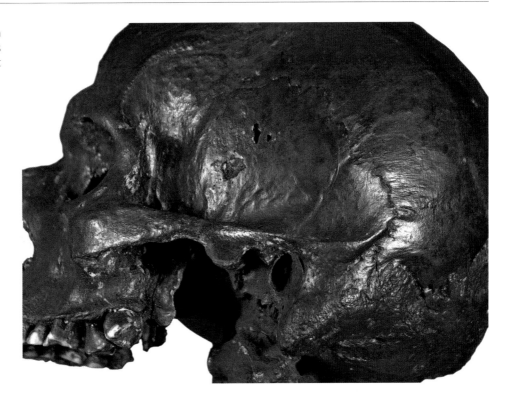

Fig. 8.17 (left) The rugose morphology of the left proximal femur with enthesophytes located in the attachment of the adductor muscles of the thigh, along the superior portions of the *linea aspera*. There is also a third trochanter and medio-lateral expansion lateral to the cranial attachment of *M. gluteus maximus*. This occurs bilaterally.

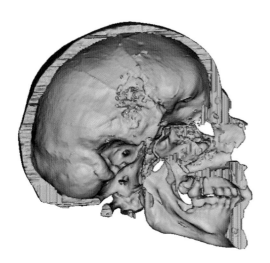

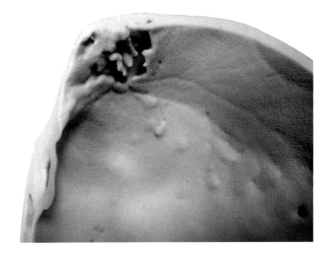

Fig. 8.19 A three-dimensional ct-image of the rounded margin, space-occupying lesion located endocranially in the left parieto-temporal region. Also visible is the expanded maxillary antrum.

Fig. 8.20 A starch reconstruction made from three-dimensional ct-scans of the left temporal area of the cranial vault. A focal, largely non-perforating, space-occupying lytic lesion with geographic and rounded margins affects the inner table and diploë layer. It disrupts the middle meningeal grooves for the middle meningeal arteries, which appear to run into the lesion. At its centre the lesion is characterised by fused, rounded, finger-like spicules of bone.

life-threatening conditions are treated with anti-biotics and drainage and, to avoid recurrent infection, surgical excision. Prior to the use of ct-scanning and the better visualisation such technology permits, mortality from such infections was as high as 40%, with 55% of individuals over 40 years of age succumbing (Alphen and Driessen 1976). These features are also consistent with the age-at-death of Gristhorpe Man. Both Whitfield (2006, 15) and Feldges et al. (1990) depict examples of such an infection in the maxillary antrum, similar in location to the cyst noted in Gristhorpe Man, but the possibility that the cranial lesion resulted from a subdural abscess from a disseminated dental infection is unlikely because such lesions usually produce a rounded, non-perforating osteolytic lesion, rather than the more irregular lesion present. Moreover, because these infections are subdural, they do not arise within the bones of the cranial vault as seems to be the case with the lesion noted in Gristhorpe Man. In addition, such abscesses most often derive from a chronic ear infection (Yang 1981), evidence for which is lacking in Gristhorpe Man. It seems, then, that an infectious origin is unlikely in this case.

Distinguishing amongst the different types of malignant tumours from their skeletal effects is difficult and secure diagnoses, even in the living, are based on biopsies performed after surgical excision of the tumour mass in most cases, but whether or not the lesion resulted from a malignant neoplasm can be addressed with more certainty due to the pattern of its effects. Radiographs and ct-scanning are important aids to this endeavour, especially when the endocranium is not easily accessed (due to the completeness of the cranial vault and wiring of the atlas to the base of the cranium), as in the current case. Malignant neoplasms are characterised by their ability to metastasise and, as a result, they are more often found in the infra-cranial skeleton (Cotran et al. 1989, 1334). In the absence of evidence for other tumour-like lesions in the rest of the skeleton, the localised expression of this lesion makes this unlikely to be a malignant neoplasm since malignant tumours are noted for their aggressive, bone-destroying and rapid development and spread (Jónsdóttir et al. 2003). Although this lesion has produced pores in the cranial vault, their size and lack of diffuse distribution (as assessed from radiographs) mitigates against a diagnosis of multiple myeloma (cf. Ortner 2003, 380–382), which develops from bone marrow. The lack of clusters of small pores and stellate, spiculated ('sunburst') lesions (cf. Aufderheide and Rodriquez-Martín 1998, 378) would tend to rule out metastatic carcinomas, as well as primary osteosarcomas.

Due to the localised nature of the lesion in Gristhorpe Man, restricted as it is to the parieto-temporal region, this would seem to be a slow-growing, indolent tumour. The resorption of the diploë and inner table of the cranial

vault, and only minimal perforation of the outer table would suggest that this tumour was not an invasive brain tumour but one with an origin in the diploë layer, an intra-osseous tumour. Today, such tumours are considered benign because they do not infiltrate the brain, and they can be excised surgically. However, their rapid growth, even if restricted, can cause destruction of surrounding normal tissues because of the pressure they exert on the dura mater and underlying arachnoid and pia mater (brain coverings) and, ultimately, the brain itself, as well as by their often highly vascularised nature (De Angelis et al. 2002: 5).

Although benign tumours like meningiomas may erode the inner table of the cranial vault, this type of cancer is most often characterised by hyperostosis (i.e. excessive new bone development) (Aufderheide and Rodriquez-Martín 1998, 251; De Angelis et al. 2002, 190; Ortner 2003, 515), the opposite of what is observed in Gristhorpe Man. Therefore, this most common form of tumour, the meningioma, seems to be unlikely in this case.

Another type of benign tumour, the hemangioma requires consideration because they can be intra-cranial, even if they are more often encountered on the skin. They consist of bundles of proliferating blood vessels. As noted above, these tumours develop from the epithelial cells lining blood vessels, and the proximity of the lesion to the meningeal grooves would be consistent with this origin. They typically involve the thin arteries of the leptomeninges (De Angelis et al. 2002, 208), the pia mater and arachnoid, the two innermost coverings of the brain, although they may occur anywhere in the central nervous system, including the cerebral hemispheres, spinal cord, optic nerve, and peripheral nerves, the most common primary tumour location in adults being the cerebellum (De Angelis et al. 2002, 208). They are rare tumours, accounting for just 0.2% of cranial tumours and 0.7% of all osseous neoplasms (Nasser et al. 2007). Although they normally develop as an expansion of the outer table of the cranial vault, they can occur as isolated tumours intracranially-that is, between the inner and outer tables of the cranial vault, and are thus termed an intraosseous cavernous hemangioma (Gottfried et al. 2004, Nasser et al. 2007). The lesions produced are osteolytic and have a 'honeycomb' internal structure (Paradowski et al. 2007, Suzuki et al. 2001), formed by lysis of the diploic trabeculae that leave only a few coarse trabeculae that traverse the lesion (Aufderheide and Rodriquez-Martin 1998, 384; Ortner 2003, 513). This morphology gives the lesion a 'sunray' appearance in tangential radiographs, without a sclerotic margin, and a honeycomb appearance in axial views (Suzuki et al. 2007). These descriptions accord with the features observed in Gristhorpe Man (see Figs. 8.10 and 8.19 and 8.20). They are slow-growing tumours that are more common in females than males by a three to one ratio (Suzuki et al. 2004). They have a peak age of incidence in the fourth or fifth decade of life but may occur at any age. Although they may appear anywhere in the cranium, most commonly they are found in the frontal, temporal, and parietal regions of the cranial vault, in that order (Gottfried *et al.* 2004). Both with regard to age, location, and appearance of the lesion, these traits seem to fit those observed in Gristhorpe Man. Although the cause of these lesions is poorly understood, they appear to be congenital in origin or related to trauma (Nasser *et al.* 2007). The occurrences of other traumatic lesions of the infra-cranial skeleton and dentition may provide some basis for support for a traumatic origin in this case, although this is only circumstantial at best.

Due to increased cranial pressure resulting from either infection or benign tumours, behavioural consequences for those suffering from such conditions are similar and may include headache, drowsiness, impaired consciousness, nausea and vomiting, as well as neurological deficits such as dysphasia (speech impairment), hemiplegia or hemiparesis (full or partial paralysis, respectively, of unilateral upper and lower limbs) and behavioural abnormalities, as well as seizures (De Angelis *et al.* 2003, Feldges *et al.* 1990, Whitfield 2005). These symptoms occur in benign intra-cranial tumours not because of direct effects on the brain, as would be found in glial (i.e. nerve cell) tumours, but due to their compression of the brain and the increased cranial pressure their expanding presence exerts. They can, however, have no behavioural effects whatsoever, and their presence in such cases would go unnoticed.

The parietal and anterior temporal location of the lesion would suggest that the functions of the left hemisphere and, most immediately, the temporal lobe of the brain would have been affected by the growth of the tissue mass. The left hemisphere of the brain is responsible for verbal ability, linguistic description, mathematical, sequential (as in sequential body movements and in speech syntax), and analytical skills (Standring 2005, 415–417). Given this wide range of capacities, it is no wonder that this hemisphere is strongly linked to what one identifies as consciousness. In addition to its primary auditory role, the temporal lobe of the brain is connected with somatosensory (control of the contralateral side of the body, i.e. producing hemiparesis in those affected) and visual cortical association pathways (Standring 2004, 399–402). The cortex of the upper part of the temporal lobe serves to process sound and the parietal and temporal areas are important association areas; they integrate information gathered by the senses (Rilling 2008). The affected area lies close to Broca's area, the left posterior inferior part of the frontal lobe, which is important in the production of language. Deficits in this area contribute to aphasia, the inability to express oneself; speech is difficult to initiate, becomes disjointed, and intonation is lost. In addition, the lateral surface of the anterior temporal lobe

also contains a visual cortex associated with recalling the names of objects. This lobe also encompasses Wernicke's area, located on the left posterior superior temporal gyrus (the name for a ridge on the cortical surface of the brain), which is linked to language comprehension (Rilling 2008). Although both hemispheres of the brain are required in the production and understanding of language, the left lobe is dominant in that it is responsible for speech output and the flow of language information goes predominantly through this side of the brain, while the right is linked more specifically to language comprehension (Cook 2002). It seems that Gristhorpe Man may have had difficulties producing and comprehending speech, had deficits in visual perception, and lack of control of the right side of his body prior to his death. The presence of this lesion, then, could have profoundly affected his behaviour towards the end of his life and if, as argued here, he occupied an elite leadership role, his lapsing ability to communicate may have severely affected the social interactions upon which his position depended.

Non-metric traits

A full record of the non-metric traits present in Gristhorpe Man can be found in Appendix 8.4. Due to the lack of a suitably large comparative sample for the Bronze Age to compare with the trait expressions in Gristhorpe Man, only those that might relate more directly to behaviour will be discussed here. In addition to the agenesis of the right third molar of Gristhorpe Man, third trochanters are present on the posterior aspect of the proximal ends of the femora, together with hypotrochanteric fossae and a medio-lateral broadening of the proximal femoral shafts (Fig. 8.21). This development suggests hypertrophy of *M. gluteus maximus,* which takes its attachment from the gluteal tuberosity, and when strongly developed is called a third trochanter (Platzer 1999, 192). *M. gluteus maximus* originates on the posterior of the sacrum, and has two parts that perform different functions. The superior part of the muscle abducts and laterally rotates the thigh, while the inferior part extends and laterally rotates the thigh, extends the trunk and assists in adduction of the thigh. It is noteworthy that this muscle is not used in normal walking, but is active in forceful extension, such as rising from a seated position, running or climbing up an incline. The presence of increased rugosity in this area indicates strenuous use of and/or age-related damage to these muscles. The enthesophytes present along the *linea aspera,* where the adductor muscles insert, indicate similar aetiologies (Figs. 8.17 and 8.21). The largest muscle, *M. adductor magnus,* adducts and extends the thigh, while *M. adductor longus* adducts and flexes the thigh, with *M. adductor brevis* adducting the thigh and assisting with

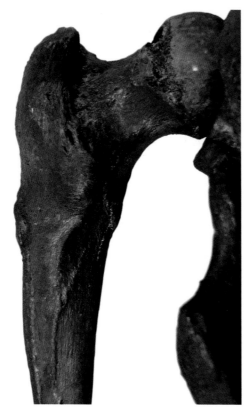

Fig. 8.21 The third trochanter of the left femur.

flexion; all assist with medial rotation. These alterations have previously been associated with hip extension and stabilization of the hip in the maintenance of an upright posture in unstable conditions (Capasso *et al.* 1999: 104). These enthesopathies tend to occur most frequently during the physical exertion associated with sport (Niepel and Sit'aj 1979), although their link to specific behaviours and strenuous use remains unclear (Zumwalt 2006).

These muscles are not involved in normal walking. Rogers *et al.* (1997) established that there are four groups of sites strongly associated with each other in the formation of osteophytes and enthesophytes. In one group are the two calcaneal sites and in another the two femoral trochanters and the tibial tubercle, indicating that biomechanical factors may lie behind such groupings (Rogers *et al.* 1997). This supports the suggestion that their presence in the Gristhorpe remains may be due to activity-related change that may also have been age-related, and given the sites of the changes in Gristhorpe Man, notably the hips and lower limbs, some powerful movement in that area can be envisioned.

Trauma

There are two well-healed rib fractures of the left side of the rib cage. The first is a transverse fracture located on

rib 6, 20 mm from the sternal end (Fig. 8.22). The second is an oblique fracture on rib 9, 60 mm from the vertebral end (Fig. 8.23). Both are well healed with no resulting malalignment and appositional displacement and likely occurred many years before death. Ribs cannot be splinted effectively, and no treatment is possible for rib fractures beyond binding the rib cage to restrict movement; most rib fractures heal without complication (Aufderheide *et al.* 1998, 25) and can be treated conservatively as 'a bad bruise' (Dandy 1993, 161).

The presence of these fractures on the same side of the body makes the possibility of a single event causing both seem conceivable, yet their differing positions on the ribs makes this assessment less obviously clear. The oblique fracture of rib 9, near the vertebral end (i.e. towards the vertebral column), would suggest a compressive force of the rib cage coming from a force directed from the posterior (cf Galloway 1999, 107, DiMaio and DiMaio 2001: 117–118), while the more sternal position of the transverse fracture of rib 6 would suggest a direct force to the chest. If the two occurred together, which may be a possibility in that both were well healed at death, then a lateral force (i.e. producing lateral compaction) to the left side of the rib cage may be indicated. Both could well have been produced at the same time (cf. Galloway 1999, DiMaio and DiMaio 2001: 118).

Fig. 8.22 A well-healed transverse fracture of rib 6, located 20 mm from the sternal end.

Fig. 8.23 A second well-healed oblique fracture of rib 9, located 60 mm from the vertebral end.

Ankylosis of cervical vertebrae

Cervical vertebrae 2 and 3 are ankylosed (i.e. fused) through the left articular facets (Fig. 8.24). Williamson (1834, 8) thought this condition could have been an indicator of advanced age-at-death, but he knew it could also possibly be the result of disease. Joint ankylosis is not a feature associated with osteoarthritis (Rogers *et al.* 1987, 2000), and is thus unlikely to be due to an age-related process. Furthermore, because the other cervical vertebrae show little degenerative change, in either their bodies or apophyseal joints, it seems highly improbable that this condition resulted from age-related degeneration. Ankylosis due to injury is known to occur (Aufderheide *et al.* 1998, 22), and this seems far more likely to have been the cause in this particular case. Given that the ankylosing is restricted to only two vertebrae, the resulting lack of flexibility would be insignificant, and probably pain-free.

The 'mistletoe berries'

Raman spectroscopic analysis of the 'mistletoe berries', previously considered to be part of the grave inclusions of the burial, demonstrates them to contain inorganic phosphates, which are not expected to be found in mistletoe, and degraded protein (Edwards *et al.* 2010, Edwards, this volume, Janaway et al., this volume). This chemical composition indicates that the 'berries' are likely to be renal stones. The absence of uric acid or urate crystals mitigates against these stones deriving from the urinary tract.

Urolithiasis, or urinary stone formation, consists of either urinary or bladder stones (lower tract) and renal stones (upper tract). Both types have previously been identified from palaeopathological studies of past populations (Steinbock, in Kiple 1999, 1091). In Britain today, the most common cause is hypercalciuria (i.e. excessive calcium in the urine) (Macpherson 1992, 319–320). This excess of calcium in the urine leads to renal stones that are more often associated with a diet high in protein that produces increased urinary phosphate. Urinary stones, on the other hand, are more often associated with a high intake of grain carbohydrate and low intake of animal protein. The latter occurs most often in young boys in economically disadvantaged circumstances, while renal stones affect all classes in developed countries (Steinbock, in Kiple 1999, 1088–1091), and predominates in adult males 35 to 55 plus years of age (Blackman *et al.* 1991). The results of this analysis support the age-at-death assessment of the Gristhorpe remains being those of an older man, but also provide insight into his social status. Such stones indicate a diet high in protein, a result that accords with the isotopic analysis that also indicates a diet high in protein (Montgomery and Gledhill, this volume).

Fig. 8.24 Ankylosis (i.e. fusion) of cervical vertebrae 2 and 3 through the left articular facets.

Acknowledgements

Mike Rouillard and Seán Goddard of the Department of Archaeology Drawing Office, University of Exeter, provided advice on and improved the images that appear in this contribution. The authors thank Rebecca Storm of the Biological Anthropology Research Centre (BARC), Archaeological Sciences, University of Bradford, who provided population asymmetry data from her doctoral research on fluctuating asymmetry. We also thank Jacqui McKinley (Wessex Archaeology), who provided stature estimates for Bronze Age individuals from Wiltshire, prior to their publication. The computer-tomographic reconstructions used in this treatment were performed using Mimics three-dimensional imaging software, through the courtesy of Carl Hitchins, UK Software Manager, Materialise, UK.

Summary

Gristhorpe Man was a physically active male who had attained the prime of life, being at least 36 to 45 years and likely much older at the time of his death (following the methods of Brothwell 1981, Işcan and Loth 1981, and Meindl and Lovejoy 1985, and Brooks and Suchey 1990). Standing between 178.27 cm (5′ 10″) and 181.2 cm (6′) (using the equations of Fully 1956 and Trotter 1970) he was of above average height for the Early Bronze Age compared with the statures of other Early Bronze Age barrow burials, whose occupants possess a mean height of 174.8 cm (standard deviation of 5.15 cm). Gristhorpe Man is at the top end of the stature range (from 185.3 to 161.6 cm) and about a standard deviation from the mean for the group. A body mass estimate, ranging between 69.8 and 74.6 kg (using the methods of Ruff *et al.* 1991, McHenry 1992, Grine *et al.* 1995) and between 78.64 and 79.57 kg. (using the method of Ruff 2000 and Ruff *et al.* 2005 based on the maximum bi-iliac breadth) suggests a body mass index of roughly 22 or between 24.5 and 25 from bi-iliac breadth, which falls towards the upper end of the normal range of 19 to 25 of modern standards (Frisancho 1993, 428). Given that the estimates of body mass are based on articular surface measurements that are set at physiological maturity (Ruff *et al.* 1991), when growth ceases, this means that in his prime, Gristhorpe Man possessed a lithe, muscular build that would be considered healthy by modern standards. Some form of strenuous physical activity involving extension and flexion, abduction and lateral rotation of the hip, resulted in bilateral third trochanters and marked hypotrochanteric fossae on the posterior surfaces of the femora, a combination of physical changes indicative of strenuous activity of the hips and lower limbs as well as due to advanced age at death. Comparing favourably with the previously analysed and very robust Towton medieval combatants (Knüsel 2000), Gristhorpe Man appears to have been right-handed and strongly lateralised indicating that he engaged in activities requiring strenuous use of his dominant right upper limb (Tables 8.3 and 8.4). This could very well have been from weapon use, although other activities requiring the use of a single hand, technological or subsistence-linked, could also have contributed to this asymmetry.

Gristhorpe Man's strontium, oxygen, and lead isotope ratios show him to have been local to the region in which he was interred (see Montgomery and Gledhill, this volume). His nitrogen isotope ratio is high and consistent with a substantial meat component to his diet. Moreover, since the carbon and nitrogen isotope values are the same from both the dentine (which provides an indication of childhood diet) and all of the bones tested (which document the last 30 years of life) his diet did not change from his childhood years to later life. Relatively reduced dental wear and lack of enamel hypoplastic lines (the presence of which would indicate a stressed growth period) and robust skeletal development testify to an individual who benefited from good nutrition and diet from birth that was not only adequate for tall stature but also contained cariogenic foodstuffs (as suggested by the presence of dental caries). His meat-based diet likely predisposed him to suffer from renal stones during his advanced years (Edwards *et al.* 2010, Edwards *et al.*, this volume). These were originally thought to have been mistletoe berries that formed part of the grave inclusions of the burial (Williamson 1834, 1872).

A brachycranic cranium (cranial index of 82.7), typical for the Bronze Age and consistent with radiocarbon determinations (see Batt, this volume), as well as the substantial height of Gristhorpe Man, supports the hypothesis that he may have been a member of a Bronze Age elite from birth. The presence of three traumatic injuries of the torso (healed fractures of left ribs 6 and 9) and neck, resulting in fusion through the left apophyseal joints of cervical vertebrae 2 and 3, in addition to vertebral degenerative changes in the form of marginal osteophytes of the vertebral bodies and a larger syndesmophyte extending from the right side of the first sacral vertebra across the lumbo-sacral intervertebral space attest to traumatic and degenerative changes. In addition to dental disease, he had suffered trauma to the lower central incisors resulting in dead tooth roots and cyst formation. A similar occurrence affected the left maxillary molars, indicated by a large cyst extending into the left maxillary antrum. These co-occurrences attest to the physical rigours to which such a social status exposed an individual in the Early Bronze Age.

Despite his healthy physique and physical evidence for social advantage for much of his life, Gristhorpe Man suffered from a slowly developing intra-osseous, benign intra-cranial tumour in the anterior left parieto-temporal region, the increased intra-cranial pressure from which may have had an impact on cerebral function. A lesion in this location may have had behavioural consequences prior to death, ranging from intermittent headaches, vomiting, aphasia (i.e. impaired speech and speech comprehension) and hemiparesis (i.e. muscle weakness) to impaired consciousness and seizure (Aufderheide and Rodriquez-Martín 1998: 250–251, De Angelis *et al.* 2002: 68). In addition to his pre-eminent social status, these adverse physical manifestations, perhaps suspected to have played a part in and certainly preceding his death, may have contributed to his unique burial treatment.

References

Alphen, H. A. M. and Dreissen, J. J. R. (1976) Brain abscesses and subdural empyema. *Journal of Neurology, Neurosurgery, and Psychiatry* 39, 481–490.

Ashbee, P. (1960) *The Bronze Age Round Barrow in Britain*. London, Phoenix House.

Auerbach, B. M. and Ruff, C. B. (2004) Human body mass estimation: a comparison of "morphometric" and "mechanical" methods. *American Journal of Physical Anthropology* 125, 331–342.

Aufderheide, A. C. and Rodriquez-Martín C. (1998) *The Cambridge Encyclopedia of Paleopathology*. Cambridge, Cambridge University Press.

Barnes, E. (1994) *Developmental Defects of the Axial Skeleton in Paleopathology*. Niwot (CO), The University Press of Colorado.

Bass, W. M. (1995) *Human Osteology: A Laboratory and Field Manual*. Columbia (MO), Missouri Archaeological Society.

Blackburn, A. and Knüsel, C. J. (2006) Bilateral asymmetry of the epicondylar breadth of the humerus. *Current Anthropology* 47, 377–382.

Blackman J., Allison, M. J., Aufderheide, A. C., Oldroyd, N. and Steinbock, R. T. (1991) Secondary hyperparathyroidism in an Andean mummy. In D. J. Ortner and A. C. Aufderheide (eds.) *Human Paleopathology: Current Syntheses and Future Options*, 291–296. Washington, D.C., Smithsonian Institution Press.

Bogin, B. (1999) *Patterns of Human Growth*, Second Edition. Cambridge, Cambridge University Press.

Brodie, N. (1994) *The Neolithic-Bronze Age Transition in Britain: A Critical Review of Some Archaeological and Craniological Concepts*. Oxford, British Archaeological Reports, British Series 238.

Brooks, S. and Suchey, J. M. (1990) Skeletal age determination based on the *os pubis*: a comparison of the Acsádi-Nemeskéri and Suchey-Brooks methods. *Human Evolution* 5, 227–238.

Brothwell, D. R. (1981) *Digging Up Bones*, Third Edition. New York, Cornell University Press.

Brothwell, D. R. and Krzanowski, W. (1974) Evidence of biological differences between early British populations from the Neolithic to Medieval times, as revealed by eleven commonly available cranial vault measurements. *Journal of Archaeological Science* 1, 249–260.

Buikstra, J. E. and Ubelaker, D. H. (eds.) (1994) *Standards for Data Collection from Human Skeletal Remains*. Fayetteville (AR), Arkansas Archaeological Survey.

Capasso, L., Kennedy, K. A. R. and Wilczak, C. (1999) *Atlas of Occupational Markers on Human Remains*. Teramo, Italy, Edigrafital S.P.A.

Christie, P. M., (1967) A barrow-cemetery of the Second Millennium BC in Wiltshire, England. *Proceedings of the Prehistoric Society* 33, 336–366.

Cook, N. D. (2002) Bihemispheric language: how the two hemispheres collaborate in the processing of language. In Crow, T. J. (ed.) *The Speciation of Modern Homo sapiens*, 169–194. Oxford, Oxford University Press.

Cotran, R. S., Kumar, V. and Robbins, S. L., (1989) *Robbins' Pathologic Basis of Disease*, Fourth Edition. Philadelphia, W.B. Saunders Co.

Dandy, D. J. (1993) *Essential Orthopaedics and Trauma*. Second Edition. Edinburgh, Churchill Livingstone.

Davis, J. B. and Thurnam, J. (1865) *Crania Britannica*. Delineations and Descriptions of the Skulls of the Aboriginal and Early Inhabitants of the British Islands: with Notices of their Other Remains (2 vols.). London, private for the subscribers.

Dawes, J. (n.d.) *Unpublished Skeletal Reports, Wetwang Slack, East Yorkshire*. Unpublished manuscript, University of Bradford.

De Angelis, L. M., Gutin, P. H., Leibel, S. A. and Posner, J. B. (2002) *Intracranial Tumours: Diagnosis and Treatment*. London, Martin Dunitz.

DiMaio, V. and DiMaio, D. (2001) *Forensic Pathology*, Second Edition. Boca Raton (FL), CRC Press.

Edwards, H. G. M., Montgomery, J., Melton, N. D., Hargreaves, M. D., Wilson, A. S. and Carter, E. A. (2010). Gristhorpe Man: Raman spectroscopic study of a Bronze Age log-coffin Burial. *Journal of Raman Spectroscopy* 41, 1533–1536.

Evans, J. G., Atkinson, R. J. C., O'Connor, T. and Green, H. S., (1984) Stonehenge- the environment in the late Neolithic and early Bronze Age and a Beaker-Age burial. *Wiltshire Archaeological and Natural History Magazine* 78, 7–30.

Eveleth, P. B. and Tanner J. M. (1976) *Worldwide Variation in Human Growth*, First Edition. Cambridge, Cambridge University Press.

Feldges, A., Heeson, J. and Schetter, D., (1990) Der odontogene Hirnabszeß. *Deutsche Zeitschrift für Mund-, Kiefer- und Gesichts-Chirurgie* 14, 297–300.

Floud, R. (2002) The achievements of anthropometric history. In M. Smith (ed.) *Human Biology and History*. Society of the Study of Human Biology Symposium 42: 152–164. London, Taylor and Francis.

Floud, R,, Wachter, K. and Gregory, A., (1990) *Height, Health, and History: Nutritional Status in the United Kingdom, 1750-1980*. Cambridge, Cambridge University Press.

Frisancho, A. R. (1993) *Human Adaptation and Accommodation*. Ann Arbor, The University of Michigan Press.

Fully, G. (1956) Une nouvelle méthode de détermination de la taille. *Annales de Médecine Légale et de Criminologie* 35, 266–273.

Galloway, A. (ed.) (1999) *Broken Bones: Anthropological Analysis of Blunt Force Trauma*. Springfield (IL), Charles C. Thomas.

Gottfried, O. N., Gluf, W. M. and Schmidt, M. H. (2004) Cavernous hemangioma of the skull presenting with subdural hematoma. *Neurosurgical Focus* 17, 1–4.

Grine, F. E., Jungers, W. L., Tobias, P. V. and Pearson, O. M. (1995) Fossil *Homo* femur from Berg Aukas, northern Namibia. *American Journal of Physical Anthropology* 97, 151–185.

Hauser, G. and de Stefano, G. F. (1989) *Epigenetic Variants of the Hman Skull*. Schweizerbart – Stuttgart.

Işcan, M. Y. and Loth, S. R. (1986) Estimation of age and determination of sex from the sternal rib. In K. J. Reichs (ed.) *Forensic Osteology*, 68–89. Springfield (IL), Charles C. Thomas.

Jónsdóttir, B., Ortner, D. J. and Frohlich, B. (2003) Probable destructive meningioma in an archaeological adult male skull from Alaska. *American Journal of Physical Anthropology* 122, 232–239.

Katz, D. and Suchey, J. M. (1986) Age determination of the male *os pubis*. *American Journal of Physical Anthropology* 69, 427–435.

Kiple, K. F. (1999) *The Cambridge World History of Human Disease*. Cambridge, Cambridge University Press.

Knüsel, C. J. (2000) Activity-related skeletal change. In V. Fiorato, A. Boylston and C. J. Knüsel (eds.), *Blood Red Roses: The Archaeology of a Mass Grave from Towton, A.D 1461*, 103–118. Oxford, Oxbow Books.

Knüsel, C. J., Göggel, S. C. and Lucy, D. J., (1997) Comparative degenerative joint disease of the vertebral column in the medieval monastic cemetery of the Gilbertine Priory of St. Andrew, Fishergate, York, England. *American Journal of Physical Anthropology* 103, 481–495.

Krogman, W. M. and Işcan, M. Y. (1986) *The Hhuman Skeleton in Forensic Medicine*. Springfield (IL), Charles C. Thomas Publishers.

Lovejoy, C. O., Meindl, R. S., Pryzbeck, T. R. and Mensforth R. P. (1985) Chronological metamorphosis of the auricular surface of the ilium: a new method for the determination of age at death. *American Journal of Physical Anthropology* 68, 15–28.

Macpherson, G. (1992) *Black's Medical Dictionary*, Thirty-seventh Edition. London, A. and C. Black.

Mays, S. (2000) Biodistance studies using craniometric variation in British archaeological skeletal material. In M. Cox and S. Mays (eds.) *Human Osteology in Archaeology and Forensic Science*, 277–288. London, Greenwich Medical Media.

Mays, S., Steele, J., and Ford, M. (1999) Directional asymmetry in the human clavicle. *International Journal of Osteoarchaeology* 9, 18–28.

McHenry, H. M. (1992) Body size and proportions in early hominids. *American Journal of Physical Anthropology* 87, 407–431.

McKern, T. and Stewart, T. D. (1957) *Skeletal age changes in young American males, analyzed from the standpoint of identification*. Technical report EP-45. Natick, Massachusetts, Headquarters, Quartermaster Research and Development Command.

McKinley, J. I. (2011) Human Remains, In A. P. Fitzpatrick (ed.) *The Amesbury Archer and the Boscombe Bowmen: Bell Beaker burials at Boscombe Down, Amesbury, Wiltshire*, 19–32. Wessex Archaeology Report 27. Old Sarum, Salisbury (Wilts.), Wessex Archaeology Ltd.

Meindl, R. S. and Lovejoy, C. O. (1985) Ectocranial suture closure: a revised method for the determination of skeletal age based on the lateral-anterior sutures. *American Journal of Physical Anthropology* 68, 57–66.

Molnar, P. (2006) Tracing prehistoric activities: musculo-skeletal stress marker analysis of a Stone Age population on the Island of Gotland in the Baltic Sea. *American Journal of Physical Anthropology* 129, 12–23.

Nasser, K., Hayashi, N., Kurosaki, K., Hasegawa, S., Kurimoto, M., Mohammed, A. and Endo, S., (2007) Intraosseous cavernous hemangioma of the frontal bone- case report. *Neurologia Medico-Chirurgica (Tokyo)* 47, 506–508.

Niepel, G. A. and Sit'aj, S. (1979) Enthesopathy. *Clinics in Rheumatic Diseases* 5, 857–872.

Ogden, A. R. (2008) Advances in the palaeopathology of teeth and jaws. In S. Mays and R. Pinhasi (eds) *Advances in Human Paleopathology*, 283–307. Chichester (UK), Wiley.

Ortner, D. J. (2003) *Identification of Pathological Conditions in Human Skeletal Remains* Second Edition. Amsterdam, Academic Press.

Ousley, S. D. and Jantz R. L. (2005) *FORDISC 3.0 Personal Computer Forensic Discriminant Functions*. Knoxville (TN), University of Tennessee.

Paradowski, B., Sasiadek, M., Zub, W., Markowska-Wojciechowska, A., Paradowski, M. (2007) Intraosseous hemangioma in parietal bone. *Neurology* 68: 44.

Platzer, W. (1999) *Color Atlas of Human Anatomy 1, Locomotor System*. Stuttgart, Thieme.

Randsborg, K. and Christensen, K. (2006) *Bronze Age Oak-Coffin Burials*. Copenhagen, Blackwell Munksgaard.

Raxter, M. H., Auerbach, B. M. and Ruff, C. B., (2006) Revision of the Fully technique for estimating statures. *American Journal of Physical Anthropology* 130, 374–384.

Richards, L. C. and Brown, T. (1986) Development of the helicoidal plane. *Human Evolution* 1, 385–398.

Rilling, J. K. (2008) Neuroscientific approaches and applications within anthropology. *Yearbook of Physical Anthropology* 51, 2–32.

Rogers, J. (2000) The palaeopathology of joint disease. In M. Cox and S. Mays (eds.) *Human Osteology in Archaeology and Forensic Science*, 163–182. London, Greenwich Medical Media.

Rogers, J. and Waldron, T. (1995) *A Field Guide to Joint Disease in Archaeology*. Chichester, John Wiley and Sons.

Rogers, J., Shepstone, L. and Dieppe, P. (1997) Bone formers: osteophyte and enthesophyte formation are positively associated. *Annals of the Rheumatic Diseases* 56, 85–90.

Rogers, J., Waldron, T., Dieppe, P. and Watt, I. (1987) Arthropathies in palaeopathology: the basis of classification according to most probable cause. *Journal of Archaeological Science* 14, 179–193.

Ruff, C. B. (2000) Body mass prediction from skeletal frame size in elite athletes. *American Journal of Physical Anthropology* 113, 507–517.

Ruff, C. B., Scott, W. W. and Liu, A. Y.-C. (1991) Articular and diaphyseal remodeling of the proximal femur with changes in body mass in adults. *American Journal of Physical Anthropology* 86, 397–413.

Ruff, C. B., Niskanen M., Junno, J.-A. and Jamison, P. (2005) Body mass prediction from stature and bi-iliac breadth in two high latitude populations, with application to earlier higher latitude humans. *Journal of Human Evolution* 48, 381–392.

Russel, A. D. (1988) *The Chilbolton Burial*. Andover, Hampshire County Museum Services.

Smith, B. H. (1984) Patterns of molar wear in hunter-gatherers and agriculturalists. *American Journal of Physical Anthropology* 63, 39–56.

Standring, S. (ed.) 2005 *Gray's Anatomy: The Anatomical Basis for Clinical Practice*, Thirty-ninth Edition. Edinburgh, Elsevier Churchill Livingstone.

Steckel, R. H. (1995) Stature and the standard of living. *Journal of Economic Literature* 33, 1903–1940.

Steele, J. (2000) Skeletal indicators of handedness. In M. Cox and S. Mays (eds.) *Human Osteology in Archaeology and Forensic Science*, 307–323. London, Greenwich Medical Media.

Storm, R. A. (2009) *Human Skeletal Asymmetry: A Study of Directional and Fluctuating Asymmetry in Assessing Health, Environmental Conditions, and Social Status in English Populations from the 7th to the 19th Century*. Unpublished PhD thesis, University of Bradford.

Suchey, J. M. (1979) Problems with the ageing of females using the os pubis. *American Journal of Physical Anthropology* 51, 467–471.

Suzuki, Y., Ikeda, H. and Matsumoto, K. (2001) Neuroradiological features of intraosseous cavernous hemangioma- case report. *Neurologia Medico-Chirurgica (Tokyo)* 41, 279–282.

Todd, T. W. (1920) Age changes in the pubic bone: the white male pubis. *American Journal of Physical Anthropology* 3, 285–334.

Trotter, M. (1970) Estimation of stature from intact limb bones. In Stewart, T. D., (ed). *Personal identification in mass disasters*, 71–83. Washington, D.C., Smithsonian Institution.

Trotter, M. and Gleser, G. C. (1952) Estimation of stature from the long bones of American whites and negroes. *American Journal of Physical Anthropology* 10, 463–514.

Trotter, M. and Gleser, G. C. (1958) A re-assessment of stature from long bones after death. *American Journal of Physical Anthropology* 16, 79–123.

Villotte, S. (2009) *Enthésopathies et Activité des Hommes Préhistoriques: Recherche Méthodologique et Application aux Fossiles Européens du Paléolithique Supérieure et du Mésolithique*. Oxford, Archaeopress.

Wallace, J. A. (1975) Did La Ferrassie I use his teeth as a tool? *Current Anthropology* 16, 393–401.

Wastling, V. J. (2006) *Gristhorpe Man: A Modern Assessment of an Early Bronze Age Tree Trunk Burial*. Unpublished MSc thesis, University of Bradford.

Webb, A. (1991) *Archaeology of Archery*. Tolworth, The Glade.

Whitfield, P. (2005) The management of intracranial abscesses. *Advances in Clinical Neuroscience and Rehabilitation* 5, 12–15.

Williamson, W. C. (1834) *Description of the Tumulus, lately opened at Gristhorpe, near Scarborough*. Scarborough, C.R. Todd.

Williamson, W. C. (1872) *Description of the Tumulus opened at Gristhorpe, near Scarborough*. Scarborough, S.W. Theakston.

Woodward, A., Hunter, J., Ixer, R., Roe, F., Potts, P. J., Webb, P. C., Watson, J. S. and Jones, M. C. (2006) Beaker age bracers in England: sources, function, and use. *Antiquity* 80, 530–543.

Woodward, A., Hunter, J., Ixer, R., Maltby, M., Potts, P. J., Webb, P. C., Watson, J. S. and Jones, M. C. 2005 Ritual in some early Bronze Age gravegoods. *Archaeological Journal* 162, 31–64.

Yang, S.-Y. (1981) Brain abscess: a review of 400 cases. *Journal of Neurosurgery* 55, 794–799.

Zumwalt, A. (2006) The effect of endurance exercise on the morphology of muscle attachment sites. *Journal of Experimental Biology* 209, 444–454.

Appendix 8.1: Sex Determination

Non-Metric Indicators:	Male	Female	?
Pelvis:			
Pelvic inlet (males heart shaped; females circular or elliptical)	x		
Pelvic outlet of true pelvis (males smaller; females oblique, shallow, spacious)	x		
Ventral arc	x		
Sub-pubic concavity	x		
Shape of the ischio-pubic ramus	x		
Sacral curvature (males more highly curved in lateral view)	x		
Sacral body proportions (males ¼, ½, ¼; females $^1/_3$, $^1/_3$, $^1/_3$)	x		
Sciatic notch (V-shaped in males and U shaped in females)	x		
Pre-auricular and post-auricular sulci ('parturition' scars, females possess higher frequencies)	x		
Pubic symphysis (higher in males than in females)			x
Obturator foramen (large ovoid in males and smaller triangular in females)	x		
Acetabulum (males large, directed laterally; females smaller, & antero-laterally)	x		
Ilium (males high and vertical : females laterally divergent)	x		
Iliac tuberosity (males large, not pointed; females small, pointed or varied)	x		
Pubic tubercle (more projected in females, rounder in males)	x		
Cranium:			
Sharpness of superior orbital border (sharp female, rounded male)	x		
Shape of orbits (larger, rectangular and lower in males than females)	x		
Supra-orbital ridges (larger in males than females)	x		
Height of forehead (steeper and more bulbous in females: receding in males)	x		
Mastoid process (larger and more delimited in males than in females)	x		
Depth of digastric fossa (deeper in males than females)	x		
Zygomatic root (extends beyond the auditory meatus in males)	x		
Supra-mastoid and supra-meatal crests (larger in males than females)	x		
Nuchal ridge (larger and more rugose in males than those in females – may meet the most inferior curve of the temporal lines in males)	x		
Temporal lines (more marked in males than in females)	x		
Height and thickness of zygomatic arches (males possess larger, more rugose, more laterally projected arches)	x		
Palate and teeth (larger and U shaped in males; smaller & parabolic in females)	x		
Parietal eminences (larger in females than those in males)	x		
Frontal eminences (larger in females than those in males)	x		
Occipital condyles (larger in males than those in females)			x

Non-Metric Indicators:	Male	Female	?
Mandible:			
Gonial flare, rugosity, and eversion of gonial angle (greater in males)	x		
Height of mandibular symphysis (greater in males than females)	x		
Breadth of the ascending ramus and its thickness (larger and thicker in males)	x		
Bilateral mental tubercles in males (square chin) single tubercle in females	x		
Non-metric Indicators (hyperostosis vs. hypostatic traits) (Hauser and de Stefano 1989)	x		
Metric Indicators:			
Maximum clavicle length (Male >150mm, Female <138)	157		
Glenoid cavity (Male >29mm, Female<26mm)	34		
Humeral head diameter (Male >47, Female<43mm)	48		
Radial head diameter (Male>23, Female<21)	24R		
Femoral head diameter (Male>48, Female<43)	49		
Femoral bicondylar width (Male>76, Female<74)	85		
Gonial angle <125° in males, >125° in females (goniometer)	120°		
Total male vs. female	39	0	2

Appendix 8.2: Age-at-Death Determination

Cranial Suture Closure (Meindl & Lovejoy 1985)	Score	Age Category
Vault Suture sites (0,1,2,3, N.A.)		
Midlambdoid	1	
lambda	1	
obelion	2	
anterior sagittal	2	
bregma	1	
midcoronal	1	
pterion	1	
Combined:	9	39.4 years
Score 7–11. Mean 39.4 years. S.D. 9.1. 24–60 years range		
Lateral-anterior suture sites (0,1,2,3, N.A.)	Score	Age Category
sphenofrontal	3	
inferior sphenotemporal	1	
superior sphenotemporal	1	
Combined (midcoronal to superior sphenotemporal)	7	45.2 years

	Score	Age Category
Cranial Suture Closure (Meindl & Lovejoy 1985)		
Score 7–8. Mean 56.2 years. S.D. 8.9. 32–65 years range		
Rib sternal end ageing (Işcan & Loth 1986)		
right fourth rib	Phase 5	33–42 years
other ribs		
Pubic Symphysis:		NA
Todd (1920)		
McKern & Stewart (1957) phase:		
McKern & Stewart (1957) component analysis		
component I (dorsal plateau):		
component II (ventral rampart):		
component III (symphyseal rim):		
Combined estimate:		
Suchey-Brooks Method (Suchey 1979, Katz & Suchey, 1986, Brooks & Suchey 1990)		NA
Auricular surface (Lovejoy *et al.* 1985):		NA
Ossified thyroid cartilage (Cerny 1983, in Krogman and Işcan 1986)		present
Tooth Wear (Brothwell 1981: 72)		
1–6	5	
1–7	2+	
1–8		NA
2–6	5+	Unequal wear
2–7		NA
2–8		NA
3–6	4	
3–7	2+	
3–8		Lost antemortem
4–6	4	
4–7	2+	
4–8		Absent due to agenesis
Total	24	33–45+

Appendix 8.3: Metrics

Cranial

1	Maximum cranial length	185	18	Inter-orbital breadth	29
2	Maximum cranial breadth	153	19	Frontal chord	122
3	Bi-zygomatic breadth	146	20	Parietal chord	130
4	Basion/Bregma height	137	21	Occipital chord	92
5	Cranial base length	98	22	Foramen magnum length	40
6	Basion-Prosthion length	92	23	Foramen magnum breadth	32
7	Maxillo-alveolar breadth	67	24	Mastoid length	35
8	Maxillo-alveolar length	53	25	Chin height	32
9	Bi-auricular breadth	137	26	Height of mandibular body	34
10	Upper facial height	67	27	Breadth of mandibular body	9
11	Minimum frontal breadth	115	28	Bi-gonial width	115
12	Upper facial breadth	112	29	Bi-condylar breadth	134
13	Nasal height	50	30	Minimum ramus breadth	32
14	Nasal breadth	39	31	Maximum ramus breadth	42
15	Orbital breadth	43	32	Maximum ramus height	68
16	Orbital height	31	33	Mandibular length	72
17	Bi-orbital breadth	112	34	Mandibular angle	120°

Infra-cranial

35	Clavicle: maximum length	157	57	Os Coxae: iliac breadth	169
36	Clavicle: antero-posterior diameter at midshaft	13	58	Os Coxae: pubis length	NA
37	Clavicle: supero-inferior diameter at midshaft	10	59	Os Coxae: ischium length	NA
38	Scapula: height	173	60	Femur: maximum length	497
39	Scapula: breadth	112	61	Femur: bicondylar length	485
40	Humerus: maximum length	341	62	Femur: epicondylar breadth	85
41	Humerus: epicondylar breadth	62	63	Femur: maximum diameter of the head	49
42	Humerus: vertical diameter of head	48	64	Femur: antero-posterior subtrochanter diameter	31
43	Humerus: maximum diameter at midshaft	21	65	Femur: medio-lateral subtrochanter diameter	42
44	Humerus: minimum diameter at midshaft	18	66	Femur: antero-posterior midshaft diameter	29
45	Radius: maximum length	270	67	Femur: medio-lateral midshaft diameter	29
46	Radius: antero-posterior diameter at midshaft	12	68	Femur: midshaft circumference	90
47	Radius: medio-lateral diameter at midshaft	15	69	Tibia: length	410
48	Ulna: maximum length	285	70	Tibia: maximum proximal epiphysis breadth	78

49	Ulna: antero-posterior diameter	14	71	Tibia: maximum distal epiphysis breadth	59
50	Ulna: medial-lateral diameter	16	72	Tibia: maximum diameter at the nutrient foramen	37
51	Ulna: physiological length	256	73	Tibia: medio-lateral diameter at the nutrient foramen	36
52	Ulna: minimum circumference	35	74	Tibia: circumference at the nutrient foramen	98
53	Sacrum: anterior length	114	75	Fibula: length	407R
54	Sacrum: anterior superior breadth	119	76	Fibula: maximum diameter at midshaft	12
55	Sacrum: maximum transverse diameter of base	69	77	Calcaneus: maximum length	84
56	Os Coxae: height	217	78	Calcaneus: middle breadth	47

All measurements are in mm. Bilateral measurements are from the left unless damaged (R indicates that the right side was used). NA= could not be assessed due to wiring (modified after Buikstra and Ubelaker (1994), attachment 21).

Appendix 8.4: Primary Non-metric Traits

	L	M	R
1. Metopic Suture:			
0 = absent		_1_	
1 = partial			
2 = complete			
9 = unobservable			

2. Supraorbital Structures:
    a. Supraorbital notch: _1_   _   1_
0 = absent
1 = present, < ½ occluded spicules
2 = present, > ½ occluded spicules
3 = present, degree of occlusion unknown
4 = multiple notches
9 = unobservable
    b. Supraorbital foramen: _0_   _   0_
0 = absent
1 = present
2 = multiple foramina
9 = unobservable

3. Infraorbital Suture: _0_   _0_
0 = absent
1 = partial
2 = complete
9 = unobservable

	L	M	R
4. Multiple Infraorbital			
Foramina:	_0_		_0_
0 = absent			
1 = internal division only			
2 = two distinct foramina			
3 = more than two distinct foramina			
9 = unobservable			

5. Zygomatico-facial

Foramina:	_6_		_5_
0 = absent			
1 = 1 large			
2 = 1 large plus a smaller foramina			
3 = 2 large			
4 = 2 large plus a smaller foramina			
5 = 1 small			
6 = multiple small			
9 = unobservable			

6. Parietal Foramen:	_0_		_0_
0 = absent			
1 = present, on parietal			
2 = present, sutural			
9 = unobservable			

7. Sutural Bones:

0 = absent
1 = present
9 = unobservable

a. epipteric bone:	_0_		_0_
b. coronal ossicle:	_0_		_0_
c. bregmatic bone:		_0_	
d. sagittal ossicle:		_0_	
e. apical bone:		_0_	
f. lambdoid ossicle:	_1_		_1_
g. asterionic bone:			
h. ossicle in occipito-mastoid suture:	_0_		_0_
i. parietal notch bone:	_0_		_0_

8. Inca Bone:		_0_	
0 = absent			
1 = complete, single bone			
2 = bipartite			
3 = tripartite			
4 = partial			
9 = unobservable			

9. Condylar Canal:	_9_		_9_
0 = not patent			
1 = patent			
9 = unobservable			

10. Divided Hypoglossal

Canal:	_9_		_9_
0 = absent			
1 = partial internal surface			
2 = partial, within canal			
3 = complete, internal surface			
4 = complete, within canal			
9 = unobservable			

	L	M	R

11. Flexure of Superior
   Sagittal Sulcus: _9_
   1 = Right
   2 = Left
   3 = Bifurcate
   9 = Unobservable

12. Foramen Ovale
   Incomplete: _0_   _0_
   0 = absent
   1 = partial formation
   2 = no definition of foramen
   9 = unobservable

13. Foramen Spinosum Incomplete:
   0 = absent   _9_   _0_
   1 = partial formation
   2 = no definition of foramen
   9 = unobservable

14. Pterygo-spinous Bridge: _9_   _9_
   0 = absent
   1 = trace (spicule only)
   2 = partial bridge
   3 = complete bridge
   9 = unobservable

15. Pterygo-alar Bridge: _9_   _9_
   0 = absent
   1 = trace (spicule only)
   2 = partial bridge
   3 = complete bridge
   9 = unobservable

16. Tympanic Dihiscence: _0_   _0_
   0 = absent
   1 = foramen only
   2 = full defect present
   9 = unobservable

17. Auditory Exostosis: _0_   _0_
   0 = absent
   1 = <1/3 canal occluded
   2 = 1/3-2/3 canal occluded
   3 =>2/3 canal occluded
   9 = unobservable

18. Mastoid Foramen
   (a) Location: _0_   _1_
   0 = absent
   1 = temporal
   2 = sutural
   3 = occipital
   4 = both sutural and temporal
   5 = both occipital and temporal
   9 = unobservable

	L	M	R
(b) Number	_0_		_1_

0 = absent
1 = 1
2 = 2
3 = more than 2
9 = unobservable

19. Mental Foramen:

	L	M	R
	_0_		_0_

0 = absent
1 = 1
2 = 2
3 = >2
9 = unobservable

20. Mandibular Torus:

	L	M	R
	_0_		_0_

0 = absent
1 = trace (can palpate but not see)
2 = moderate: elevation between 2-5mm.
3 = marked: elevation greater than 5mm.
9 = unobservable

21. Mylohyoid Bridge

	L	M	R
(a) Location:	_0_		_0_

0 = absent
1 = near Mandibular foramen
2 = centre of groove
3 = both bridges described in 1) and 2), with hiatus
4 = both bridges described in 1) and 2), no hiatus
9 = unobservable

	L	M	R
(b) Degree	_0_		_0_

0 = absent
1 = partial
2 = complete
9 = unobservable

22. Atlas Bridging

	L	M	R
(a) Lateral Bridging	_0_		_0_

0 = absent
1 = partial
2 = complete
9 = unobservable

	L	M	R
(b) Posterior Bridging	_0_		_0_

0 = absent
1 = partial
2 = complete
9 = unobservable

23. Accessory Transverse Foramina: (in 7th vertebra)

	L	M	R
	_9_		_9_

0 = absent
1 = partial
2 = complete
9 = unobservable

24. Septal Aperture (distal humerus):

	L	M	R
	_0_		_0_

0 = absent
1 = small foramen (pinhole) only
2 = true perforation
9 = unobservable

M indicates that the trait is located in the mid-line. R= right, L= left

9

RAMAN SPECTROSCOPY OF THE GRISTHORPE MAN 'MISTLETOE BERRIES': LASER ILLUMINATION OF AN ANCIENT MYSTERY

Howell G. M. Edwards

Introduction

The recovery and preservation of artefacts from archaeological excavations involving biomaterials and skeletal remains requires the adoption of special techniques designed to identify and to minimise the further bio-deterioration of sensitive specimens exacerbated by their exposure to aerobic oxidation. In particular, the desiccation of specimens from wet depositional environments to minimise microbial decay is not favoured as this can cause undue mechanical stresses to be created within the artefact. A primary conservation exercise usually involves the cleaning and spraying of an artefact with protective materials, such as an aqueous solution of polyethylene glycol, as used for the on-going preservation of ships' timbers, such as those from the submerged warships *Vasa* and the *Mary Rose*. Added to this are the effects of corrosion of metal objects in damp depositional environments, the growth of biological colonies of cyanobacteria, lichen and fungi on a variety of substrates and the erosion of exposed materials by atmospheric pollutants and waterborne chemicals. The analysis of these artefacts must recognise and allow for these scenarios, whilst attempting to deliver the molecular structural information that is frequently required urgently to assist conservators in the selection of the proper protocols that need to be adopted for the preservation of the excavated materials.

Raman spectroscopy, a laser-based scattering technique, has been demonstrated to be viable for the non-destructive molecular analysis of a range of archaeological materials in which the major advantages are that no chemical or mechanical pre-treatment of the specimens is necessary. Desiccation of the specimen is not required as the sensitivity of the Raman effect to the presence of water is low, and the use of Raman microscopy affords access to specimen quantities with masses from 1 pg to several kg (Long, 2002; Edwards, 2005; Edwards, 2009 a and b). For especially large or unusually shaped artefacts, the use of fibre optical probe heads to bring the incident laser radiation onto the selected region of the specimen and to collect the scattered radiation for spectroscopic analysis affords a useful adjunct for the non-destructive acquisition of data. Of particular interest is that the Raman spectral molecular signatures of complex mixtures containing both inorganic and organic components can be identified in the same spectrum without the need for separation methods; this is a useful facility for the analytical study of archaeological materials that have been subjected to mineralisation during burial and for establishing the interactions that have occurred between minerals and degraded organic deposits in grave sites. An example is provided by the Raman spectroscopic analysis of the female skeleton from a 7th-century cist burial at Tywyn-y-Capel, UK, in which the de-calcification and embrittlement of the cervical vertebrae could be attributed to the formation of newberyite crystals at the interface of the vertebrae and scalp hair (Edwards *et al.* 2007). Despite these advantages, Raman spectroscopy has only been applied to archaeological and art problems in museum conservation science relatively recently in comparison with the more widely encountered infrared spectroscopic technique. The reason for this can probably be attributed to the invention of the Raman microscope with laser excitation and sensitive detection which facilitated the analytical observation of the Raman spectra of materials on a microscale. The first published Raman spectrum of an art object appeared in 1989 from the laboratory of Guineau in Paris (Guineau 1989) when mineral pigments in manuscripts were studied using microRaman spectroscopy; this quickly became adopted in several key studies and is summarised in an early review by Clark (1995). Nevertheless, it was almost a decade later before the application to organic biomaterials in an art and archaeological context appeared (Edwards 2004; Vandenabeele *et al.* 2007). The diagnostic capability of vibrational spectroscopy for the non-destructive discrimination between different resins and biomaterials from several geographical sources, and for the detection of thermal and environmental specimen degradation, is a powerful aid to the provision of novel information for historical provenancing for museum curators. In this context, the Raman spectra of resin specimens from archaeological excavations has revealed some key vibrational features that facilitate the botanical or generic classification of the specimen; examples include the important resins prized by ancient cultures, such as ambers, myrrh and frankincense. The degradation suffered by resins in archaeological burial environments has also been studied and the effects on the spectra were evaluated

(Edwards and Farwell, 1996; Edwards and Falk 1997; Edwards *et al.* 2008; De Faria *et al.* 2004; Brody *et al.* 2001, 2002).

Often, the first evidence of structural degradation in human burials has been provided by Raman spectroscopic signatures associated with protein and lipid components in human mummified skin, and the relative degradation of keratotic materials in claw, bone, skin and feathers found in a 1000 years old ice-mummified Antarctic penguin (Edwards *et al.* 1999) have indicated regions of interest and relevance that require immediate conservation and preservation procedures to be undertaken. In a similar study by Petersen *et al.* (2003) of the mummified remains of Nekht-Ankh, found in one of the two sarcophagi in the 'Tomb of the Two Brothers' in Der Rifeh, Egypt, in 1906 by Flinders Petrie, Raman spectroscopy showed that whilst certain regions of the skin were well-preserved and exhibited significant retention of alpha-helical protein structure others were very badly degraded and, furthermore, indicated that residues of sodium sulphate salts still remained from the natron desiccant adopted for the mummification ritual in the XIIth Dynasty, around 4000 BCE.

In the case of the Gristhorpe Man burial, the Raman spectroscopic analysis centred upon the characterisation of one of three small spherical nodules about 3 mm in diameter, stained black in colour from tannins in the oak coffin. This nodule, showing a natural fissure exposing a white substrate, is shown in Figure 9.1. An initial tentative

Fig. 9.1 Three spherical nodular objects were found underneath the skeleton in the coffin base; one of these has a fissure, shown here, which exposes the white inner region (Figure reproduced courtesy of John Wiley and Sons from Edwards *et al.* (2010) *Journal Raman Spectroscopy* 41, 1244).

classification of these nodules as '*a few dried berries... about the size of the mistletoe*' was made after '*distinguish[ing] a long laceolate leaf, resembling that of the mistletoe*' in the bed of vegetation upon which the body had been placed (Williamson 1834, 10). Williamson assumed them to have been placed in the coffin as part of an ancient funerary rite, and later likened them to '*dried fruit or seeds*' (Williamson 1872, 15). Scarborough Museums Trust requested that any scientific procedure to investigate them must be completely non-destructive and non-invasive.

Raman spectroscopy

Raman spectra were excited using a Renishaw InVia Raman microscope (Renishaw plc., Wotton-under-Edge, UK). Excitation was effected with a 785 nm laser, with a maximum power delivered of 500 mW, and a spectral footprint at the sample of about 5 microns diameter was achieved with a X50 lens objective. Spectra were recorded over the range 200–2000 cm^{-1} with a resolution of 2 cm^{-1}

and the spectral accumulation of ten scans each of ten seconds duration to increase the signal-to-noise ratio. Wavenumber calibration was effected using a silicon standard with a band at 520.50 ± 0.10 cm^{-1}. The laser power at the specimen was maintained at several milliwatts only to minimise the possibility of sample damage arising from absorption of the laser radiation – it can be calculated that the adoption of full laser power densities into micron-size diameter spectral footprints at the specimen can result in an irradiance of several GW/cm^2, which can be destructive of samples which exhibit absorption of the laser radiation. Care needs to be taken with archaeological specimens in this respect since their exposure to the depositional environment often results in the acquisition of materials from the geological and hydrological records that are subject to fluorescence emission upon laser irradiation. Although the fluorescence emission, which can be several orders of magnitude greater in intensity than the Raman spectral scattering, is significantly reduced by the adoption of long wavelength laser excitation that does not probe the

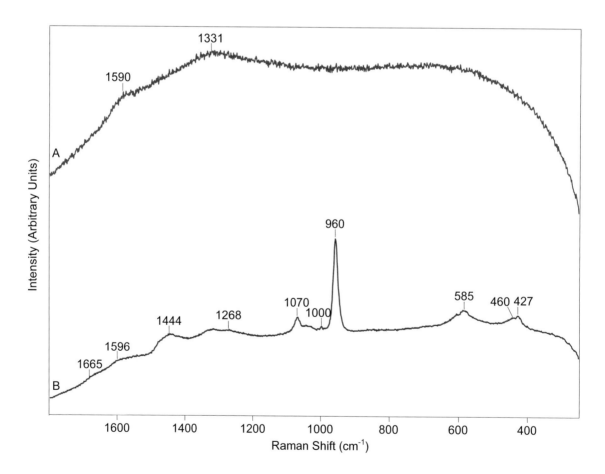

Fig. 9.2 Raman spectra of spherical nodule specimen from the Gristhorpe burial coffin; A, outer surface of the specimen; B, inner core as exposed via a fissure in the nodule, as shown in Fig. 9.1. (Figure reproduced courtesy of John Wiley and Sons from Edwards *et al.* (2010) *Journal of Raman Spectroscopy* 41, 1245).

electronic energy levels of exogenous materials and give rise to fluorescence phenomena. Inspection of the Raman spectra obtained from the spherical nodules reveals that some background emission is still present, although this is not sufficient to compromise the interpretation of the Raman spectral data.

The spherical nodule presented for analysis was dark brown in colour due to the absorption of materials from the burial environment, and the Raman spectra were, in fact, swamped by fluorescence emission; however, the nodule exhibited a small fissure which exposed the white underlying substrate and, using the confocal microscope facility, it was possible to obtain Raman spectra directly from the underlying substrate, which were relatively free from background interference, as can be seen in the example shown in Figure 9.2.

Spectra were obtained from several points and under different conditions to verify that the laser radiation had not caused degradation of the specimen under illumination to occur. In previous studies of archaeological specimens

of biomaterials such as skin, bone, textiles, hair and ivory, it was found that laser absorption resulted in localised thermal heating and decomposition – which could be observed visually microscopically as a crater and spectrally as carbon. In this case, the so-called D and G bands of sp^3 and sp^2 hybridised amorphous carbon are observed as broad spectral features centred at 1320 and 1580 cm^{-1}, respectively; in the case of the spherical nodules the protocol of use of low laser power densities to interrogate the specimen did not result in specimen degradation and we can therefore attribute any spectral signatures to the specimen itself without modification by the laser irradiation (Carter and Edwards 2001).

The Raman spectra from the fissure in the 'mistletoe berry' spherical nodule indicates that this attribution is false; the spectral signatures from Figure 9.2 clearly show peaks at 960, 600 and 450 cm^{-1}, which are assignable to a phosphatic matrix that contains an organic component evident from the proteinaceous bands at 1650, 1440 and 1230 cm^{-1}, all of which show spectral broadening as

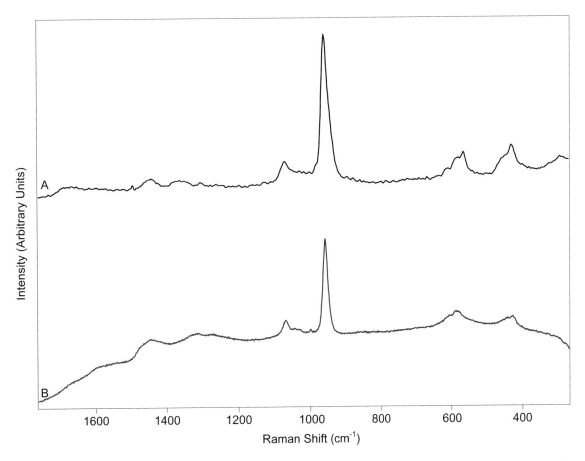

Fig. 9.3 Comparison of the Raman spectra of A, clinically excised kidney stone; B, inner core of the spherical nodular specimen from the Gristhorpe burial coffin. (Figure reproduced courtesy of John Wiley and Sons from Edwards *et al.* (2010), *Journal Raman Spectroscopy* 41, 1245).

expected form their degradation in the burial environment. In particular, the amide I CONH protein stretching modes are contained in the broad band envelope from 1670–1625 cm^{-1} which has contributions from the alpha-helix, beta-sheet and random coil conformations. Clearly, this spectrum is not compatible with an assignment to a seed or berry, which would have spectral signatures of lignin and cellulose – the next questions are then generated, of course.... what is it , and where did it come from?

The presence of both the phosphatic and proteinaceous components is highly indicative of a gall stone calculus or renal stone; the absence of Raman signatures due to calcium oxalate and oxalic acid renders the exclusion of gall stones as a possible source, which therefore leaves renal stones as a possibility. A comparison of the Raman spectra of the spherical nodule termed 'mistletoe berry' and a modern excised renal stone revealed a match (Fig. 9.3). Hence, we can assert that the idea originally proposed that the three spherical nodular 'mistletoe berries' were placed in the log coffin as part of the funerary rites is no longer tenable, and that the occupant of the coffin, Gristhorpe Man, possessed renal calculi which were deposited in the base of his coffin as his cadaver decomposed. It appears that the observation of the presence of these renal calculi in the skeletal remains of Gristhorpe Man is consistent with his having a high protein diet (Montgomery and Gledhill, this volume). Further details of the spectroscopic interpretation and assignment of the Raman spectra of these calculi are available for the interested reader in a recent specialist Raman spectroscopic paper (Edwards *et al.* 2010).

References

Brody, R. H., Edwards, H. G. M. and Pollard, A. M. (2001) A study of amber and copal samples using FT-Raman spectroscopy. *Spectrochimica Acta*, Part A, 57, 1325–1328.

Brody, R. H., Edwards, H. G. M. and Pollard, A. M. (2002) FT-Raman spectroscopic study of natural resins of archaeological interest. *Biopolymers* 67, 129–141.

Carter, E. A. and Edwards, H. G. M. (2001) Biological Applications of Raman Spectroscopy. In H. U. Gremlich, and B. Yan (eds.) *Infrared and Raman Spectroscopy of Biological Materials*, 421–475. New York, Marcel Dekker.

Clark, R. J. H. (1995) Raman spectroscopy of pigments on ancient historiated manuscripts. *Chemical Reviews* 42, 187–196.

De Faria, D. L. A., Edwards, H. G. M., Afonso, M. C., Brody, M. C. and Morais, J. L. (2004) Raman spectroscopic analysis of a resin tembeta an archaeological artefact in need of conservation. *Spectrochimica Acta*, Part A, 60, 1505–1513.

Edwards, H. G. M. (2004) ArchaeoRaman: probing history with Raman spectroscopy. *Analyst* 129, 870–879.

Edwards, H. G. M. (2005) Biological Materials and Degradation. In Edwards, H. G. M. and Chalmers, J. M. *Raman Spectroscopy in Archaeology and Art History*, 231–279. Cambridge, Royal Society of Chemistry.

Edwards, H. G. M. (2009a) Raman Spectroscopy in Art and Archaeology: A New Light on Historical Mysteries. In Laane J. (ed.). *Frontiers of Molecular Spectroscopy*. 133–173. Amsterdam, Elsevier Science.

Edwards, H. G. M. (2009b) Raman Spectroscopy of Inorganic Materials. in Art and Archaeology. In J. Yarwood, R. Douthwaite, and S.B. Duckett, (eds.), *Spectroscopic Properties of Inorganic and Organometallic Compounds: Materials and Applications*, 16–48. Specialist Periodical Reports. Cambridge, Royal Society of Chemistry Publishing.

Edwards, H. G. M. and Falk, M. J. (1997) FT-Raman spectroscopy and ancient resins: a feasibility study of application to archaeological artefacts. *Journal of Raman Spectroscopy* 28, 211–218.

Edwards, H. G. M. and Farwell, D. W. (1996) FT-Raman spectroscopy of amber. *Spectrochimica Acta*, Part A, 52, 1119–1125.

Edwards, H. G. M., David, A. R. and Brody, R. H. (2008) FT-Raman spectroscopy of archaeological resins. *Journal of Raman Spectroscopy*, 39, 966– 971.

Edwards, H. G. M., Farwell, D. W. and Wynn-Williams, D. D. (1999) FT Raman spectroscopy of avian mummified tissue of archaeological relevance. *Spectrochimica Acta*, Part A, 55, 2691–2703.

Edwards, H. G. M., Montgomery, J., Melton, N. D., Wilson, A. S., Hargreaves, M. D. and Carter, E. A. (2010) Gristhorpe Man; a Raman spectroscopic study of 'mistletoe berries' in a Bronze Age log coffin burial. *Journal of Raman Spectroscopy* 41, 1243–1246.

Edwards, H. G. M., Wilson, A. S., Nikhassan, N. F., Davidson, A. and Burnett, A. (2007) Raman spectroscopic analysis of human remains from a 7th century cist burial on Anglesey. *Analytical and Bioanalytical Chemistry* 387, 821–828).

Guineau, B. (1989) Raman spectroscopic characterisation of pigments on manuscripts. *Studies in Conservation* 34, 38–42.

Long, D. A. (2002) *The Raman Effect: A Unified Treatment of the Theory of Raman Scattering by Molecules*. Chichester, UK: John Wiley & Sons.

Petersen, S., Nielsen, O. F., Christensen, D. H., Edwards, H. G. M., Farwell, D. W., David, A. R., Lambert, P., Gniadecka, M., Hart Hansen, J. P. and Wulf, H. C. (2003) NIR FT-Raman spectroscopic study of skin samples from the "Tomb of the Two Brothers", Khnum-Nakht and Nekht-Ankh, XIIth Dynasty Egyptian mummies (*ca*. 2000 BC). *Journal of Raman Spectroscopy* 34, 375–379.

Vandenabeele, P., Edwards, H. G. M. and Moens, L. (2007) A decade of Raman spectroscopy in art and archaeology. *Chemical Reviews* 107, 675–686.

Williamson, W. C. (1834) *Description of the Tumulus, lately opened at Gristhorpe, Near Scarborough*. Scarborough, C. R.Todd.

Williamson, W. C. (1872) *Description of the Tumulus opened at Gristhorpe, Near Scarborough*. Scarborough, S. W. Theakston.

10

DIET AND ORIGINS:
THE ISOTOPE EVIDENCE

Janet Montgomery and Andrew R. Gledhill

Archaeologists use isotope analysis to complement their traditional arsenal of techniques for identifying human behaviours such as transhumance, trade and migration. The technique is often portrayed as straightforward providing results as clear and unambiguous as reading a passport and opening an atlas. Unfortunately, this is seldom the case. Isotope ratios obtained from the teeth of a person derive primarily from the food they ate and the water they drank when the tooth was forming. If these were sourced locally, teeth will contain isotope ratios characteristic of the place of origin. For example, the isotope ratios of strontium originate from the rock that produces the soil on which crops are grown (Bentley 2006; Montgomery 2010), whilst those of oxygen testify to the climatic zone in which drinking water fell as rain (Fricke *et al.* 1995; Ehleringer *et al.* 2008). In prehistory, lead isotopes can be used in a similar way to those of strontium to identify an individual's geographic origin, until the pollution of the environment with anthropogenic lead during the Roman period (Molleson *et al.* 1986; Montgomery *et al.* 2010). In addition, carbon and nitrogen isotope ratios of dentine and bone collagen are well established as tools to provide dietary information, especially if used in conjunction with contemporaneous dietary fauna (Jay and Richards 2007). Use of marine resources can be particularly well characterised. Thus people with non-local diets can sometimes be identified (Barrett and Richards 2004; Müldner *et al.* 2011).

If a skeleton in a cemetery has very different ratios from the other individuals or to what would be expected from the place of burial, it is highly likely they ate food sourced from somewhere else as a child. There may, of course, be many reasons for this, and the first assumption to be made is that the individual went to the food rather than that the food was brought to the individual. Today, food and water may move very large distances across the world and be consumed far away from their source, but in most archaeological contexts it is highly unlikely that a person imported the bulk of their diet from elsewhere. The crucial thing to remember when interpreting isotope data is that the technique is 'exclusive' – it is very good at ruling out places of origin but not so good at identifying them. The reason for this is that for any given isotope ratio, or combination of isotope ratios, there will be many places in Britain, Europe or the world where such a combination exists. There may, of course, be very good archaeological reasons why most of these places can be ignored in interpretations, but isotope analysis alone cannot distinguish them – it is up to the researcher to consider and interpret the data in context.

At the outset of the project, we planned to undertake what is relatively routine (in application if not yet interpretation) isotope analysis of Gristhorpe Man's teeth and bones to obtain direct evidence for:

1. His diet – how it compared to other prehistoric people and whether he experienced any significant changes in diet, for example the consumption of meat, which might be related to changes in status between childhood and adulthood, possibly as a result of his achieving '*high rank*' during his lifetime (Williamson 1834, 6).
2. His origins - whether he was indigenous to the region and may thus have been a locally born '*Brigantian*

chief', or if he had come to the area during later life or for burial.

However, it soon became clear that the combination of unique organic preservation and the fascinating historical 'back story' to this remarkable assemblage, documented elsewhere in this volume, posed other intriguing questions to which we might fruitfully be able to contribute. Once Gristhorpe Man was ensconced in the conservation laboratory at the University of Bradford, he had amongst his numerous early visitors several eminent Bronze Age prehistorians, osteoarchaeologists, dentists and doctors – which was unsurprising as he struck, even 4,000 years after his demise, an awe-inspiring figure. Slowly, however, their various comments on how odd, unique and unusual this burial was, placed a seed of doubt about the integrity of the skeleton itself, despite its well-known provenance and the corroborating historical documentation such as the detailed osteological report in 1834 and the drawing in Davis and Thurnam's *Crania Britannica* in 1865, which clearly shows the same skull. In short, there were so many unusual things about this Bronze Age skeleton, each on its own perhaps not sufficient to warrant more than a passing comment, but together they raised the question: was Gristhorpe Man a 19th-century fake?

Compared with other contemporaneous individuals, Gristhorpe Man was very tall, he had caries in an age before refined sugar, and he had remarkably little tooth wear for his age suggesting a softer diet (see Knüsel *et al.*, this volume). Bronze Age experts Mike Parker Pearson, Alison Sheridan, Stuart Needham and Alex Gibson all remarked on the completeness of the skeleton (only a few small bones were missing – see Knüsel *et al.*, this volume), something rarely encountered with Bronze Age burials. Moreover, although Williamson had written in his report of 1834 that the skeleton was '*quite perfect and of an ebony colour*' (1834, 6), it had clearly at some stage been 'touched up' with a black substance particularly on the anterior parts of the skeleton. Raman spectroscopy by Janet Ambers at the British Museum subsequently determined this to be Indian ink, a carbon-based compound. Was this something done merely as a minor cosmetic improvement, or was it possible some other skeleton had been painted to replicate the original ebony colour? Could a far more recent skeleton have been substituted, painted black and wired up for display?

That the bone mineral of the blackened skeleton had survived largely intact for 4,000 years in the tannic acid of an oak coffin was somewhat perplexing in itself, as such environments, like peat bogs, tend to support the preservation of collagenous or keratinous soft tissues such as skin, hair and nails but not tooth enamel and bone mineral. Indeed, prior to the discovery of Gristhorpe Man in 1834, no previously excavated log coffin in Denmark had produced any evidence that a body had been deposited; they were either empty or contained only hair and clothes. It was thus assumed they were:

'*simply repositories for the dead person's possessions placed down in the middle of the great burial mounds to protect them against robbery while the dead themselves were burnt and their ashes put into the urns which were in many instances found in the sides of the same burial mound*' (Glob, 1974, 19).

Although skeletal remnants were present in the log coffin discovered in Stoborough in Dorset in the 18th century, which most closely parallels the Gristhorpe burial and in which the few surviving human bones were '*black, and soft*' (Hutchins 1797), it is exceedingly rare for bone mineral, as opposed to the organic collagen fraction and other proteinaceous soft tissues, to survive in any great quantity. Williamson was aware of this and cites communications from Canon William Greenwell and Barnard Davis of instances of finds from bogs and log coffins where the skin was blackened and tanned like leather (Williamson 1872, 8). In the case of Gristhorpe Man, no human hair, skin or nails were reported, but both collagen and bone mineral were present in the form of bones, teeth and mineralised cartilage (Knüsel *et al.*, this volume). All the teeth had enamel, which is almost entirely mineral, and it showed no sign of acid erosion. All the bones articulated normally with no evidence of the pliability or warping that would be expected if bone mineral had been irrevocably lost. Nonetheless, it is clear from Williamson's account of 1834 that several organic artefacts, rarely encountered in prehistoric burials in Britain, were observed at the coffin's opening, although none could be recovered wholly intact. For example, they observed and identified '*a singular variety of adipocere, which likewise proved that the actual body of the Ancient Briton had been deposited, and not merely the bones*' (1834, 18) – leading perhaps to one of the first forensic deductions recorded. There was a '*soft and fine*' animal skin that wrapped the body (1834, 6); the '*shallow basket of wickerwork*' that agonisingly '*fell in pieces on exposure to the atmosphere*' (1834, 9); amongst the mass of vegetable matter the '*long lanceolate leaf, resembling that of the mistletoe*' (1834, 10); and, perhaps, most regrettably:

'*Laid upon the lower part of the breast of the Skeleton was a very singular ornament, in the form of a double rose of a ribband, with two loose ends, but of what it is composed, I am not able to say; it appears to have been an appendage of some belt or girdle, but like the basket, it fell into small fragments immediately on removal. Its composition is exceedingly brittle, something resembling thin horn, but is more opaque and not elastic: the surface has been simply though curiously ornamented with small elevated lines.*' (Williamson 1834, 10)

This all too fleeting sight of the richness of the rarely seen organic components of a high-status burial is made even more bittersweet because the excavation took place on the eve of the invention of the camera; if it had occurred just a few short years later, the learned and scientific gentlemen of the Scarborough Philosophical Society would surely have had a newly-invented camera to hand to capture this for posterity. In the case of Gristhorpe, it appears that the sealed and waterlogged environment inside the coffin buried deep and surrounded by clay, or as Williamson wrote 'The peculiarity of being inclosed in such an antiseptic case' (1834, 17), ensured neutral, stable and anaerobic conditions during the 4000 years of burial that promoted the survival of both mineral and organic artefacts and remains until the day the coffin lid was removed.

If organic survival inside the coffin was good (and the small section removed from the right femur was indeed surprisingly dense and visibly greasy, almost resembling fresh bone) why was the post-excavation conservation of simmering the skeleton in gelatine for eight hours required? And could such a treatment have had the effect of removing collagen from the skeleton, rather than consolidating the bones? 'Animal jelly, or gelatine, is glue, whereas vegetable jelly is rather analogous to gum' (Beeton 1865, 165) and as any good 19th-century cook would know, simmering of bones has the effect of extracting gelatine, rather than of adding it. Gelatine is hydrolysed collagen and is extracted from animal skins, bones and hooves by boiling them in water for several hours or 'from cod sounds, or other fishy matters capable of yielding gelatine' (Hassal 1857, 463–4). By this process, cooks have historically thickened stocks and soups and produced such delicacies as calves' foot jelly: 'Bones ought always to form a component part of the stock-pot... Two ounces of them contain as much gelatine as one pound of meat' (Beeton 1861, 52). Nor do the bones need to be fresh, as Hassal (1857, 463) records, citing Pereira: 'Gelatine has been extracted from antediluvian bones. A soup was prepared from the bones of the great mastodon by a préfet of one of the departments of France'. That is, the process of lengthy simmering in water removes collagen from animal and fish bones, although it is admittedly unclear whether this process would have been initiated in a solution already thickened with glue. This notwithstanding, gelatine 'is more readily procured by employing bones which have been previously digested in hydrochloric acid to extract the phosphate of lime' (Hassal 1857, 463). Whether an acidic environment existed for some period of time within the coffin cannot now be determined but an analysis of the coffin water by Dr. Murray showed that it 'contained much sulphate of lime, but no appreciable animal matter or tannin' (Williamson 1834, 17). Sulphate of lime (calcium sulphate) in the coffin water, would counter any acidity from tannin, and the largest source of calcium inside the coffin was arguably the bones of Gristhorpe Man.

Did the animal glue replace collagen lost from the bones? Why had collagen been lost in such a burial environment

in the first place? Williamson's account of the preservation state of the skeleton appears contradictory. In 1834, he states that, on opening, 'the coffin contained a perfect skeleton' (page 5), that it was 'quite perfect and of an ebony colour' (page 6), that 'these fragile bones are nearly as perfect, as on the day they were placed in the ground' (page 17) and that 'it remains a matter of astonishment how they should have been preserved so strong and perfect as to enable them to be articulated' (page 16), attributing their survival to the tannic or gallic acids and waterlogging. In 1872, however, he precedes his recollection of the conservation that was carried out in 1834 by saying, 'The bones were very rotten and of an ink-black colour. The former condition was obviously the result of their prolonged maceration in water' (1872, 7). He then describes the process of simmering them in gelatine 'through many weary hours guarding lest the ebullition should become too violent for the brittle bones. After simmering for about eight hours the bones were removed from the boiler, exposed for some days to currents of air, and then articulated with little difficulty.'

What Williamson meant by the terms 'perfect', 'fragile', 'rotten' and 'brittle' is unclear, and it should be remembered that he was not present at the excavation, although he was given the duty of watching the bones as they simmered in the laundry boiler (Fig. 10.1). Why did simmering in glue consolidate and harden the bones sufficiently to permit them to be 'articulated as readily as recent bones could have been' (Williamson 1896, 45) in the manner of an anatomical specimen? Given that the extant skeleton appears not to have lost a significant amount of collagen or bone mineral, that having been waterlogged, all it may have needed was to dry out, that adhering remnants of soft tissue may have given the bones the appearance of being 'rotten', and that the conservation method was not considered sufficiently important to feature in his 1834 report at all, despite Williamson expressing astonishment that the skeleton had

Fig. 10.1 Cartoon drawn by a friend of the Beswick family in 1900 depicting the young Williamson monitoring the conservation process 'through many weary hours' (Courtesy of Mrs D. Beswick†).

survived in so perfect a condition, did it actually take place? There is a somewhat tetchy comment in this section where Williamson notes that *'When Mr. Layard brought home some friable ivories from his Eastern excavations, the late Dr. Buckland obtained some applause – if I mistake not – for his ingenious recommendation that they should be boiled in a solution of gelatine. This is exactly what we did with the Gristhorpe Skeleton many years previously'* (1872, 7). Williamson, writing now as a Professor of Natural History and Fellow of the Royal Society, was evidently unhappy that someone else, and especially perhaps the eminent William Buckland, had received all the credit for this novel method. It is possible Buckland, who created a *'flutter of excitement'* when he visited Scarborough in 1834 with Louis Agassiz (Williamson 1877, 196) had got the idea from Williamson himself. His involvement in identifying the small animal bones found amongst the Gristhorpe assemblage as weasel (Williamson 1872, 15) and his pivotal role in bringing Williamson's 1834 report to wide attention in the *Literary Gazette* that same year (Williamson 1896, 46) are a matter of record. Nonetheless, five years after Williamson documented his method, he still clearly regarded Buckland highly describing him as earnest and enthusiastic and that *'it was impossible to spend an hour in his bright, genial presence, without becoming infected with his scientific enthusiasm'* (Williamson 1877, 196). Whatever was at the source of Williamson's apparent annoyance, if the conservation had taken place, and he was not just mis-remembering his one and only archaeological project nearly 40 years later, he was clearly rueing omitting this from his report of 1834. It may be pertinent that the timing of the 1872 edition coincided with a flurry of recent Early Bronze Age barrow excavations undertaken by the like of Greenwell, Bateman and Mortimer and a burgeoning interest in the conservation of archaeological bones. This may have prompted Williamson's somewhat belated attempt to stamp his authority on the practice and establish the conservators of Gristhorpe Man as trailblazers. Contemporary evidence for the conservation is elusive: the cartoon (Figure 10.1) that illustrates Williamson watching the simmering bones was dated August 1900 and was drawn by Harry Woolsey, a friend of the Beswick family (according to the late Mrs. Beswick). It thus seems more likely that it draws on Williamson's 1872 report rather than first-hand knowledge from 1834. The Minute Books of the Scarborough Philosophical Society for the 12th July 1834 (the day after the skeleton was recovered) note that *'W. Travis, Rt. Tindall, W. Smith, F. Weddell, W. Harland and P. Murray are appointed a committee to ... to ascertain the best method of preserving the skeleton etc and to carry the whole into effect'* (see Melton and Beswick this volume for full transcript). They clearly expedited this request, enabling The *'Hull Packet'* to record on 22nd August 1834 that *'the human bones found in the coffin have been beautifully articulated by the liberal exertions of Messrs. Weddell and Harland, two*

medical practitioners in Scarbro'. But neither allude to the novel conservation method which we can assume had taken place between these two dates. Williamson's 1834 report was indubitably promptly prepared and published within six months of the discovery, but there was, nonetheless, still time for Dr. Murray to analyse the water from the coffin and the *'singular variety of adipocere'* floating upon it and for Williamson to include these experiments *'after the other parts had gone to Press'* (Williamson 1834, 17–18). Why did a procedure completed by the 22nd August not warrant a mention?

It seems unlikely that Williamson would have per-petuated a deception in his second edition of 1872, where he described Gristhorpe Man in the preface as an *'old friend'* – one who, Williamson's widow later recounted in a posthumous addition to his autobiography, he never tired of visiting in his latter years and that *'he almost embraced the brown old skeleton'* (Williamson 1896, 209). Writing in his autobiography he recalled that *'It was then suggested, probably by Dr. Harland, one of the most intelligent of the medical men then residing in the town, that these bones should be carefully washed and put into a common laundry boiler filled with a thin solution of glue.'* (Williamson 1896, 45). Is it possible, then, that William Harland, charged with wiring up the 'rotten' skeleton, had given up and replaced it with one he had acquired from elsewhere? Could this explain the many unusual factors surrounding the skeleton, including its completeness, height, dental caries, lack of tooth wear, the black paint and the evidently un-rotten state?

Two main problems thus presented themselves: was the skeleton of Early Bronze Age date or of 19th-century vintage, and had the conservation taken place? A radiocarbon date was required, but how would we know if we were dating a 19th-century human or, if the glue had penetrated the genuine skeleton (as Williamson seemed to think), 19th-century horses or fish, from which the glue was derived? Could we separate the two sources of collagen and possibly identify the type of glue? If the skeleton were not a fake, had the simmering itself destroyed the integrity of Gristhorpe Man's collagen, thus making radiocarbon dating and isotope analysis of his bone collagen impossible? In addition to the first two aims stated previously, we now had two more:

1. To determine whether the skeleton was a 19th-century fake.
2. To determine whether the novel conservation methods of simmering the skeleton in *'a thin solution of glue'* (Williamson 1872, 7) could be demonstrated; if it was hydrolysed animal collagen, what sort of animal it may have been; and if the conservation in 1834 meant we could no longer retrieve intact Early Bronze Age human collagen from the skeleton for dating and isotope analysis.

Samples and Methods

A right mandibular second molar was extracted from the mandible (Figs. 10.2, 10.3 and 10.4) and a replica tooth made by Cosmadent Ltd. Halifax, prior to sampling for isotope analysis and radiocarbon dating. The replica tooth was inserted into the mandible (Fig. 10.5) for display in the museum. The enamel surface was cleaned of all adhering material and surface enamel with tungsten carbide dental burrs prior to the removal of core enamel samples for strontium, oxygen and lead isotope analysis. In addition, a sample of crown dentine was removed for strontium isotope analysis to assess post-mortem change (Montgomery et al. 2007). Samples of enamel were sealed in containers for transport to the clean laboratory suite at the NERC Isotope Geosciences Laboratory at the British Geological Survey, Nottingham. Further sample preparation and measurement were performed following standard laboratory protocols and additional information on methods, standards and errors can be found in Table

10.1 and: for phosphate oxygen isotopes in Chenery et al. (2012); for lead isotopes and concentrations in Montgomery et al. (2010); and for strontium isotopes in Montgomery et al. (2007). The enamel of the sampled tooth mineralizes between the approximate ages of 2 and 8 years (AlQahtani et al. 2010) and because enamel, unlike bone, is acellular and avascular there is no subsequent replacement or turnover of the tissue. Consequently, these results provide information about place of origin during early childhood. In addition to the enamel sample, the bronze dagger was also subjected to lead isotope analysis by MC-ICP-MS at the NERC Isotope Geosciences Laboratory at the British Geological Survey, Nottingham.

Dentine from the lower half of the tooth root was removed for radiocarbon dating and carbon and nitrogen isotope analysis. This sample contains bone collagen deriving from approximately 6 years of life between the ages of 9.5 and 15.5 (AlQahtani et al. 2010). In addition, cortical bone from the femur was removed from the

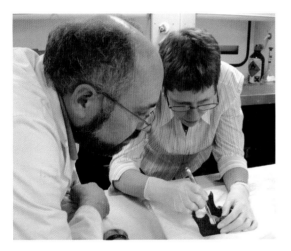 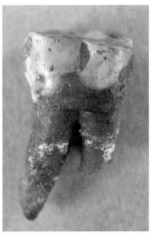 

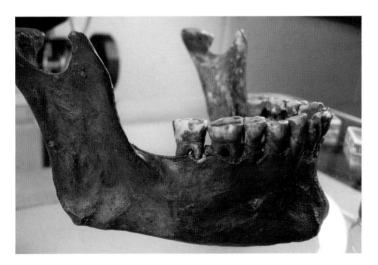

Above, left to right:

Fig. 10.2 Photograph of Christopher Knüsel and Julia Beaumont, BDS, extracting the right second molar for analysis.

Fig. 10.3 Photograph of the buccal view of the extracted right second molar.

Fig. 10.4 Photograph of the occlusal view of the extracted right second molar.

Fig. 10.5 (left) Photograph of the mandible with the replica second molar in place.

anterior right mid-femoral shaft with a small dental saw (Fig. 10.6). The sampled section was moulded, replaced and coloured by Dr. Sonia O'Connor (see Janaway *et al.*, this volume) prior to display in the museum. The femur was sub-sampled for radiocarbon dating and carbon and nitrogen isotope analysis and the sample submitted expected to represent a long-term average over most of Gristhorpe Man's adult life (Hedges *et al.* 2007). In addition to these robust and dense bone tissues, several other samples were selected specifically because their biogenic integrity was most likely to be compromised by the post-excavation conservation process: a periosteal flake from a rib, other loose bone flakes and surface bone 'dust'. Under normal circumstances such samples would never be taken for isotope analysis through choice, but it was hoped that such friable, poorly preserved, outer surfaces would be where evidence for the presence and species of animal glue would be found. The dentine and femoral bone samples to be dated were transferred to the NERC Radiocarbon Facility at Oxford University (see Batt, this volume) and those for carbon and nitrogen isotope analysis to the Stable Isotope Facility at the University of Bradford. Carbon and nitrogen isotope determinations were also carried out on a sample of 'brain' and carbon isotopes on the 'beeswax' (which contained only trace nitrogen), found inside the cranium.

Collagen was prepared using the modified Longin method (Brown *et al.* 1988; O'Connell and Hedges 1999). For dentine surface debris was removed by air-abrasion. For the femur, the surface was removed and retained for analysis. No pre-cleaning was undertaken on the surface flakes of bone (dust) or the rib sample. For dentine, femur and rib, a sample of *c.* 300 mg was demineralised in 0.5M hydrochloric acid at 4°C. Samples were rinsed with de-ionised water, placed in sealed tubes with pH3 HCl at 70°C

for 48 hours until the collagen fibrils had solubilized. Samples were filtered using an 8μm Ezee® filter to remove large debris and 30,000 molecular weight ultrafilters to retain intact collagen. For some samples, the 'small fraction' (the filtrate from the ultrafilter) which is normally discarded, was retained and processed to establish if it contained hydrolysed collagen from the animal glue used in the conservation process in 1834. The samples were then freeze-dried to sublimate remaining water.

Results and Discussion

The results of the isotope analysis, along with details of standards and analytical errors, are presented in Tables 10.1 and 10.2.

Lead isotopes and concentration

The first question addressed was whether Gristhorpe Man was a fake. A significantly different level of anthropogenic pollution, using the level of lead as a proxy, would have been experienced by someone living in early Bronze Age England compared to an England in the throes of the Industrial Revolution. Changes in the level of lead in human teeth in Britain have been documented from the Neolithic through to the 19th century (Montgomery *et al.* 2010; Millard *et al.* in press), and they increase from *c.* less than 0.1 mg kg⁻¹ to levels approaching 100 mg kg⁻¹, i.e. a 1,000–fold increase. The level of lead in the enamel of Gristhorpe Man was 0.003 mg kg⁻¹, and is, to date, the lowest amount of lead yet measured in human tooth enamel from Britain (Montgomery *et al.* 2010). It is exceedingly low, and it is highly unlikely that anyone living in England during the post-medieval period would have such a low level of lead exposure. It is, therefore, indicative of an individual inhabiting a pristine and unpolluted environment and strongly suggests the tooth, and by extrapolation the skeleton, is of prehistoric date.

Gristhorpe is located to the north of the Cretaceous Chalk Wolds in a complex region of sedimentary rocks (mudstones, siltstones, limestones and sandstones) of Jurassic date which are largely overlain by Quaternary till (British Geological Survey 1977, 2001) (Fig. 10.7). The isotope ratio of the lead in Gristhorpe Man's tooth enamel places him within the field of other archaeological humans from England and thus suggests an English origin (Fig. 10.8). Place of origin can be constrained further: such values are not consistent with origins on marine carbonate rocks such as the Chalk uplands of the Yorkshire Wolds to the south of Gristhorpe (green areas on Fig. 10.7), and the Jurassic, Carboniferous or Permian limestones that occur to the north and west (blue and green areas on Fig. 10.7).

1cm

Fig. 10.6 Photograph of the right anterior femur showing the location of the removed sample of cortical bone for radiocarbon dating and isotope analysis and the restoration prior to colour matching to the original bone surface.

Table 10.1. Lead, strontium and oxygen isotope data for Gristhorpe Man and his dagger. Data source: Melton *et al.* 2010.

Sample	^{206}Pb/^{204}Pb[1]	^{207}Pb/^{204}Pb	^{208}Pb/^{204}Pb	^{207}Pb/^{206}Pb	^{208}Pb/^{206}Pb	Pb mg kg^{-1}	Sr mg kg^{-1}	^{87}Sr/^{86}Sr[2]	δ^{18}O$_{p\ vsmow}$ ‰[3]	δ^{18}O$_{dw\ vsmow}$ ‰[4]
Bronze Dagger	18.2428	15.6308	38.2600	0.85684	2.09736					
Second molar enamel	18.45	15.63	38.44	0.847	2.083	0.003	66.3	0.71069	17.2 ±0.18	-7.8 ±0.4
Second molar dentine							173.9	0.71062		

[1] External reproducibility for the dagger measured by MC-ICP-MS at NIGL, Keyworth: ±0.0124% for ^{208}Pb/^{204}Pb; ±0.0108% for ^{207}Pb/^{204}Pb; ±0.0078% for ^{206}Pb/^{204}Pb; ±0.0043% for ^{207}Pb/^{206}Pb; ±0.0068% for ^{208}Pb/^{206}Pb 2σ and data are normalised and errors propagated to within run measurements of NBS 981. For the tooth measured by TIMS: ±0.15% for ^{208}Pb/^{204}Pb; ±0.11% for ^{207}Pb/^{204}Pb; ±0.07% for ^{206}Pb/^{204}Pb; ±0.04% for ^{207}Pb/^{206}Pb and ±0.08% for ^{208}Pb/^{206}Pb (2σ, n=19).
[2] External reproducibility was estimated at ±0.004% (2σ).
[3] External and sample reproducibility for phosphate oxygen measurements was estimated at ±0.18‰ (1σ).
[4] Calculated using Levinson's equation (Levinson *et al.* 1987) after correction for the difference between the average published values for NBS120C and NBS120B used by Levinson (Chenery *et al.* 2010). For comparison, Daux *et al.* 2008 Eq. 4 and 6 would produce drinking water values of -7.5‰ and -7.2‰ respectively which would not change the interpretation of local origins.

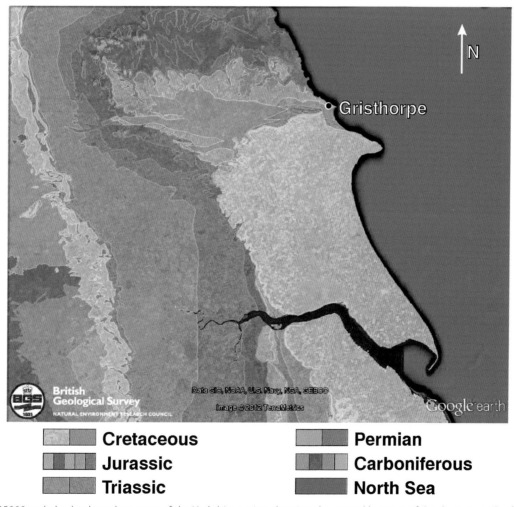

Cretaceous   Permian
Jurassic   Carboniferous
Triassic   North Sea

Fig. 10.7 1:625000 scale bedrock geology map of the Yorkshire region showing the coastal location of Gristhorpe, north of the Yorkshire Wolds on Jurassic sedimentary rocks. Reproduced with the permission of the British Geological Survey ©NERC. All rights Reserved.

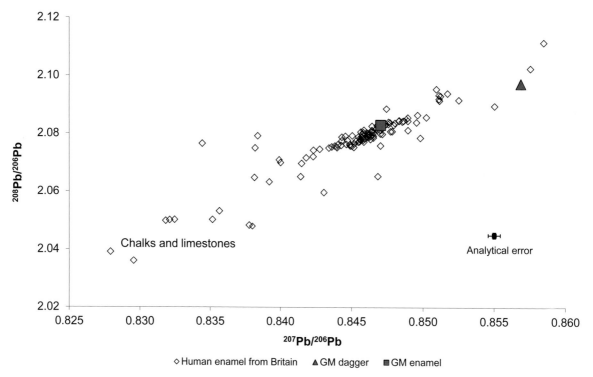

Fig. 10.8 Lead isotope plot showing data for Gristhorpe Man and his dagger. Comparative data for other humans from Britain is shown (Montgomery 2002; Montgomery *et al.* 2010). Analytical error for the enamel samples is shown as ±2σ.

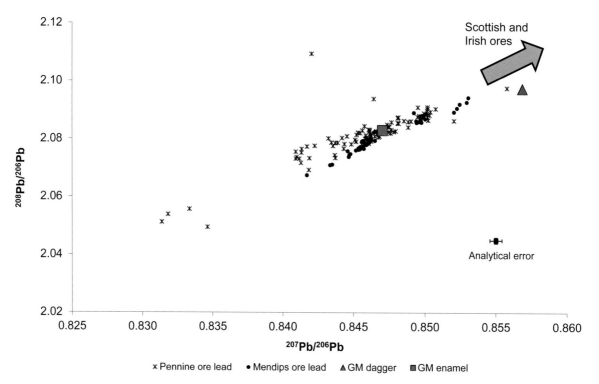

Fig. 10.9 Lead isotope plot showing data for Gristhorpe Man and his dagger. Comparative data for the Mendips (Haggerty *et al.* 1996) and Pennine (Barreiro 1995) orefields are shown. Analytical error for the enamel samples is shown as ±2σ.

The lead isotope ratio of the bronze dagger is different to that of Gristhorpe Man and falls on the outer edge of the main English lead and copper ore sources in the Pennines and southwest England (Fig. 10.9). It is, therefore, highly unlikely to be composed solely of English copper, although the data cannot rule out some contribution through mixing and recycling. Older metal deposits from Scotland and Ireland may have provided all or most of the copper in the Gristhorpe dagger (Rohl 1996). Northover (this volume) notes that the lead isotope ratios from the dagger are consistent with Chalcolithic 'A' metal from Ireland or Wales.

Strontium and oxygen isotopes

The enamel sample from Gristhorpe Man produced a strontium isotope ratio of 0.7107 and had a strontium concentration of 66 mg kg⁻¹. This level of strontium is in line with archaeological populations from Britain which have a median value of 84 mg kg⁻¹ (Evans *et al.* 2012). The dentine sample was higher, at 174 mg kg⁻¹, which is often the case in archaeological humans as dentine and bone are susceptible to post-mortem contamination (Trickett *et al.*

2003). The lack of any change in the isotope ratio between the enamel and dentine, however, suggests the value in the enamel was the same as that of the strontium in the waters percolating through the coffin (Montgomery *et al.* 2007). The enamel strontium isotope ratio corroborates the conclusion drawn from the lead isotopes, and rules out origins on marine carbonates such as chalk and limestone (Fig. 10.10). However, such a ratio is hardly unique and is therefore somewhat undiagnostic: it is extremely common amongst humans excavated from both Britain and the Continent because it can be obtained from a wide range of sedimentary silicate terrains found across northern Europe. These include the Jurassic rocks and Quaternary till at Gristhorpe, and the Permo-Triassic sediments and drift deposits of the Vale of Pickering in the wider Yorkshire region (Fig. 10.7). The oxygen isotope ratio obtained from the tooth enamel phosphate provided a $\delta^{18}O$ value of 17.2‰, which is in close agreement with the mean value for humans from eastern Britain of 17.2‰ ± 1.3‰ (Evans *et al.* 2012) (Fig. 10.10). All three isotope systems are, therefore, in agreement and are consistent with origins on the Jurassic silicate sedimentary rocks of north Yorkshire. They cannot,

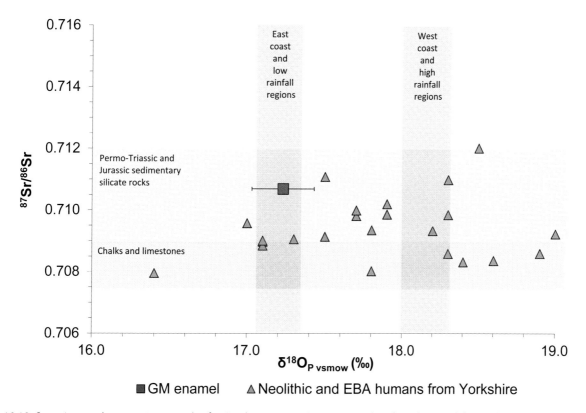

Fig. 10.10 Strontium and oxygen isotope plot for Gristhorpe Man. Comparative data for other Neolithic and Early Bronze age humans excavated from Yorkshire (Evans *et al.* 2012; Montgomery *et al.* 2005, 2007) is shown with expected strontium isotope ranges for humans originating on the main geological terrains in Yorkshire (Evans *et al.* 2010). The vertical blue rectangles are the 95% confidence intervals for oxygen isotope ratios of humans inhabiting the eastern and western seaboards of England (Evans *et al.* 2012). Analytical error for the Gristhorpe Man sample is within symbol for $^{87}Sr/^{86}Sr$ (2σ) and ±0.2 ‰ (1σ) for $\delta^{18}O$.

Table 10.2 Carbon and nitrogen isotope data for Gristhorpe Man. Stable isotopes were measured by continuous-flow isotope ratio mass spectrometry at the Stable Light Isotope Facility, University of Bradford. 'Small fraction' refers to the collagenous proteins that, unlike intact collagen, go through the ultrafilter and are usually discarded. Highlighted boxes indicate samples which did not meet the quality criteria for well-preserved collagen established by van Klinken (1999) and have not been plotted in Figure 10.11. Analytical error determined from repeat measurements of internal and international standards was ±0.2 ‰ or better.

Sample	$\delta^{13}C$‰	$\delta^{15}N$‰	%C	%N	C/N	n
Bone samples taken for dietary analysis						
Femur – surface removed	-21.2	10.7	44.7	16.4	3.2	2
Femur – surface removed repeat	-21.2	10.8	43.6	16.1	3.2	2
Dentine from second molar	-21.0	11.3	45.0	16.9	3.1	2
Bone samples taken to identify glue						
Femur – surface removed small fraction	-21.3	10.6	42.3	15.2	3.2	2
Femur – surface removed small fraction repeat	-21.4	10.7	42.3	15.1	3.2	2
Femur surface – small fraction	-21.4	10.5	40.3	13.5	3.4	2
Femur surface – small fraction repeat	-21.7	10.5	40.0	13.1	3.6	1
Bone "dust"	-21.6	10.5	45.0	15.6	3.4	1
Bone "dust" small fraction	-21.1	10.7	40.6	14.3	3.3	2
Bone "dust" small fraction repeat	-21.2	10.7	41.4	14.4	3.2	1
Rib surface flake	-21.2	12.0	46.0	14.3	3.7	2
Rib surface flake – small fraction	-21.2	11.9	43.4	13.4	3.8	2
mean of bone samples (n = 12)	-21.3	10.9	42.9	14.9	3.4	
1 sd	0.2	0.5	2.0	1.2	0.2	
Miscellaneous samples						
"Brain"	-23.6	11.7	54.9	8.1	7.9	2
Beeswax from inside the cranium	-26.8	n/a	81.8	0.1	n/a	2

however, rule out origins in other places of Britain and Europe, where a similar combination of values may possibly be found but the most parsimonious interpretation is that Gristhorpe Man spent his childhood in Yorkshire.

Carbon and nitrogen isotopes

The samples of dentine, bone and bone flakes and fractions produced a small range of carbon and nitrogen isotope ratios. The mean of the carbon isotope ratios is -21.3‰ ± 0.2‰ and for nitrogen isotope ratios 10.9 ‰ ± 0.5‰ (1σ, n = 12) (Table 10.2). All samples produced collagen which fell within the quality indicators for well-preserved collagen (van Klinken 1999) apart from the two rib flake samples which gave similar carbon isotope ratios to the other bone samples but slightly higher nitrogen isotope ratios (Table 10.2). Such values are typical of humans

from Britain and highly untypical of herbivores such as sheep, cow and horse, which would have lower values (Fig. 10.11), and marine fish, which would have higher values. All the results are within the expected range for Bronze Age individuals from east Yorkshire and Britain (Fig. 10.11) and indicate a diet with a high level of animal protein from terrestrial sources such as beef, pork or lamb, with no measurable consumption of marine resources (Jay et al. 2012). Given the location of Gristhorpe on the Yorkshire coast, it might be expected that marine resources would be exploited to a greater degree, but this appears not to be the case throughout Britain during the Bronze Age (Montgomery and Jay 2012; Jay et al. 2012). There is, therefore, no difference between the samples taken from the bone surfaces and those of cortical bone or dentine, no difference between the collagen from the 'small fraction' (<30,000 molecular weight) and the intact collagen which

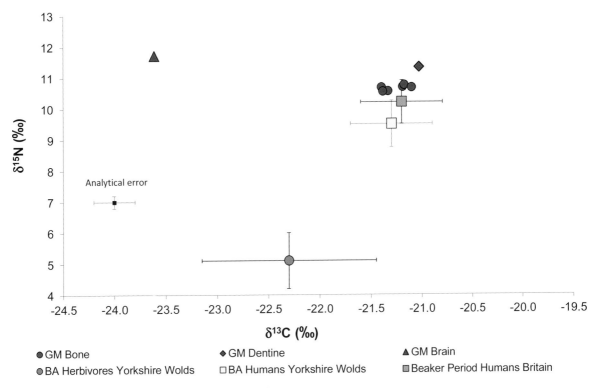

Fig. 10.11 Carbon and nitrogen isotope plot of all samples measured from Gristhorpe Man (GM). Comparative populations are mean values ±1σ of Bronze Age humans and herbivores from the Yorkshire Wolds (Montgomery and Jay 2013) and Beaker period humans from across Britain (Jay *et al.* 2012). Analytical error for the Gristhorpe Man samples is ±0.2‰ (1σ).

might have been expected to separate out degraded animal collagen from well-preserved human collagen, and no interpretable difference between the thick cortical bone of the femur and the thin rib flake fragment. Indeed, if the poor quality collagen obtained from the rib was poor because it was contaminated with glue, the isotope ratios did not support this conclusion, as herbivore collagen would have been lower for both δ¹⁵N and δ¹³C and marine fish would have higher δ¹³C values. Following these puzzling results, a fresh flake of surface bone was submitted to Mike Buckley for proteomics analysis as he raised the possibility that animal glue may have been present but, being soluble in water, was lost in the initial weak acid demineralization step of the collagen extraction procedure. However, proteomics could find no evidence for the presence of non-human collagen on the surface of Gristhorpe Man's bones (Buckley, this volume). The radiocarbon dates for the bone collagen (dentine: 2150–1940 cal BC; femur: 2280–2030 cal BC, see Batt, this volume) likewise showed no evidence of contamination with 19th-century collagen, effectively ruling out the somewhat gruesome conclusion that Gristhorpe Man had been simmered in glue produced from human bones; the dates for the skeleton were in good agreement with the dates for the coffin (Batt, this volume).

The carbon and nitrogen isotope ratios of the black substance in a test tube labelled as 'brain' produced results that would be broadly consistent with brain tissue from Gristhorpe Man: the nitrogen isotope ratio of 11.7‰ was comparable with the dentine sample and the carbon isotope ratio of -23.6‰ was is 2.6‰ lower than that for the dentine. This is consistent with the expected carbon isotope ratio offset between collagen and a fatty, lipid rich tissue such as the brain (Jim *et al.* 2004). GC-MS of a small sample of the putative brain tissue by Carl Heron showed it to be rich in stanols and stanones which are microbial alteration products of cholesterol which makes up 25% of the lipids present in brain tissue (Melton *et al.* 2010). This combined evidence strongly suggests this material is indeed 4000–year-old degraded brain tissue. And, finally, the solid substance recovered from inside the cranium also proved not to be the elusive glue: in stark contrast to collagen, it contained virtually no nitrogen (Table 10.2) and was determined using GC-MS to be degraded beeswax (Carl Heron, pers. comm.). It is not known when beeswax was applied to the skeleton, or why it is present inside the cranium, but it may date to the drilling of the hole in the top of the cranium (see Janaway *et al.*, this volume).

Conclusions

All the evidence suggests that, if it did indeed take place, the process of simmering the bones for eight hours did not adversely affect the recovery of good quality collagen, and hence the integrity of the stable isotope data or the radiocarbon dates. No trace of animal glue was found and evidence that the glue had impregnated, or coated the skeletal tissues that were analysed proved elusive. The evidence thus provides no support for the claim that the bones had been simmered in glue. A contemporary written record predating Williamson's 1872 revised report has yet to be found, and thus what sort of glue was used and why Williamson thought it had worked as a treatment remains a mystery. It may be pertinent that the timing of the 1872 edition coincided with a flurry of recent Early Bronze Age barrow excavations undertaken by Greenwell, Bateman and Mortimer and a new interest in the preservation of archaeological bones.

That Gristhorpe Man was consuming a diet rich in terrestrial animal protein such as meat is further supported by the identification of renal stones (Edwards; Knüsel *et al.,* this volume) and the presence of bovine products amongst the assemblage (Buckley, this volume). What is perhaps most interesting is that there was no increase in animal protein between later childhood and adulthood; similar amounts and sources of protein seemed to have been consumed between the ages of nine and sixteen, as in later life. If he had been elevated to the '*high rank of a Brigantian chief*' (Williamson 1834, 16) through prowess in adulthood, this change in status does not seem to be reflected in a new diet. Moreover, if he was well-nourished from an early age with a relatively soft diet containing meat and sugars/carbohydrates, such a diet may provide an explanation for many of the attributes that marked him out as rather unusual for the Early Bronze Age - such as his tall stature, tooth decay and limited tooth wear, which all point to him being well-nourished since early childhood. Williamson's conclusion that '*the man was likely to belong to the Brigantes, the tribe resident in Yorkshire when the Romans arrived*' (1834, 16) is supported by the lead, strontium and oxygen data, although they clearly cannot determine either his tribal affiliation or whether the Brigantes were already resident in Yorkshire in the Early Bronze Age. The new data presented here would perhaps enable a small amendment: Gristhorpe Man appears to have been a high-ranking member, throughout his life, of the tribe resident in what was a pristine and salubrious Yorkshire - until the Romans arrived and polluted it.

Acknowledgements
We are indebted to the Rotunda Museum, Scarborough, and Karen Snowdon for allowing us to carry out this research on Gristhorpe Man. We thank: Janet Ambers at the British Museum for identifying the Indian ink; Carl Heron, University of Bradford, for undertaking GC-MS analysis on the brain and beeswax; Julia Beaumont, who used her skills in dentistry to extract the tooth; and Mandy Jay for invaluable advice and insights.

References

AlQahtani, S. J., Hector, M. P. and Liversidge, H. M. (2010) Brief communication: The London atlas of human tooth development and eruption, *American Journal of Physical Anthropology* 142(3), 481–490.

Barreiro, B. A. (1995) *Lead isotopic composition of galenas for the North Pennine ore field*, NIGL Report No. 75, Nottingham, UK.

Barrett, J. H. and Richards, M. P. (2004) Identity, gender, religion and economy: new isotope and radiocarbon evidence for marine resource intensification in early historic Orkney, Scotland, UK. *European Journal of Archaeology* 7(8), 249–271.

Beeton, I. (1861) *The Book of Household Management.* London, S.O. Beeton.

Beeton, I. (1865) *Mrs. Beeton's Dictionary of Every-Day Cookery.* London, S.O. Beeton.

Bentley, R. A. (2006) Strontium isotopes from the earth to the archaeological skeleton: A review. *Journal of Archaeological Method and Theory* 13(3), 135–187.

British Geological Survey 1977. *Quaternary map of the United Kingdom South*, Ordnance Survey/NERC, Southampton.

British Geological Survey 2001. *Solid Geology Map UK South Sheet*, Ordnance Survey/NERC, Southampton.

Brown, T. A., Nelson, D. E., Vogel, J. S. and Southon, J. R. (1988) Improved collagen extraction by modified Longin method. *Radiocarbon* 30, 171–177.

Chenery, C., Müldner, G., Evans, J., Eckardt, H. and Lewis, M. (2010) Strontium and stable isotope evidence for diet and mobility in Roman Gloucester, UK. *Journal of Archaeological Science* 37(1), 150–163.

Chenery, C., Pashley, V., Lamb, A., Sloane, H. and Evans, J. (2012) The oxygen isotope relationship between the phosphate and structural carbonate fractions of human bioapatite, *Rapid Communications in Mass Spectrometry* 26, 309–319.

Daux, V., Lécuyer, C., Héran, M.-A., Amiot, R., Simon, L., Fourel, F., Martineau, F., Lynnerup, N., Reychler, H. and Escarguel, G. (2008) Oxygen isotope fractionation between human phosphate and water revisited. *Journal of Human Evolution* 55(6), 1138–1147.

Davis, J. B. and Thurnam, J. (1865) *Crania Britannica. Delineations and Descriptions of the Skulls of the Aboriginal and Early Inhabitants of the British Islands: with Notices of their Other Remains.* Vol. 2. London, printed for the subscribers.

Glob, P. V. (1974) *The Mound People: Danish Bronze-Age Man Preserved.* New York (NY), Cornell University Press.

Ehleringer, J. R., Bowen, G. J., Chesson, L. A., West, A. G., Podlesak, D. W. and Cerling, T. E. (2008) Hydrogen and oxygen isotope ratios in human hair are related to geography. *Proceedings of* the *National Academy of Sciences of the United States of America* 105(8), 2788–2793.

Evans, J., Chenery, C. A. and Montgomery, J. (2012) A summary of strontium and oxygen isotope variation in archaeological human tooth enamel excavated from Britain. *Journal of Analytical Atomic Spectroscopy* 27, 754–764.

Evans, J., Montgomery, J., Wildman, G. and Boulton, N. (2010) Spatial variations in biosphere ^{87}Sr/^{86}Sr in Britain. *Journal of the Geological Society* 167(1), 1–4.

Fricke, H. C., O'Neil, J. R. and Lynnerup, N. (1995) Oxygen isotope composition of human tooth enamel from Medieval Greenland: linking climate and society, *Geology* 23(10), 869–872.

Haggerty, R., Budd, P., Rohl, B. and Gale, N. H. (1996) Pb-isotope evidence for the role of Mesozoic basins in the Genesis of Mississippi Valley-type mineralization in Somerset, UK. *Journal of the Geological Society, London* 153, 673–676.

Hassal, A. H. (1857) *Adulterations detected: or plain instructions for the discovery of frauds in food and medicine.* London, Longman, Brown, Green, Longmans and Roberts.

Hedges, R. E. M., Clement, J. G., Thomas, C. D. L. and O'Connell, T. C. (2007) Collagen turnover in the adult femoral mid-shaft: Modeled from anthropogenic radiocarbon tracer measurements. *American Journal of Physical Anthropology*, 133(2), 808–816.

Hutchins, J. (1767) Archaeology, Part 1. *Gentlemans' Magazine* 37, 94–95.

Jay, M. and Richards, M. P. (2007) British Iron Age diet: stable isotopes and other evidence. *Proceedings of the Prehistoric Society* 73, 169–190.

Jay, M., Parker Pearson, M., Richards, M., Nehlich, O., Montgomery, J., Chamberlain, A. and Sheridan, A. (2012) The Beaker People Project: an interim report on the progress of the isotopic analysis of the organic skeletal material. In M. J. Allen, J. Gardiner and A. Sheridan, (eds.) *Is there a British Chalcolithic? People, place and polity in the later 3rd millennium*, Prehistoric Society Research Papers 4, 226–236. Oxford, Oxbow Books.

Jim, S., Ambrose, S. H. and Evershed, R. P. (2004) Stable carbon isotopic evidence for differences in the biosynthetic origin of bone cholesterol, collagen and apatite: implications for their use in palaeodietary reconstruction. *Geochimica et Cosmochimica Acta* 6861–72.

Levinson, A. A., Luz, B. and Kolodny, Y. (1987) Variations in Oxygen Isotope Compositions of Human Teeth and Urinary Stones. *Applied Geochemistry* 2, 367–371.

Melton, N., Montgomery, J., Knusel, C., Batt, C., Needham, S., Parker Pearson, M., Sheridan, A., Heron, C., Horsley, T., Schmidt, A., Evans, A., Carter, E., Edwards, H., Hargreaves, M., Janaway, R., Lynnerup, N., Northover, P., O'Connor, S., Ogden, A., Taylor, T., Wastling, V. and Wilson, A. (2010) Gristhorpe Man: an Early Bronze Age log-coffin burial scientifically defined. *Antiquity* 84(325), 796–815.

Millard, A., Montgomery, J., Trickett, M., Beaumont, J., Evans, J. and Chenery, S. (in press) Childhood lead exposure in the British Isles during the Industrial Revolution. In M. Zuckerman (ed.) *Are Modern Environments Bad for Human Health? Revisiting the Second Epidemiological Transition.* Columbia, SC, University of South Carolina Press.

Montgomery, J. (2002) Lead and Strontium Isotope Compositions of Human Dental Tissues as an Indicator of Ancient Exposure and Population Dynamics. Unpublished PhD thesis, University of Bradford.

Montgomery, J. (2010) Passports from the past: Investigating human dispersals using strontium isotope analysis of tooth enamel, *Annals of Human Biology* 37(3), 325–346.

Montgomery, J. and Jay, M. (2013) The contribution of skeletal isotope analysis to understanding the Bronze Age in Europe. In A. Harding and H. Fokkens, (eds.) *The Handbook of Bronze Age Europe*, 179–196. Oxford, Oxford University Press.

Montgomery, J., Evans, J. and Cooper, R. (2007). Resolving archaeological populations with Sr-isotope mixing models. *Applied Geochemistry* 22(7), 1502–1514.

Montgomery, J., Evans, J., Powlesland, D. and Roberts, C. (2005) Continuity or colonization in Anglo-Saxon England? Isotope evidence for mobility, subsistence practice, and status at West Heslerton. *American Journal of Physical Anthropology* 126(2), 123–138.

Montgomery, J., Evans, J. A., Chenery, S. R., Pashley, V. and Killgrove, K. (2010) "Gleaming, white and deadly": the use of lead to track human exposure and geographic origins in the Roman period in Britain. In H. Eckardt (ed.) *Roman diasporas: archaeological approaches to mobility and diversity in the Roman Empire*, 199–226, Journal of Roman Archaeology Supplement 78, Portsmouth, Rhode Island.

Molleson, T., Eldridge, D. and Gale, N. H. (1986) Identification of lead sources by stable isotope ratios in bones and lead from Poundbury Camp, Dorset. *Oxford Journal of Archaeology* 5(2), 249–253.

Müldner, G., Chenery, C. and Eckardt, H. (2011) The 'Headless Romans': multi-isotope investigations of an unusual burial ground from Roman Britain. *Journal of Archaeological Science* 38(2), 280–290.

O'Connell, T. C. and Hedges, R. E. M. (1999) Isotopic Comparison of Hair and Bone: Archaeological Analyses. *Journal of Archaeological Science* 26(6), 661–665.

Rohl, B. (1996) Lead isotope data from the Isotrace Laboratory, Oxford: archaeometry data base 2, galena from Britain and Ireland. *Archaeometry* 38, 165–180.

Trickett, M. A., Budd, P., Montgomery, J. and Evans, J. (2003) An assessment of solubility profiling as a decontamination procedure for the Sr-87/Sr-86 analysis of archaeological human skeletal tissue. *Applied Geochemistry* 18(5), 653–658.

van Klinken, G. J. (1999) Bone Collagen Quality Indicators for Palaeodietary and Radiocarbon Measurements. *Journal of Archaeological Science* 26(6), 687–695.

Williamson, W. C. (1834) *Description of the Tumulus, lately opened at Gristhorpe, near Scarborough.* Scarborough, Yorks., C. R. Todd.

Williamson, W. C. (1872) *Description of the Tumulus opened at Gristhorpe, near Scarborough, with engravings of the coffin, weapons, etc.* Scarborough, Yorks., S.W. Theakston.

Williamson, W. C. (1877) Reminiscences of a Yorkshire Naturalist. *Good Words* 18, 62–66, 133–136 and 194–197.

Williamson, W. C. (1896) *Reminiscences of a Yorkshire Naturalist.* London, George Redway.

11

THE FACIAL RECONSTRUCTION

Alan R. Ogden

Introduction

The superb preservation condition of the Gristhorpe Man, offered the rare opportunity to produce a facial reconstruction using modern forensic techniques. Unusually for an archaeological reconstruction no parts of the skull-cranium, facial skeleton or mandible, were missing, offering a precious opportunity to reconstruct a face from the past. The reconstruction is now part of the new display at the Rotunda Museum of Gristhorpe Man with his coffin, that brings the Bronze Age in East Yorkshire to life. In doing this we are following in the tradition of Victorian predecessors, in particular William Crawford Williamson's 1872 third edition of the pamphlet describing the discovery. In this, he included illustrations of the skull that had been published in *Crania Britannica* (Davis and Thurnam 1865), and which he described as '*the reappearance of an old friend but emphatically with a new face*' (Williamson 1872, 3).

Methods and materials

The cranium was articulated with the mandible in its normal resting position with the dental arches separated vertically by 2 mm. The skull was wrapped in a layer of 1cm thick bubble-wrap to act as a spacer, and a two-part supporting shell for the impression was constructed in Plaster of Paris using a 1mm wax layer along the antero-posterior midline to separate the two halves. This shell was left for two hours to set and gain strength. The shell was then gently prized apart and the bubble-wrap removed. A layer of cotton wool and gauze was glued to the inner surface of both shells for anchorage of the impression material.

Eyeballs of clay (24 mm diameter) were positioned with

the plane of the iris/sclera junction tangential to the mid-supraorbital and infra-orbital points, as is suggested by Wilkinson (2004, 166), supported in position with crumpled acid-free paper. Deep cavities and undercuts on the skull that would make its withdrawal from the mould impossible without risking damage to the fragile bones were blocked

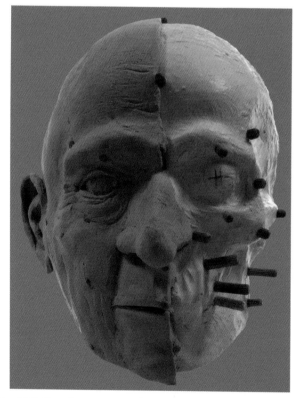

Fig. 11.1 The clay reconstruction in progress showing the tissue depth markers glued to the plaster replica and the completed right-hand side.

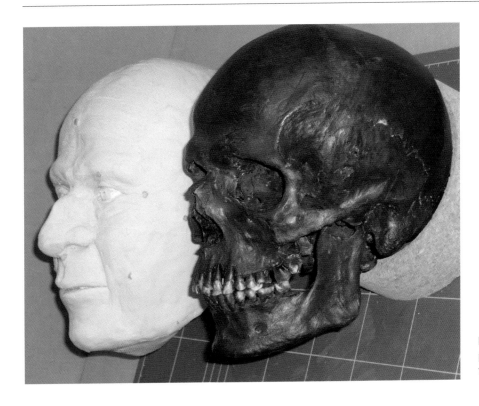

Fig. 11.2 The clay reconstruction compared with the original skull showing the prominent glabella and nasal bones.

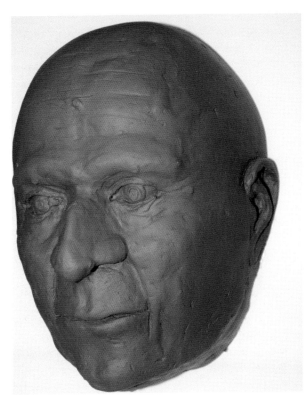

Fig. 11.3 The finished reconstruction, now on display at the Rotunda Museum. Note that the tissue-depth markers are just visible, confirming that the mean tissue depths are correct at each point.

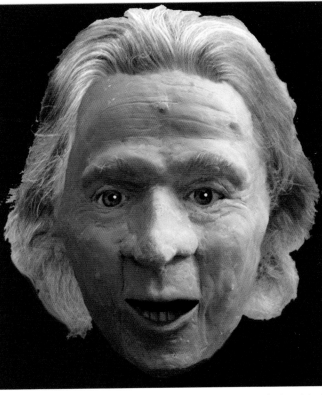

Fig. 11.4 A still from the three-minute animation which added colouring, hair and expression to the head. It shows Gristhorpe Man welcoming the public to the Rotunda Museum and describing the investigations that he has undergone whilst at Bradford University.

out with crumpled acid-free paper and masking tape. The skull with its applied blocking-out materials was then swathed in 'Cling-Film' low density polyethylene (LDPE), to prevent any direct contact of the impression material with the surface of the bone. The shell was then fixed together and an alginate dental impression material was used to take an impression of the skull and its covering, as its water-based formula and low tear-resistance minimised any risk of damage to the delicate bones. The impression material was mixed with cold water to ensure slow setting, placed in the mould, the skull was then gently lowered into position, and the alginate left to set.

The plaster shell and impression was then gently prised open and the undamaged skull removed from the mould and cleaned of masking tape and paper. A cast of the skull was then poured in resin-strengthened Plaster of Paris.

Facial reconstruction was by the 'Manchester Method' (Prag & Neave 1997; Wilkinson 2004). Tissue thickness indicators, 4 mm width wooden dowels cut to the correct length for the location, based on ultrasound data for a 55-year-old European male (Helmer, 1984, modified by Wilkinson 2004, 137) were glued to the plaster replica, carefully placed on skeletal landmarks (Figure 11.1). The muscles were then built up in modelling clay, according to the strength of their muscle markings on the skull. The anatomical modelling was covered by a layer of clay, laid over the surface to simulate the outer layer of subcutaneous tissues and skin allowing them to mirror the form beneath, but always using the markers to control their thickness. The tissues were thereby built up to the average depth over each landmark and, for permanence, a resin cast was made (Figures 11.2 and 11.3).

Unfortunately, such a model bears only as much likeness to a living person as a formal passport photograph. Modern software techniques (Adobe Photoshop Elements 8: Reallusion Crazytalk v6.2 PRO) were therefore used to render the hair and to animate the reconstruction as he speaks in English to a modern audience (Figure 11.4). The visitor to the Museum can thus visualise the reconstruction as a living man, a senior figure in his society, used to being obeyed and perhaps even revered. A three-minute animation was made from a photograph of the finished reconstruction, to inform, educate and entertain museum visitors. This animation added colour, hair, expression and movement to the head. Although there was no direct evidence for hair or colouring, long greying hair in keeping with his biological age was applied and left ungroomed (Wilkinson 2006). The video animation with the cast representing Gristhorpe Man welcoming the public to the Rotunda Museum and, as requested by the Museum Curator, describing the investigations that the skeletal remains had undergone whilst at Bradford University, have been on public display alongside the skeleton ever since.

Discussion

Several methods are available for facial reconstruction from the skull. Modern scientific methods of forensic facial reconstruction can be said to have begun with the Russian Gerasimov working in the 1930s, who developed an anatomical method that involved modelling every facial muscle onto the skull, one by one (Gerasimov 1971). Krogman and Snow in the US later developed what has become known as the American 3D method which employs tissue thickness data from tables relating to different ages, ethnic groups and sexes (Snow et al. 1970; Taylor 2001), and this was further developed in Germany by Helmer (Işcan and Helmer 1993; Helmer 1993). However, these methods can produce a very unrealistic and characterless, shop dummy appearance (see Byers 2002, 382 for an example). Recently computerised systems have been developed, but so far have produced similar disappointing results since they use tissue depth data and general determinants only, rather than the extensive information that can be determined from the bony details (Vanezis et al. 2000; Wilkinson 2004). The ability of computerised systems to represent realistic face morphology is 'currently limited in contrast to manual methods.' (Stephan 2009, 305).

Regarding the choice between the anatomical method and the tissue depth method, Anderson (1990, 14) states: 'It should be noted that these two methods are not mutually exclusive or contradictory. Many reconstruction practitioners use a combination of both', whilst Taylor (2001, 344) has opined 'It is our belief, too, that the wise reconstruction artist takes advantage of the best aspects of each method. Therefore, a combination approach is likely the best approach'.

Richard Neave is a medical artist who also uses tissue depth information and was joint founder with John Prag of 'The Manchester Method' (Prag and Neave 1997), and this has been further developed by Caroline Wilkinson (2004). Their reconstructions are done on plaster castings of human skulls and, in the opinion of this author, are outstanding in their realism. After preparing the casting, they examine the muscle attachments evident on the skull and, based on their robusticity, develop the facial musculature, muscle by muscle. At the stage where all the precisely calculated anatomical modeling is covered up by a layer of clay, to simulate the outer layers of subcutaneous tissues and skin, the artist must allow them to mirror the form underneath but always use the measurements to dictate their thickness. 'This ensures that the hand of the artist does not and cannot influence the final shape of the head and face. The measurements still rule supreme.' (Prag and Neave 1997, 31). The combination method of facial reconstruction, 'appears to be the most accurate technique .... Although the tissue depth data are very important, it must be noted that these are only mean sets of tissue thickness and, as such, cannot take into *account the individuality of each skull and, therefore, each face. The Manchester method involves the study of facial anatomy, expression, anthropometry, anthropology and the relationship between the soft and hard tissues of the face'* (Wilkinson 2004).

The author has endeavored to meet these ideals and hopes that the viewing public will consider that this reconstruction has succeeded in bringing an old friend, on public display since 1834, to new life.

Acknowledgements
Thanks are offered to Dr Nigel Melton and Dr Janet Montgomery of the Department of Archaeology, Durham University, and Dr Karen Snowden (Head of Collections, Scarborough Museums Trust) for the opportunity to work with these precious remains. Grateful thanks are also offered to Julia Beaumont and Nivien Speith who were invaluable assistants on the occasions when the author simply did not have enough hands.

References

Anderson, M. (1990) Fleshing out the past: reconstructing fossil faces. *Discovery,* 22 (1), 11–15.

Byers, S. N. (2002) *Introduction to Forensic Anthropology: A Textbook.* Boston, Allyn & Bacon.

Davis, J. B. and Thurnam, J. (1865) *Crania Britannica. Delineations and Descriptions of the Skulls of the Aboriginal and Early Inhabitants of the British Islands: with Notices of their Other Remains* (2 vols.). London, printed for the Subscribers.

Gerasimov, M. (1971) *The Face Finder.* London, Hutchinson & Co.

Helmer, R. R., Rohricht, S., Petersen, D. and Mohr, F. (1993) Assessment of the reliability of facial reconstruction. In Iscan, M. Y. and Helmer. R. P. (eds.) *Forensic Analysis of the Skull,* 229–246. New York, Wiley-Liss.

Işcan, M. Y. and Helmer, R. P. (1993) *Forensic Analysis of the Skull.* New York (NY), Wiley-Liss Inc.

Prag, J. and Neave, R. (1997) *Making Faces.* London, British Museum Press.

Stephan, C. N. (2009) Craniofacial identification: techniques of facial approximation and craniofacial superimposition. In Blau, S. and D. H. Ubelaker (eds.) *Handbook of Forensic Anthropology and Archaeology,* 304–321. Walnut Creek (CA), Left Coast Press Inc.

Snow, C. C., Gatliff, B. P. and McWilliams, K. R. (1970) Reconstruction of facial features from the skull: an evaluation of its usefulness in forensic anthropology. *American Journal of Physical Anthropology* 33, 221–8.

Taylor, K. T. (2001) *Forensic Art and Illustration.* Boca Raton (FL), CRC Press.

Vanezis, P., Vanezis, M., McCombe, G., Niblett, T. (2000) Facial reconstruction using 3–D computer graphics. *Forensic Science International* 108, 81–95.

Wilkinson, C. (2004) *Forensic Facial Reconstruction.* Cambridge, Cambridge University Press.

Wilkinson, C. (2006) Facial anthropology and reconstruction. In Thompson, T. and S. Black, (eds.) *Forensic Human Identification,* 231–255. Boca Raton (FL), CRC Press.

Williamson, W. C. (1872) *Description of the Tumulus, opened at Gristhorpe, near Scarborough,* third edition. Scarborough, S. W. Theakston.

The grave goods

12

THE GRISTHORPE COFFIN AND ITS CONTENTS

Alison Sheridan, Stuart Needham, Sonia O'Connor, Nigel Melton, Rob Janaway, Esther Cameron and Adrian Evans

Introduction

Gristhorpe Man is rightly famous for the remarkable preservation of his skeleton and for the fact that he had been accorded the special treatment of burial in a tree-trunk coffin, but his grave goods and the other items found in that coffin are equally worthy of note, especially because they include some types of organic object that normally do not survive from Early Bronze Age graves, due to the specific conditions of preservation within the coffin (Janaway *et al.*, this volume). They also confirm the impression that he was buried as a high status man, in accordance with the norms of the day, and they offer us fascinating insights into Early Bronze Age beliefs about (and indeed knowledge of) what happens to the dead. This chapter describes these finds, and the coffin in which they were discovered, firstly presenting the excavator William Williamson's observations and identifications (Williamson 1834; 1872) and then offering an up-to-date version in the light of the scientific research that was undertaken as part of the Gristhorpe Man Project. It then discusses the *comparanda* for the artefacts and assesses their significance in comparison with other British Early Bronze Age funerary assemblages, thereby complementing the discussion of tree-trunk coffin graves presented by Parker Pearson *et al.* elsewhere in this volume.

Williamson's descriptions of the coffin and of the items found in it

Williamson's initial description and illustration of the coffin and its contents (the latter reproduced in Rowley-Conwy this volume, Fig. 3.1) was admirable even if, as we now know, his identifications were not always correct. Investigations by Dr Sonia O'Connor have revealed that his '*ring of horn...most probably...used for fastening a light scarf over the shoulder*' (No. 11 in that illustration; Williamson 1834, 9) is, in fact, ossified fragments of tracheal cartilage rings

Fig. 12.1 The face-like carving at the narrow, northern end of the coffin lid. Photograph by Nigel Melton

from Gristhorpe Man's windpipe that had been preserved in the burial environment (Knüsel *et al.*, this volume), while as for the '*few dried berries...about the size of those of the mistletoe*' found among plant material (*ibid.*, 10), one has been confirmed, by analysis, to be a renal calculus (kidney stone: Edwards, this volume), while another has been found to be a human sesamoid bone. The third extant example is most likely to be another kidney stone. (Others, which crumbled away shortly after excavation, could have been genuine berries of some kind; we shall never know.) As will be seen below, some of the artefacts were also misidentified. However, by the time Williamson produced the third edition of his report in 1872, having become more familiar with prehistoric finds from elsewhere and benefiting from discussions with the distinguished antiquary and barrow excavator Canon William Greenwell (Rowley-Conwy, this volume), he was able to correct some of his errors.

Williamson's description of the coffin is especially valuable since only the cover and a few fragments of the base now survive. When freshly uncovered, not only was the bark perfectly preserved, but there was also '*a coating of a species of Lichen upon the bark, which at first was beautifully distinct*' (Williamson 1834, 15). The coffin was orientated north-south and measured 7′6″ (*c.* 2.29 m) in length and between 3′3″ (*c.* 0.99 m) and 2′10″ (*c.* 0.86 m) in width. The log had been split close to its mid-point. The broadest end – which corresponds to the lower end of the tree trunk – is rounded, with relatively broad and deep hollows being interpreted by Williamson as the marks left by the axe used to fell the tree. (He argued that these 3″/*c.* 7.5 cm-wide marks had been made by a stone axehead, possibly of flint.) The other (north) end is squared off and has a teardrop-shaped carving on the lid's upper surface, its tip pointing towards the broad end of the coffin (Fig. 12.1). This was interpreted as a stylised face, and it was noted that its position did not correspond with that of the occupant's head, which had lain instead at the broader end of the coffin. Both the underside and the lid had been hollowed to form a burial chamber (Fig. 12.2; cf. Fig. 3.1, no.1). This is sub-rectangular in plan; in cross-section it is roughly semi-circular on the base. Williamson did not describe the shape of the hollow on the underside of the lid, but information about this has been obtained subsequently, as detailed below and shown in Fig. 12.2. The chamber measured 5′4″ (*c.* 1.52 m) long, between 2′3″ (*c.* 0.69 m) and 2′7½″ (*c.* 0.8 m) wide, and between 2′3″ (*c.* 0.69 m) and 1′10″ (*c.* 0.56 m) deep overall (i.e. including the measurements for both the base and the lid). This hollowing had been effected using a narrower blade than that used to chop the exterior; the cut marks are 2″ (*c.* 5 cm) wide. Williamson suggested that a flint chisel had been used, but as will be argued below, it is more likely that the tool had been a metal adze. A small (around 3″ × 1″/*c.* 8 × 3 cm), rectangular hole near

the centre of the hollow in the base, and extending to the exterior, was interpreted as having been carved to allow bodily fluids to escape during the body's decomposition – thereby suggesting knowledge of the process of *post-mortem* changes. No form of sealant had been used to join the two halves of the log, which had fitted neatly together along the wedge-split plane. Outside the coffin, a single oak branch had been placed standing upright at one end, '*apparently to steady it*' (Williamson 1832, 11), while other oak branches, between 5″ and 8″ (*c.* 13–20 cm) in diameter and with their bark still intact, had been '*carelessly thrown over the coffin*' (*ibid.*).

The artefacts and other items found in the coffin comprise the following:

1. An **animal hide**, described by Williamson as '*the skin of some animal, but of what kind it is impossible to say, the hair of which is soft and fine, much resembling that of a sheep, or perhaps still nearer that of a goat, but not quite so long*' (Williamson 1834, 8; 1872, 12). The skin was in a poor condition when found, and Williamson admitted that it was further damaged during the excavation. However, enough survived for Williamson to conclude that the skin had originally been wrapped around the body and fastened at the chest with...

2. A **bone pin**, which Williamson thought to have been of horn or whalebone (Fig. 3.1, no.10; Williamson 1834, 9; 1872, 12). Also present were:

3. A **dagger (or knife)**, comprising a copper alloy blade with two rivets (of which only one now survives), and a fine bone pommel, the latter with holes for three rivets (Fig. 3.1, nos. 3 and 6–8). In 1834 Williamson wrongly described its blade as '*the head of a spear or javelin, formed either of brass or some other composition of copper, on which time appears to have exerted considerable influence, as it is much corroded and has lost a considerable quantity of metal at the point. At the broad end there are two small rivets, which have doubtless been used to attach the Head to a shaft, which from the shortness of the rivets still remaining, must have been broad and thin*' (Williamson 1834, 8). He opined that the pommel had been '*the ornamental handle of a Javelin, of which the metal Head...formed the opposite extremity*', and he described its material as being '*of either horn, or the bone of some of the larger cetaceous tribe of Fishes*' (*ibid.*, 9) – the same substance, he thought, as that used for the pin. By 1872 Williamson had realised that the blade had not been a projectile head, but rather a '*Dagger or Knife, formed of bronze...*', and cited parallels from elsewhere in Britain, including one in Canon Greenwell's collection where the blade had been associated with a bone pommel (Williamson

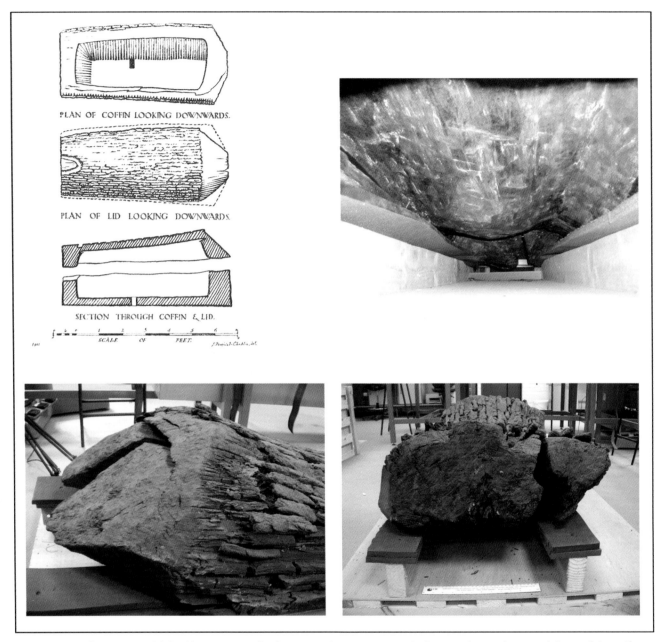

Fig. 12.2 Top left: drawing published by Mortimer Wheeler in 1931 (in Rowntree 1931), showing the condition and shape of the coffin at that time. Top right: The underside of the coffin lid in 2006. Bottom left: the curving (southern) end of the coffin lid in 2006. Bottom right: the straight (northern) end of the coffin lid in 2006. Photographs by Nigel Melton

1872, 13–14). Not remarked upon by Williamson, yet clearly visible in his published engraving, are the remains of an organic sheath or (perhaps more likely) scabbard, the latter being a rigid, composite article made from wood and hide, rather than just hide; its truncated narrow end shows how it had fitted snugly around the blade.

4. **Three flint artefacts**, all initially believed by Williamson (again wrongly) to be projectile points – the largest (Fig. 3.1, no. 4) being described as a '*javelin*' and the smaller two, '*rude heads of Arrows*' (Fig. 3.1, nos. 7–8) (Williamson 1834, 8, 9). By 1872 he had changed his identification of the largest object to that of a knife or scraper, and of the smaller objects

to flakes 'of the class frequently found with ancient British interments. The use to which they were applied appears very doubtful' (Williamson 1872, 14).

5. A **wooden object with one tapering and one rounded end** (Fig. 3.1, no. 9). This puzzled Williamson, who described it as 'a pin, or something allied to it, made of wood…I cannot give any idea of the purpose for which it has been employed, as there is no record of anything similar having been met with' (Williamson 1834, 9). He was still none the wiser in 1872, when he described it as resembling 'a miniature spatula with a round handle' (Williamson 1872, 14).

6. A **container, made of sewn bark** (not illustrated by Williamson; see below). In 1834 Williamson described this object as 'a kind of dish, or shallow basket of wicker work: it is of a round form, and about six inches in diameter; the bottom has been formed of a single flat piece of bark, and the sides composed of the same, stitched together by the sinews of animals; which, though the basket fell in pieces on exposure to the atmosphere, are still easily to be observed in the fragments and round the edges of the bottom. Attached to the bottom is a quantity of decomposed matter, which has not been analysed. The most likely opinion concerning this Basket is, that it has contained offerings of food, either for the dead, or as gifts to the Gods' (Williamson 1834, 9). In 1872 he added that the container had probably played a similar role to that of the Food Vessel pots that were frequently found associated with ancient interments (Williamson 1872, 15). Here, he was alluding to the finds from northern English barrows, many of which had been excavated in the interim between his two publications on Gristhorpe (e.g. Bateman 1861; Greenwell 1890; Mortimer 1905, the last two including the results of excavations carried out before 1872).

7. An **organic ornament** (not illustrated by Williamson), described in 1834 as 'a very singular ornament, in the form of a double rose of a ribband, with two loose ends, but of what it is composed, I am not able to say; it appears to have been an appendage of some belt or girdle, but like the basket, it fell into small fragments immediately on removal. Its composition is exceedingly brittle, something resembling thin horn, but is more opaque and not elastic: the surface has been simply though curiously ornamented with small elevated lines.' (Williamson 1834, 10).

8. A quantity of **plant material** (not illustrated by Williamson), initially thought to be dried rushes. Some of this material was macerated in order to identify the species, but it was found that most of it was so decomposed that nothing but the fibre remained. However, 'in one or two instances we have been so far successful, as to clearly distinguish a long lanceolate leaf, resembling that of the mistletoe, which plant it has most probably been' (ibid.; cf. Williamson 1872, 15). The aforementioned kidney stones were found among this plant material, and at first Williamson suspected that they may be mistletoe berries, but in his 1872 publication he stated that they had probably belonged to some leguminous plant. Also present among the plant material (and among fragments of the aforementioned decomposed animal hide) were:

9. A few small **animal bones** (not illustrated by Williamson), comprising phalanges (paw bones), 'about the size of those of a small dog…as though the foot of some animal had been buried with the body' (Williamson 1834, 14). By 1836, when Williamson published the second edition of his account, he was able to report that Dr Buckland had considered the bones to be from a weasel (Williamson 1836, 14).

As regards where in the coffin each of these items had been found, Williamson's description is less detailed than one would like; he admitted as much, when observing in relation to the pommel and blade of the dagger or knife that 'notice was not taken when the Coffin was opened of their relative situations.' (Williamson 1834, 9). Nevertheless, from the information provided in the 1834 account, we can form some idea of the disposition of the skeleton and of the location of at least some of the artefacts.

Williamson reported that the body had been laid on its right side, with the head to the south, 'and its face turned towards the rising Sun' (i.e., east: ibid., 8). The feet lay at the narrow, northern end of the coffin – the end with the teardrop-shaped, face-like carving (Fig. 3.1, no. 1). He noted that the discrepancy between the length of the chamber (5'4"/c. 152 cm) and the estimated height of the individual ('rather more than 6 feet 2 inches': ibid., 8 and cf. Knüsel et al., this volume) meant that his lower limbs must have been drawn up into a flexed position, and he noted that this would 'account for the disordered state the lower extremities were found in' (Williamson 1834, 8). Whether they were slightly flexed, or whether the body had been contracted, as is the norm with other Early Bronze Age interments, is unknown, but the width of the chamber is certainly sufficient to have accommodated a contracted body. Its depth, around 69 cm, would have allowed plenty of headroom.

The old man's body had been wrapped in the animal hide (No. 1, above), its ends fastened together with the bone pin (No. 2), found in the chest region. Few details are given about the findspot locations of the other items in the coffin; the organic ornament (No. 7) was described as having been laid 'upon the lower part of the breast of the Skeleton' (ibid., 10); and the bark container (No. 6) was found 'By the side of the bones' (ibid., 9). It is not stated whether either of these had been inside or outside the hide. The fact that the kidney stones and the phalanges (No. 9) were found among the plant material (No. 8) suggests that the latter had probably been laid in the base of the hollow, as a lining.

The coffin and the items within: revised descriptions in the light of the Gristhorpe Man Project

As part of the research carried out for the Gristhorpe Man Project, a team of specialists and students studied and analysed all of the surviving items from the coffin, along with the coffin lid, and the results are presented below. Unfortunately, no remains of the organic ornament (No. 7) or the plant material (No. 8) had survived to make their way into the Rotunda Museum in Scarborough. However, to judge from Williamson's description of the former, and bearing in mind the range of materials that survived in the coffin, it is likely that this had been made from animal skin or sinew; such a material could have taken the decoration mentioned by Williamson.

The coffin

As mentioned above, the base of the coffin does not survive (except as a few fragments), having suffered firstly from having been displayed outside the museum in a brick, stone and wood 'sarcophagus' until 1853, and subsequently from damp and dry rot, as discussed by Janaway et al. (this volume). The lid was studied by David Maron (Maron 2007) and by Dr Nigel Melton, and confirmation of the species identification as oak was provided by Dr Ian Tyres.

The coffin lid has clearly undergone significant shrinkage, deformation and splitting since its discovery. Some idea of the extent of the shrinkage, particularly at the rounded end, is provided by a drawing published by Mortimer Wheeler in 1931 (Fig. 12.2 and Wheeler in Rowntree 1931), and the sagging of the central part is clear from photographs taken in 2006 (Fig. 12.2, bottom). The 1931 drawing is valuable in providing a longitudinal cross-section view of the lid, showing that the ends of the hollowed chamber taper inwards (with an undercut at one end where the adze blade had penetrated too far). The photograph of the underside of the lid (Fig. 12.2, top right) shows that the hollowed area now dips towards the centre, but this is due to the post-excavation deformation, and the chamber would originally have been flat-topped. As for the rounded shape of the coffin's exterior at its broader, southern end (Fig. 3.1, nos. 1–2; Fig. 12.2, bottom left), while Williamson had implied that this represented the shape

of the tree-trunk after its felling, this is only partly true: this end had evidently been 'tidied up' to create a smooth, rounded shape and there had clearly been the intention to create such a rounded end, in contrast to the squared-off northern end of the coffin (Fig. 12.2, bottom right). It may indeed be the case that the makers had wanted to evoke the shape of a logboat, as discussed by Parker Pearson et al. elsewhere in this volume.

While it was not possible to undertake a study of the toolmarks on the coffin lid during the Gristhorpe Man Project, enough clues exist from Williamson's original description (cited above) and from photographs taken in 2006 (Fig. 12.2) to argue that the broad, deep and curving-sectioned marks on the rounded end are most likely to have been made by a stone axehead (with the term 'stone' encompassing flint), while the well-preserved marks on the underside of the lid, which are narrower, shallower and straighter, must have been made using a metal blade, hafted as an adze. Additional confirmation comes from the shape of the aforementioned undercut. The same tool could arguably have been used to create the straight end of the lid (Fig. 12.2, bottom right).

Regarding the 'rude figure of a human face' (Williamson 1834, 5–6) carved on the outside of the coffin's lid, Williamson's illustration shows its position incorrectly, as being set a short distance in from the narrow (northern) end of the coffin. In fact, as can be seen from Fig. 12.1, its broad edge is coincident with the coffin's end. It appears that the error in Williamson's illustration was not noticed until Wheeler published the correct version in 1931 (Fig. 12.2, top left); previous versions by Jewitt (Jewitt 1870) and Elgee (Elgee 1930, plate IX, facing p.72) had simply replicated, or been based on, Williamson's. The shape is in false relief, having been created by adzing away a band around it. In its current state, the 'face' does not appear to have any bark on it; its uneven surface includes an area of flattened sapwood, and a curving gash. Williamson had reported that 'unfortunately, it was much damaged by the feet of the workmen' (Williamson 1872, 6) but the nature of this damage was not specified. One feature that has not previously been recorded is a flaring of the carved area towards the edge of the lid (Maron 2007; Fig. 12.1).

The items within the coffin

1. The animal hide
This has survived only as a few small fragments, none larger than 150 × 60 mm (Fig. 12.3, top). However, the application of proteomics analysis to examine the protein in a hair from this hide was able to confirm that the species had been cattle (Buckley, this volume), a conclusion supported by the scanning electron microscope images taken by Rob Janaway (Fig. 12.3, bottom). Examination of these images

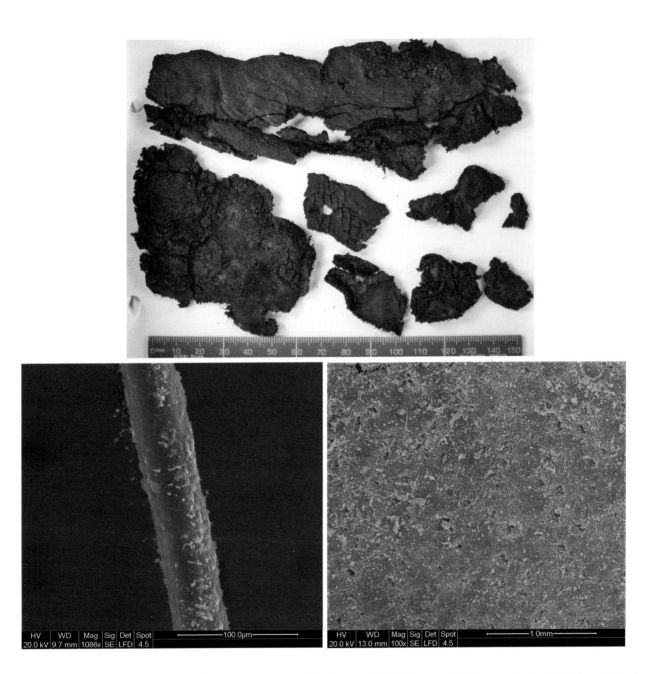

Fig. 12.3 The animal hide. Top: surviving fragments, prior to analysis; bottom left: highly magnified image of a single hair from the hide, taken using a scanning electron microscope (SEM); bottom right: SEM image of the hide, showing its 'grain', including follicles for individual hairs. Photograph by Andrew Wilson; SEM images by Rob Janaway

by Dr Esther Cameron has led to the conclusion that, to judge from the density of the hair follicles (namely 42 per 2mm²), an adult animal is represented. It is, however, not possible to determine from these images whether the item had been an oxhide or a cowhide.

Similarly, it is impossible to determine whether the hide

had been deposited with its hairy side outermost (although intuitively this arrangement seems most likely), or whether it had originally enclosed the whole of Gristhorpe Man's body, shroud-like, or had left his head exposed to view, cloak-like. The fact that the hide had survived at all, while all traces of the human skin had perished, raises the question as to whether it had been treated (e.g. through vegetable tanning). The issue of when tanning was first practised in Europe has been investigated by Willy Groenman-van Waateringe and colleagues (Groenman-van Waateringe *et al.* 1999), who have concluded that there is no unequivocal evidence for deliberate tanning prior to the Roman period. Secondary tanning, as caused by the acid milieu of peat bogs, by the interior of tree-trunk coffins and by the salty environment of salt mines, is well attested and, given the evidence presented by Groenman-van Waateringe *et al.* (*ibid.*), it seems most likely that the hide's preservation is due to this natural process, rather than to human agency (Groenman-van Waateringe, pers. comm.). Natural tanning of the parts of the hide that had been in immediate contact with the oak coffin could arguably account for the observed pattern of partial and differential preservation, with the human skin not surviving because it had not been in contact with the wood.

2. The bone pin (Fig. 3.1, no. 10, Fig. 12.4)

This is short, straight and slender, with a sharp point at one end; the other end has been gently squared off. For most of its length it is roughly rectangular in cross-section, with rounded sides. It is 71.7 mm long, with a maximum thickness and width (at its head) of 5.0 × 2.9 mm. It had been smoothed and polished to a fairly high sheen over most of its surface (although we cannot rule out the

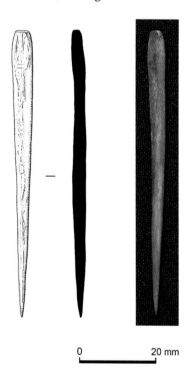

0   20 mm

Fig. 12.4 The pin made from a pig fibula. Drawing by Daniel Bashford; photograph by Alison Sheridan

possibility that, to some extent, this sheen may relate to a coating of a consolidant, as noted with the pommel. No obvious traces of such a consolidant were noted with the naked eye). Osteological identification by Professor Terry O'Connor concluded that the pin had been made from the fibula of a domestic pig.

3. The dagger or knife (Fig. 3.1, nos. 3,5,6 and Figs. 12.5–6)

In its current condition, this comprises a pommel along with a short, only slightly corroded blade, with one rivet *in situ* and with small patches of surviving organic material from the scabbard or sheath attached to its surface. Clearly, over the years it has lost most of the scabbard/ sheath remains that were present when the blade was first illustrated in 1834 (Fig. 3.1, no. 3). Indeed, Janaway *et al.* (this volume) argue that the blade had been stripped chemically as a 'conservation' measure in the past, and it is clear, from Fig. 15.17, that this had happened by 1954 (when the dagger or knife is shown mounted on a piece of card, with a plastic hilt). This stripping process will have removed most of the remains of the scabbard/sheath. It is also clear, from the photograph, that the blade had lost one of its metal rivets by that time; a drawing of the dagger that appeared in Sabine Gerloff's 1975 *corpus* of British daggers and knife-daggers (Gerloff 1975, 51 and plate 5, 55) is misleading, as it is based on Williamson's 1834 engraving and shows both rivets as being present.

The blade is short, flat and very thin, with a straight butt (i.e. hilt end) with rounded edges. The rivets had been placed close to each corner of the butt. Below the level of the rivets, the minimally-concave sides taper towards a round-pointed tip (Fig. 12.5). There is no evidence to support Williamson's assertion that '*a considerable quantity of metal*' had been lost from the tip (1834, 8). Likewise, Gerloff's illustration offers a misleading impression of a badly-damaged tip, due to the fact that the drawing seems to have been traced from Williamson's engraving, which of course included parts of the scabbard or sheath. In cross-section, the blade is flat for most of its width. There are signs of a very shallow bevel along one edge on one side of the blade, with near-imperceptible traces of a similar feature along the other edge on the same side, and along both edges on the other side. This feature can be seen with varying degrees of clarity in the views presented in Figure 12.5. This bevelling is so shallow that it does not materially affect the flat cross-section shape of the blade. As discussed in Northover (this volume), it may well have resulted from cold-hammering to re-sharpen the edges of the blade, following wear through use. Use may also have been responsible for the very slightly concave shape of the sides of the blade; when new, it might have had straight, or even minimally convex sides.

The blade is 82.7 mm long; its maximum width is

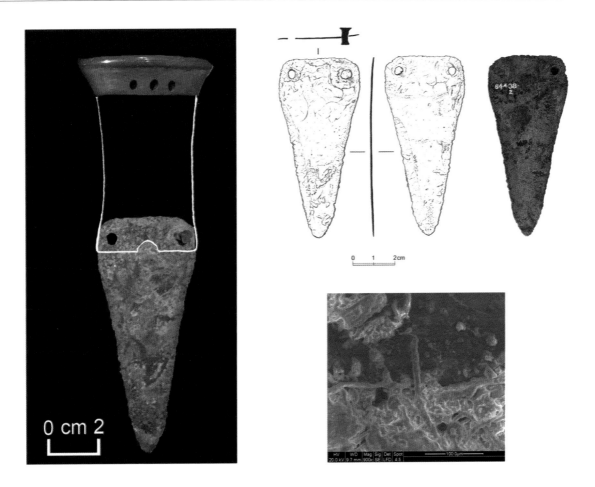

Fig. 12.5 The dagger blade. Top: drawing by Daniel Bashford, showing traces of bevelling on both sides. Top right: photograph of one side of the blade; the omega-shaped line left by the lower edge of the hilt is visible immediately above the object label. Photograph by Sonia O'Connor. Left: the dagger and pommel laid out to replicate the estimated original length of the dagger. Photograph: Alison Sheridan. Bottom right: SEM image of animal collagen traces on the dagger blade, probably from the sheath/scabbard. Image by Rob Janaway

37.8 mm, and its thickness, 1.2 mm. The rivet hole has a diameter of 3.7 × 4.65 mm and the surviving rivet, which has flattened and slightly expanded ends, is 7.5 mm long and measures 2.7 × 2.8 mm across its slightly angular shaft and 3.75 mm across its top. (In terms of rivet terminology, it falls between 'peg' and 'plug' shape, but is closer to 'peg' shape.) The rivet's length indicates that the hilt had been just 7.5 mm thick where it clamped the blade, and the width of the blade's butt indicates that it had been at least *c.* 38 mm wide at its lower edge. The original shape of this lower edge of the hilt is revealed by the shadow of an omega-shaped central hollow, its innermost edge lying just below the mid-point of the rivets. This is most clearly visible in Figure 12.5, top right), and is also implicit in Williamson's engraving (Fig. 3.1, no. 3), where the slightly darker shading around the rivets indicates the last traces, or stain, of the hilt. That same illustration also shows that

the bottom of the hilt abuts the top of the sheath/scabbard. The typology of the blade is discussed below, and details of the metallurgical analysis are presented in Northover, this volume; essentially, Northover concluded that the blade had been made from an unleaded tin bronze with 12% tin, thoroughly worked and annealed. The copper had originated in south-west Ireland and the tin is most likely to have originated in south-west England, but the metal had probably been recycled several times before being used to make the blade, a conclusion that is supported by lead isotope analysis (Montgomery and Gledhill, this volume). Although the surviving rivet has not been analysed, it is most likely to have been of copper alloy (Northover, pers. comm.).

As for whether the object protecting the blade had been a sheath or a scabbard – the difference being that the former is exclusively made from animal skin and

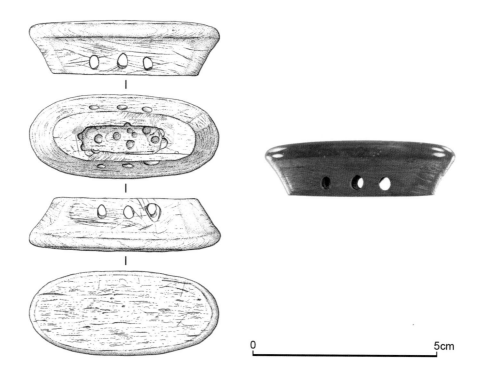

0   5cm

Fig. 12.6   The dagger pommel. Drawing by Daniel Bashford; photograph by Sonia O'Connor

may be flexible, whereas the latter is a rigid composite that usually consists of a layer of wood, coated on the interior and exterior with animal skin (Cameron 2003) – inspection of Williamson's 1834 engraving by Dr Esther Cameron concluded that not enough had survived to allow a confident identification. However, given that a fairly substantial object was represented, it was quite possible that the object had been a scabbard. Imaging using a scanning electron microscope, undertaken by Rob Janaway, has confirmed the presence of animal collagen on the blade (Fig. 12.5, bottom right), although further research would be required to determine from which species it derives. At least one other Early Bronze Age scabbard or sheath (from Seafield West, Inverness: Gabra-Sanders *et al.* 2003) has been found to comprise cattle skin.

By comparison with the relatively slight blade, the pommel (Fig. 3.1, nos. 5–6 and Fig. 12.6) appears disproportionately large and robust. It has a broad, flat, expanded top, fat-elliptical in plan and measuring 51.75 × 22.2 mm, and below its rounded edge it curves in to a flat base, with three narrow transverse rivet holes perforating each of the long sides just above this base. From top to bottom it is 13.6 mm high, and the diameters of the rivet holes range from 2.9 × 3.65 mm to 4.5 × 4.8 mm. Its width at its base – and hence the width of the hilt that it had been designed to adorn – is *c.* 40 mm. A sub-rectangular hollow,

roughly 25 mm long, had been cut from its underside to accommodate the tang of the hilt. The edges of this hollow are slightly ragged and at its base are several circular depressions, each *c.* 2.3 mm wide, which could have been made by the same drill as that used to create the rivet holes. It may be, then, that this hollow had been (at least partly) drilled out. Other tool marks consist of possible gouge marks around the edge of the hollow, together with shallow but clear grinding striations on the underside and below the top of the pommel. The latter had not been erased by the polishing that was applied to the whole of the exterior (except the underside) and which, along with probable use-wear, had given the top and upper edge a brilliant sheen. (See also Janaway *et al.*, this volume, on the coating of the pommel with an acetone-soluble resin in the past.) There is also some faceting on the lower part of the pommel, caused by the shaping process. The rivet holes must have been bored from the exterior inwards, but their outer edges are flush with the surface, rather than cupped, which indicates that they had been drilled when the pommel was still in its roughed-out state; subsequent work to the surface would have removed any marks from the drill's entry. These drill-hole edges are also crisp, with only minor smoothing from the organic – probably wooden – rivets that they had housed. The fact that Williamson made no mention of having found any wooden pommel rivets should not occasion surprise, as they would have been very small and easy to miss, had they survived at all.

The pommel is an orange-brown colour, stained by the tannin from the coffin, but it would originally have been a creamy colour. The material has been identified by Professor Terry O'Connor and Dr Sonia O'Connor as bone from the cortex of a lower jaw (mandible) of a whale; the distinguishing features are the densely-packed secondary osteons that have completely remodelled the bone, removing all evidence of its lamellar structure.

It is likely, by analogy with other Early Bronze Age examples, that the Gristhorpe dagger or knife had had a short, broad, fairly thin hilt, with concave sides and an omega-shaped base; assuming that it had been designed to fit both the blade and the pommel, its width around its base must have been at least *c*. 38 mm, while its width at its top will have been *c*. 40 mm. Given the fact that its material had completely decayed away, the material had probably been horn. Therefore, four materials are represented (or at least are likely to have existed) in the dagger: bronze, used for the blade (and almost certainly also for the blade rivets); horn, for the hilt; whalebone, for the pommel, and wood, for the pommel rivets. By analogy with other Early Bronze Age daggers and knife-daggers, its overall length could have been *c*. 145 mm, in which case the pommel top is unlikely to have projected beyond the fist when the dagger was held (Fig. 12.5, bottom left).

4. The flint artefacts (Fig. 3.1, nos. 4 and 7 and 8, Figs. 12.7–8)
The largest of the three objects is a plano-convex knife made from a blade of mottled, medium- to dark grey flint, probably obtained locally. It is 69 mm long, 18 mm wide at its broadest, proximal end and up to *c*. 5 mm thick. The knife is asymmetrical in plan and narrows from its roundish, proximal end to a point at its distal end (Fig. 3.1, no. 4, Fig. 12.7). The outer edges of the convex, dorsal side have retouch all round, with the proximal 20 mm having steep blunting retouch (to aid hafting), while the rest of the edges have flat invasive retouch. Traces of ancient organic residue were noted adhering to the dorsal surface; in addition, traces of glue were present, from when the knife had been stuck to cardboard, probably for the 1954 re-display. Microwear analysis and residue analysis were carried out by Dr Adrian Evans. The microwear analysis was undertaken using a 20–80x stereomicroscope and a modified metallurgical microscope at 200x magnification. This revealed two related forms of wear along the right edge, between the mid-point and the pointed end, and also showed that the knife had been re-sharpened through repeated retouching. That this re-sharpening had taken place while the blade was hafted is clear from the presence of a haft margin (Fig. 12.7), separating the parts of the blade with this secondary retouch from those with primary, manufacturing retouch. The first form of wear is a well-developed hide polish that survives on protrusions

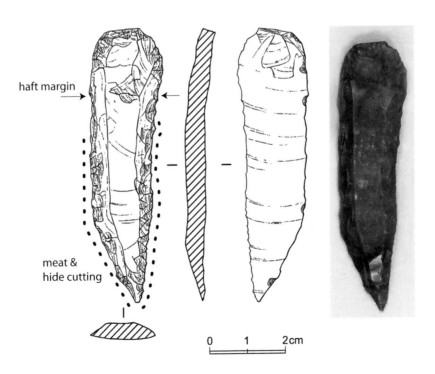

haft margin

meat &
hide cutting

0   1   2cm

Fig. 12.7 The flint knife. Drawing by Daniel Bashford; photograph by Andrew Wilson

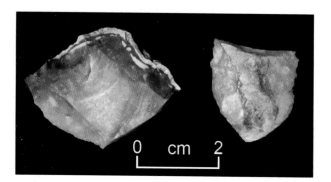

Fig. 12.8 The two flint flakes. Photograph by Alison Sheridan

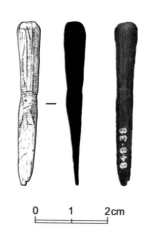

Fig. 12.9 The wooden object, probably a fastener. Drawing by Daniel Bashford; photograph by Alison Sheridan

that had survived the second phase of sharpening retouch. The second is a weakly developed hide/meat polish which also exists sporadically and is limited to protrusions, but which overlies the last phase of blade modification. The organic residue analysis took the form of lipid analysis using GC-MS (gas chromatography-mass spectrometry) to examine the residue from the proximal (butt) end, and quantification of protein residue from the remainder of the dorsal surface using SDS-PAGE (sodium dodecyl sulfate polyacrylamide gel electrophoresis). The GC-MS results demonstrated the presence of a tree resin, of unspecified species; unfortunately, the SDS-PAGE analysis failed to produce sufficient quantities of protein residue to justify taking the analysis any further. Taken together, however, the microwear and organic residue analysis confirmed that the knife had been hafted at its butt end, secured to its handle with resin (and probably with binding as well, although no trace of that was found), and that it had seen at least two episodes of use prior to being deposited in the coffin. It had been heavily used to cut and/or scrape fresh hide and then, following sharpening through fresh retouch, it had been used lightly to cut hide and/or meat.

As for the other two flint objects (Fig. 3.1, nos. 7–8, Fig. 12.8), one is a flake and the other, a blade. Both are made of a mottled mid- to dark-grey flint and both have weathered cortex; on the flake the cortex runs around the outer edge, while on the blade it runs across part of one surface. It is likely that the parent material had been small cobbles picked up from the shore nearby; this may also be the case with the knife. The flake measures 34.4 × 25.3 × 4.9 mm, and the blade, 21.9 × 19.2 × 3.7 mm. Neither shows any signs of retouch or of use.

5. The wooden object, probably a fastener (Fig. 3.1, no. 9, Fig. 12.9)
This small object, 43.2 mm long and 6.0 mm in maximum diameter, is straight and round-sectioned at one end, with sides that taper to a central waist (diameter: 4.4 mm) before swelling out slightly and tapering again to a round-pointed end. (The latter has suffered minor damage since

Williamson illustrated it.) A sliver had been cut from between the waist and the round-pointed end, giving this half of the artefact a wedge-shaped profile. A small piece of roundwood had been used; its ring pattern is clearly visible. The species of the wood could not be identified. The surface of the object is smooth, although there are slight surface irregularities running around part of the waist (on the non-cut side), possibly relating to wear. The most likely use for this object is as a fastener, perhaps for a pouch or – had it been lidded – for the bark and wood container described below. The wedge-shaped end would have been slid through, and held in place by, a cord loop, to sit with its cut side touching the side of the pouch or container.

6. The bark and wood container (Fig. 12.10)
This survives as several curving (and badly-warped) fragments of bark from the side of the container, along with two fragments of thin, mineralised wood from its base. There has been very significant shrinkage and warping since the container was found, when Williamson was able to report that it had been circular and had a diameter of 6″ (c. 150 mm). One of the surviving fragments of bark has two holes in its side, but these are not necessarily thread-holes (although Williamson's report had made it clear that the bark strips had been sewn together with animal sinew). It was not possible to identify the species of the bark, but it is most likely to have been of birch. The largest basal fragment is 139 mm long, 25.4 mm wide and 5.5 mm thick. It had been made from split wood, and the structure of the wood is clearly visible (although it was not possible to identify its species as the cells had collapsed). No holes are present, even though the sides would almost certainly have been sewn to the base. The two basal fragments now describe an oval shape. The fact that Williamson made no mention of a lid suggests that the container had probably not had one – in which case, the wooden fastener described above is arguably more likely to have served as a pouch fastener than as one for the container.

Specimens of the so-called 'food' residue – including detached fragments that had been stored in a test tube – were analysed by Joanne Hawkins and Professor Carl Heron using a variety of methods, including pollen analysis, micro-

Fig. 12.10 Remains of the container with bark sides and a wooden base. Top: bark fragments; Bottom: remains of the base. Photographs by Andrew Wilson and Alison Sheridan, respectively

imaging with a scanning electron microscope (SEM) and compositional analysis using an electron microprobe and GC-MS (Hawkins 2006). The pollen analysis revealed that no ancient pollen was present, but that contamination from the ambient pollen at the time of the grave's excavation in 1834 had taken place. The micro-structural SEM analysis led to the conclusion that the material had been viscous, bubbly and burnt; electron microprobe analysis confirmed that it was an organic substance; and the GC-MS analysis indicated that it contained plant-derived terpenoids, suggesting that it had been a gum, resin or tar. The most likely explanation for its presence is that it had been birch bark tar, used to waterproof the interior of the vessel. This, in turn, suggests that the vessel's contents had been liquid, or semi-liquid. This conclusion is supported by proteomics analysis (Buckley *et al.*, 2013), which identified the presence of bovine milk casein in a sample of the 'sinews of animals' (Williamson 1834, 9) that had been used to stitch the bark sides to the wooden base of the vessel. The same analysis confirmed that the stitching was composed of bovine hair and sinew.

9. The animal bones

These were identified as a metatarsal from a fox and phalanges from a pine marten, by Drs Julie Bond and Nigel Melton, respectively; in other words, these come from the animals' paws. They may represent the former presence of fox and pine marten pelts, since paws are often retained when an animal is skinned for its fur. Alternatively, they could have been detached paws, perhaps used as amulets.

Discussion: *comparanda* for the items in the coffin, and the significance of Gristhorpe within the context of Early Bronze Age funerary practices

This section will focus mainly on the items in the coffin, since *comparanda* for the practice of tree-trunk coffin burial have already been discussed by Parker Pearson *et al.* (this volume). It should, however, be noted that while there is no exact parallel for the carved face-like design on the coffin cover, a canoe-shaped probable tree-trunk coffin from Loose Howe, North Yorkshire did have a hollowed triangular area carved into its underside (Elgee and Elgee 1949, 92 and fig. 4). As will be demonstrated below, this is one of several points of similarity between the Loose Howe find (which also included a lidded tree-trunk coffin in addition to the object mentioned above) and the Gristhorpe coffin; the two sites lie around 45 km apart as the crow flies and may have been closely contemporary. It is a moot point whether these carvings are representations, however abstract, of a face; they are certainly not handle-like features. The interpretation of the Gristhorpe carving (and perhaps that at Loose Howe) as a stylised face – perhaps portraying the occupant as an ancestor or spirit – is not implausible, given that the whole of the funerary process had been concerned with ensuring Gristhorpe Man's safe passage into the Otherworld and his accession into the world of the gods and ancestors. As discussed elsewhere in this volume (by Parker Pearson *et al.*), the possible boat imagery of the coffin's shape may well have symbolised that journey, and the orientation of the body to face the rising sun in the east also accords with such a belief. Furthermore, the care with which the log coffin was interred may reflect a concern with ensuring some kind of physical 'immortality'.

At Gristhorpe, from all the evidence currently available, it would appear that the funerary ritual involved first lining the base of the hollow with plant material, before laying the body in this 'chamber'. What species of plant had been used, we are unlikely ever to know, unless the specimens referred to by Williamson ever come to light in the future; it is therefore impossible to determine whether he was correct in suggesting that the plant with long lanceolate leaves had been mistletoe. Similarly, we do not know whether any of the plant material had been mounded to form a pillow (as had been the case at Loose Howe, in the lidded tree-trunk coffin found beside the aforementioned canoe-shaped object: *ibid.*, 90). Having lined the hollow, the burial party then lowered the body of Gristhorpe Man into the coffin, on his right side, his lower limbs flexed, and his body wrapped within the cattle hide, fastened at the chest with the bone pin. As noted above, it is unclear whether or not the skin had been used as a cloak or as a shroud-like garment. In any case it is likely, by analogy with other Early Bronze Age graves in Britain, that the corpse had been buried fully dressed: a fragment of a shoe (presumably of animal skin) had been found at Loose Howe, in the aforementioned lidded coffin (*ibid.*, 90) and there are several examples from northern England and Scotland where sets of V-perforated buttons of jet or similar material are believed to have belonged to jackets (I. A. G. Shepherd 2009, 346). It may be that Gristhorpe Man had been buried wearing clothes made from wool, or perhaps linen, which had decomposed in the specific micro-environment of the coffin. Parallels for the use of both materials are known from other Early Bronze Age graves: for example, woollen cloth was found in a tree-trunk coffin at Rylstone, North Yorkshire, where it had been used either as clothing or as a shroud-like garment (Greenwell 1877, 375–377), while the presence of large amounts of linen fabric in a high status (and tall) male's cist at Kelleythorpe, North Yorkshire, led Mortimer to conclude that the deceased had probably been '*wrapped in linen from head to foot*' (Mortimer 1905, 275). Flax fibre was also present in the Loose Howe coffin, and at Garton Slack barrow 82, North Yorkshire (as a coarse linen fabric: *ibid.*, lxxiii and fig. 595).

As for the mysterious organic ornament that decomposed upon discovery, but which was described as '*a double rose of a ribband, with two loose ends*', found in the lower chest area (Williamson 1834, 10), this might have been some kind of fastener for a garment, although no obvious parallels are known from Early Bronze Age contexts. Alternatively, if Williamson was correct in suggesting that '*...it appears to have been an appendage of some belt or girdle*', then it might have been an ornament for a pouch that could have been suspended from a belt and fastened with the spatulate wooden object. The presence of such pouches in contemporary graves is suggested by several instances where fire-making equipment has been found in a tight cluster, sometimes in the immediate vicinity of a jet V-perforated button which could have been used as the pouch fastener (*ibid.*, 347; Greenwell 1877, 265). If that is the case, then candidates for the contents of such a pouch at Gristhorpe are the flint knife and the two flint flakes – everyday tools that would be of use to the deceased in the Otherworld, according to Early Bronze Age beliefs. If the

fox and pine marten paw bones indicate the presence of paws from these animals (rather than entire pelts), then these, too, are candidates for pouch contents, perhaps as amulets to protect the deceased in the Afterlife. However, given that the bones were found among the plant material, it is perhaps equally likely that we are dealing with fine fur pelts, laid on the base of the coffin. The dagger or knife, in its scabbard, would have been close to the body, and would have been included not only as a useful tool or weapon for Otherworldly use, but also as an indicator of the wealth and importance of Gristhorpe Man. The bark and wood container which, as noted above, seems to have contained milk (or some other substance containing dairy fat) for the deceased's journey into the Otherworld, was placed beside the body, either inside or outside the hide. As noted above, and will be discussed further below, the dagger or knife and the flint knife had clearly seen some use before they were deposited; the evidence is less clear with the bone pin and wooden item but these, too, need not have been made expressly for the grave.

Comparanda among British Early Bronze Age graves can be found for most of the contents of the coffin. As indicated above, the placing of plant matter as a lining for the coffin 'chamber' finds a parallel in the aforementioned tree-trunk coffin grave at Loose Howe. Here, rushes, reeds or straw had lined the base of the hollow, and fragments of a pillow of grass or straw were found where the head had rested (Elgee and Elgee 1949, 90). There are several other instances where plant material has been found in Early Bronze Age graves. Some of these – as at a 'dagger grave' cist at Forteviot, Perth and Kinross – represent the deposition of large amounts of meadowsweet on top of the corpse, perhaps to counteract the smell of incipient decay (Noble and Brophy 2011; cf. Davies and Tipping's 2007 discussion of the presence of meadowsweet in Early Bronze Age graves). At Ashgrove, Fife, another 'dagger grave' cist contained a thick layer of plant material of various species including fern, birch, cross-leaved heath and moss (Henshall 1964); this appeared to lie over the body.

A few parallels can also be cited for the inclusion of remains of fur-bearing animals in Early Bronze Age graves. At Tillicoultry, Clackmannanshire, the remains of a pelt that had lain under the head of the deceased, on top of a 'pillow' of quartz pebbles, in a stone cist (Robertson *et al.* 1895, 192) were identified as being possibly from a stoat (Ryder 1964, 176). In a tree-trunk coffin at Dysgwlfa Fawr, Dyfed, a piece of animal fur, unidentified as to species, had been found lying on top of a Food Vessel and cremated human bones (Green 1987, 47), while at Whitehorse Hill cist, Devon, cremated remains had been wrapped in a pelt (Jones *et al.* 2012). Elsewhere, a calcined cervical vertebra of a mustelid species, probably a polecat, was found among the cremated remains of a child in a Collared Urn at Lesmurdie Road,

Elgin, Moray (Andrew Kitchener pers. comm.; Suddaby forthcoming). Furthermore, Mortimer refers to several finds of bones of fox in Early Bronze Age graves under barrows in Yorkshire, although not necessarily present as parts of pelts (e.g. at Painsthorpe Wold barrow 118, North Yorkshire: Mortimer 1905, 127).

As for *comparanda* for the presence of the cattle hide, a review of the Scottish evidence by Ellen McAdam (McAdam 1982, 126 and table 4) was able to identify nine Early Bronze Age instances, with a tenth having been found more recently in the aforementioned 'dagger grave' cist at Forteviot, Perth and Kinross (Noble and Brophy 2011). Where species identification has been undertaken, it has been found to be of cattle in the case of Ashgrove, Fife and Masterton, Fife, and more specifically of ox in the case of Collessie, Fife (Ryder 1964); the Forteviot hide, examined by Dr Esther Cameron, may also be of cattle. The rare English examples include sewn hides found in tree-trunk coffins at Cartington, Rothbury, Northumberland (Dixon 1913) and Stoborough, Dorset (Hutchins 1767; Elgee and Elgee 1949, 105, 106), with the former being claimed to be of calf- or kidskin in the former case, and deer in the latter. The deployment of these hides seems to have varied, with some (such as the last two examples) being used to wrap the body, as at Gristhorpe, while at Masterton the hide had been lain over the floor of the cist (McAdam 1982, 126 and table 4) and at Barns Farm, Fife (cist 1), it seems to have been used as a pillow (Watkins 1982, 61–62). Elsewhere, as noted above, woollen and linen fabric may have been used as alternatives to animal hides as a material used to wrap the body. What unites all of these examples is that they come from graves where there are additional indications of the special status of the occupant: the grave itself may have taken more effort than usual to construct (as in the case of the tree-trunk coffins and the large and/or elaborate cists), and rare types of grave good – in particular, a dagger – are often present. The inclusion of an animal hide (or indeed of a considerable amount of woollen or linen fabric) represents a significant expenditure of resources, and while many examples are likely to have perished completely or been missed by excavators, it is reasonable to argue that burial with an animal hide (or wrapped in fine textile) had been an exceptional act and an indicator of high status.

Regarding the bone pin, there are numerous Early Bronze Age *comparanda*, both from Yorkshire (e.g. in a woman's grave at Huggate and Waterwold barrow 249, East Yorkshire: Mortimer 1905, fig. 936) and further afield. Contextually and in terms of its associations, the bone pin from a rich grave of a relatively old man at Acklam Wold (barrow 124), North Yorkshire offers the closest parallel to the Gristhorpe example (*ibid.*, fig. 215). Both unburnt (e.g. *ibid.*, fig. 617) and burnt (e.g. *ibid.*, fig. 463) pins of a size comparable to the Gristhorpe example are believed to

have been used as fasteners for funerary garments, with the calcined ones having been burnt as the body was consumed on the pyre. (See Sheridan 2007 for some radiocarbon-dated Scottish examples of calcined bone and antler pins.) Not all pins need to have been clothing fasteners, however; Mortimer (1905, 76 and fig. 167) argued that a set of six, found in the area of a woman's head at Aldro barrow 113, North Yorkshire, had probably been used as hair pins.

Parallels for the flint artefacts are similarly numerous, as can be seen from Mortimer's summary listing of finds from barrows in what had, in 1905, been the East Riding of Yorkshire (*ibid.*, table following p. 442; part of this area is now North Yorkshire). While his total of 147 'flint tools and flakes' encompasses some Neolithic examples and some Early Bronze Age flint daggers, strike-a-lights and other tools not closely comparable with the Gristhorpe objects, nevertheless this figure conveys a sense of the frequency with which flint items were included as grave goods. While most of the flint knives found in Early Bronze Age graves in Yorkshire, and elsewhere in Britain, tend to be of plano-convex 'slug' form, with retouch all over their dorsal surface (e.g. *ibid.*, fig. 610), examples with less extensive retouch – and hence more closely comparable to the Gristhorpe knife – are known (e.g. Garton Slack barrow 74, East Yorkshire: *ibid.*, 221 and fig. 567).

Before considering the knife or dagger, the container and the wooden 'fastener' can be dealt with rapidly since parallels are far harder to find. (The birch bark containers known from Danish Bronze Age log coffins can be excluded from the discussion here since they are both geographically remote and several centuries later than the Gristhorpe example, dating to the 14th century BC: Randsborg and Christensen 2006). Objects made from bark are extremely rare in Britain, since they are so prone to decay except in waterlogged conditions (Coles *et al.* 1978). There is, however, evidence for the use of sewn birch bark in an Early Bronze Age context: at Dalrigh, near Oban, Argyll and Bute, a tree-trunk coffin (which may have been a re-used logboat) contained fragments of sewn birch bark, which may have covered or enclosed a body that had disintegrated completely by the time of the coffin's discovery (Mapleton 1879). One of the fragments of this birch bark was radiocarbon dated, as part of National Museums' Scotland ongoing programme of radiocarbon dating ancient material in its collections, producing a date of 3555±60 BP, OxA-6813, 2120–1730 cal BC at 95.4% probability using OxCal 4.1 (Sheridan *et al.* 2002). More recently, criss-cross strips of birch bark, probably forming a bier upon which the deceased had been borne to the grave, were found in the Forteviot 'dagger grave' cist (Noble and Brophy 2011).

The authors know of no obvious parallel for the wooden 'fastener' from Gristhorpe (although no exhaustive review has been attempted of all British waterlogged organic artefacts). It does not resemble any of the variously-shaped bone or jet/jet-like clothes fasteners of the Early Bronze Age. However, as discussed above, its use as a pouch fastener seems the most plausible explanation for its presence in the coffin.

Despite the difficulties of finding Early Bronze Age British *comparanda* for the Gristhorpe container, the presence of an object containing drink or food for the journey into the Otherworld is a regular feature of Early Bronze Age graves, in the form of the ceramic Food Vessel and late Beaker pots that are well attested in Yorkshire (as illustrated, for example, in Mortimer 1905. The Food Vessels include a few lidded examples.). The discovery of milk or milk-product traces within the Gristhorpe container is also paralleled in Food Vessel and Beaker funerary pottery, as a recent project of absorbed lipid analysis undertaken by Lucija Šoberl has revealed (Šoberl pers. comm.).

The knife or dagger is in some respects easy to parallel (as a prestigious Early Bronze Age flat metal-bladed weapon), while exact parallels for the morphology of its blade are more elusive. It would be easy to become embroiled in the finer points of typological debate, and to worry over whether it had been designed and/or used as a dagger or as a knife; typological considerations are summarised below. The key point to note is that it would have been instantly recognisable, during its owner's lifetime, as a precious and rare possession that signalled his standing in society and indicated his ability to slit the throat of an animal or a foe. Furthermore, it may have had a particularly interesting biography of its own, since the fact that the whale bone pommel appears disproportionately large with respect to the blade, when compared with other broadly contemporary metal daggers and knives (Gerloff 1975, plates 3–7, 23, 28), suggests that the pommel and blade had not originally been made together. Indeed, given that the blade shows obvious signs of wear and re-sharpening, while the pommel appears far less worn, it may be that Gristhorpe Man had arranged for a new, ostentatious pommel of whalebone – a material both rare and probably redolent in symbolism – to be fitted to an already-old blade (with a new horn hilt being required to fit the two components together).

Regarding the question of the typological classification of the Gristhorpe blade, it should be noted that this specimen blade poses problems since it shares some features with other Early Bronze Age blades that have been classified as 'daggers', while also sharing characteristics (such as the presence of only two rivets) with a series of generally smaller blades that have traditionally, and somewhat unhelpfully, been classed as 'knife-daggers' (Gerloff 1975). While both classes may actually have been used as knives – with the shape of the 'dagger' blades suggesting that

they were principally designed to deliver a slashing *coup de grâce* as noted above – and while there is an overlap in length, there is a distinction to be drawn between these two classes of blade, since they tend to have different patterns of association and may well have had a different social significance (Needham forthcoming). Morphologically the Gristhorpe blade is difficult to pigeonhole, but bearing in mind these patterns of association and the overall 'vocabular and grammar' of Early Bronze Age high status male grave goods, it finds its closest parallels among Early Bronze Age daggers. This was the opinion of Sabine Gerloff, who classed it as a 'Type Merthyr Mawr, variant Parwich' flat dagger (Gerloff 1975, 50, 51), contemporary with the earliest flat bronze dagger blades of her 'Type Butterwick' and differing from them in having two, rather than three, rivets fixing the blade to the haft. ('Variant Parwich' consists of three relatively heterogeneous blades.) According to the most up-to-date version of dagger and knife typology (Needham forthcoming), the Gristhorpe blade is clearly a 'Series 2' blade, being flat and very thin. Some Series 2 dagger blades are almost as short as the Gristhorpe blade, with that from Eynsham, Oxfordshire (Gerloff 1975, no. 41) being only c. 90 mm long and that from Kenslow Knoll, Middleton & Smerrill, Derbyshire (*ibid.*, no. 24) being 88 mm (in comparison with Gristhorpe's length of c. 83 mm). The Gristhorpe blade is around 30 mm shorter than the 'type Merthyr Mawr', Series 2 dagger blade from the aforementioned lidded tree-trunk coffin from Loose Howe. (Note that Elgee and Elgee's reconstruction of that blade as having four rivets may well be incorrect: Elgee and Elgee 1949, fig. 3).

Typologically, the pommel belongs to a widespread class of pommel characterised by having a top with a long oval shape and a pronounced lipping of its edge. In his review of such pommels, Stuart Needham (Needham 2011) was able to cite a dozen examples, including that from Gristhorpe; an additional example has since come to light at Shaw Cairn, Greater Manchester. The date range for these pommels extends from c. 2050 BC to c. 1500 BC; the Gristhorpe example therefore lies early within this series, which accords with the fact that the lipping is not quite as pronounced as in some later examples. The association of this kind of pommel with a knife ('knife-dagger') is attested at Winterbourne Stoke barrow G66, Wiltshire (*ibid.*, table SS3.1), while at Irthlingborough, Northamptonshire, the pommel was found with a dagger blade. The fact that the Gristhorpe pommel is of whale bone fits with a broader pattern whereby unusual materials, especially of marine species, were used as pommels for Early Bronze Age blades. Regarding the example from Ashgrove, Fife, the pommel was found to be probably of sperm whale tooth (Clarke 1964), while the same material seems to have been used for the pommel of the Forteviot dagger (as identified by

Dr Sonia O'Connor) and possibly also for that of the dagger from Standlow, Derbyshire (Kinnes 1985). Elsewhere (and slightly later), the special materials included amber, as found on the now-destroyed dagger from Hammeldon, Devon (Gerloff 1975, no. 194). Clearly, the pommel – as the most prominently-visible element of a dagger or knife, when being carried in its scabbard or sheath – was the focus for competitive conspicuous consumption, and in this respect Gristhorpe Man seems to have 'played the game', compensating for a relatively unassuming blade with a fancy pommel.

The use of horn (presumably cattle horn) for the hilt of the Gristhorpe dagger or knife is readily paralleled among Early Bronze Age daggers from northern Britain (Cameron 2003); *comparanda* for the use of animal hide for scabbards and sheaths, as at Rameldry, Fife, Seafield West, Highland and Forteviot, Perth & Kinross, have already been mentioned (*ibid.*; Gabra-Sanders *et al.* 2003).

The practice of depositing daggers or knives in high-status male graves had a long currency, having been introduced as one of several novelties including the use of Beaker pottery during the 25th century BC and persisting until the second quarter of the second millennium BC (Needham 2012). The radiocarbon dates for the kind of flat-bladed daggers that were in contemporary use with the Gristhorpe blade are presented by Stuart Needham (*ibid.*, table 1.1). The distribution of Early Bronze Age 'dagger graves' is not even, but tends to show regional clustering, with Yorkshire forming one such cluster, the Peak District another (Bateman 1861) and – as far as the early second millennium is concerned – coastal and inland Wessex yet another (Gerloff 1975, plate 29; several more have been found since this was published. See also Needham 2000 and Needham *et al.* 2006 on the Wessex finds, and see Baker *et al.* 2003, illus 12 and table 4 for the Scottish distribution – to which the Forteviot example now needs to be added.)

Finally, some comments can be offered regarding the fact that Gristhorpe Man had been lain in the coffin on his right side – a side more commonly associated with female interments during the Early Bronze Age and the preceding Chalcolithic period. Thanks to research by Alexandra Shepherd on 'sidedness' in the graves of these periods in Yorkshire and in north-east Scotland (A. Shepherd 2012), it is clear that the more rigid distinction between male, left-side interments vs. female, right-sided interments that had obtained during the early currency of Beaker pottery use had begun to break down by the time that Gristhorpe man was buried. At this time, when Food Vessels and late Beakers were in use, males were regularly being buried on their right side (*ibid.*, 263).

Conclusions: Gristhorpe Man within Early Bronze Age society in Yorkshire (and beyond)

This review, and that of Parker Pearson *et al.* (this volume) of the *comparanda* for Gristhorpe Man's coffin, will have made it clear that this grave belongs to the highest echelon of Early Bronze Age society, with much effort being expended on its creation and on the appropriate kitting-out of its occupant for his journey into the Otherworld. Both as a tree-trunk coffin grave and as a 'dagger grave', it is one of several to have been found in Yorkshire, which seems to have had a relatively high concentration of high-status Early Bronze Age graves; the density of 'dagger graves' of this period is exceeded only in the Peak District. While some of the objects found in the coffin (such as the flint objects and bone pin) will have been relatively common, and some others (i.e. the bark and wood container and the wooden 'fastener') may appear rarer than had been the case, due to the vagaries of organic preservation, nevertheless the dagger or knife will have been a rare and precious object. Along with the cattle hide, the coffin itself and the overall construction of the grave, it will have underlined the fact that Gristhorpe Man had been singled out as a special member of the community. As demonstrated above and in Parker Pearson *et al.* (this volume), the Gristhorpe grave complied with a 'vocabulary of esteem' that was widespread across Britain in the period between the first use of bronze, during the 22nd century BC, and around 1900 BC. This period saw a marked increase in expressions of social differentiation (Needham 2004), with the opportunities afforded by control over metal and other scarce resources (along with the generation of agricultural surplus, in some areas) allowing some families and individuals to indulge in the kind of competitive conspicuous consumption as attested at Gristhorpe.

References

Baker, L., Sheridan, J. A. and Cowie, T. G. (2003) An Early Bronze Age 'dagger grave' from Rameldry Farm, near Kingskettle, Fife. *Proceedings of the Society of Antiquaries of Scotland* 133, 85–123.

Bateman, T. (1861) *Ten Years' Diggings in Celtic and Saxon Grave Hills in the Counties of Derby, Stafford and York....* London and Derby, J. R. Smith and W. Bemrose and Sons.

Buckley, M., Melton, N. D. and Montgomery, J. (2013) Proteomics analysis of ancient food vessel stitchng reveals >4,000-year-old milk protein, *Rapid Communications in Mass Spectrometry*, 23, 1–8.

Cameron, E. (2003) The dagger – hilt and scabbard. Pp. 99–101 in L. Baker, J. A. Sheridan and T. G. Cowie, An Early Bronze Age 'dagger grave' from Rameldry Farm, near Kingskettle, Fife. *Proceedings of the Society of Antiquaries of Scotland* 133, 85–123.

Clarke, A. S. (1964) Identification of materials in the dagger haft. Pp. 176–7 in A. S. Henshall, A dagger-grave and other cist burials at Ashgrove, Methilhill, Fife. *Proceedings of the Society of Antiquaries of Scotland* 97 (1963–1964), 166–179.

Coles, J. M., Heal, S. V. E. and Orme, B. J. (1978) The use and character of wood in prehistoric Britain and Ireland. *Proceedings of the Prehistoric Society* 44, 1–45.

Davies, A. and Tipping, R. (2007) The pollen. Pp. 44–55 in H. K. Murray and I. A. G. Shepherd, Excavation of a beaker cist burial with meadowsweet at Home Farm, Udny, Aberdeenshire. *Proceedings of the Society of Antiquaries of Scotland* 137, 35–58.

Dixon, D. D. (1913) Cartington oak coffin, &c. *Proceedings of the Society of Antiquaries of Newcastle* (3rd Series), 6, 79–84.

Elgee, F. (1930) *Early Man in North-East Yorkshire.* Gloucester, John Bellows.

Elgee, H. W. and Elgee, F. (1949) An Early Bronze Age burial in a boat-shaped wooden coffin from North-east Yorkshire. *Proceedings of the Prehistoric Society* 15, 87–106.

Gabra-Sanders, T., Cressey, M. and Clarke, C. (2003) The scabbard. Pp. 62–63 in M. Cressey and J. A. Sheridan, The excavation of a Bronze Age cemetery at Seafield West, near Inverness, Highland. *Proceedings of the Society of Antiquaries of Scotland* 133, 47–84.

Gerloff, S. (1975) *The Early Bronze Age Daggers in Great Britain and a Reconsideration of the Wessex Culture.* Munich, C.H. Beck'sche (Prähistorische Bronzefunde Series 6(2)).

Green, H. S. (1987) The Disgwylfa Fawr round barrow, Ceredigion, Dyfed. *Archaeologia Cambrensis* 136, 43–50.

Greenwell, W. (1877) *British Barrows.* Oxford, Clarendon Press.

Greenwell, W. (1890) Recent researches in barrows in Yorkshire, Wiltshire, Berkshire, etc. *Archaeologia* 52, 1–72.

Groenman-van Waateringe, W., Kilian, M. and Londen, H. van (1999) The curing of hides and skins in European prehistory. *Antiquity* 73, 884–890.

Hawkins, J. M. F. (2006) *Gristhorpe Man: Molecular and Microscopic Analysis of an Artefact/Eco-assemblage found within a Burial Context.* Unpublished MSc dissertation, University of Bradford.

Henshall, A. S. (1964) A dagger-grave and other cist burials at Ashgrove, Methilhill, Fife. *Proceedings of the Society of Antiquaries of Scotland* 97 (1963–1964), 166–179.

Hutchins J. (1767) Archaeology, Part I. *The Gentleman's Magazine*, 37, 94–5.

Jewitt, L. (1870) *Grave-Mounds and their Contents: a Manual of Archaeology.* London, Groombridge.

Jones, A. M., Marchand, J., Sheridan, J. A., Straker, V. and Quinnell, H. (2012) Excavations at the Whitehorse Hill Cist, Dartmoor. *PAST* 70, 14–16.

Kinnes, I. A. (1985) *Beaker and Early Bronze Age Grave Groups.* British Bronze Age Metalwork, Associated Finds Series, A7–16. London, British Museum Publications.

McAdam, E. (1982) Comparative background: the cemetery. Pp. 120–129 in T. Watkins, The excavation of an Early Bronze Age cemetery at Barns Farm, Dalgety, Fife. *Proceedings of the Society of Antiquaries of Scotland* 112, 48–141.

Mapleton, R. J. (1879) Notice of the discovery of an old canoe in a peat-bog at Oban. *Proceedings of the Society of Antiquaries of Scotland* 13 (1878–1879), 336–338.

Maron, D. R. (2007) *The Bronze Age Tree Trunk Coffin from*

Gristhorpe, East Yorkshire: Curation, Scholarship, and New Research Agenda. Unpublished MSc dissertation, University of Bradford.

Mortimer, J. (1905) *Forty Years' Researches in British and Saxon Burial Mounds of East Yorkshire.* London, A. Brown and Sons.

Needham, S. P. (2000) Power pulses across a cultural divide: cosmologically driven exchange between Armorica and Wessex. *Proceedings of the Prehistoric Society* 66, 151–207.

Needham, S. P. (2004) Migdale-Marnoch: sunburst of Scottish metallurgy. In I. A. G. Shepherd and G. J. Barclay (eds.) *Scotland in Ancient Europe: The Neolithic and Early Bronze Age of Scotland in their European Context*, 217–245. Edinburgh, Society of Antiquaries of Scotland.

Needham, S. P. (2011) The dagger and pommel from Barrow 1. In J. Harding and F. Healy (eds.) *The Raunds Area Project. A Neolithic and Bronze Age Landscape in Northamptonshire. Volume 2 Supplementary Series*, 383–388. London, Engliah Heritage. http://www.english-heritage.org.uk/publications/neolithic-and-bronze-age-landscape-vol2/raundsareaproj2-ss3.pdf, accessed January 2013.

Needham, S. P. (2012) Case and place for the British Chalcolithic. In M. J. Allen, J. P. Gardiner and J. A. Sheridan (eds.) *Is There a British Chalcolithic? People, Place and Polity in the Late 3rd Millennium*, 1–26. Oxford, Oxbow/Prehistoric Society (Prehistoric Society Research Paper 4).

Needham, S. P. (forthcoming) A revised classification and chronology for daggers and knives. Appendix 1 in A. Woodward, J. Hunter and D. Bukach, *Ritual and Dress in the Early Bronze Age.* Oxford, Oxbow.

Needham, S. P., Parfitt, K. and Varndell, G. (2006) *The Ringlemere Cup. Precious Cups and the Beginning of the Channel Bronze Age.* London, The British Museum.

Noble, G. and Brophy, K. (2011) Ritual and remembrance at a prehistoric ceremonial complex in central Scotland: excavations at Forteviot, Perth and Kinross. *Antiquity* 85, 787–804.

Randsborg, K. and Christensen, K. (2006) *Bronze Age oak-coffin graves: archaeology and dendro-dating.* Copenhagen, Blackwell Munksgaard (*Acta Archaeologica* 77, Supplementa VII).

Robertson, R., Black, G. F. and Struthers, J. (1895) Notice of the discovery of a stone cist and urns at the Cununghar, Tillicoultry; with notes on the contents and the sculptured covering stone of the cist; and on the microscopical examination of the fibrous or hairy substance found in the cist. *Proceedings of the Society of Antiquaries of Scotland* 29 (1894–1895), 190–197.

Rowntree, A. (ed.) (1931) *The History of Scarborough.* London, J. M. Dent and Sons.

Ryder, M. L. (1964) Report on hair and skin remains from Ashgrove Farm, Methil, Fife and other Bronze Age sites. Pp. 174–176. In A. S. Henshall, A dagger-grave and other cist burials at Ashgrove, Methilhill, Fife. *Proceedings of the Society of Antiquaries of Scotland* 97 (1963–1964), 166–179.

Shepherd, A. N. (2012) Stepping out together: men, women and their Beakers in time and space. In M. J. Allen, J. P. Gardiner and J. A. Sheridan (eds.) *Is There a British Chalcolithic? People, Place and Polity in the Late 3rd Millennium*, 257–280. Oxford, Oxbow/ Prehistoric Society (Prehistoric Society Research Paper 4).

Shepherd, I. A. G. (2009) The V-bored buttons of Great Britain and Ireland. *Proceedings of the Prehistoric Society* 75, 335–369.

Sheridan, J. A. (2007) Dating the Scottish Bronze Age: "There is clearly much that the material can still tell us". In C. Burgess, P. Topping and F. Lynch (eds.), *Beyond Stonehenge: Essays on the Bronze Age in Honour of Colin Burgess*, 162–185. Oxford, Oxbow.

Sheridan, J. A. Cowie, T. G. and Hunter, F. J. (2002) National Museums' of Scotland dating programme: 1994–98. In C. Bronk Ramsey, T. F. G. Higham, D. C. Owen, A. W. G. Pike and R. E. M. Hedges, Radiocarbon dates from the Oxford AMS system: *Archaeometry* datelist 31. *Archaeometry* 44(3), Supplement s1, 55–61.

Suddaby, I. (forthcoming) *Excavation of two Mesolithic post-circles, Neolithic pits and Bronze Age Funerary remains at Silverscrest, Lesmurdie road Elgin, Moray, 2002.* Scottish Archaeological Internet Report, www.sair.org.uk/

Watkins, T. (1982) The excavation of an Early Bronze Age cemetery at Barns Farm, Dalgety, Fife. *Proceedings of the Society of Antiquaries of Scotland* 112, 48–141.

Williamson, W. C. (1834) *Description of the Tumulus, lately opened at Gristhorpe, near Scarborough.* Scarborough, C. R. Todd.

Williamson, W. C. (1836) *Description of the Tumulus, lately opened at Gristhorpe, near Scarborough*, second edition. Scarborough, C. R. Todd.

Williamson, W. C. (1872) *Description of the Tumulus opened at Gristhorpe, near Scarborough*, third edition. Scarborough, S. W. Theakston.

13

ANALYSIS AND METALLOGRAPHY OF THE GRISTHORPE DAGGER

Peter Northover

The metallurgy of the Gristhorpe dagger

The dagger, found with a male skeleton from an oak coffin burial at Gristhorpe, near Filey, North Yorkshire, and illustrated in Figures 13.1 and 13.2, was submitted for metallurgical study. The problems surrounding the identification of this object as either a dagger or a knife (or 'knife-dagger') have been discussed already (Sheridan *et al.*, this volume), and the typological arguments need not be rehearsed again here. Suffice it to remind the reader that there are aspects of the blade that suggest links not only with Early Bronze Age flat daggers – as was acknowledged by Sabine Gerloff in her classification of the blade as a 'Variant *Parwich* of Type *Merthyr Mawr*' flat dagger (Gerloff 1975) – but also with what Gerloff terms 'knife-daggers', a class of object with somewhat different associations. Moving the Gristhorpe blade into the 'knife-dagger' group would have an impact on how the importance of the individual buried in the coffin is appreciated, so one aim of this study was to ascertain how the blade compares technically with the flat daggers on the one hand and with the knife-daggers on the other.

It is also important to utilise what information the analysis gives us from a chronological point of view as knife-daggers are chronologically and typologically less well defined than daggers. If, however, it is legitimate to equate the blade to Gerloff's *Parwich* variant of Type *Merthyr Mawr* flat daggers, we can be relatively precise about dating. Flat daggers generally pre-date the more elaborate blades of the first phase of the Wessex Culture, commonly referred to as Armorico-British daggers. The earliest dated form of the flat bronze dagger is that of Gerloff's Type *Butterwick*,

with the example from Gravelly Guy, Stanton Harcourt, Oxfordshire, being dated to 2280–1980 cal BC (Gerloff 2005, Northover 2005). Taking Type *Merthyr Mawr* and its variants as derivative from Type *Butterwick*, it is reasonable, on the basis of form, to place the Gristhorpe blade at *c.* 2000 BC. If it should, indeed, be classed with the knife-daggers, rather than with the larger flat blades, the possible date range would expand, but a date either side of 2000 BC would still be the most credible. This date is consistent both with the radiocarbon dates obtained from Gristhorpe Man and his coffin, and with Stuart Needham's allocation of the blade to his 'Series 2' thin flat blades, as discussed in Sheridan *et al.* (this volume).

Sampling and analysis

A single sample, labelled #R3005, was cut from the edge of the blade using a fine jeweller's saw. The sample was hot-mounted in a carbon-filled thermosetting resin, then ground and polished to a 1μm diamond finish. Analysis was by electron probe microanalysis with wavelength dispersive spectroscopy; operating conditions were an accelerating voltage of 20kV, a beam current of 30nA, and an X-ray take-off angle of 40°. Seventeen elements were sought, as listed in Table 1; pure element and mineral standards were used with a counting time of 10s per element. Detection limits were typically 100–200ppm, with the exception of 400ppm for gold.

Five areas, each 30x50μm were analysed on the sample; the individual compositions and their means, normalised

Fig. 13.1 The Gristhorpe dagger blade photographed in 2005 (Photograph: S. O'Connor).

Fig. 13.2 The Gristhorpe dagger blade as illustrated in 1834 (Williamson 1834, frontispiece).

Table 13.1 Analysis of the Gristhorpe dagger.

Sample	Object	Part	Fe	Ca	Ni	Cu	Zn	As	Sb	Sn	Ag	Bi	Pb	Au	Cd	S	Al	Si	Mn
R3005/1	Flat Dagger: Parwich Variant	Edge	0.06	0.00	0.01	87.25	0.00	0.33	0.08	12.06	0.13	0.03	0.03	0.00	0.00	0.01	0.00	0.00	0.00
R3005/2			0.17	0.01	0.03	87.08	0.08	0.36	0.11	11.89	0.13	0.00	0.08	0.04	0.00	0.00	0.00	0.02	0.00
R3005/3			0.16	0.00	0.00	87.41	0.06	0.45	0.06	11.56	0.15	0.06	0.09	0.00	0.00	0.00	0.00	0.00	0.02
R3005/4			0.13	0.01	0.00	86.68	0.00	0.38	0.07	12.47	0.20	0.02	0.02	0.00	0.00	0.00	0.00	0.00	0.01
R3005/5			0.05	0.00	0.01	87.23	0.02	0.37	0.11	11.89	0.11	0.00	0.12	0.04	0.00	0.00	0.00	0.01	0.02
R3005/ Mean			0.11	0.00	0.01	87.13	0.03	0.38	0.09	11.97	0.14	0.02	0.07	0.02	0.00	0.00	0.00	0.00	0.01

to 100%, are shown in the table. All concentrations are in weight %. After analysis the sample was examined metallographically in the as-polished and etched states. The etch used was an acidified aqueous solution of ferric chloride further diluted with ethanol. Because of the very small size of the prepared sample the metallography is not illustrated.

The alloy

The blade was formed from an unleaded medium tin bronze with 12.00% tin. The principal impurities were 0.11% iron, 0.38% arsenic, 0.09% antimony, 0.14% silver, and 0.07% lead. There were also small traces of nickel, zinc, bismuth and, just possibly, manganese.

Approximately 50% of the daggers and knife-daggers catalogued by Gerloff have been analysed, as have a number of subsequent discoveries, so there is a more than adequate body of comparative data. Bronze was fully adopted for axes and daggers by the end of the 22nd century BC (Northover 1999). The process of adoption was rapid and in most areas of Britain and Ireland an alloy with 9–12% tin became standard, with a tendency towards the higher end of the scale. Although the literature has traditionally cited a 10% tin bronze as representing the best compromise between 'hardenability', toughness and ductility, 12% bronze often suited the Bronze Age smith's purposes better, giving a useful increase in the possible ductility of the blade with only a small diminution in hardness. Although the sample was too small for the hardness of the blade edge to be measured, a Vickers hardness number in excess of 200VPN is highly probable.

The impurity pattern and the origins of the metal

To assist in interpreting the impurity pattern, in which iron, arsenic and silver are the main impurities, with lesser amounts of antimony and lead, it is helpful to use the classification of Bronze Age impurity patterns devised by the present writer for the metalwork from Wales (Northover 1980). In this system the Gristhorpe dagger can be described as most probably belonging to Group 'A3'. 'A' metal, with an arsenic/antimony/silver impurity pattern, has long been attributed to Ireland and recent research for the Ross Island/Early Bronze Age Mines Project (O'Brien *et al.* 2004), and in the use of lead isotope analysis in the British Bronze Age (Rohl and Needham 1998), has confirmed this. Although some 'A' copper also appears to have been mined in Scotland in the Migdale phase of the Early Bronze Age,

the dagger does not fit the Scottish pattern as both arsenic and antimony contents are too low.

The producton of 'A' copper from south-west Ireland, especially attested from Ross Island, Co. Kerry, dates back to the beginnings of copper metallurgy in these Islands, around or soon after 2500 BC. The arsenic content of the metal exported from the source area often had arsenic contents in excess of 1%. As the metal could be re-melted and cast in non-reducing conditions there was a tendency for arsenic and antimony to be lost by oxidation and, as the amount of recycled metal in circulation increased, so there was a tendency for arsenic contents overall to decrease. The use of this metal continued after the adoption of bronze, still with a tendency for arsenic contents to decrease. At the same time there was a gradual change in the composition of the ore minerals being smelted, with a gradual reduction in the antimony content. Study of the axe and copper from the Toormore, Co. Cork wedge tomb site (O'Brien *et al.* 1992) showed that this metal was made of 'F' metal, i.e. with just arsenic and silver as the characteristic impurities with only a very small amount of antimony, with lead isotopes linking this to the Ross Island source. The deposition of the Toormore material took place about 1800 BC, which helps give us a *terminus ante quem* for the possible production of the Gristhorpe blade. The effects of recycling have to be balanced against the shift in composition of the ore source, but the period from c. 2000 BC, as suggested by the typology, to the completion of the shift to 'F' compositions and the cessation of production at Ross Island, and the date of the Toormore deposit c. 1800 BC surely encompasses the life of the Gristhorpe dagger.

We should here consider two related questions, the compositions of contemporary daggers in Britain, and the possibility that, since Irish metal contributed to the manufacture of the dagger, it might have been made in Ireland. This last can be dealt with readily by comparison with the corpus of Irish Early Bronze Age daggers (Harbison 1969); there is no reasonable parallel for the Gristhorpe dagger. Turning to the British flat daggers we find a strong tendency for the earliest flat blades of Type *Butterwick*, as with many of the earliest bronze axes in Britain, to be made from 'A' metal, with five out of eight analysed examples, but thereafter the occurrence of 'A' metal is sporadic, and it has effectively disappeared by the time of the first Armorico-British daggers. The available analyses also suggest that the Gristhorpe dagger should indeed be classified with the daggers, albeit as a small one, rather than with the knife-daggers, which tend to have a heterogeneous collection of compositions with antimony often being accompanied by nickel.

The contribution of lead isotope analysis to these arguments is discussed in a separate chapter (Montgomery and Gledhill, this volume), but it is useful to note here that the lead isotope ratios of the Gristhorpe dagger overlap with those of Chalcolithic 'A' metal from Ireland and Wales, the match being slightly better with those from Wales, supporting the idea that recycling, in addition to some mixing with a small amount of other metal has formed the composition of the Gristhorpe dagger.

Metallography

As already noted, the small size of the sample and the degree of corrosion restricted the possibility of metallographic study. The effects of corrosion have removed the very edge of the blade in the sample area. However, enough remains to show that, as would be expected, the cutting-edge was cold-worked and annealed through several cycles, the annealing temperature being high enough to ensure homogenisation of the bronze. It was not possible to determine a mean grain size from so few grains, but it would appear to be medium to large with, away from the edge, only a modest amount of final cold work. The near-imperceptible bevel that is visible around parts of the blade's edge is likely to have resulted from cold-hammering to re-sharpen the blade following use.

Conclusions

The Gristhorpe dagger belongs to one of a number of small variant groups of flat blades that developed from the first flat bronze daggers in Britain, Gerloff's Type *Butterwick*. This attribution would place the date of the dagger about or soon after 2000 BC. This is supported not only by the radiocarbon dates obtained for Gristhorpe Man and his coffin, but also by the use of 'A' metal of ultimate Irish origin for making the bronze, although the metal had probably already been recycled a number of times. The choice of an unleaded tin bronze with 12% tin and the thorough working and annealing of the bronze are typical of contemporary practice.

References

Gerloff, S. (1975) *The Early Bronze Age Daggers in Great Britain and a Reconsideration of the Wessex Culture.* Munich, Beck (Prähistorische Bronzefunde 6: 2).

Gerloff, S. (2005) The dagger from grave 4013/12. In G. Lambrick, and T. Allen (eds.) *Gravelly Guy, Stanton Harcourt, the Development of a Prehistoric and Romano-British Community*, 82–86. Oxford, Oxford Archaeology (Thames Valley Landscapes Monograph 21).

Harbison, P. (1969) *The Daggers and the Halberds of the Early Bronze Age in Ireland.* Munich, Beck (Prähistorische Bronzefunde 6: 1).

Northover, J. P. (1980) The analysis of Welsh Bronze Age metalwork, appendix to Savory, H. N. (ed.) *Guide catalogue to the Bronze Age collections.* Cardiff, National Museum of Wales.

Northover, J. P. (1999) The earliest metalworking in southern Britain. In A. Hauptman, E. Pernicka, Th. Rehren, and Ü. Yalçin (eds.) *The Beginnings of Metallurgy*, 211–226. Bochum, Deutsches Bergbau-Museum (*Der Anschnitt*, Beiheft 9).

Northover, J. P. (2005) The Bronze Age metalwork. In G. Lambrick and T. Allen (eds.) *Gravelly Guy, Stanton Harcourt, the Development of a Prehistoric and Romano-British Community)*, 88–89. Oxford, Oxford Archaeology (Thames Valley Landscapes Monograph 21).

O'Brien, W., Northover, J. P. and Cameron, E. (1992) An Early Bronze Age metal hoard from a wedge tomb at Toormore, Co. Cork. *Journal of Irish Archaeology* 5 (1989–1992), 9–17.

O'Brien, W., Northover, J. P. and Stos, S. (2004) Lead isotopes and metal circulation. In W. O'Brien (ed.) *Ross Island: Mining, Metal and Society in Early Ireland.*, 538–551. Galway, Department of Archaeology, National University of Ireland (Bronze Age Studies 6).

Rohl, B. M. and Needham, S. P. (1998) *The Circulation of Metal in the British Bronze Age: The Application of Lead Isotope Analysis.* London, British Museum (Occasional Paper 102).

Williamson, W. C. (1834) *Description of the Tumulus, lately opened at Gristhorpe, near Scarborough.* C. R. Todd, Scarborough.

14

PROTEOMICS ANALYSIS OF GRISTHORPE MAN 'GELATINE' AND SPECIES IDENTIFICATION OF THE ANIMAL HIDE KERATIN

Mike Buckley

Introduction

The exceptional preservation of the Gristhorpe Man burial led to the survival of a remarkable range of hard and soft tissues that have now been widely investigated by various scientific techniques, including the log coffin (usually recognised only as soil stains), the skeletal material (bones and teeth), brain tissue (Melton *et al*, 2010; Montgomery and Gledhill, this volume), and a range of grave inclusions that included animal hide wrapped around the body, a bone pin, a whalebone pommel, a small wooden fastener, animal phalanges and a bark container (Williamson 1834, 9; 1872,15; Sheridan *et al.*, this volume) that '*fell in pieces*' when exposed to air at the time of excavation.

Despite several lines of scientific inquiry, including stable isotope analysis and gas chromatography-mass spectrometry (GC-MS) (Melton *et al.* 2010), several unanswered questions remain with regard to the source

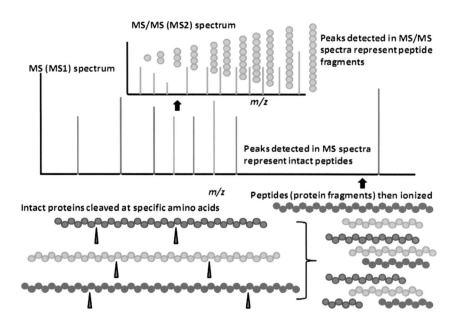

Fig. 14.1 The methodology employed in typical 'bottom up' proteomics techniques, where intact proteins are extracted from a sample and digested with a protease that cleaves at known amino acid residues. The resulting peptides are then analysed by soft-ionization mass spectrometry to produce a peptide mass fingerprint. Each peptide can then be further fragmented to yield a fragment ion spectrum representing the amino acid sequence.

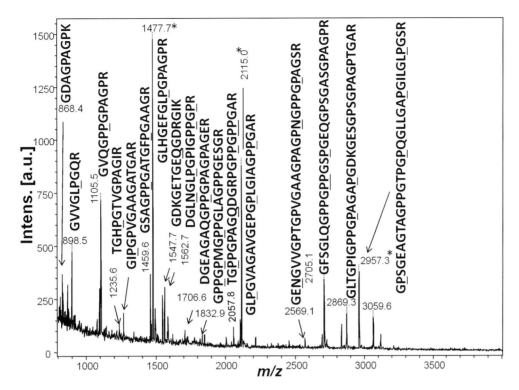

Fig. 14.2 MALDI-ToF-MS peptide mass fingerprint showing collagen digestion peaks. Although most peaks present are found in a wide range of vertebrate type 1 collagens (including that of humans), the three peptides marked by * indicate the dominance of human collagen in this sample.

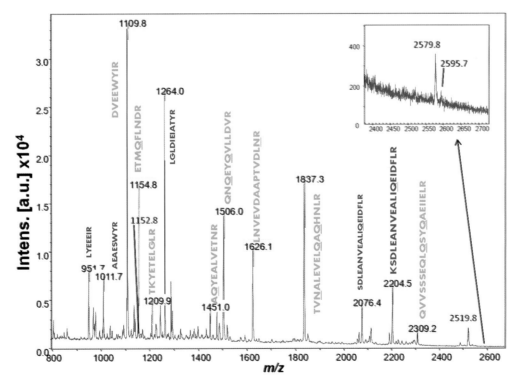

Fig. 14.3 MALDI-ToF-MS PMF of Gristhorpe hair sample digested with trypsin. Labels indicate matches from LC-MS data where green indicates bovine Type I keratin red indicates bovine Type II keratin. A relatively low-abundant bovine-specific marker at m/z 2595 is shown inset.

of some of these soft-tissue materials associated with Gristhorpe Man. Newer techniques of protein sequencing by mass spectrometry, called proteomics, may be able to address some of these questions. In a typical 'bottom up' proteomics experiment, the protein component of a given sample is solubilised, the mixture of proteins present is then cleaved into peptides using an enzyme (usually the protease trypsin which cuts specifically at the amino acids arginine (R) and lysine (K)), and the peptides analysed using a form of soft-ionization mass spectrometry (commonly using either Matrix Assisted Laser Desorption Ionization (MALDI) or Electrospray Ionization (ESI)). Peptide sequences can be inferred following induced fragmentation of the peptides and further analysis in the mass spectrometer (Fig. 14.1). The quality of the results can be improved by the additional use of liquid chromatography (LC), often coupled with the mass spectrometer (LC-MS).

Proteomics analyses are conventionally used to infer the proteins present within a particular sample. However, a number of analyses have also focussed on species identification of animal tissues, particularly in archaeological bone (Buckley *et al.* 2008; 2009; Buckley and Kansa 2011; Buckley and Collins 2011) and animal furs (Hollemeyer *et al.* 2008; 2012). The first part of this study uses proteomics to investigate the presence of animal collagen that may be present in the human skeletal material (a conservation technique reportedly used shortly after its discovery in 1834 in which the bones were gently boiled for eight hours in a glue solution (Williamson 1872, 7)). The second part concerns the identification of the species from which the animal hide surrounding the body was sourced using a hair from the skin that had been curated in the Museum.

Animal Glue Determination

Investigation of the human skeletal material itself was carried out to ascertain whether any 19th-century animal glue could be detected. If present, the introduced animal collagen could affect the radiocarbon dating and stable isotope analysis of Gristhorpe Man's collagen. Stable isotope analysis of various bone tissues had provided no evidence for the presence of non-human 19th-century collagen (Montgomery and Gledhill, this volume); the radiocarbon dates from bone and dentine were consistent with the Early Bronze Age coffin and the stable carbon and nitrogen isotope ratios were inconsistent with terrestrial herbivores, marine fish or marine mammal (Melton *et al.* 2010). Given the degraded nature of gelatine when used as a consolidating agent, it would be readily solubilised in the initial acid-demineralisation steps used in typical stable isotope analyses. Thus it is entirely plausible that the

gelatine glue is present, but that the analytical methodology removes this prior to the stable isotope measurements. A small sample consisting of a flake of periosteal bone, which was deemed most likely to have been in contact with the glue solution during the conservation undertaken in 1834, was investigated using proteomics analysis.

To ensure that no gelatine was lost, soluble protein was extracted with 50 mM ammonium bicarbonate (ABC; pH 7.4) buffer without prior demineralisation, eliminating the need for any buffer exchange step that may result in loss of small molecular weight degraded gelatine peptides. The protein mixture was then digested with the protease trypsin (18 hours at 37 °C) in order to cleave intact proteins into peptides, which were then purified using C18 ZipTips (e.g. Buckley *et al.* 2009), co-cystalised onto a stainless steel target plate with hydoxycinnamic acid and analysed by MALDI; the cleavage into peptides is to produce fragments that are within the ideal range for accurate analysis in the mass spectrometer using reflectron mode) following Buckley and Kansa (2011). However, the resulting MALDI peptide mass fingerprint (PMF) spectrum (Fig. 14.2) was an almost identical match to that of human type 1 collagen (Buckley and Kansa 2011). LC-MS analyses were also carried out in order to ascribe sequence information to each peak identified in the PMF. Digested samples were analysed by LC-MS/MS (NanoAcquity LC coupled to a Orbitrap Elite mass spectrometer) on which the peptides were concentrated on a pre-column (20 mm × 180 μm) then separated on a 1.7 μM BEH C18 analytical column (75 mm × 250 μm i.d.), using a gradient from 99% buffer A (0.1 % formic acid (FA) in H_2O)/1% buffer B (0.1% FA in acetonitrates) to 25% B in 45 min at 200 nL min^{-1}. Peptides were selected for fragmentation automatically by data dependent analysis. Proteomics data files were searched using Mascot v2.2.06 against the UniProt public database. Standard searches were carried out using two missed cleavages, error tolerances of 0.5 Da (MS and MS/MS) and variable pyro-glutamic acid (Q), phosphorylation (S and T), oxidation (P, K and M) and deamidation modifications. All peaks are accounted for by the known human bone collagen (I) sequences publicly available (Appendix 1) and no exogenous collagen peptides (i.e. from other species potentially used as sources of animal glue) could be detected. Other proteins identified in the ABC soluble fraction included human prothrombin, chondroadherin, lumican and biglycan (Table 14.1).

The most likely reason for this result and those from previous stable isotope analyses (Melton *et al.* 2010, Montgomery and Gledhill, this volume) is that little or no non-human animal glue was utilised. If gelatine based animal glue was used, it must have derived from poor quality/highly degraded material. However, even this should be considered highly unlikely given that we

Table 14.1 Top protein matches in LC-MS analyses of Gristhorpe Man 'gelatine' with ion score cut-off 50 and with at least two unique peptide matches. Further details given in Appendices I and II.

Protein	Species	Mascot Score	Peptides Matched (Unique)
Type 1 Collagen Alpha 1	Human	4047	311 (96)
Type 1 Collagen Alpha 2	Human	3863	188 (79)
Prothrombin	Human	172	6 (4)
Chondroadherin	Human/Dog	151	4 (4)
Lumican	Human	147	9 (4)
Biglycan	Human	136	4 (3)

would still expect to observe at least some 'novel' peptide signatures representing additional peptides, whereas in our spectra we can account for all peaks as present in human bone collagen.

Hair Identification

Hair was obtained from the animal skin in which the body of Gristhorpe Man had been wrapped. This skin, described when first revealed as '*of some animal... the hair of which is soft and fine, resembling that of a sheep, or perhaps nearer that of a goat, but not as long*' (Williamson 1834, 8) was sampled for proteomics analysis. This involved a relatively simple protein solubilisation in 50 mM ABC buffer (3 hours at 75°C) containing the reducing agent dithiothreitol (DTT; 100 mM), tryptic digestion and peptides purified as described above, and initial analysis by MALDI-ToF-MS

(Fig. 14.3), followed by in-depth analyses using LC-MS. Two further experiments were carried out; one followed the above methodology but included an acetylation step (with 100 mM iodoacetamide) following the reduction step, the other following the Hollemeyer *et al.* (2012). In brief, this used a similar protein extraction technique, but where the extraction was only over 20 min at 95°C (instead of 3 hours at 75°C) and the tryptic digest only 2 hours (instead of 18 hours). By comparing the MALDI-ToF-MS PMFs (e.g., Fig. 14.2) to the species biomarkers given by Hollemeyer *et al.* (2008; 2012), we could confirm that not only were the keratins the key structural component present, but also infer that this sample derived from cattle. Based on the presence of peaks at m/z 1109, 1449 (found in all artiodactyls except pigs), m/z 1505 (found in all artiodactyls), m/z 2519 (found only in bovines, red deer and elk) and a low abundant peak at m/z 2595 (unique to bovines – see Hollemeyer *et al.* 2008), we can infer that

Table 14.2 Top protein matches in LC-MS analyses of animal hide hair with ion score cut-off 50 and with at least 2 unique peptide matches. Further details given in Appendices 1 and 2.

Protein	Species	Mascot Score	Peptides Matched (Unique)
Keratin Hb3	Bovine	2790	124 (51)
Keratin Hb1	Bovine	2659	129 (51)
Keratin Ha1	Bovine	2571	168 (46)
Keratin Ha3	Bovine	2544	187 (45)
Keratin Ha5	Bovine	412	63 (25)
Keratin-associated protein 3-3	Bovine	111	2 (2)
Keratin 79	Bovine	90	13 (7)
Selenium-binding protein	Bovine	65	5 (4)
Histone H4	Bovine + most organisms in database	52	3 (2)

the hair is that of cattle (although m/z 1151 peak, used to separate cattle from red deer in Hollemeyer *et al.* 2012 is absent, a small peak at m/z 1152 may derive from the deamidated cattle peptide). LC-MS analyses as described above were carried out in order to identify the sequences of each peptide (Fig. 14.3; Appendix 2), as well as any other proteins present within archaeological hair (Table 14.2).

Hair, which grows from follicles in the skin of mammals, is typically made up of dead, cornified cells that are dominated by keratin proteins, as well as the pigment melanin and trace amounts of metal elements. The mammalian keratins are composed of polymers of two keratin molecular type, types 1 (acidic) and 2 (neutral-basic). The LC-MS analyses of the hair specimen gives us in-depth details regarding the protein components present (Table 14.2), including bovine Type 1 (Ha1, Ha3 and Ha5) and 2 (Hb1 and Hb3) keratins, as well as several other keratin-associated proteins. The only protein identified not closely associated with hair keratin was the histone, which plays a role in structuring the chromatin in eukaryotic cells. All of the proteins identified showed highest similarity to bovine-specific sequences, with the only exception being the highly conserved histone protein that is similar throughout most animals.

Concluding Remarks

Detecting traces of a gelatine-based glue in a sample that is dominated by the same protein (collagen) can be difficult, even with the current knowledge on species biomarkers. Although we cannot rule out that it once was present, we can infer that the suggested animal glue is not currently present, at least not enough to be of concern in adversely affecting the radiocarbon dating results. The species identification of the animal hide proved to be in agreement with other evidence for cattle within the grave goods of Gristhorpe Man. It is clear that he was buried with artefacts reflecting the widespread use of cattle remains, not only for clothing such as the animal hide analysed in this study, but the identification of cattle hair, sinews and milk residues within the remains of stitching from the associated bark container (Buckley *et al.*, 2013) are highly suggestive of the importance of domesticated cattle in the British Early Bronze Age.

Acknowledgements
The author would like to thank the NERC for grant NE/H015132/1; the Michael Barber Centre for Mass Spectrometry, the Manchester Life Sciences Proteomics Core Facility; Julian Selley for bioinformatics support; and Karen Snowden, Scarborough Museums Trust, for giving permission to sample the materials studied herein.

References

Buckley, M., Collins, M. J. and Thomas-Oates, J. (2008) A method of isolating the collagen (I) alpha 2 chain carboxytelopeptide for species identification in bone fragments. *Analytical Biochemistry* 374, 325–334.

Buckley, M., Collins, M. J., Thomas-Oates, J. and Wilson, J. (2009) Species identification of bone collagen using Matrix-Assisted Laser Desorption/Ionization Mass Spectrometry. *Rapid Communications in Mass Spectrometry* 23, 3843–3854.

Buckley, M. and Kansa, S. W. (2011) Collagen fingerprinting of archaeological bone and teeth remains from Domuztepe, South Eastern Turkey. *Archaeological and Anthropological Sciences* 3(3), 271–280.

Buckley, M. and Collins, M. J. (2011) Collagen survival and its use for species identification in Holocene-lower Pleistocene bone fragments from British archaeological and palaeontological sites. *Antiqua* 1(1), e1.

Buckley, M. Melton, N. D. and Montgomery, J. (2013) Proteomics analysis of ancient food vessel stitching reveals >4,000–year-old milk protein. *Rapid Communications in Mass Spectrometry*, 43, 1–8.

Hollemeyer, K., Altmeyer, W., Heinzle, E. and Pitra, C. (2008) Species identification of Oetzi's clothing with matrix-assisted laser desorption/ionization time-of-flight mass spectrometry based on peptide pattern similarities of hair digests. *Rapid Communications in Mass Spectrometry* 22 (18), 2751–2767.

Hollemeyer, K., Altmeyer, W., Heinzle, E. and Pitra, C. (2012) Matrix-assisted laser desorption/ionization time-of-flight mass spectrometry combined with multidimensional scaling, binary hierarchical cluster tree and selected diagnostic masses improves species identification of Neolithic keratin sequences from furs of the Tyrolean Iceman Oetzi. *Rapid Communications in Mass Spectrometry* 26 (16), 1735–45.

Melton, N., Montgomery, J., Knüsel C. J., Batt, C., Needham, S., Parker Pearson, M., Sheridan, A., Heron, C., Horsley, T., Schmidt, A., Evans, A., Carter, E., Edwards, H., Hargreaves, M., Janaway, R., Lynnerup, N., Northover, P., O'Connor, S., Ogden, A, Taylor, T., Wastling, V. and Wilson, A. (2010) Gristhorpe Man: an Early Bronze Age log-coffin burial scientifically defined. *Antiquity* 84, 796–815.

Williamson, W. C. (1834) *Description of the Tumulus, lately opened at Gristhorpe, near Scarborough.* Scarborough, C. R. Todd.

Williamson, W. C. (1872) *Description of the Tumulus opened at Gristhorpe, near Scarborough.* Scarborough, S.W. Theakston.

Appendix 14.1. Mascot search results for LC-MS analysis of tryptic digest from Gristhorpe Man gelatine sample showing the experimental and calculated molecular weights, peptide ion and expect score and sequence for each uniquely matched peptide.

Mr (expt)	Mr (calc)	Score	Expect	Peptide
Collagen alpha-1(l)				
547.2603	547.2602	14	4.3e+03	K.GDTGAK.G
737.3706	737.3708	24	3.9e+02	R.GPPGPPGK.N
768.3774	768.3766	23	3.3e+02	K.GDAGPAGPK.G
782.4288	782.4286	41	6.9	R.GAAGLPGPK.G
850.4186	850.4185	44	4.3	R.GFSGLDGAK.G
851.4254	851.4250	41	8.6	R.GPPGPQGAR.G
867.4578	867.4199	41	7.3	R.GPAGPQGPR.G
881.4350	881.4355	33	51	R.PGAPGPAGAR.G
886.4164	886.4145	52	0.82	R.GSEGPQGVR.G
897.5032	897.5032	51	0.84	R.GVVGLPGQR.G
926.4454	926.4458	27	1.8e+02	R.GPPGSAGAPGK.D
927.4396	927.4662	26	2.8e+02	R.PGEAGLPGAK.G
928.4994	928.3886	25	3.9e+02	K.QGPSGASGER.G
947.3956	947.3945	27	3e+02	K.GETGEQGDR.G
949.4622	949.4618	54	0.57	R.PGPPGPPGAR.G
1072.4804	1072.4785	24	6.6e+02	K.GNSGEPGAPGSK.G
1087.5292	1087.5298	72	0.01	R.GFPGADGVAGPK.G
1094.5586	1094.5581	44	5.7	R.GRPGAPGPAGAR.G
1105.5526	1105.5516	59	0.18	R.GVQGPPGPAGPR.G
1115.4846	1115.4843	19	2.1e+03	R.EGAPGAEGSPGR.D
1125.5068	1125.5051	44	5	K.TGPPGPAGQDGR.P
1126.5742	1126.5731	45	3.8	R.GAAGLPGPKGDR.G
1130.5302	1130.5316	45	4.8	K.GADGSPGKDGVR.G
1145.5760	1145.5751	41	12	R.GLPGTAGLPGMK.G
1177.5456	1177.5438	75	0.0052	R.GQAGVMGFPGPK.G
1191.6260	1191.6248	57	0.32	R.GVPGPPGAVGPAGK.D
1240.6532	1240.6524	38	25	R.GVVGLPGQRGER.G
1241.5908	1241.5888	54	0.61	K.GLTGSPGSPGPDGK.T
1263.5334	1263.5327	38	26	R.GDKGETGEQGDR.G
1296.6082	1296.6058	41	13	K.GESGPSGPAGPTGAR.G
1301.6388	1301.6364	78	0.0029	R.GPSGPQGPGGPPGPK.G
1343.6368	1343.6358	82	0.001	R.GFPGLPGPSGEPGK.Q
1349.6698	1349.6688	43	9.5	K.GPAGERGSPGPAGPK.G
1458.6850	1458.6852	88	0.00027	R.GSAGPPGATGFPGAAGR.V
1464.6868	1464.6845	86	0.00042	R.GEPGPTGLPGPPGER.G
1489.7070	1489.7049	42	14	R.PGEVGPPGPPGPAGEK.G

Mr (expt)	Mr (calc)	Score	Expect	Peptide
1495.6736	1495.7566	22	1.1e+03	R.GLPGTAGLPGMKGHR.G
1546.6888	1546.7223	40	23	R.GDKGETGEQGDRGIK.G
1561.7738	1561.7737	58	0.32	K.DGLNGLPGPIGPPGPR.G
1568.7644	1568.7617	39	24	K.STGGISVPGPMGPSGPR.G
1584.7672	1584.7645	84	0.0008	K.GANGAPGIAGAPGFPGAR.G
1589.8051	1589.8050	14	7.2e+03	R.GLTGPIGPPGPAGAPGDK.G
1601.7310	1601.7281	35	69	K.GNSGEPGAPGSKGDTGAK.G
1604.8276	1604.8271	14	9e+03	K.AGERGVPGPPGAVGPAGK.D
1614.7759	1614.7751	24	7.4e+02	R.GGPGSRGFPGADGVAGPK.G
1616.7793	1616.7795	18	3e+03	R.GFSGLDGAKGDAGPAGPK.G
1635.8356	1635.8329	53	1	R.GAAGLPGPKGDRGDAGPK.G
1642.7322	1642.7295	31	1.6e+02	K.NGDDGEAGKPGRPGER.G
1654.7926	1654.7911	58	0.3	K.GSPGEAGRPGEAGLPGAK.G
1689.7724	1689.7707	100	2e-05	K.DGEAGAQGPPGPAGPAGER.G
1719.8784	1719.8765	20	2.3e+03	R.GLPGERGRPGAPGPAGAR.G
1742.8468	1742.8449	48	3.1	K.GARGSAGPPGATGFPGAAGR.V
1743.7684	1743.7660	59	0.29	R.EGAPGAEGSPGRDGSPGAK.G
1748.8462	1748.8442	24	9.1e+02	R.GARGEPGPTGLPGPPGER.G
1759.7002	1759.6955	85	0.00064	K.GEPGSPGENGAPGQMGPR.G
1765.8278	1765.8231	53	1	K.PGEQGVPGDLGAPGPSGAR.G
1815.8612	1815.8574	108	3.5e-06	R.GPPGPMGPPGLAGPPGESGR.E
1827.8772	1827.8752	55	0.65	R.VGPPGPSGNAGPPGPPGPAGK.E
1846.8716	1846.8698	71	0.017	K.GEPGPVGVQGPPGPAGEEGK.R
1860.8653	1860.8676	17	4.6e+03	R.GQAGVMGFPGPKGAAGEPGK.A
1904.9458	1904.9453	22	1.5e+03	K.RGARGEPGPTGLPGPPGER.G
2003.9574	2003.9549	63	0.15	K.GEPGPVGVQGPPGPAGEEGKR.G
2056.9627	2056.9563	53	1.3	K.TGPPGPAGQDGRPGPPGPPGAR.G
2064.9571	2064.9573	25	7.4e+02	R.GPAGPQGPRGDKGETGEQGDR.G
2071.9198	2071.9155	28	4.2e+02	R.EGAPGAEGSPGRDGSPGAKGDR.G
2088.9854	2088.9825	80	0.0024	K.GSPGADGPAGAPGTPGPQGIAGQR.G
2133.9634	2133.9604	49	2.8	R.GEPGPPGPAGFAGPPGADGQPGAK.G
2152.0554	2152.0549	65	0.077	R.GETGPAGPPGAPGAPGAPGPVGPAGK.S
2214.9474	2214.9448	54	0.95	K.GDAGAPGAPGSQGAPGLQGMPGER.G
2215.0531	2215.0506	36	61	R.GETGPAGRPGEVGPPGPPGPAGEK.G
2281.0994	2281.0975	70	0.024	K.GDAGPPGPAGPAGPPGPIGNVGAPGAK.G
2316.0322	2316.0255	55	0.92	R.GEPGPPGPAGAAGPAGNPGADGQPGAK.G
2372.1058	2372.0993	26	6.1e+02	R.GPSGPQGPGGPPGPKGNSGEPGAPGSK.G
2377.1107	2377.1034	28	4.2e+02	K.GDTGAKGEPGPVGVQGPPGPAGEEGK.R
2434.1908	2434.2023	16	7.2e+03	R.PGERGPPGPQGARGLPGTAGLPGMK.G
2435.1703	2435.1677	22	1.8e+03	R.GSPGPAGPKGSPGEAGRPGEAGLPGAK.G
2469.2290	2469.2249	54	1.1	R.GPPGSAGAPGKDGLNGLPGPIGPPGPR.G
2496.2041	2496.1994	48	4.7	K.GDRGETGPAGPPGAPGAPGAPGPVGPAGK.S
2508.1015	2508.0936	44	12	K.GDAGPAGPKGEPGSPGENGAPGQMGPR.G
2532.2266	2532.2205	47	5.3	K.GDTGAKGEPGPVGVQGPPGPAGEEGKR.G

Mr (expt)	Mr (calc)	Score	Expect	Peptide
2541.1494	2541.2208	22	1.7e+03	K.GPRGETGPAGRPGEVGPPGPPGPAGEK.G
2547.2029	2547.1991	48	5.1	R.GNDGATGAAGPPGPTGPAGPPGFPGAVGAK.G
2615.2699	2615.2212	16	7.7e+03	R.GETGPAGPPGAPGAPGAPGPVGPAGKSGDR.G
2688.2554	2688.2529	85	0.0008	R.GFSGLQGPPGPPGSPGEQGPSGASGPAGPR.G
2718.2278	2718.2271	49	3.6	R.GAPGDRGEPGPPGPAGFAGPPGADGQPGAK.G
2741.2507	2741.2464	58	0.43	K.QGPSGASGERGPPGPMGPPGLAGPPGESGR.E
2868.4051	2868.4003	36	78	R.GLTGPIGPPGPAGAPGDKGESGPSGPAGPTGAR.G
2880.3670	2880.3639	40	31	R.GVPGPPGAVGPAGKDGEAGAQGPPGPAGPAGER.G
2929.3213	2929.3261	20	2.9e+03	R.GPPGPMGPPGLAGPPGESGREGAPGAEGSPGR.D
3079.4482	3079.4483	52	1.8	K.GEPGDAGAKGDAGPPGPAGPAGPPGPIGNVGAPGAK.G
3100.3852	3100.3833	30	2.7e+02	R.GLPGPPGAPGPQGFQGPPGEPGEPGASGPMGPR.G
3182.4652	3182.4613	44	12	R.GSEGPQGVRGEPGPPGPAGAAGPAGNPGADGQPGAK.G
3242.3902	3242.3654	51	2.7	R.GANGAPGNDGAKGDAGAPGAPGSQGAPGLQGMPGER.G
3257.6332	3257.5549	17	6e+03	R.PGEAGLPGAKGLTGSPGSPGPDGKTGPPGPAGQDGR.P
3414.5722	3414.5713	40	33	R.GNDGATGAAGPPGPTGPAGPPGFPGAVGAKGEAGPQGPR.G
3711.7462	3711.7370	17	5.4e+03	R.TGDAGPVGPPGPPGPPGPPGPPSAGFDFSFLPQPPQEK.A
Collagen alpha-2(I)				
742.3982	742.3974	17	1.7e+03	R.GAAGIPGGK.G
770.4042	770.4035	47	1.8	R.GASGPAGVR.G
785.3672	785.3668	36	27	R.GDQGPVGR.T
808.4310	808.4304	35	34	K.GHAGLAGAR.G
840.4466	840.4454	45	3.2	R.GVVGPQGAR.G
867.4578	867.4563	61	0.081	R.GPSGPQGIR.G
867.4590	867.4563	55	0.29	R.VGAPGPAGAR.G
891.4934	891.4926	47	2.9	R.PGPIGPAGAR.G
894.4562	894.4559	28	1.6e+02	R.GPAGPSGPAGK.D
909.4670	909.4668	35	36	R.GHNGLDGLK.G
959.4500	959.4495	54	0.65	R.AGVMGPPGSR.G
1057.4868	1057.4863	50	1.5	R.PGEPGLMGPR.G
1080.5806	1080.5788	38	19	R.GRVGAPGPAGAR.G
1083.5568	1083.5560	55	0.39	R.GLVGEPGPAGSK.G
1095.5058	1095.5057	33	56	R.DGQPGHKGER.G
1167.5998	1167.5996	18	2e+03	R.GPSGPQGIRGDK.G
1181.6034	1181.6041	40	12	K.EGPVGLPGIDGR.P
1183.4862	1183.4854	55	0.4	R.DGNPGNDGPPGR.D
1200.5780	1200.5775	67	0.033	R.GEPGNIGFPGPK.G
1221.6016	1221.6030	44	7.2	R.GFPGTPGLPGFK.G
1222.6075	1222.6055	40	15	R.GPAGPSGPAGKDGR.T
1222.6172	1222.6167	43	7.8	K.NGDKGHAGLAGAR.G
1234.6066	1234.6054	31	1.2e+02	R.GEAGAAGPAGPAGPR.G
1234.6423	1234.6419	35	54	R.TGHPGTVGPAGIR.G
1252.6436	1252.6412	79	0.0018	R.GLPGSPGNIGPAGK.E
1266.6700	1266.6681	95	4.8e-05	R.GIPGPVGAAGATGAR.G
1426.7056	1426.7061	38	26	K.GVGLGPGPMGLMGPR.G

Mr (expt)	Mr (calc)	Score	Expect	Peptide
1439.7124	1439.7117	27	3.3e+02	K.GEPGLRGEIGNPGR.D
1476.7498	1476.7474	66	0.044	R.GLHGEFGLPGPAGPR.G
1487.7290	1487.7256	58	0.31	R.TGEVGAVGPPGFAGEK.G
1509.7202	1509.7172	72	0.012	R.GAPGAVGAPGPAGATGDR.G
1546.7870	1546.7852	97	4.3e-05	K.GEIGAVGNAGPAGPAGPR.G
1548.6664	1548.6627	63	0.11	R.GDGGPPGMTGFPGAAGR.T
1561.7862	1561.7849	81	0.0015	R.GETGPSGPVGPAGAVGPR.G
1561.8224	1561.8213	68	0.036	K.GAAGLPGVAGAPGLPGPR.G
1563.8044	1563.8046	26	4.8e+02	R.GFPGTPGLPGFKGIR.G
1579.7612	1579.7591	66	0.044	R.GPPGESGAAGPTGPIGSR.G
1618.7728	1618.7700	83	0.0011	R.GPNGEAGSAGPPGPPGLR.G
1647.7754	1647.7713	29	2.5e+02	K.AGEDGHPGKPGRPGER.G
1655.8132	1655.8115	65	0.059	R.GLVGEPGPAGSKGESGNK.G
1699.7422	1699.7398	76	0.0048	K.GEPGAPGENGTPGQTGAR.G
1713.8652	1713.8646	35	61	R.GAAGIPGGKGEKGEPGLR.G
1732.8523	1732.8857	19	2.5e+03	R.GHNGLDGLKGQPGAPGVK.G
1751.8096	1751.8075	89	0.00027	R.GPPGAVGSPGVNGAPGEAGR.D
1753.8712	1753.8707	41	19	K.GEKGEPGLRGEIGNPGR.D
1774.8738	1774.8711	91	0.00017	K.RGPNGEAGSAGPPGPPGLR.G
1780.8796	1780.8704	39	29	R.GPSGPQGIRGDKGEPGEK.G
1781.8138	1781.8115	52	1.3	R.GPNGDAGRPGEPGLMGPR.G
1822.8000	1822.7970	71	0.017	K.GEPGSAGPQGPPGPSGEEGK.R
1828.8978	1828.8956	52	1.4	R.TGPPGPSGISGPPGPPGPAGK.E
1921.9272	1921.9242	77	0.0043	R.GERGPPGESGAAGPTGPIGSR.G
1947.9508	1947.9511	45	7.7	K.GPTGDPGKNGDKGHAGLAGAR.G
2025.9793	2026.0093	61	0.18	K.HGNRGETGPSGPVGPAGAVGPR.G
2055.0886	2055.0862	33	1.4e+02	K.EGPVGLPGIDGRPGPIGPAGAR.G
2066.9714	2066.9658	83	0.0012	R.GEVGPAGPNGFAGPAGAAGQPGAK.G
2075.1034	2075.0436	9	3.1e+04	R.PGPIGPAGARGEPGNIGFPGPK.G
2114.1174	2114.1120	109	2.9e-06	R.GLPGVAGAVGEPGPLGIAGPPGAR.G
2136.0514	2136.0448	69	0.034	K.GEPGVVGAVGTAGPSGPSGLPGER.G
2145.9652	2145.9676	24	9.8e+02	R.GAPGPDGNNGAQGPPGPQGVQGGK.G
2284.1503	2284.1448	19	3.7e+03	R.TGPPGPSGISGPPGPPGPAGKEGLR.G
2315.1325	2315.1295	18	4.5e+03	R.GYPGNIGPVGAAGAPGPHGPVGPAGK.H
2395.0636	2395.0524	36	71	K.GESGNKGEPGSAGPQGPPGPSGEEGK.R
2409.1333	2409.1309	58	0.41	R.GEVGPAGPNGFAGPAGAAGQPGAKGER.G
2417.2214	2417.2187	62	0.17	R.GEVGLPGLSGPVGPPGNPGANGLTGAK.G
2456.2342	2456.2772	70	0.026	R.GERGLPGVAGAVGEPGPLGIAGPPGAR.G
2539.1617	2539.1535	22	1.8e+03	K.GQPGAPGVKGEPGAPGENGTPGQTGAR.G
2551.1578	2551.1535	29	3.5e+02	K.GESGNKGEPGSAGPQGPPGPSGEEGKR.G
2568.2413	2568.2205	48	4.1	K.GENGVVGPTGPVGAAGPAGPNGPPGPAGSR.G
2572.1869	2572.2558	26	7.6e+02	R.GSDGSVGPVGPAGPIGSAGPPGFPGAPGPK.G
2650.2457	2650.2372	61	0.23	R.GSPGERGEVGPAGPNGFAGPAGAAGQPGAK.G
2742.3133	2742.3070	68	0.046	R.GAPGAVGAPGPAGATGDRGEAGAAGPAGPAGPR.G

Mr (expt)	Mr (calc)	Score	Expect	Peptide
2849.4088	2849.4057	69	0.035	K.GPKGENGVVGPTGPVGAAGPAGPNGPPGPAGSR.G
2916.3004	2916.2983	23	1.5e+03	R.GPPGAVGSPGVNGAPGEAGRDGNPGNDGPPGR.D
2956.4954	2956.4891	58	0.5	K.GPSGEAGTAGPPGTPGPQGLLGAPGILGLPGSR.G
2959.3375	2959.3333	22	1.7e+03	R.GPPGAAGAPGPQGFQGPAGEPGEPGQTGPAGAR.G
3229.5172	3229.5124	61	0.27	R.GPSGPPGPDGNKGEPGVVGAVGTAGPSGPSGLPGER.G
3299.6632	3299.6382	98	5e-05	K.GPSGEAGTAGPPGTPGPQGLLGAPGILGLPGSRGER.G
3978.0382	3978.0083	75	0.0091	R.GEVGLPGLSGPVGPPGNPGANGLTGAKGAAGLPGVAGAPGLPGPR.G
Prothrombin				
797.4544	797.4548	35	23	K.IYIHPR.Y
1193.5962	1193.5928	34	61	R.ELLESYIDGR.I
1250.6512	1250.6506	61	0.14	R.ETAASLLQAGYK.G
1560.6932	1560.7209	42	13	R.TATSEYQTFFNPR.T
Chondroadherin				
713.4064	713.4072	22	5.1e+02	K.VTELPR.G
749.3692	749.3708	23	5.8e+02	R.AGAFQGAK.D
1348.6920	1348.6888	23	8.2e+02	R.NNFPVLAANSFR.A
1354.6836	1354.7133	84	0.00068	K.FSDGAFLGVTTLK.H
Biglycan				
924.5274	924.5280	37	20	R.VPSGLPDLK.L
1312.7254	1312.7238	61	0.12	K.IQAIELEDLLR.Y
1593.8094	1593.8072	41	15	R.MIENGSLSFLPTLR.E
Lumican				
726.4062	726.4064	24	2.6e+02	K.YLYLR.N
1024.5366	1024.5341	46	3.1	R.FNALQYLR.L
1177.6333	1177.6343	28	2.7e+02	R.LKEDAVSAAFK.G
1669.8202	1669.8199	50	2.1	K.SLEYLDLSFNQIAR.L

Appendix 14.2. Mascot search results for LC-MS analysis of tryptic digest from hair sample showing the experimental and calculated molecular weights, peptide ion and expect score and sequence for each uniquely matched peptide.

Mr (expt)	Mr (calc)	Score	Expect	Peptide
Keratin, type II Hb3				
781.3544	781.3541	3	1.5e+03	R.SVCGGFR.A
810.4280	810.4276	43	0.17	R.FAAFIDK.V
850.4308	850.4297	50	0.033	R.GLTGGFGSR.S
905.4606	905.4607	45	0.1	R.FLEQQNK.L
950.4714	950.4709	44	0.15	R.LYEEEIR.V
967.4398	967.4875	46	0.085	K.LQFYQNR.Q
973.4722	973.4716	48	0.07	R.LLEGEEQR.L
973.5090	973.5080	35	1.6	R.LTAEVENAK.C

Mr (expt)	Mr (calc)	Score	Expect	Peptide
978.4510	978.4514	32	2.7	K.QDMACLLK.E
1007.4620	1007.4923	18	68	K.YEEEVALR.A
1010.4454	1010.4457	45	0.14	R.AEAESWYR.S
1010.4492	1010.4491	38	0.74	K.DVDCAYIR.K
1015.4936	1015.4934	31	3.4	K.EEINELNR.L
1038.4624	1038.4618	60	0.0039	K.AQYDDIASR.S
1065.5962	1065.5971	58	0.0059	R.FAAFIDKVR.F
1071.5816	1071.5811	72	0.00029	K.LAGLEEALQK.A
1106.5730	1106.5720	46	0.11	R.RLYEEEIR.V
1110.4960	1110.4950	35	1.4	R.CCITAAPYR.G
1126.4978	1126.4964	36	1.1	K.EYQEVMNSK.L
1129.5736	1129.5727	45	0.17	R.RLLEGEEQR.L
1135.5884	1135.5873	50	0.048	K.KYEEEVALR.A
1138.5444	1138.5441	36	1.1	K.KDVDCAYIR.K
1177.5834	1177.5835	49	0.061	K.AKQDMACLLK.E
1191.6142	1191.6135	60	0.0049	R.ATAENEFVALK.K
1210.5202	1210.5223	13	2.6e+02	R.AFSCVSACGPR.P
1245.6212	1245.6200	54	0.022	R.TKEEINELNR.L
1253.5796	1253.5789	56	0.014	R.SRAEAESWYR.S
1262.6870	1262.6870	73	0.00028	K.LGLDIEIATYR.R
1263.6104	1263.6823	24	20	K.KKYEEEVALR.A
1269.7290	1269.7292	44	0.23	K.LAGLEEALQKAK.Q
1315.6816	1315.6806	76	0.00015	R.GLNMDNIVAEIK.A
1319.7086	1319.7085	75	0.00019	R.ATAENEFVALKK.D
1358.7228	1358.7227	43	0.3	R.CKLAGLEEALQK.A
1400.7379	1400.7371	55	0.018	R.RTKEEINELNR.L
1421.6404	1421.6392	29	8	R.GGVVCGDLCVSGSR.P
1485.8412	1485.8403	77	0.00013	R.VLQANISDTSVIVK.M
1491.7828	1491.7820	63	0.0035	R.FLEQQNKLLETK.L
1593.7196	1593.7192	40	0.64	R.LTAEVENAKCQNSK.L
1692.7950	1692.7924	92	4.5e-06	R.LCEGVGAVNVCVSSSR.G
1844.8690	1844.9156	105	3e-07	R.LSSELNHVQEVLEGYK.K
1973.0150	1973.0105	71	0.0007	R.LSSELNHVQEVLEGYKK.K
2063.9934	2063.9898	102	5.5e-07	K.SDLEANSEALIQEIDFLR.R
2115.9834	2115.9807	127	2.1e-09	K.LEAAVTQAEQQGEVALNDAR.C
2191.1074	2191.1008	116	2.6e-08	R.KSDLEANSEALIQEIDFLR.R
2347.2064	2347.2019	40	1.1	R.KSDLEANSEALIQEIDFLRR.L
2358.0769	2358.0508	38	1.6	R.QCCESNLEPLFEGYIETLR.R
2389.1377	2389.1358	22	72	K.EYQEVMNSKLGLDIEIATYR.R
2403.1228	2403.1223	20	1.2e+02	K.LEAAVTQAEQQGEVALNDARCK.L
2514.1654	2514.1519	38	1.8	R.QCCESNLEPLFEGYIETLRR.E
2648.2603	2648.2534	21	1.1e+02	R.LLEGEEQRLCEGVGAVNVCVSSSR.G
2733.2590	2733.2399	29	15	K.CQNSKLEAAVTQAEQQGEVALNDAR.C

Mr (expt)	Mr (calc)	Score	Expect	Peptide
Keratin, type II Hb1				
795.3702	795.3698	17	54	R.SICGGFR.A
810.4280	810.4276	43	0.17	R.FAAFIDK.V
850.4308	850.4297	50	0.033	R.GLTGGFGSR.S
905.4606	905.4607	45	0.1	R.FLEQQNK.L
950.4714	950.4709	44	0.15	R.LYEEEIR.V
967.4398	967.4875	46	0.085	K.LQFYQNR.Q
973.4722	973.4716	48	0.07	R.LLEGEEQR.L
973.5090	973.5080	35	1.6	R.LTAEVENAK.C
978.4510	978.4514	32	2.7	K.QDMACLLK.E
1007.4620	1007.4923	18	68	K.YEEEVALR.A
1010.4454	1010.4457	45	0.14	R.AEAESWYR.S
1010.4492	1010.4491	38	0.74	K.DVDCAYLR.K
1015.4936	1015.4934	31	3.4	K.EEINELNR.V
1038.4624	1038.4618	60	0.0039	K.AQYDDIASR.S
1065.5962	1065.5971	58	0.0059	R.FAAFIDKVR.F
1071.5816	1071.5811	72	0.00029	K.LAGLEEALQK.A
1106.5730	1106.5720	46	0.11	R.RLYEEEIR.V
1110.4960	1110.4950	35	1.4	R.CCITAAPYR.G
1126.4978	1126.4964	36	1.1	K.EYQEVMNSK.L
1129.5736	1129.5727	45	0.17	R.RLLEGEEQR.L
1135.5884	1135.5873	50	0.048	K.KYEEEVALR.A
1138.5444	1138.5441	36	1.1	K.KDVDCAYLR.K
1177.5834	1177.5835	49	0.061	K.AKQDMACLLK.E
1191.6142	1191.6135	60	0.0049	R.ATAENEFVALK.K
1210.5202	1210.5223	13	2.6e+02	R.AFSCVSACGPR.P
1245.6212	1245.6200	54	0.022	R.TKEEINELNR.V
1253.5796	1253.5789	56	0.014	R.SRAEAESWYR.S
1262.6870	1262.6870	73	0.00028	K.LGLDIEIATYR.R
1263.6104	1263.6823	24	20	K.KKYEEEVALR.A
1269.7290	1269.7292	44	0.23	K.LAGLEEALQKAK.Q
1319.7086	1319.7085	75	0.00019	R.ATAENEFVALKK.D
1358.7228	1358.7227	43	0.3	K.CKLAGLEEALQK.A
1373.6876	1373.6860	76	0.00014	R.DLNMDNIVAEIK.A
1400.7379	1400.7371	55	0.018	R.RTKEEINELNR.V
1421.6404	1421.6392	29	8	R.GGVVCGDLCVSGSR.P
1491.7828	1491.7820	63	0.0035	R.FLEQQNKLLETK.L
1508.8580	1508.8562	65	0.0021	R.VLQAHISDTSVIVK.M
1593.7196	1593.7192	40	0.64	R.LTAEVENAKCQNSK.L
1709.7734	1709.7713	101	6.9e-07	R.LCEGVGSVNVCVSSSR.G
1743.8986	1743.9002	34	3.3	R.TKEEINELNRVIQR.L
1808.9070	1808.9043	93	4.3e-06	R.LSSELNSLQEVLEGYK.K
1936.0196	1936.0153	70	0.0009	R.LSSELNSLQEVLEGYKK.K
2056.9954	2056.9912	132	6.8e-10	K.LEAAVTQAEQQGEAALNDAK.C

Mr (expt)	Mr (calc)	Score	Expect	Peptide
2075.0454	2075.0422	85	2.8e-05	K.SDLEANVEALIQEIDFLR.R
2202.1574	2202.1532	147	2.2e-11	R.KSDLEANVEALIQEIDFLR.R
2344.0514	2344.0351	99	1.3e-06	R.QCCESNLEPLFNGYIETLR.R
2359.2436	2359.2383	33	6.2	R.KSDLEANVEALIQEIDFLRR.L
2389.1377	2389.1358	22	72	K.EYQEVMNSKLGLDIEIATYR.R
2500.1386	2500.1362	47	0.23	R.QCCESNLEPLFNGYIETLRR.E
2664.2494	2664.2483	17	2.3e+02	R.LLEGEEQRLCEGVGSVNVCVSSSR.G
2675.2345	2675.2344	31	11	K.CQNSKLEAAVTQAEQQGEAALNDAK.C
Keratin, type I Ha3				
822.3880	822.3872	36	0.7	K.LASDDFR.T
822.4482	822.4487	38	0.48	R.LASYLEK.V
903.4730	903.4735	22	27	K.EELICLK.Q
988.5086	988.5077	52	0.029	R.TIEELQQK.I
995.4910	995.4924	30	4	K.YETEVSLR.Q
999.5598	999.5600	57	0.009	R.LVVQIDNAK.L
1035.4548	1035.4543	35	1.4	R.GLLDSEDCK.L
1077.6181	1077.6182	29	5.7	R.LASYLEKVR.Q
1091.4176	1091.4165	22	25	R.CGPCNTFVH.-
1103.5896	1103.5896	62	0.0027	R.ILDELTLCK.S
1108.5172	1108.5189	43	0.23	R.DVEEWYIR.Q
1152.4994	1152.5233	48	0.077	K.ETMQFLNDR.L
1197.5342	1197.5336	67	0.0011	R.LECEINTYR.G
1224.6343	1224.6350	49	0.057	R.TKYETEVSLR.Q
1227.6446	1227.6459	53	0.03	R.QLVEADLNGLR.R
1259.6899	1259.6907	27	10	R.RILDELTLCK.S
1264.6198	1264.6200	27	11	R.RDVEEWYIR.Q
1293.6208	1293.6201	63	0.0027	R.AQYEALVETNR.R
1351.6018	1351.6004	53	0.028	K.QNHEQEVNTLR.S
1384.7316	1384.7310	27	12	R.QLVEADLNGLRR.I
1423.6898	1423.6878	43	0.32	R.ARLECEINTYR.G
1449.7224	1449.7212	46	0.17	R.AQYEALVETNRR.D
1459.7941	1459.7956	24	28	R.VESLKEELICLK.Q
1460.6758	1460.6743	55	0.022	R.QLERDNAELESR.I
1478.6754	1478.6736	80	6.5e-05	R.DSLENTLTETEAR.Y
1487.7274	1487.7256	68	0.00094	R.QNQEYQVLLDVR.A
1589.7988	1589.8334	63	0.0033	R.TIEELQQKILCSK.S
1624.8424	1624.8420	76	0.0002	R.LNVEVDAAPTVDLNR.V
1714.8866	1714.8638	18	1.2e+02	R.QNQEYQVLLDVRAR.L
1715.8492	1715.8438	48	0.11	K.VRQLERDNAELESR.I
1803.8928	1803.9367	38	1.3	R.LVVQIDNAKLASDDFR.T
1836.9326	1836.9217	101	7.1e-07	R.TVNALEVELQAQHNLR.D
1958.9356	1958.9295	51	0.079	K.ETMQFLNDRLASYLEK.V
1991.0562	1991.0548	96	2.4e-06	R.RTVNALEVELQAQHNLR.D
2005.9579	2005.9566	16	2.3e+02	K.QNHEQEVNTLRSQLGDR.L

Mr (expt)	Mr (calc)	Score	Expect	Peptide
2106.0254	2106.0229	61	0.0085	R.SDLERQNQEYQVLLDVR.A
2143.9694	2143.9633	55	0.034	R.SQQQEPLVCPNYQSYFR.T
2164.0771	2164.0760	25	32	R.VLNETRAQYEALVETNRR.D
2283.1374	2283.1342	58	0.016	R.SQLGDRLNVEVDAAPTVDLNR.V
2308.1434	2308.1434	106	2.9e-07	K.QVVSSSEQLQSYQAEIIELR.R
2464.2424	2464.2445	36	2.9	K.QVVSSSEQLQSYQAEIIELRR.T
2575.3134	2575.3064	167	2.7e-13	R.YSCQLAQVQGLIGNVESQLAEIR.S
2681.1454	2681.1190	31	11	R.GLLDSEDCKLPCNPCATTNACER.P
3151.5502	3151.5408	45	0.46	R.QTEELNKQVVSSSEQLQSYQAEIIELR.R
3298.6102	3298.5688	58	0.026	R.TVNALEVELQAQHNLRDSLENTLTETEAR.Y
Keratin, type I Ha5				
760.3902	760.3901	31	2.9	R.VLNEMR.C
806.3932	806.3923	44	0.13	K.LAADDFR.T
822.4482	822.4487	38	0.48	R.LASYLEK.C
903.4730	903.4735	22	27	K.EELLCLK.K
999.5598	999.5600	57	0.009	R.LVVQIDNAK.L
1013.4488	1013.4488	28	7.2	K.YETEVSMR.Q
1035.4548	1035.4543	35	1.4	R.GLLDSEDCK.L
1089.5732	1089.5740	55	0.015	R.ILDDLTLCK.A
1152.4994	1152.5233	48	0.077	K.ETMQFLNDR.L
1197.5342	1197.5336	67	0.0011	R.LECEINTYR.G
1201.6190	1201.6190	49	0.076	K.ADLEAQVESLK.E
1226.5536	1226.5527	38	0.93	K.NHEEEVNSLR.C
1243.6414	1243.5867	29	7.3	R.QLVESDMNGLR.R
1354.6506	1354.6477	19	68	K.KNHEEEVNSLR.C
1404.6742	1404.6732	60	0.0059	R.DALESTLAETEAR.Y
1423.6898	1423.6878	43	0.32	R.ARLECEINTYR.G
1487.7274	1487.7256	68	0.00094	R.QNQEYQVLLDVR.A
1620.7770	1620.8471	16	1.9e+02	R.LNVEVDAAPPVDLNR.V
1714.8866	1714.8638	18	1.2e+02	R.QNQEYQVLLDVRAR.L
1788.8912	1788.9258	56	0.022	R.LVVQIDNAKLAADDFR.T
1855.9134	1855.9098	56	0.022	R.TVNALEIELQAQHSMR.D
1958.9356	1958.9295	51	0.079	K.ETMQFLNDRLASYLEK.C
1988.8716	1988.7795	11	7.8e+02	K.ASFSSGSLKVPGGAGGGSAR.V
2088.0714	2088.0660	79	0.00013	K.ADLEAQVESLKEELLCLK.K
2634.3014	2634.1771	56	0.033	R.YSSQLAQMQGLIGNVESQLAEIR.C
Keratin, type I Ha1				
806.3932	806.3923	44	0.13	K.LAADDFR.T
822.4482	822.4487	38	0.48	R.LASYLEK.V
903.4730	903.4735	22	27	K.EELICLK.S
979.4974	979.4974	39	0.44	K.YETELGLR.Q
988.5086	988.5077	52	0.029	R.TIEELQQK.I
999.5598	999.5600	57	0.009	R.LVVQIDNAK.L
1035.4548	1035.4543	35	1.4	R.GLLDSEDCK.L

Mr (expt)	Mr (calc)	Score	Expect	Peptide
1077.6181	1077.6182	29	5.7	R.LASYLEKVR.Q
1103.5896	1103.5896	62	0.0027	R.ILDELTLCK.S
1108.5172	1108.5189	43	0.23	R.DVEEWYIR.Q
1112.4376	1112.4379	29	5.6	R.CGPCNSYVR.-
1152.4994	1152.5233	48	0.077	K.ETMQFLNDR.L
1197.5342	1197.5336	67	0.0011	R.LECEINTYR.G
1208.6401	1208.6401	45	0.16	R.TKYETELGLR.Q
1218.5978	1218.5979	44	0.2	K.SDLEAQVESLK.E
1243.6412	1243.6408	62	0.0031	R.QLVESDINGLR.R
1259.6899	1259.6907	27	10	R.RILDELTLCK.S
1264.6198	1264.6200	27	11	R.RDVEEWYIR.Q
1293.6208	1293.6201	63	0.0027	R.AQYEALVETNR.R
1327.6010	1327.6004	39	0.71	K.SNHEEEVNTLR.S
1399.7425	1399.7419	36	1.7	R.QLVESDINGLRR.I
1423.6898	1423.6878	43	0.32	R.ARLECEINTYR.G
1449.7224	1449.7212	46	0.17	R.AQYEALVETNRR.D
1474.6924	1474.6899	36	1.7	R.QLERENAELESR.I
1478.6754	1478.6736	80	6.5e-05	R.DSLENTLTETEAR.Y
1487.7274	1487.7256	68	0.00094	R.QNQEYQVLLDVR.A
1518.6854	1518.6813	42	0.45	M.SYNFCLPNLSFR.S
1564.6632	1564.6320	27	13	K.LPCNPCATTNACGK.T
1573.8032	1573.8385	57	0.015	R.TIEELQQKILCAK.S
1624.8424	1624.8420	76	0.0002	R.LNVEVDAAPTVDLNR.V
1714.8866	1714.8638	18	1.2e+02	R.QNQEYQVLLDVRAR.L
1788.8912	1788.9258	56	0.022	R.LVVQIDNAKLAADDFR.T
1836.9326	1836.9217	101	7.1e-07	R.TVNALEVELQAQHNLR.D
1958.9356	1958.9295	51	0.079	K.ETMQFLNDRLASYLEK.V
1982.9456	1982.9406	45	0.28	K.SNHEEEVNTLRSQLGDR.L
1991.0562	1991.0548	96	2.4e-06	R.RTVNALEVELQAQHNLR.D
2104.0674	2104.0609	85	3.3e-05	K.SDLEAQVESLKEELICLK.S
2106.0254	2106.0229	61	0.0085	R.SDLERQNQEYQVLLDVR.A
2157.9814	2157.9789	68	0.0015	R.SQQQEPLLCPNYQSYFR.T
2164.0771	2164.0760	25	32	R.VLNETRAQYEALVETNRR.D
2283.1374	2283.1342	58	0.016	R.SQLGDRLNVEVDAAPTVDLNR.V
2334.1390	2334.1373	74	0.00049	K.QVVSSSEQLQSCQTEIIELR.R
2575.3134	2575.3064	167	2.7e-13	R.YSCQLAQVQGLIGNVESQLAEIR.S
2580.1075	2580.1077	50	0.11	R.GLLDSEDCKLPCNPCATTNACGK.T
3179.5282	3179.5027	37	3.2	R.QTEELNKQVVSSSEQLQSCQTEIIELR.R
3298.6102	3298.5688	58	0.026	R.TVNALEVELQAQHNLRDSLENTLTETEAR.Y

GRISTHORPE MAN: PRESERVATION, TAPHONOMY AND CONSERVATION, PAST AND PRESENT

Rob C. Janaway, Sonia O'Connor and Andrew S. Wilson

Introduction

This chapter provides a holistic overview of the circumstances that resulted in the preservation of materials discovered by the original excavators of Gristhorpe Man. It documents the 'cutting edge' treatment of its day that resulted in the survival of so many of the remains and the evidence that they embodied, and now has enabled the systematic re-evaluation of both the body and its associated artefacts.

Throughout this chapter the term 'preservation' refers to the survival of physical remains both within the depositional environment and through the curation history of this assemblage. 'Conservation' is used to denote measures taken to arrest physical deterioration of the remains from the point of discovery, through the recovery process and subsequent post-excavation treatments. We also intend a broader meaning for the term conservation to include actions to identify, reveal, interpret and preserve the information surviving in archaeological finds (O'Connor 1996). This is investigative conservation and by carefully integrating this work with the project to re-examine Gristhorpe Man it has been possible to maximise the new information gained, to elucidate the object biographies and to challenge and correct past errors of identification and interpretation.

A second strand of the conservation work has been preventative conservation, which encompasses all the actions necessary to reduce the risk of future deterioration of an object, for instance by securing loose fragments that might otherwise be lost, specifying the conditions of storage and display environments, or developing safe handling and sampling protocols. These considerations had implications for every aspect of the Gristhorpe Man project, including the packing for transportation to and from the museum, the CT-scanning, the isotope sampling of the skeletal remains, and the preparation of the coffin lid for dendrochronological and radiocarbon dating.

Since the time of the excavation of Gristhorpe Man, archaeological conservation has emerged as a profession and gradually matured into a fully-fledged branch of archaeological science. Today's conservation interventions are based on an understanding of the chemistry and structure of materials and how they decay in various environments, coupled with an appreciation of object fabrication techniques and taphonomy. An important aspect of conservation ethics is that the treatment undertaken should not substantially alter the scientific attributes or invalidate the authenticity or originality of the object. This philosophy makes modern conservation approaches more investigative and often less interventive than those of the past. The final appearance of the object will have more to do with preserving information than some preconceived idea of restoring it to its 'original' state. In developing conservation strategies and methods for archaeological assemblages, the long-term survival of the material is still central, but the needs of other strands of their scientific investigation (such as technological studies, dating, chemical and biomolecular studies) increasingly have a great bearing on the approach taken.

This greater integration of conservation with other areas of archaeological science has changed the perspective of its practitioners, making it increasingly easy to criticise past treatments, even those undertaken relatively recently, for hindering new lines of investigation. However, hindsight should not blind us to the fact that such is the speed of scientific development in the study of the human past that many of our current conservation treatments are liable to be viewed in a similar way far sooner. The vindication of today's conservation treatments will be in ensuring a longevity of survival of archaeological objects that at least matches that achieved by the early pioneers who conserved the Gristhorpe finds nearly 200 years ago.

To understand why so many organic materials have survived in the Gristhorpe assemblage, and the condition of the skeleton and artefacts as a whole, it is first necessary to explore briefly the taphonomic pathways that can be followed by organic and inorganic materials in different burial environments. Then, by examining what is known of the construction of the burial mound, the preservation treatments of the day, and the scant records of the display history and subsequent re-treatments of the assemblage, it becomes possible to appreciate more fully the significance of the evidence presented by these objects.

This chapter brings together what is known of the recovery and past treatment of the Gristhorpe assemblage and discusses the approaches to, and outcomes of, the conservation work undertaken at Bradford, from the initial conservation assessment and condition recording of the assemblage, through to its packing for transportation and return to the Rotunda Museum as the centrepiece of the newly refurbished displays.

Taphonomy: Decay and preservation of body remains

Gristhorpe Man and his oak coffin were excavated on Friday, 11th July 1834, and a detailed report of the excavation featured in the Saturday, 19th July edition of *The York Herald, and General Advertiser* (York, England), Saturday, July 19, 1834; Issue 3227. By the 22nd of August the skeleton had been re-articulated and was on display within the museum, whilst the coffin was on public view outside the museum, where it must have continued to decay. The initial drying of the wood cell walls will have caused shrinkage and deep longitudinal splits. In addition, contact with damp ground in an uncontrolled environment will undoubtedly have contributed to fresh fungal decay of the lower coffin.

Contemporary accounts of the excavation provide tantalising insight into the variables affecting the state of preservation of the assemblage. The waterlogged coffin discovered at an approximate depth of 7–8 ft (*c.* 2.1–2.4 m), beneath layers of loose stones and clay, was solid enough that the oak lid could be carefully hoisted from the coffin

using a windlass to reveal black bones wrapped in animal hide and '*minute flocculent pieces of a pure white colour*', which were observed on the interior of the lid and in the water within the coffin (*The York Herald*, and *General Advertiser* (York, England), Saturday, July 19, 1834; Issue 3227). Dr Murray examined this substance at the time and identified it as adipocere. This is an intermediate degradation product of fat formed as it degrades into fatty acids, and it was described by Fourcroy (1791; 1793), some 40 years earlier. Adipocere is often associated with bodies from damp conditions or submerged in water, e.g. waterlogged graveyards. This would have been known in the medical literature of the day where, for instance, Mansfield (1800) describes the case of the body of a young woman exhibiting adipocere formation who was recovered from a river after one year's immersion. Murray goes on to speculate that the white crumbled, almost powdery appearance of this adipocere differed from the '*more usual appearance in consequence of partial decomposition, resulting without doubt from its vast age, and the peculiarity of being enclosed in such an antiseptic case*'. It was concluded that the presence of adipocere demonstrated that the whole body and not just the bones had been buried in the mound (Williamson 1834, 17–18). It was not until 1917, with the publication by Ruttan and Marshall (1917) that a detailed quantification of adipocere chemistry was published.

The body itself was skeletonised in the coffin and described as '*quite perfect, and of an ebony colour*' (Williamson 1834, 6) and that the bones were fragile but '*nearly as perfect, as on the day they were placed in the ground*' (Williamson 1834, 17). Later, Williamson (1872, 7) expands on his description saying that the bone itself was '*very rotten*'. The black colouration of the bones was suggested to be the result of a combination of iron from the clay and tannic acid from the wood (Williamson 1872, 7–8). This far-reaching interpretation is probably very close to the mark. These early descriptions of Gristhorpe Man's condition illustrate how the 19th-century research team were trying to make sense of the immediate depositional environment and its effect on the body. These same contemporary accounts place the waterlogged coffin at some considerable depth into the solid natural clay beneath a low-rising mound (with the coffin base roughly 10 feet (*circa* 3 m) below the top of the mound), which is why a windlass was required to hoist it from the ground. The stratigraphic sequence suggests that immediately above the coffin were oak branches and a '*puddle of blue clay*', above which were loose stones, more clay and a '*vegetable soil*' capping (Williamson 1872, 16). By marrying the contemporary descriptions of the excavation and archaeological stratigraphy with evidence observed during the 2008 excavation and taking into account the preservation and range of organic materials recovered (including proteinaceous materials – bone, teeth, skin, hair and brain matter; and ligno-cellulosics – wood and plant remains such as the bark container and 'berries'), we can propose the following:

Firstly, the clay pit into which the coffin was placed must have acted as a sump for any precipitation, and this would have been enhanced by moisture percolation through the loose stones that lay above the coffin (Breuning-Madsen and Holst 1998). The mound itself, which retained evidence of a part turf-construction, similar to other examples of barrows in Denmark, would also function as a moisture trap, soaking up and holding a lens of water. The 'puddle' of blue clay immediately below the loose stone could be partly due to a natural accumulation of fine clay particulates settling at the base of these stones, through percolation, but it is more likely a deliberate capping. The blue colouration would have been due to the establishment of anaerobic conditions within the mound as a whole and indicated the reduced state of iron salts in the clay particles. It would generally be expected that soft tissues and ligaments would disintegrate over the timeframe involved (Janaway *et al.* 2009). In the circumstances of the Gristhorpe interment the combination of tannic acid derived from the oak coffin and the formation of waterlogged low-redox conditions, effectively encapsulating the barrow core, has led to enhanced preservation.

This interpretation of the burial conditions is consistent with work undertaken from the mid-1990s at the Historical-Archaeological Research Centre at Lejre, 30 km west of Copenhagen in Denmark, where experimental studies were set up to mimic the conditions of the Bronze Age Egtved Storhøj oak coffin burials. Parallels can be drawn between these preservation conditions and those that resulted in the survival of the organic material in the Gristhorpe assemblage. The Danish studies suggest that the construction sequence involved producing a compacted turf structure sealing the core of the mound and then an outer, more porous mantle of subsoil was mounded over this. This structure maintained high water levels and anoxic conditions in the core of the mound (Breuning-Madsen and Holst 1998). These studies found that with increasingly anaerobic conditions in the core of the mound, immobile ferric iron Fe^{3+} and manganese Mn^{4+} was reduced to mobile ferrous iron Fe^{2+} and Mn^{2+}. At the boundary with the aerobic subsoil of the mound, part of the Fe^{2+} and Mn^{2+} was precipitated as Fe^{3+} and Mn^{4+} to form a thin, strongly cemented iron pan (Breuning-Madsen *et al.* 2001). The preservation produced by these mounds varies considerably. The inside of the coffin of Egtved Girl, discovered in 1921 (Glob 1974, 56–60), was coated with a fatty substance '*like white paint*' believed to have been derived from the body. Soft tissues, including hair, facial skin and brain, had been preserved but, apart

from her teeth, no bone survived. In contrast, the multiple oak trunk coffin burials of Borum Eshøj preserved bones '*stained by tannic acid*' and one of the coffins, excavated in 1875, contained an old man whose bones were recovered still held together by '*dried muscle*' (Glob 1974, 31–40).

Decay and Preservation of artefactual materials

As with the Danish mound burials the anoxic waterlogged environment at Gristhorpe has led to the preservation of a wide range of ephemeral organic objects such as the animal skin (1938.853), and the wood and bark container (1938.855). However, in contrast the Gristhorpe assemblage also contains a range of well-preserved osseous items, such as the pommel (1938. 844.1), bone pin (1938.849) and the human skeleton itself (1938.861) and the tracheal rings (1938.851), which in considerably more acidic sites would be either absent or in much more degraded condition. Whereas flints artefacts are relatively stable in any burial environment, copper alloys are vulnerable to corrosion under conditions of low pH and high redox. The copper alloy dagger blade (1938.844.2) from Gristhorpe has a substantial metal core with only superficial surface corrosion consistent with anoxic waterlogged and mid range pH.

What are absent, and presumably were originally present are fingernail, hair and, perhaps, woollen textiles all based on the protein keratin. These are regularly found in acidic, anoxic environments, their absence at Gristhorpe again reflects a set of depositional conditions, which, while favouring the preservation of wood and bone, were less forgiving to keratin-based materials. Curiously, the animal skin consisting of both hair (keratin) and the hide (collagen) has survived in a sufficiently recognisable state to be recovered by the original excavators. Current scholarship indicates that there is no evidence for deliberate tanning of hides in prehistory and those pre-Roman leather items that have been recovered survived as the result of secondary tanning due to the depositional environment – such as peat bogs and inside oak coffins (Groenman-van Waateringe *et al.* 1999). This cannot be ruled out in the Gristhorpe assemblage, although in this case the lack of human hair and nail is perplexing.

Documentation of the recovery, treatment and display history of the Gristhorpe Man assemblage

With the medical interest and involvement in the recovery of Gristhorpe Man (Melton and Beswick, this volume), it

Fig. 15.1 The display of Gristhorpe Man, dated 1938, detail of wider view shown in Fig. 15.9 (Photo credit and permission: Scarborough Museums Trust).

Fig. 15.2 The dismantling of the display in 1950 due to damp, with glazing removed (Photo credit and permission: Scarborough Museums Trust).

Fig. 15.3 The dismantling of the display in 1950 due to damp, revealing brick and plaster construction of the replica base (Photo credit and permission: Scarborough Museums Trust).

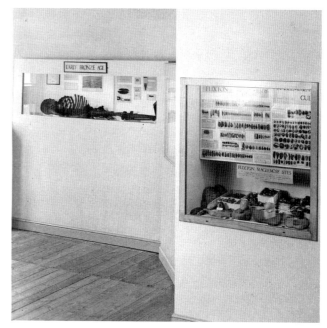

Fig. 15.4 The 1954 display (Photo credit and permission: Scarborough Museums Trust).

is hardly surprising that anatomical preparation methods were employed. In the third edition of his report, Williamson (1872, 7) reports that the bones were consolidated 'in a large laundry boiler filled with a thin solution of glue' for 8 hours after which they were air dried over several days and then 'articulated with little difficulty' which involved the wiring of the skeleton as an anatomical specimen. Notwithstanding Williamson's claims, no evidence for the

presence of glue has been found on the skeleton (Buckley, this volume; Montgomery and Gledhill, this volume). For the other finds it is extremely difficult to reconstruct the immediate post-excavation conservation treatment. From the scant records available, apart from the initial post-excavation work that presumably involved little more than cleaning and air-drying, there seems to have been little or no conservation intervention. The only formal

Fig. 15.5 The display post-1954 (Photo credit and permission: Scarborough Museums Trust).

conservation records surviving relate to fungal growths on small fragments of wood from the museum's store, treated in 1983.

The assemblage was accessioned in 1938 and, from an image of that date (Fig. 15.1), it appears that the small objects were displayed at either end of the skeleton in shallow cardboard trays in a manner similar to the practice used for geological specimens, a practice consistent with the origins of the collections housed in the Rotunda Museum. This approach would have enabled the objects to be readily accessible for scholarly study. This image appears to record the Gristhorpe display as it must have remained since its installation in the 19th century, within the ground-floor apsidal recess of the southwest wing of the building. The entire exhibit was glazed, with the lower portion containing the coffin lid and base being stepped forward to accommodate its greater width. The display was backed by vertically-oriented painted wood panelling. The wired skeleton is shown on a shelf above the coffin lid which in turn is held on a long supporting wooden bar with lateral brackets. Beneath this is the coffin base, mostly hidden behind a high skirting board but in photographs, taken during remedial work to the gallery, the base is revealed as largely being a replica in plastered brick, edged with a few surviving fragments of wood Figs. 15.2 and 15.3.

In a photograph dated to 1954 (Fig. 15.4) the finds have been re-displayed in a rather more minimalist environment. The skeleton of Gristhorpe Man is seen lain on a glass shelf. Some of the small finds are seen adhered onto grey card mounted on the wall of the display. These include the 'horn ring' (1938.851), animal bones (1938.850), the 'mistletoe berries' in a glass tube (1938.852), the flint blade (1938.845), the wood and bark container (1938.855), fragments of food remains (1938.858), the dagger with bronze blade and whalebone pommel mounted using a plastic hilt (1938.844). From this image it does not appear that the coffin lid and remains of the base are included in the display; it is possible that they could be viewed by looking down through the glass shelf, as if seeing down into the heart of the barrow.

The grey card used to mount the small finds persisted into later versions of this display, because the finds were stuck directly to it. At some point, however, the card was cut up to separate the finds from each other and each separate find on its section of card remounted on board of a different colour. One photograph of the display shows the remounted pieces on a large board placed in the replica lower coffin (Fig. 15.5). The finds were never removed from the card, merely restyled with different labels and masks and when the assemblage eventually travelled to Bradford, they were still stuck to card which was mounted on dark grey-brown display board (Fig. 15.6).

The first report of the display of the coffin itself was in

Fig. 15.6 The 'horn ring' stuck to earlier display card with later dark card mask (Photo: R. C. Janaway).

Fig. 15.7 The Rotunda Museum, Scarborough, in 2010. The southwest wing is to the left of picture (Photo: T. O'Connor).

the *Hull Packet* 22nd Aug 1834 and this account notes that the coffin was being displayed in a sarcophagus erected for its protection near the '*entrance into the museum*'. The wording suggests that this structure, described as having '*two folding-doors in front ... tastefully ornamented with bark of the larch; and the whole of the brick-work rusticated with the calcareous tufa*' was actually sited outside the museum itself at that time. Despite standing on a brick plinth the coffin base continued to decay until in the spring of 1853 the museum council decided to move it inside the museum (Snowden, this volume). A bespoke glass case

was constructed for its display and '*such measures taken for its preservation as .... may appear desirable*' (Minutes of Committee of Management 18th April 1853).

Between 1828 and 1829 the Rotunda Museum was purpose-built to house one of the foremost geological collections of the day (Snowden, this volume) (Fig. 15.7). The rotunda has two-storeys and is constructed in ashlar stone, with a rusticated ground floor on a moulded plinth. Gristhorpe man was initially displayed within the upper room in the rotunda (Snowden, this volume) but, after the addition of the new low wings in 1860, it was displayed in

Fig. 15.8 A photograph of Rotunda Museum taken in 1950 showing the flowerbeds adjacent to the apse that contained the display of the Gristhorpe finds (Photo credit and permission: Scarborough Museums Trust).

Fig. 15.9 A view of the Gristhorpe display in 1938 (Photo credit and permission: Scarborough Museums Trust).

the new gallery in the SW wing. These wings are each of three bays, with a cornice crowned with a stellate ornament and segmental bowed ends, [details from Listed Buildings Database 445581]. A 19th-century photograph (Fig. 15.8) shows municipal flowerbeds built up adjacent to the ground-floor level of the exterior of the south west wing of the building where today the ground level is still high as it rises to the road and buildings behind. Modern images, taken prior to the recent refurbishment, show the stone of the cornice is green, indicating problems with roof drainage, and staining of the exterior stonework apse may well have been caused by a combination of water penetrating from the roof and rising damp from the raised flowerbeds. It is in this apse that Gristhorpe Man is displayed with his coffin and grave goods shown in a photograph of 1938 (Fig. 15.9), and where it was still being displayed in 1950 (Figs. 15.2 and 15.3) when the extent of damp in the walls and rot in the panelling was clearly apparent.

During the Second World War some at least of the Gristhorpe display (namely the skeleton and presumably other portable items) were removed for safe-keeping and stored close to the museum at the 'report centre' at Valley Bridge, but later were moved to a heated cave near Huddersfield for the remainder of the war. The contemporary newspaper account of this move in the *Scarborough Evening News*, 2nd July 1943, suggested that this latter move was because '*the exhibit had begun to show signs of dampness*'. If the coffin base was already largely a replica in 1938, this at least must have remained *in situ* in the Rotunda Museum for the duration.

By 1950, the serious damp problems in the exhibit were manifest most notably in the warping of the painted wooden panelling visible in the photographs (Figs. 15.2 and 15.3) that record the dismantling of the exhibit. The display glazing, coupled with the water retention of the decorative features of the building and the high exterior soil levels, will have produced a microclimate perfect for the development of dry-rot. The photograph of the inset windowed display case in the 1954 re-display seems to indicate that this is no longer located in the apse (Fig. 15.4).

The only recorded conservation treatment was carried out during 1983 (February-August) when the wood fragments from the coffin were conserved by the staff of the Doncaster Museum and Arts Service Conservation Department (John Greenwood and Hazel Page). The wood was reported to have been affected by dry-rot and following initial advice it was frozen before being sent for conservation. The conservation records describe the wood as badly cracked, fragile and broken into numerous pieces. Some pieces had large deposits of white fungal mycelia and most pieces had spores identified as viable dry rot (*Serpula lacrymans*). The conservation treatment focused on reducing the water content of the timbers through freeze-drying, initially to below 20% RH (Relative Humidity) and physical removal of visible spores by brushing. Future storage at 50% RH was recommended. Although the treatment was an emergency response, current thinking would question the validity of using freeze-drying as a technique on timber that had already undergone air-drying with consequent cellular collapse, followed by re-wetting.

By the time that the Gristhorpe assemblage was packaged for transport to the University of Bradford in November 2005 the coffin lid was supported on a steel beam or joist below which the wired skeleton was displayed on a plate glass shelf suspended on metal chains from steel joists (Fig. 15.5). Beneath the skeleton was a fibreglass replica of the base of the coffin. Three large fragments of timber were displayed against the sides of the case, whilst the remainder of the fragments were in store. Small finds from the excavation, still adhering to card, were mounted on a board lying inside the replica base.

The contemporary context for the treatment of the Gristhorpe coffin

When excavated the coffin base and lid seem to have been equally well preserved, as were associated timbers (often referred to in the records as 'branches') that were lying on top of it. But, by 2005, the largest surviving piece of timber was the coffin lid (Fig. 15.5). Two of the 'branches' were on display, and possible remnants from the coffin base were in store. All this timber had been subjected to air-drying in the past and exhibited the expected shrinkage, warping and cross-grain cracking. The coffin lid, which consisted of a substantial section of oak, including heartwood, sapwood and bark, as might be expected, had exhibited most of the collapse in the sapwood, although there were significant radial cracks in the heartwood as well (Fig. 15.10). Comparing the original illustrations from the 1834 publication (Williamson, 1834) to the current condition of the lid, two corners (Figs. 15.10 and 15.11) have been sawn off (top and bottom to the right of the head motif). This appears to have been done to accommodate the coffin lid in the apsidal display. This is despite the lower part of the glazed display being stepped out to provide a greater depth (Fig. 15.1) The bark which had been left on in the original construction was largely intact, although many sections had become detached during the display life of the object and had been reattached using various adhesives (Fig. 15.12). The surviving bark of the coffin lid provided a highly textured surface in which dust, paint, plaster, building rubble, and cobwebs accumulated.

Currently, the surface of the coffin lid is very dark in colour and is covered in decades of surface dirt. It is entirely

Fig. 15.10 A large radial crack in coffin lid (centre) and sawn corner (to right), 2006 (Photo: R. C. Janaway).

Fig. 15.11 The coffin lid in 2006 showing sawn corner (Photo: R. C. Janaway).

possible that in addition to the dirt and natural oxidation that it had been coated at sometime in the past with a 'preservative' treatment. The light catalysed oxidation of wood has been well understood for a considerable time. This ultraviolet catalysed oxidation of lignin, and perhaps hemicellulose, causes timber to turn brown. Then, in time, the leaching out of soluble lignin products results in the greying evident in old exposed timbers (Stamm 1971).

It is clear that the coffin base had a much more chequered curation history than the lid. Due to its size and weight it had initially been displayed outside on the

ground supported on a brick plinth in the 'sarcophagus' outside the museum. It is not clear how much of the base survived to be brought inside the museum in the 1850s but by 1938 little remained except for fragments that adorned the top of the brick and plaster reconstruction (Fig. 15.1) and these were still in position in the 1950s (Fig. 15.3) when the full extent of the damp problem became apparent. This may be the root cause of the fungal problem that led to the 1985 conservation of these fragments held in store.

One might consider that the treatment of the timbers showed a callous disregard for what was clearly a major archaeological find of international significance. However, when set against the methodological context for water-logged wood conservation in Britain and Europe at that time, the treatment of the Gristhorpe timbers was at the forefront of contemporary developments.

Development of preservation treatments for waterlogged timbers

The extraction and display of the oak coffin from Gristhorpe in 1834 considerably pre-dates a number of the notable 19th and 20th-century discoveries of large pieces or large quantities of waterlogged wood. It is generally accepted that apart from chance finds, wetland archaeology, and hence the deliberate investigation of artefacts associated with timber structures, really begins in earnest in the mid 19th century. In 1854, prehistoric wooden piles were discovered in Lake Bienne, Switzerland (Coles 1984, 19). During the winter of 1853–4 low lake levels in Lake Zurich (Switzerland) revealed further wooden piles lining areas of the lake bed (Keller 1866). Interest in Lakeland waterlogged deposits continued throughout the 19th century with the publication in English of Ferdinand

Fig. 15.12 The top side of detached bark (top) and underside of same fragment showing old adhesive (below) (Photo: R. C. Janaway).

Keller's *The Lake Dwellings of Switzerland and other parts of Europe* (Keller 1866), followed by R. Munro's *Ancient Scottish Lake Dwellings or Crannogs* (Munro 1882). From 1888, Arthur Bulleid, inspired by the Swiss lake village studies, began to search for similar sites in the Somerset Levels, excavating a series of finds near Glastonbury between 1892 and 1907 (Bulleid and Gray 1911 and 1917). However, these investigations were generally concerned with the retention of far smaller timbers than those of the Gristhorpe coffin. Indeed, as late as the 1980s Morrison (1985, 96) states that '*it is not feasible to conserve and retain all the products of a crannog excavation*'. These early archaeologists simply did not have the resources or techniques to conserve large or complex waterlogged timbers and air-drying was normal procedure. Munro's report of an excavation from Lochlee (Ayrshire) in 1878 describes the excavation of a wooden trough carved out from a single piece of wood and recounts that '*upon drying it quickly crumbled to dust*' (Munro, 1882, 93). This was, though, fortunately recorded in a beautifully executed drawing. Later archaeologists would call this 'preservation by record'.

A combination of dredging and engineering works in waterlogged deposits through the 19th and early 20th centuries brought about the chance finds of a number of log boats, but, as Barker observed in his 1975 survey of the conservation of log boats: '*It is almost impossible to find any well documented information concerning attempts at the conservation of waterlogged wooden artefacts in Britain prior to the Second World War*' (Barker 1975, 61–64). The Giggleswick Tarn boat is typical of such chance finds. Recovered from the anoxic deposits of the silted up tarn near Settle in Craven, North Yorkshire, in 1863, this logboat consisted of a single ash log which had clearly been allowed to air dry after excavation. In 1941, it was bomb damaged and when eventually it was sent to the National Maritime Museum, Greenwich, London, for study in the mid 1970s, it arrived in fragments. During the reconstruction of the logboat it was observed that at some point since its discovery the surface had been painted with two or more coats of a brown creosote-like substance but analysis was not undertaken to confirm this (O'Connor 1979).

The British Museum has three early log boat finds. The first was recovered from between North and South Stoke in Sussex in 1834. The second, a dugout canoe from excavations of the Royal Albert Dock, Woolwich, was found in 1878. The third was found in 1900 in the River Lee at Walthamstow. Barker (1975, 61–64) could find no records for their conservation amongst the British Museum's archives and concluded that '*judging by their present condition, it seems likely that they were simply allowed to dry out naturally*'. The British museum archives, however, have preserved a letter of 1936 from W. Anderson, of Edinburgh, to Dr Plenderlieth recommending a three-step process for log

boat conservation. While Barker in his 1975 paper implies this conservation treatment is intended for one of the three existing boats, it is clear that this is a technique for dealing with wet timber where there was still a danger of warping upon drying. It seems more likely that this correspondence relates to the conservation of freshly excavated material in the care of the museum (Barker 1975). In summary, the procedure Barker (1975, 61–64) recounts is as follows:

> '*Firstly the boat was to be lined internally with a paper separating over which is placed a thick layer of Plaster of Paris which on setting will act to minimise distortion during the second stage; the air drying of the boat. This drying process was to be enhanced by the application of a layer of cotton wool wadding, impregnated with desiccated calcium chloride, to the exposed wood surfaces. This layer was in turn covered by 'some waterproof material'. When the impregnated cotton wool became wet it was to be removed and replaced; the process being repeated several times until the wood was considered to be dry. Finally, when the wood was dry, it was 'hardened' by the application of a surface consolidant such as poly-vinyl acetate or several applications of sodium silicate solution*'.

In 1938, 1940 and 1963 three boats were discovered from the Humber near North Ferriby. The conservation treatments of these finds are particularly interesting because they span the period when some re-conservation of the Gristhorpe coffin may have occurred. Boats number 1 and 2 were taken to the National Maritime Museum for treatment. The British Museum Research laboratory recommended gradual dehydration in baths of Glycerine followed by an alum-based treatment, although it is not entirely clear what the evidence base was for this approach. The Kenmere boat from Westmorland, was discovered during this period, in 1955, and was slowly air-dried over a 12-month period before consolidation with epoxy resin (Araldite) (Barker 1975). At least here we get some hint of experimental work being carried out before hand. These experiments, carried out by Dr Werner of the British Museum, were small-scale and involved the use of a mixture of methods including alum and ether/dammar resin. However, for the boat itself, a more conventional route was taken (Barker 1975).

In Scandinavia, especially in Denmark, treatments for the conservation of waterlogged wood got off to an early start. The National Museum in Copenhagen was established in 1807, by Royal Ordinance, as the Commission for the Preservation of Artefacts (Sease 1996). In 1816 Christian Jürgensen Thomsen was appointed to the post of secretary and was curator of this collection from then until his death in 1865. In 1831, he published *Om nordiske Oldsager og deres Opbevaring* (On Nordic artefacts and their preservation) (Thomsen 1831). Despite the early state funded start to this work, and familiarity with organic finds from peat sites, Thomsen states that:

'No small amount of the most peculiar artefacts have been found during peat-digging: they have usually been better preserved, with better and more distinct remains of wood and leather and even cloth. The earth may be either carefully removed with water, or they may be dried in the air, after which they can be taken up: whereas the objects should not be placed in the sun or in strong heat, since those parts are not of metal or stone are easily shrunk' (Brinch Madsen 1987).

Thomsen's approach to the conservation of timber was no more sophisticated than that carried out at Gristhorpe at about the same date with the same reliance on cleaning followed by air drying. At least by 1845, when Thomsen and others excavated the Hvidegard grave (Lyngby, north of Copenhagen), their conservation techniques had advanced. C. F. Herbst, one of Thomsen's assistants, did most of the subsequent conservation of the artefacts, initially storing the organic materials in either water or 'spirits' (Brinch Madsen 1987), a very early version of the modern first-aid practices of storing waterlogged finds immediately post-excavation. At excavations in 1859, Herbst started to experiment with the use of supersaturated alum solutions to displace the water in the wood. The technique relied on the alum solution crystallising in the wood cells and providing a solid support for the cells during drying and so reduce shrinkage. Herbst published his work in 1861 (Herbst 1861), and this method, with modifications, was used in the National Museum in Copenhagen up until the early 1950s, nearly 100 years later. In the early 20th century the alum method was pre-eminent, and even in 1956 was still recommended as a wood treatment in the first really comprehensive work on archaeological conservation published by Plenderlieth (1956), keeper of the Restoration Laboratory of the British Museum (1924–1959). But by then major changes were taking hold of the conservation of freshly excavated waterlogged wood as the Danish conservator Christen Christensen had started to experiment with the use of water soluble Polyethylene Glycol (PEG) as a baulking agent for waterlogged wood (Håfors 1989).

From 1959 there were a number of papers in *Studies in Conservation* on PEG treatments for wood, including papers by Anna Rosenquist (Rosenquist 1959a, 1959b) on the re-conservation of the Oseberg ship. In 1904, this Viking age ship, over 21 metres long and 5.1 metres wide, was excavated at Oseberg, Norway. It had rested on a bed of blue clay and was covered by a stone cairn topped with peat. The sealing by clay and peat enhanced the preservation of the oak timbers to the extent that it was possible to steam them back into their original shape using the standard steaming technology used in wooden boat building. At the time of their recovery the ship's timbers were dried and coated with creosote and linseed oil and, in 1957, they were re-coated with linseed oil and white spirit. Most of the smaller wooden items were conserved using the alum method, immersing the objects in the solutions at 100° C, and after drying impregnating them with linseed oil and lacquer. A number of carved fragments not treated at the time of excavation (due to limitations of the alum method) were stored between 1904 and 1954 in water and formalin. In the 1950s these were treated by a variety of methods, including the newly developed Polyethylene Glycol treatment as well as solvent drying using ethyl alcohol (Rosenquist 1959a; 1959b).

Despite the widespread use of the alum method it might seem surprising that this, or one of the treatments that followed, were not used to re-treat the Gristhorpe timber. These treatments, however, were for freshly excavated wood, and there would have been no advantage to subsequently applying them to already air-dried timber as the largely irreversible cell collapse and shrinkage had already occurred. So, in hindsight there really was no viable contemporary alternative to air-drying the Gristhorpe coffin; however, the decision to initially display it outside the museum was unfortunate but probably due to limited space inside at that time.

Conservation and analysis 2005

Personnel from the Rotunda Museum and the Bradford team packaged the Gristhorpe assemblage for transport at the Rotunda Museum on 17th November 2005. The entire assemblage comprised the crated coffin lid, a metal casket containing the wired skeleton of Gristhorpe Man and six further boxes containing the associated small finds and fragments of wood. To minimise damage to the wired skeleton, joints were carefully wrapped with acid-free tissue and immobilised / secured to minimise vibration (Fig. 15.13). The packaged assemblage was received at Bradford and unwrapped on 23rd November 2005. The conservation assessment was undertaken later that month to serve as part of the custody records and to serve as a primary costing/strategy document to inform both the remedial conservation measures and scanning electron microscopy that were required.

Throughout the initial stages of the project, conservation oversight was also provided to both investigative and sampling measures that were undertaken, including overseeing the safe packaging and transport of Gristhorpe Man to St Luke's Hospital, Bradford, to undergo CT-scanning. Conservation input also aided discussions for both the sampling of coffin wood for dendrochronology (14th August 2006) and the removal of a section of femur for isotopic analysis and radiocarbon dating. Involvement at these stages helped to balance the need for maximising potential information by selecting the optimum size, location and orientation of sampling needs, whilst informing the reconstructive measures that were required by way of dowelling and gap-filling.

All the surviving finds from the Gristhorpe barrow were examined to gauge their condition and conservation needs. This process started at the museum with a photographic record of the finds to capture the condition of the objects and any outward signs of continued deterioration whilst still on their display mounts or in their storage containers. Individually packed to immobilise and physically protect the objects, the skeleton, coffin and associated finds were then transferred to the University of Bradford, where the conservation assessment could proceed using the facilities of the Archaeological Sciences Conservation Laboratory.

The initial conservation assessment document provides a brief description of each item, detailing its physical condition, how it is mounted or housed, and making recommendations for its conservation. This information facilitated the selection of objects requiring conservation before inclusion in the new display.

To examine many of the objects further meant removing them from their display mounts. This was not particularly problematic for the fragments housed in glazed panels or glass phials but where the objects were stuck down directly to card, this procedure was not without risk to the object. With no record as to the adhesive used, it was decided that the least hazardous approach was to cut away the surface of the card with a scalpel so that the object could be removed with the adhesive still *in situ* (Fig. 15.14). The adhesive could then be sampled for testing to determine the best approach to its removal in each instance.

An essential pre-requisite to any conservation work is the correct identification of the materials to be treated and now that the de-mounted objects could be more easily examined in the round, microscopy confirmed the identification of the dagger pommel (1938.844.1)

Fig. 15.13 Gristhorpe Man immobilised using acid free tissue pads prior to transportation from Scarborough to Bradford (Photo: A. S. Wilson).

Fig. 15.14: The dagger pommel (1938.8441) with the remains of the card mount still attached by adhesive (Photo: Sonia O'Connor).

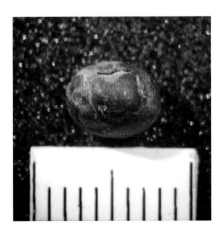 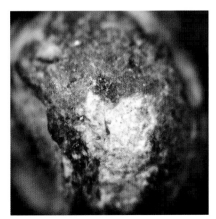 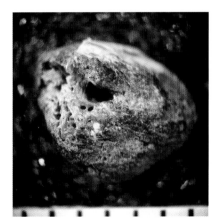

Fig. 15.15: Photomicrographs of the three 'mistletoe berries' (1938.852): a, micro photograph showing the lamellar structure of one urinary tract stone, b, detail of the granular surface of the second urinary tract stone and c, the sesamoid bone (Photo: Sonia O'Connor).

as cetacean bone (Sheridan *et al.*, this volume) but also revealed that two of the finds were not what they had seemed. Under magnification the horn ring (1938.851) did not have the characteristic structure of horn (cf. O'Connor 1987), nor did it show any surface evidence of working, such as cut or polish marks. Instead, the surfaces of the connected double hoop shape were smoothly sculptured with lacunae redolent of ossified cartilage, leading the conservator to suggest that this was not an artefact but a natural structure, perhaps a tracheal ring. This object was then passed to the osteological team who confirmed that it was indeed a tracheal ring (Knüsel *et al.*, this volume). All three of the 'mistletoe berries' (1938.852) were blackened, irregular, flattened-spherical objects, below 5mm in diameter, but none showed any evidence of plant features and under magnification there was no trace of the expected cellular structure. Two were dense and of a finely lamellar, granular material that was quite white where the surface had crumbled (Fig. 15.15 a and b). The third was not laminated but was perforated by rounded tunnels (Fig. 15.15 c). The conservator identified the two lamellar 'berries' as possibly being urinary tract stones and the third as a small sesamoid bone and passed both to the osteological team (Knüsel *et al.*, this volume; Edwards, this volume).

Conservation treatments

Many of the objects were extremely fragile but, with continued careful support and appropriately controlled environments, there was little doubt that they could survive as they were without further interventive conservation treatment. Of the small list of objects selected for conservation by the museum, the impetus for this work was mostly preparation for display. The treatments undertaken are detailed in the conservation records, copies of which have been deposited with the site archive at Scarborough Museum. Here, we give only a summary of this work and the findings this revealed. Throughout, the aim has been to achieve this with minimum impact on future studies of the material.

Cleaning

Even the objects not selected for conservation required some degree of cleaning to remove accumulated dust, except for those specimens, such as the 'berries', that were protected within closed glass containers. This was largely done using an array of paintbrushes and a vacuum cleaner adapted for the purpose. Brushes of different shape and softness of bristle were selected depending on the scale of the object and material from which it was made. This

approach proved very effective in cleaning the many-surfaced and complex shape of the mounted skeleton (1938.861). The vacuum cleaner had a variable suctions control and the diameter of the pipe was stepped down to an appropriate size. In the case of the coffin lid (1938.856) and the associated branches, a narrow rubber tube of about 1 cm diameter was connected to the end of the hose to reach into the deep fissures of the wood. A fine textile net was secured over the end of the hose, which allowed the dust to be removed but also trapped larger detritus so that it could be examined before being retained or discarded. This cleaning retrieved fallen fragments of wood, lumps of what might have been plaster or building rubble, cobwebs and dead spiders. Mechanical cleaning, using a scalpel, was required to remove old paint splashes and excess adhesives from old repairs to the brittle surface of the coffin lid.

The cleaning of the smaller and more friable objects was mostly performed under the microscope, the dust mobilised using the brushes then being drawn away on the air by bench-mounted dust extractors. It was during the cleaning of the animal hide fragments under the microscope that the remains of a dead woodworm beetle, *Anobium punctatum* (Fig. 15.16) was discovered amongst the remains of the hide (1938.853). This beetle would not have been feeding on the leather, and the coffin and other wood finds show no evidence of woodworm infestation of any period. From the colour and condition of the beetle this is probably modern contamination originating from before the remedial work on the museum in the 1950s. Microscopy also revealed, trapped in the crazed surface of this embrittled skin, hundreds of cotton wool fibres, each of which had to be removed using fine tweezers. Once a popular material for packing and cushioning fragile archaeological finds, this tendency for the fibres to catch on

Fig. 15.16 The deceased woodworm found on the remains of the skin cloak (1938.852) (Photo: Sonia O'Connor).

any roughened surface illustrates the intrinsic unsuitability of cotton wool for this purpose.

The removal of the adhesive used to attach the wood, bone, flint and metal small finds to their card mounts, involved a combination of softening the adhesive through the local application of the organic solvent acetone and mechanical removal using a fine wooden point or scalpel blade tip. The adhesive was entirely soluble in acetone but this controlled and localised approach avoided flooding the object with acetone, spreading the adhesive over the surface or driving it deeper into the structure of the porous materials.

Evidence of past treatments

The skeleton itself is in remarkably good condition, and here at least there are accounts of the blackened appearance on discovery and the subsequent simmering in glue and wiring in the manner of anatomical specimen preparation of the day (Scarborough Philosophical Society Minute Book for 1834 (K. Snowden, pers. comm.); Harland 1932). Of the treatment of the other finds, then and later,

rather less is known, as already discussed. Examination of the skeleton revealed a range of materials used in its re-articulation and subsequent running repairs, including leather washers and cork spacers between the vertebral bodies and sacro-iliac joint. Notably, cotton wool fibres and brush hairs were found amongst the detritus stuck to the surface of the underside of the cranium suggesting that, at some point, it had been coated with paint or lacquer (Montgomery and Gledhill, this volume).

The cleaning of the other finds revealed evidence of several unrecorded interventions, such as the adhesive joins in the dagger pommel and the collection of small animal bones (1938.850). It also revealed patches of iridescent particles on the skin surface of the animal hide that could be the remains of a solution applied to preserve the leather after discovery, perhaps as a baulking agent, fungicide or insecticide, or perhaps it relates to the minute flocculent deposit identified as adipocere that was observed over the interior of the coffin lid and floating in the water around the body, upon the opening of the coffin (Williamson 1834). Unfortunately, analysis of this material was beyond the scope of the project, but the demise of the woodworm

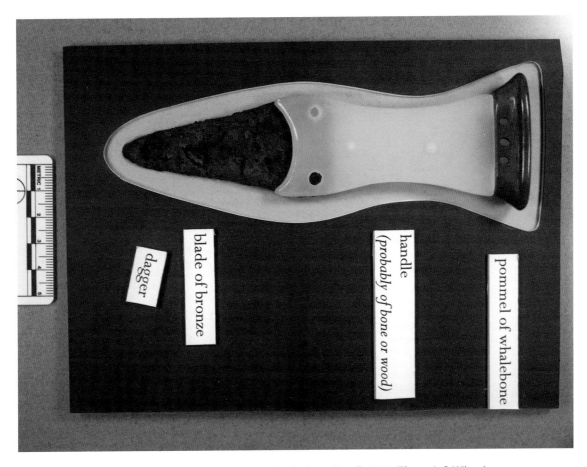

Fig. 15.17 Dagger mounted on card with plastic handle 2005 (Photo: A. S. Wilson).

amongst the hide fragments provides circumstantial evidence, at least, that the skin might have been treated with a biocide making it essential that protective gloves are worn if these fragments are handled in the future.

Another indication of previous treatments became apparent upon removal of the card and adhesive from the bone pommel. Where acetone has been used on absorbent swabs to remove the last traces of the adhesive from the bone the surface became dulled on drying. Microscopy revealed that the whole of the outside of the pommel had been coated with an acetone soluble resin to heighten the surface polish. That the interior of the pommel was not coated probably indicated that this was applied at the time when the dagger was reconstructed around the replica plastic hilt, first seen in the photograph of the re-display of the finds in the 1950s (Figs. 15.4, 15.17). At one time, lacquers were applied to bone objects almost unthinkingly, but today this is only done if consolidation of a friable surface is an unavoidable necessity and actions are taken to avoid this giving a sheen to the surface. Surface coatings can disguise or hide significant surface finishes and working marks important to fabrication and use-wear studies. With the refinement of collagen extraction techniques for radiocarbon dating these coatings pose less of a problem than in the past but could, potentially, interfere with future biomolecular analysis in this rapidly developing field.

Once removed from the replica plastic hilt, the cleaning and investigation of the dagger blade (1938.844.2) revealed further evidence of perhaps the original treatment of the blade. The appearance was that of a chemically or electro-chemically stripped object with only dark, powdery deposits in places over a finely pitted, tarnished metal surface.

The original drawings of the dagger indicate that there were remains of a possible scabbard (Williamson 1834). This would have been constructed from thin sheets of organic materials, such as wood, leather or horn, and have only survived because of the waterlogged, anoxic burial environment combined with the proximity of the corroding blade. In these conditions the copper in the blade alloy will have produced a biocidal solution, enhancing the preservation of this intrinsically ephemeral structure (Janaway and Scott 1989; English Heritage 2008). Organic materials preserved in this way are termed 'mineral preserved organic' remains; commonly abbreviated to MPO remains. Unless the organic materials are exceptionally well preserved, they can easily be dismissed as insignificant detritus and be removed in an attempt to reveal the detail of the underlying metal object. The importance and widespread occurrence of MPO remains have only become appreciated since incident light microscopy has been a standard tool of the conservator.

Microscopy combined with developments in mechanical cleaning techniques have also lead to a greater appreciation that much of the original surface detail of metal objects from archaeological deposits is preserved not at the surface of the surviving metal but within the encapsulating layers of the corrosion. By controlled and selective mechanical removal of these corrosion layers more information can be preserved *in situ*, and where MPO remains obscure underlying features this detail can still be retrieved through X-radiography of the object (Lang and Middleton 2005, English Heritage 2006). In the early 19th century there was little appreciation of these matters and the Gristhorpe dagger blade, like so many metal finds of that time and through much of the 20th century, were stripped of all their corrosion down to the surface of any surviving metal core.

Re-attachment of loose fragments

The skeleton required some attention including the re-alignment of the original wiring where this had become bent. The mandible was re-attached to the cranium using the original wiring holes and replacement wire painted to tone in with the original wiring. The broken and lose teeth and the resin replica of the tooth removed for isotope studies where all secured with Paraloid B72 adhesive. A fracture in the delicate ossified thyroid cartilage in the throat had been identified at Bradford and was secured with a small strip of non-woven polyester fabric and Paraloid B72 adhesive. Given the fragility of this bone, it was decided to leave this support *in situ* and to colour it with acrylic paint so that it toned in with the blackened colour of the bone (Fig. 15.18). The top of the shaft of the right tibia was also broken, but as the skeleton was to be displayed horizontally it was not required that this bone should be mended.

Most of the surviving objects required no reconstruction and those fragments that had been re-attached in the past seemed to be sound so removing and replacing the unknown adhesives with conservation approved products would have posed more risk to the objects than leaving them as they were. The intention with the animal hide had been to re-assemble the fragments once they were cleaned. In the event, it became apparent that the positions of the fragments in their original glazed mount had no real significance. There were no recognisable joins between fragments, and it appeared that they had been arranged purely to fill the space available. Some consolidation of crumbling surfaces was required, and this was done with a dilute solution of a conservation grade acrylic co-polymer (Paraloid B72). Elsewhere, deeply cracked fragments were re-enforced with patches of non-woven polyester fabric applied, to the flesh-side of the hide, with an adhesive of the same resin.

Fig. 15.18 Re-inforcement of the ossified thyroid cartilage of the skeleton: a, before and b, after painting to tone with the bone (Photo: Sonia O'Connor).

Despite its size, the wood of the coffin lid was very brittle and prone to damage. The top of the coffin, in particular, was deeply cracked longitudinally, and its uppermost surface, possibly including the remains of the bark, was coarsely reticulated and not well attached to the underlying wood. There was much evidence here of past re-adhesion of fragments and of recent loss. Numerous small fragments were collected from around and beneath the lid when it was removed from the museum and their positions recorded photographically in an attempt to tie-down their probable original locations on the lid. After cleaning the wood, however, it was apparent that whilst some of the fragments re-adhered in the past were in their correct positions, others had been placed to give a 'best fit' in the gaps between them. It was possible to find joins for some of the loose fragments, and these were re-adhered with Paraloid B72 adhesive, but others could not be re-located with any confidence. After discussions it was agreed to re-attach these pieces where possible to provide the best appearance for display and ensure their continued survival.

The re-attachment of the section cut from the broadest end of the coffin lid, which had been sawn off to provide surfaces for combined dendro-chronological and radiocarbon dating (see Batt, this volume), posed rather different problems. This block weighed several kilograms and needed to be fixed in a position in a way that allowed it to be easily removed if re-examination or further sampling was required in the future. This was achieved using three *circa* 5 mm threaded, stainless steel dowels, which were screwed a few centimetres into holes drilled in the cut end of the coffin lid. These dowels protruded a similar distance from this surface and located into slightly larger holes drilled in the surface of the block (Fig. 15.19). These

Fig. 15.19 The cut faces of the coffin lid showing the stainless steel dowels and corresponding dowel holes. The rectangular features in the right-hand face are where the samples for radiocarbon dating had been removed (Photo: Sonia O'Connor).

safely held the block in its correct position for display, but for transportation the block was removed and packed separately.

Chemical stability

Only one of the finds from the assemblage showed any hint of chemical deterioration since its excavation, and this was the dagger blade (Fig. 15.17). This had been held between the front and back portions of the plastic hilt. In the photograph of the new display from the 1950s the replica handle appears to be quite transparent, but by

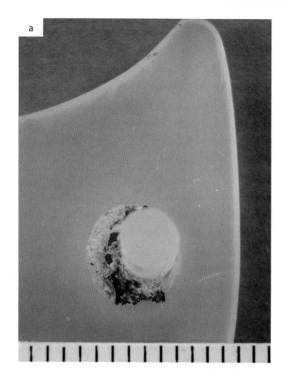

Fig. 15.20 Traces of corrosion on the dagger (1938.844): a, around the peg on the plastic replica handle and b, on the blade (1938.844.2) (Photo: Sonia O'Connor).

2005 it had become translucent white. The top end of the handle was fitted into the underside of the pommel. Two plastic pegs in the centre-line of the handle attached the front panel to the back. A third peg was located through an empty rivet hole in one corner of the blade, whilst a surviving copper alloy rivet in the other corner of the blade fitted into corresponding holes in the handle panels. When the handle was dismantled it revealed an apparent concentration of corrosion around the empty rivet hole and also around the plastic peg that had fitted into it (Fig. 15.20a and b). It is not clear whether this corrosion was related to the deterioration of the plastic or an adhesive used to attach the peg. In addition, there were small spots of light green, powdery corrosion towards the edge of the

blade that may have been caused by residual chemicals from the stripping process (Fig. 15.20b) but seemed no longer to be actively corroding.

Improved mounts and packaging for transportation

The objects that had been stuck to card were mostly quite robust and only needed to be cradled in recessed inserts of polythene foam (Plasterzoate) and repacked in stable plastic or acid-free boxes. The original mount for the remains of the animal hide had been backed with compressed fibreboard that was itself deteriorating and had possibly contributed to the poor condition of the hide through the production of acid vapours. As the decision was taken not to include these remains in the new display a series of stacking storage trays were fabricated from corrugated plastic board with lifting handles of unbleached cotton twill tape. Foam blocks under the corners of each tray maintained enough space to accommodate the far from flat hide fragments when the trays were stacked in their storage box.

The wooden base of the wood and bark container (1938.855), although far from flat, had also been stuck to a card mount (Fig. 15.21). The thin board was shrunken, warped and broken into two pieces that no longer fitted to each other. The original mount only acted to keep the two pieces together and did not really afford any physical support. After removal of the dust and spots of adhesive, a new support was made for the wooden base, shaped to fit its curves. Mounded sand in a deep box was covered in a layer of thin plastic film and the base fragments were placed face-down on to this surface. The positions of the pieces were adjusted until a 'best fit' was found, using the

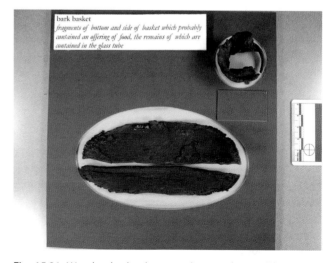

Fig. 15.21 Wooden basket base stuck to card 2005 (Photo: A. S. Wilson).

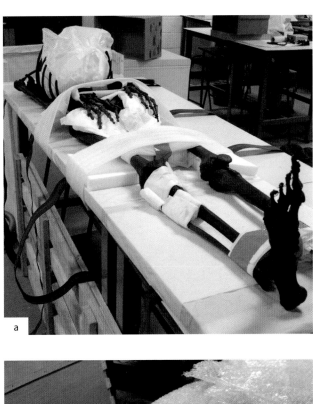
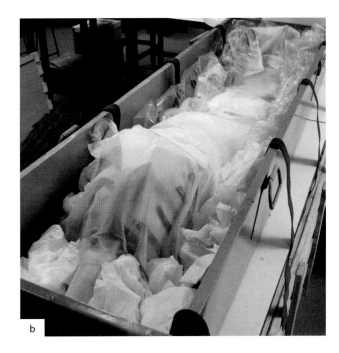

Fig. 15.22 Stages in the packing of the post-cranial skeleton (1938.861): a, immobilising the limbs and supporting the rib cage, b, bracing the skeleton within the metal coffin, c padding out the dome of the lid whilst avoiding pressure on the rib cage and d, transfer into an air-sprung vehicle for transportation to the museum (Photo: Sonia O'Connor).

sand as a support. A separating layer of the thin plastic film was laid over the base fragments, and the support was formed over this using Modrock™, a fine plaster bandage used for modelling. Each layer was formed from small, overlapping oblongs of the moistened bandage and, as this began to set, another layer was added with the oblongs lying in a different orientation, until 4 or 5 layers had been applied. Within minutes the Modrock™ had become stiff enough to allow it to be removed and, when fully set and dry, it provided a relatively thin but rigid support for the wooden base. The mount was trimmed to shape and the inner surface of it lined to prevent the plaster from

Polythene foam wedges to support deeply cracked areas

Polythene foam wrapped cable tie

Folded acid free tissue sheet

Modrock support with cling film seperating layer

Polythene foam blocks to prevent the branch making contact with base board

Plastic cable tie passing through the base board

Detail of the support construction

Fig. 15.23 Protection for the branches associated with the coffin (1938.856): a, two branches secured to their support board, and b, detail of the customised support structure (Photo: Sonia O'Connor).

marking the object. Polythene foam pads were adhered to the underside so that the mount did not rock when placed in its storage box.

The re-packaging of the skeleton, the coffin and its associated branches for transportation to the new gallery were more complex processes. The skeleton was physically protected by the padded supporting board on which it was always lifted and by the steel coffin in which it would be transported. However, it could still be damaged if it was free to move around within this space, so the first stage of the packing was to support the ribs, immobilise the limbs and inhibit movement between the supporting board and the skeleton in general. The thoracic cavity was lined with acid free tissue paper and filled with plastic airbags. Polythene foam blocks, wrapped in acid free tissue were then inserted between the lower limbs and folded sheets of tissue were taped around them to hold the bones against the blocks. Jiffy foam sheeting was then passed over these areas and stapled to the supporting board. The upper limbs were secured in the same way with the hands supported within the pelvis by crumpled balls of acid free tissue (Fig. 15.22a). The skeleton and its supporting board were then lifted into the steel coffin, covered in a layer of acid free

tissue, braced against the insides of the coffin with blocks and sheets of polythene foam and packed around with more air bags (Fig. 15.22b). Finally, the remaining space in the coffin was filled with bubble wrap and rolls of bubble wrap were laid on top (avoiding the thoracic area) to fill the space under the dome of the lid, which was screwed into position (Fig. 15.22c and d). This provided a light-weight but secure and robust packaging system that was successful in protecting the skeleton, despite the fact that it had to be manhandled up a spiral staircase to reach its final destination in the museum.

The packing of the coffin lid in its wooden crate followed a similar pattern. To protect the (in places) tenuously attached 'bark' layer, lengths of Jiffy foam, interleaved with acid free tissue paper, were stapled to the base of the coffin's crate either side of the lid. Plastic foam blocks and tightly rolled wads of bubble wrap were then inserted between the coffin lid and the sides of the crate before the lid was re-attached.

Perhaps the objects most difficult to pack were the branches associated with the coffin. When received these roughly hewn, brittle and deeply fissured timbers were wrapped in bubble-wrap with many fragments broken from the fin-like remains of the collapsed sapwood. After cleaning and re-attachment of the larger fragments, a support system was devised that minimised contact with the surface of the branches. This was achieved by suspending the branches above a rigid support board using individually tailored mounts.

First, the branches were examined to determine the most suitable positions for the mounts, i.e. areas that looked most robust and with the fewest projections on what would become the weight bearing surfaces. Two areas were selected on each branch and, using a plastic film separating layer, Modrock™ was applied to these surfaces to make a mould of the surface. These moulds were designed to spread the weight of the branches, protecting any projecting surfaces from further damage. Polythene foam blocks were then used to provide cushioned surfaces for the moulded supports and to lift the branches clear of the wooden support board. The surfaces of the branch above the mounts were protected with a pad of folded acid-free tissue and wedges of polythene foam were inserted betweens the fins of sapwood before plastic cable ties, sheathed in rolls of polythene foam, were passed over the top to secure the branches to the support blocks and the board (Fig. 15.23a and b). The branches were then covered with a semi-rigid tent of polythene foam sheet (Jiffy foam) that was tightly stapled to the edges of the board. This covering was held clear of the surface of the wood by the foam sheathing around the cable ties.

Finally, the contactors engaged to transport and install the Gristhorpe material in the new museum displays inspected and approved the packing arrangements and agreed procedures for safe-handling of the branches, coffin lid and skeleton with the conservation team before they were transferred to the contractors' care.

Conclusion

Given the limited understanding and techniques available at the time, post-excavation practice was resourceful and intelligently applied, particularly as conservation practice had not yet emerged as a rigorous scientific discipline. Reasoned scientific choices are particularly evident in the preservation of the body itself, which was a classic exercise in anatomical preparation. Without the anatomical wiring it is highly likely that the skeleton would not have survived as intact throughout its lengthy curation history. With no realistic alternatives the practice of air-drying a large prehistoric wooden coffin was pragmatic. The more vulnerable objects, such as the wood and bark container and the hide, provided more of challenge and, although surviving, are fragmentary and now difficult to interpret. In addition some material, although observed during the excavation, was not successfully recovered and curated, for instance vegetable fibres and 'a very singular ornament in the form of double rose of a ribband.... something resembling thin horn, but is more opaque and more elastic... but... which fell into small fragments on removal' (Williamson 1834,10).

The Gristhorpe assemblage was returned to Scarborough Rotunda Museum on the 13th of March 2008 to form the centrepiece of the newly refurbished archaeology galleries. Its conservation has allowed us to return to the primary evidence and to correct a number of errors, some of which reflected the attitudes and expectations of the day.

Acknowledgements
The authors wish to thank Stuart Fox for his technical support to the process of re-aligning the dendrochronological sample and the safe packaging of the branches and Terry O'Connor for the photograph in Figure15. 7.

References

Barker, H. (1975) Early work on the conservation of waterlogged wood in the UK. In W. A. Oddy (ed.) *Problems in the Conservation of Waterlogged Wood*, 61–63. Greenwich, National Maritime Museum.

Breuning-Madsen, H. and Holst, M. K. (1998) Recent studies on the formation of iron pans around the oaken log coffins of the Bronze Age burial mounds of Denmark. *Journal of Archaeological Science* 25, 1103–1110.

Breuning-Madsen, Holst, M. K. and Rasmussen, M. (2001) The chemical environment in a burial mound shortly after construction- an archaeological-pedological experiment. *Journal of Archaeological Science* 28, 691–697.

Brinch Madsen, H. (1987) Artefact conservation in Denmark at the begining of the last century. In J. Black (ed.) *Recent Advances in the Conservation and Analysis of Artefacts*, 343–345. London, Summer Schools Press, University of London Institute of Archaeology.

Bulleid, A. and Gray, S. G. (1911 and 1917) *The Glastonbury Lake Village*. Glastonbury, Glastonbury Antiquarian Society.

Coles, J. (1984) *The Archaeology of Wetlands*. Edinburgh, Edinburgh University Press.

English Heritage (2006) *Guidelines on the X-Radiography of Archaeological Metalwork*. London, English Heritage.

English Heritage (2008) *Investigative Conservation*. London, English Heritage.

Fourcroy, A. F. (1791) Deuxième mémoire sur les matières animales trouvées dans la Cimetière des Innocens à Paris, pendant les fouilles qu'on a faites en 1786 et 1787. Examen chimique de la matière grasse des cadavres contenus dans les fosses, *Annales de Chimie* 8, 17–73.

Fourcroy, A. F. (1793) Examen chimique du cerveau de plusieurs animaux. *Annales de Chimie* 16, 282–322.

Glob, P. V. (1974) *The Bog People*. London, Faber and Faber.

Groenman-van Waateringe, W., Kilian, M. and Van Londen, H.

(1999) The curing of hides and skins in European prehistory. *Antiquity* 73, 884–890.

Håfors, B. (1989) The Role of the Wasa in the Development of the Polyethylene Glycol Preservation Method. In R. M. Powell and R. J. Barbour (eds.) *Archaeological Wood: Properties, Chemistry and Preservation*, 195–216. ACS Advances in Chemistry Series No. 225. Washington, D. C., American Chemical Society.

Harland, N. (1932) Letter to F. Elgee dated 28th February 1932. Frank Elgee Archive, Yorkshire Archaeological Society, 23 Clarendon Road, Leeds LS2 9NZ, UK.

Herbst, C. F. (1861) Om bevaring af oldsager af trae fundne i torvemoster. *Antiquarisk Tidsskrift* 1858–1860, Copenhagen, 174–176.

Janaway, R. C. and Scott, B. G. (eds.) (1989) *Evidence Preserved in Corrosion Products: New Fields in Artifact Studies*. London, Institute for Conservation.

Janaway, R. C., Percival, S. L. and Wilson, A. S. (2009) Decomposition of human remains. In S. L. Percival (ed.) *Microbiology and aging*, 313–334. New York, Springer.

Keller, F. (1866) *The Lake Dwellings of Swizerland and other parts of Europe*. London, Longman.

Lang, J. and Middleton, A. (eds.) (2005) *Radiography of Cultural Material* (second revised edition). London, Elsevier.

Mansfield, S. M. (1800) Account of a Remarkable Case, in which a Considerable Part of a Woman's Body was Converted into Fatty Matter. *The Medical and Physical Journal*, 3, 10–11.

Morrison, I. (1985). *Landscape with Lake Dwellings: The Crannogs of Scotland*. Edinburgh, Edinburgh Unviversity Press.

Munro, R. (1882) *Ancient Scottish Lake Dwellings or Crannogs*. Edinburgh, David Douglas.

O'Connor, S. (1987) The identification of osseous and keratinaceous materials at York. In K. Starling and D. Watkinson (eds.) *Archaeological Bone, Antler and Ivory*, 9–21. London, United Kingdom Institute for Conservation. Occasional Papers 5.

O'Connor, S. A. (1979) The conservation of the Giggleswick Tarn Boat. *The Conservator* 3, 36–38.

O'Connor, S. A. (1996) Developing a conservation strategy in a rescue archaeology environment. In A. Roy and P. Smith (eds.) *Archaeological Conservation and its Consequences: Preprints of the Contributions to the IIC Copenhagen Congress 26-30 August 1996*, 133–136. London, Institute for Conservation.

Plenderleith, H. J. (1956) *The Conservation of Antiqities and Works of Art*. London, Oxford University Press.

Rosenqvist, A. M. (1959a) The stabilizing of wood found in the Viking ship of Oseberg. Part I. *Studies in Conservation* 4 (1), 13–22.

Rosenquist, A. M. (1959b) The stabilizing of wood found in the Viking ship of Oseberg. Part II. *Studies in Conservation* 4(1), 62–72.

Ruttan, R. G. and Marshall, M. J. (1917) The composition of adipocere. *Journal of Biological Chemistry* 39, 319–327.

Sease, C. (1996) A short history of archaeological conservation. In A. Roy and P. Smith (eds.) *Archaeological Conservation and its Consequences: Preprints of the Contributions to the Copenhagen Congress, 26-30 August 1996*, 157–161. London, Institute for Conservation of Historic and Artistic Works.

Stamm, A. J. (1971) Wood deterioration and its prevention. In G. Thomson (ed.) *Conservation of Wooden Objects: Preprints of the Contributions to the New York Conference on Conservation of Stone and Wooden Objects 7-13 June 1971*. London, International Institute for Conservation 2, 1–9.

Thomsen, C. J. (1831) *Om nordiske Oldsager og deres Opbevaring (On Nordic artefacts and their preservation)*. Copenhagen, Det Kongelige Nordiske Oldskriftelskab.

Williamson, W. (1834) *Description of the Tumulus, lately opened at Gristhorpe, near Scarborough*. Scarborough, C. R. Todd.

Williamson, W. (1872) *Description of the Tumulus opened at Gristhorpe, near Scarborough*. Scarborough, S.W. Theakston.

Conclusions

THE GRISTHORPE MAN PROJECT 2005–2008

Nigel D. Melton, Janet Montgomery and Christopher J. Knüsel

The Contribution of the Present Project

The Gristhorpe Man burial occupies a significant and unique place in British archaeology. It remains the best-preserved of the growing body of Early Bronze Age tree-trunk burials in Britain (Parker Pearson *et al.*, this volume), and the exceptional range of organic material preserved within the waterlogged coffin offers an unparalleled insight into aspects of high-status society and burial ritual at the end of the 3rd millennium BC. The majority of these items have survived to this day but others, such as the '*double rose of a ribband*' seen on the chest of the skeleton when the coffin was first opened, and the layer of vegetation on which the body had been placed, which was considered at the time to be composed of rushes and to contain mistletoe (Williamson 1834, 10), sadly have not. They exist only as vivid and intriguing contemporary descriptions in Williamson's report. Of the objects that have survived in variable states of preservation, it is not possible to gauge precisely how much they have deteriorated since recovery or what treatments may have been applied since 1834 to mitigate the changes caused by drying and microbial activity (Janaway *et al.*, this volume).

Gristhorpe Man's retrieval marked an extremely early example of an excavation by individuals who were able to identify and deal competently with human remains. In part, this was due to the serendipitous timing of the excavation. In the 1760s a similar log coffin burial unearthed during road construction works at Stoborough in Dorset was ripped apart in a search for treasure and has not survived (Ashbee 1960, 86–88), and in the decades following the Gristhorpe discovery, barrow digging became a popular antiquarian pursuit. Vast numbers of barrows were opened, the excavations often being conducted by local diggers hired by distantly located antiquarians (Marsden 1999). Such diggers were effectively paid for the grave goods and skulls they retrieved in order to enhance the private collections of the antiquarians. Standards of recovery and recording, and speed of publication (if this took place at all) were, generally, inferior to those seen at Gristhorpe in 1834. This failure to record is illustrated by the example of William Beswick himself, who never published his 1824 excavations of the two outlying barrows at Gristhorpe, with the result that Canon William Greenwell was unaware of Beswick's earlier work when he investigated the northern barrow in 1887. It is unlikely that many of the organic grave goods that were preserved within the Gristhorpe coffin, and which have provided such a rich resource for modern analytical methods, would ever have been available for study had the excavation been undertaken under these circumstances.

The existence of the Scarborough Philosophical Society, and the opening of its remarkable museum a few years prior to the Gristhorpe barrow excavation (K. Snowden, this volume), are further key elements that contributed to the quality of the recording, recovery, and preservation of the log coffin and its contents. The presence of prominent members of the Society at the opening of the coffin and the retrieval of its contents on the cliff-top at Gristhorpe on 11th July 1834 may be seen as pivotal to the subsequent prompt donation of the finds to the Society's museum (Melton and Beswick, this volume). The account published in the *York Herald* on 19th July 1834 records that William Travis, a surgeon, and Peter Murray, a physician, were both present at the opening of the coffin and removal of its contents. Similarly, William Harland, a physician, and Thomas Weddell, a surgeon, undertook the preparation and articulation of the skeleton. This, and their involvement in the subsequent curation of the skeleton, coffin and grave goods, has ensured that this important discovery has remained available for study using scientific techniques that even these learned medics and polymaths could not have dreamed of in 1834. The coffin lid is one of the earliest survivals of a large timber object and, although its treatment at the time might seem crude compared to today's array of conservation procedures, it was in fact extremely advanced for its day (Janaway *et al.*, this volume). The treatment of the skeleton itself can also not be criticized, given that it would then have been impossible to predict the array of analytical interrogations to which it would later be subjected. On the contrary, it has contributed, or at least has not been detrimental to, the survival of the bone tissue in relatively good condition and with virtually all the skeletal elements still extant (Knüsel *et al.*, this volume). The importance of the Society in ensuring that local antiquarian endeavours were of the highest possible standard is further demonstrated by the publication in 1836 by William Travis of a pamphlet on the excavation of a cist grave near Scarborough (Rowley-Conwy, this volume).

As Karen Snowden (this volume) has concluded, the range of modern analytical methods that have formed the core of the current project are likely to have met with the approval of those learned members of the Society who were involved in 1834. The find was probably the first British case in which such scientific techniques were employed. The reported novel method of conservation of the skeleton was suggested by Dr Harland (Williamson 1896, 45), the chemical analysis of the water in the coffin was undertaken by physician Dr Peter Murray, and the identification of adipocere and its interpretation as demonstrating that a fleshed corpse had been interred (Williamson 1834, 17fn.) all marked a significant moment in British archaeology.

Furthermore, the publication of the excavation was prompt and, although lacking a plan and sections, was advanced for its time in that details of the layers excavated were provided, as were details of the position of the skeleton. Although the location of the grave goods within the coffin was not so well recorded, their interpretation by the youthful William Williamson as an assemblage (Rowley-Conwy, this volume) was progressive and, once again, ahead of its time. The three editions of Williamson's report on the findings and, in particular, his revisiting of the project for the third (1872) edition after an interval of nearly four decades provide a fascinating insight into the development of archaeology and archaeological thought in the middle decades of the 19th century. The Gristhorpe

find played a central role in these changes, not least in the introduction of C. J. Thomsen's 'Three Age System' into British archaeology (Rowley-Conwy, this volume).

Investigations on the barrow site

The description of William Beswick's excavation of the log coffin burial in 1834 (Williamson 1834), whilst clearly innovative, left many questions unanswered, including the extent of Beswick's excavations on the site the previous year. The lack of a plan or section precluded aspects of interpretation: for example, many barrows exhibit a number of phases of construction and use, but whether or not this was the case in the 'Gristhorpe Man' barrow remained unresolved. This latter point was particularly pertinent, given the anomalous dating evidence from the oak 'branches' that were found lying on top of the coffin (Batt, this volume) and the evidence from the northern barrow in the group of three on the cliff-top at Gristhorpe. That barrow, excavated by Beswick in the 1820s, was re-examined by Canon William Greenwell in 1887 (Greenwell 1890), and a secondary interment consisting of a small cist containing cremated remains that had been missed by Beswick was located. Furthermore, the site of the central barrow which contained the log coffin burial lay within an area where there had been extensive landscaping in the 1950s and, although there was promising visual evidence that the barrow had escaped destruction (Melton and Russ, this volume), the extent of the preservation or destruction of the archaeological stratigraphy in the nearly two centuries since the original excavation was not known.

The non-invasive geophysical surveys and small evaluation trench excavated in 2007 answered many of these questions. The geophysics, resistivity, magnetometry and ground-probing radar surveys confirmed that there were *in situ* archaeological remains and hinted at something unusual, identifying an inner circular feature with an outer, slightly offset, circle of discrete, fairly regularly spaced, anomalies, suggesting at least two phases of barrow construction (Schmidt *el al.*, this volume).

The evaluation trench (Melton and Russ, this volume) identified these anomalies and confirmed that, given the extensive landscaping of the surrounding area, the archaeological preservation of the barrow is remarkably good. A later, kerbed, phase of barrow construction was uncovered, and a cut for either Beswick's 1833 or 1834 excavations located. Although the evidence for any activity that would explain the discrepancy between the coffin and its contents and the 'branches' that lay on top of it (Batt, this volume) had been obliterated in 1834, it may be that the construction sequence of the barrow provides a possible explanation. Another point of interest lay in the outer ring of discrete anomalies on the magnetometer survey. These were identified as relating to different types of stone being used in the kerb of the later phase of barrow construction, perhaps selected on the basis of their colour (Melton and Russ, this volume). Their regular spacing raised the question of their deliberate placement (Schmidt *et al.*, this volume).

The skeleton

Gristhorpe Man is now one of the earliest individuals in Britain to have undergone a complete bioarchaeological treatment encompassing osteological, palaeopathological and isotopic analysis, along with AMS radiocarbon dating of his remains, of the coffin and of the associated 'branches' (axe-trimmed logs). Estimates of his age, stature and body mass were made, revealing him to have reached a considerable age and to have been relatively tall for the period and robust. An anatomically-based facial reconstruction has suggested how he would have looked. Palaeopathological analysis was augmented by ct-scanning and the use of *Mimics* software to reconstruct the appearance of an intra-cranial pathological condition. Isotope analyses to investigate his place of origin were all consistent (but not uniquely so) with Gristhorpe Man being born and bred in the Scarborough region. They provided fascinating evidence for lifelong access to an animal protein-rich diet that enabled him to reach optimal stature and corroborated the relatively low level of tooth wear for his age at death, as well as the presence of renal stones, a likely consequence of his protein-rich diet. In addition, AMS radiocarbon and dendrochronological dating of his body and of the coffin and associated axe-trimmed logs (described in Williamson's original reports as 'branches') have provided valuable new dates for the practice of burial in a tree-trunk coffin, and helped to refine the Bronze Age chronology in the region.

Analyses of the items found in the coffin provide an insight into the materials used in their manufacture, their origins and use. Proteomics and SEM analyses of the hide in which the body had been wrapped have confirmed that it was bovine in origin (Buckley, this volume; Sheridan *et al.*, this volume), in contrast to the 19th-century identification of it being most likely that of a sheep or goat. The identification of the Gristhorpe animal skin as bovine is paralleled in number of other British Early Bronze Age graves (Sheridan *et al.*, this volume), as well as in some of the later Bronze Age Danish log coffin burials, such as that containing the 'Egtved girl' (Hvass 2000). The identification of the species of animal skin, together with evidence for predominantly terrestrial animal protein in the diet of 'Gristhorpe Man' (Montgomery and Gledhill, this volume),

in conjunction with the predisposition of this type of diet to lead to the development of renal stones, suggest that cattle husbandry and the consumption of beef and dairy products had an important role in defining the elite of Early Bronze Age society.

Similarly, analysis of apparent Victorian conservation practices helps to evaluate the written record of the treatment of the human remains and, in combination with the dating programme, establishes the authenticity of the remains, while clarifying the events surrounding their curation. It is curious that anatomical parts (tracheal rings and abdominal stones) were apparently mis-identified as grave inclusions. The revised identifications substantiate the age-at-death estimate and shed light on his health status and diet. The identification of brain tissue (Montgomery and Gledhill, this volume) is remarkable for this period and predates the next earliest identified British example by more than two millennia (O'Connor *et al.* 2011). The preservation of the brain points to rapid burial and the effects of the waterlogged burial environment. If this was the case, then the time taken for coffin preparation, site selection and excavation of the grave must have been brief, requiring a high degree of social cohesion and pre-planning of the funerary rites.

The integration of conservation in all aspects of the current study (Janaway *et al.*, this volume) has produced many benefits. It informed the safe handling and packaging of the assemblage in its journeys to and from Bradford, it greatly improved the appearance of the material for the new display, and it helped to ensure that Gristhorpe Man, his coffin and grave goods would survive in good order for further study in the future. But perhaps most importantly, the project benefited from the investigative aspects of the conservation work, which helped uncover mis-identified objects and materials, and helped in the piecing together of the taphonomic history of the assemblage and the individual object biographies (Janaway *et al.*, this volume; Sheridan *et al.*, this volume).

The date of the burial

Dating the burial is an endeavour that perhaps most clearly illustrates the advances made in archaeological investigations since the time of the discovery. In 1834, Williamson was only able to conjecture that the coffin was interred some time '*before the Roman Invasion*' (1834, 11). Subsequent advances during the mid-19th century, in which the find played a key role (Rowley-Conwy, this volume), enabled Williamson to assign it chronologically to the Bronze Age in 1872. The arrival of radiocarbon dating in the mid-20th century provided for the first time an absolute date, albeit to a wide range of 2280–1680 cal

BC (for one of the overlying 'branches'), and the modern AMS dates now permit the death of 'Gristhorpe Man' to be much more closely assigned. The body has now been dated to 2280–2030 cal BC and to 2150–1950 cal BC (Batt, this volume). This, together with the wiggle-matching technique that has refined the date of the felling of the tree used to manufacture the coffin to 2110–2030 cal BC (ibid.), establish the Gristhorpe burial as the most closely-dated British Early Bronze Age log coffin burial. It is hoped this date will be further refined when a local dendrochronological master sequence becomes available.

The dates obtained from the skeleton and the coffin lid also shed important new light on the artefacts found inside the coffin, and in particular the dagger, with its slightly unusual blade (Sheridan et al., this volume; Northover, this volume). The increased dating precision has also raised the intriguing question of whether the burial was re-visited some centuries later or remained open in some way. One of the axe-trimmed logs in the museum display (presumed to be Williamson's 'oak branches' that were found covering the coffin) was dated to 1750–1540 cal BC, a minimum of 270 years later than the felling of the tree from which the coffin was made (Batt, this volume). If this is not simply due to random error, then it suggests that the 'branches' were deposited some considerable time after the coffin. On the one hand, the evidence of additional phases of barrow construction (Schmidt et al., this volume; Melton and Russ, this volume), which went undetected in the original excavation, provides physical evidence of later site use. If, as suggested by Schmidt et al. (this volume), William Beswick's initial attempt on the barrow in 1833 failed because he located his investigation on the summit of the barrow, which was an artefact of a later phase of construction, then it is surprising that he did not discover an interment associated with this later phase. On the other hand, it must be borne in mind that the logs lay directly on top of the coffin and were sealed within the grave cut by a layer of clay that Williamson (1834, 10) described as 'Puddle, or Blue Clay' and which he considered was not from the immediate neighbourhood. This layer of clay could, therefore, be interpreted as a deliberate sealing of both the coffin and overlying logs, but it has been suggested (Janaway et al., this volume) that whilst this is the most likely explanation, this layer could be the result of the natural accumulation of fine clay particles percolating through the overlying layer of stones, and that the blue colour of the clay was the result of anaerobic conditions within the mound rather than an exotic origin. Interpretation of the origin of this 0.3 m thick layer is crucial to the understanding of the preservation of the coffin and oak 'branches', and to whether it represents a form of ritual sealing. A small, but significant, typological difference in the description of the clay layer in the 1834

and 1872 editions of Williamson's report creates further uncertainty. In the former it is described as 'Puddle, or Blue Clay', suggesting that its texture was similar to that of puddled (i.e. refined) clay, but in 1872 this text becomes 'Puddle of blue clay'. The sequence of layers within the barrow provided by Williamson may help to clarify the issue; the clay lies below a 0.3 m thick layer of 'Loose Stones' and directly above the 'Oak branches' that appeared to have been 'carelessly thrown over the coffin' (Williamson 1834, 11; 1872, 16). For the 0.3m of clay to accumulate naturally over the centuries, there would have to have been a significant void, which is possible if the axe-trimmed logs (Williamson's 'branches') represented a mortuary structure that had subsequently collapsed. However, this would have also required that the loose stones above such a void, whilst allowing the free percolation of fine particles through them, did not themselves collapse into it and, whilst some are described as 'having sunk into it [the clay]' (Williamson 1834, 11), this does not seem to have occurred. Furthermore, the 'carelessly thrown' description of the branches suggests that there could well have been voids between them into which the clay, for some reason, did not continue to permeate. On balance, therefore, the evidence suggests that, as Williamson in 1834 and Janaway et al. (this volume) have suggested, the clay most likely represents an anthropogenically-placed, deliberate sealing of the coffin. The clay-sealed log coffins that have been found elsewhere in Yorkshire, including examples where it was thought that the clay had been brought in from elsewhere (Parker Pearson et al., this volume), may point to the existence of a local rite relating to these high-status burials.

Williamson's account states that one of the 'branches' or axe-trimmed logs was 'placed perpendicularly at the foot of the coffin, apparently to steady it' (1834, 5). It appears from this description that the logs and coffin co-existed at some period. The circa three centuries difference in the radiocarbon dates between these logs and the coffin (Batt, this volume) is therefore, difficult to explain, especially considering Williamson's (1834, 5) description of the appearance of the coffin bark when first recovered as in a state of 'good preservation', still retaining a coating of 'a species of lichen' (ibid., 15). Furthermore, the remarkable preservation of the organic remains within the coffin suggests both its rapid water-logging and the likelihood that it was not re-opened in antiquity. As oak is most easily worked when 'green', it seems unlikely that the coffin had been fashioned from a log that had been curated since it was felled some three centuries or so earlier. This is backed up by the radiocarbon dates obtained from the skeleton and by the 19th-century observation of adipocere within the coffin and its interpretation as demonstrating that a fleshed body, rather than curated remains, had been interred. Only further radiocarbon dating of the 'branches' can show whether the recently-obtained date (and indeed the earlier date obtained in the 1980s with a far larger standard deviation) had been faulty.

The coffin and its contents

The coffin

Although raised intact, the initial display of the coffin in a specially constructed stone shelter outside the entrance of the museum, during which time the condition of the base began to deteriorate, and subsequently within the museum where decay continued (Janaway *et al.*, this volume), has meant that only the lid and fragments of the base have survived. The survival of the coffin lid is fortunate, as this permitted both dendrochronlogical and 'wiggle-match' radiocarbon dates to be undertaken, as well as a re-appraisal of both the manufacture of the coffin, and of its unique feature: the '*rude figure of a human face*' (Williamson 1834, 5–6) carved on the 'foot end' of the coffin lid. The original identification of this feature as anthropomorphic was fairly quickly replaced by the suggestion that it was a functional feature (Jewitt 1870, 48). Sheridan *et al.* (this volume) suggest that the original interpretation is not implausible, and that the carving formed part of a complex funerary process revealed in unprecedented detail by the survival of the organic grave goods in the waterlogged coffin; the closest parallels are to be seen in another of the North Yorkshire group of log coffin burials, excavated at Loose Howe (Elgee and Elgee, 1949), near Danby, some 45 km to the north of Gristhorpe.

The contents of the coffin

A significant outcome from the project has been the incorporation of its findings into the new exhibit of the Gristhorpe finds in the Rotunda Museum in Scarborough. Items are now displayed with their descriptions from the original 1834 report alongside the new information in order to demonstrate how advances in scientific analytical techniques have contributed to the modern archaeological interpretations.

The animal hide

The animal hide in which the body had been wrapped was described by Williamson (1834, 8) as having '*hair which is soft and fine, much resembling that of a sheep, or perhaps still nearer that of a goat, but not quite so long*'. The skin had suffered badly from both the retrieval of the human remains that it enveloped and from its subsequent drying out (Janaway *et al.*, this volume) and survived only as a few small scraps of skin and samples of hair. Proteomic analysis (Buckley, this volume) and scanning electron microscopy (Sheridan *et al.*, this volume) have confirmed that 19th-century identification was incorrect and that the hide is bovine in origin. It has also been suggested that, by analogy with other Early Bronze Age graves in Britain, the body had probably been buried fully dressed, but whereas there had been preservation of the animal skin due to natural tanning, conditions within the coffin had not been conducive to the survival of either woollen or linen cloth (Sheridan *et al.*, this volume).

The bone pin

The only item for which the precise location within the coffin was noted was the bone pin which was '*laid on the breast of the Skeleton, having been used to secure the skin in which the body had been wrapped*'. This pin, thought in 1834 to be bone or horn (Williamson 1834, 9), has now been identified as having been manufactured from the fibula of a domestic pig, and displays possible signs of wear prior to its final use to fasten the animal skin (Sheridan *et al.*, this volume).

The dagger blade and pommel

The dagger blade was incorrectly identified by Williamson (1834, 8) as '*the head of a spear or javelin, formed either of brass or some other composition of copper*', although, intriguingly, a poem entitled 'Lines addressed to the skeleton in the Scarbro' Museum' that appeared in the local paper shortly after the discovery, and which was written on 'Gristhorpe Cliff' by 'WB' – almost certainly William Beswick – refers to the coffin's occupant's '*brazen dagger*'. This raises the question of whether Beswick, who was present when the coffin was first opened, had seen and made a mental note of its position (Melton and Beswick, this volume). Whether this was the case or not, Williamson was quick to revise his opinion, as when the second edition of his report appeared (Williamson 1836) he had changed the description of it to a '*spear or dagger*' (*ibid.*, 8).

By 1872 Williamson had realised that the blade was that of a '*Dagger or Knife, formed of bronze*', and was able to cite parallels from elsewhere in Britain. With regard to the pommel, he was able to state that there was '*no doubt that this*' had been associated with the blade, quoting information received from Canon William Greenwell about a similar example (Williamson 1872, 13–14). Nowhere in any of the three editions of his report does Williamson comment on the evidence of a sheath or scabbard being present, although his illustration of the blade appears to show this. Examination of the blade during conservation suggested that it had been chemically or electro-chemically stripped at some time (Janaway *et al.*, this volume), presumably for display purposes, although scanning electron microscopy of the blade has revealed that traces of animal collagen that may belong to a sheath or scabbard are still present (Sheridan *et al.*, this volume).

In the 20th century, the dagger was classified as a *Type Methyr Mawr, Variant Parwich* (Gerloff 1975, 51). Northover (this volume) concludes that the blade was made from an unleaded tin bronze with 12% tin, that had been thoroughly worked and annealed, and that the copper had originated in Ireland, although the metal had probably undergone several phases of recycling. Lead isotope analysis (Montgomery and Gledhill, this volume) has also suggested that a variety of ore sources are constituents of the artefact.

The pommel was also incorrectly identified initially, with Williamson (1834, 9) describing it as '*the ornamental handle of a Javelin, of which the metal Head... formed the opposite extremity*', and bemoaning that notice had not been taken of the relative positions of the two items. He described the pommel as being manufactured from '*either horn, or the bone of some of the larger cetaceous tribe of Fishes*' (*ibid.*). The latter suggestion has now been confirmed; the pommel had been fashioned from a whale jaw-bone. A detailed examination of the object has elucidated many details of its manufacture (Sheridan *et al.*, this volume).

The flints
The three flints found within the coffin were described by Williamson (1834, 8–9) as '*a beautifully formed flint... head of a small javelin*' and two '*rude heads of arrows*'. In 1872, he revised his description to a '*well-formed implement of flint, of a common type ... probably used as knives, or occasionally as scrapers for cleaning skins*' (Williamson 1872, 14). The other two pieces were described as flint flakes. The latter descriptions remain valid (Sheridan *et al.*, this volume), but additional study now reveals the knife blade to have been hafted and residue analysis has identified traces of the tree resin used for this purpose. Two phases of re-sharpening after hafting have been recognised, and microwear analysis has revealed that it had been used to cut and scrape hide and/or meat.

The wooden object
Described by a perplexed Williamson (1834, 9) as '*a Pin, or something allied to it*', and later as '*a curious object made of wood, like a miniature spatula with a round handle*' (Williamson 1872, 14), the function of this object remains elusive due to a lack of known parallels. It has been suggested that it is most likely to be a fastener, for either a pouch or, possibly, for a lid to the bark and wood container – although no lid is mentioned as being present when the latter was first seen in 1834.

The bark and wood container
In 1834, Williamson (p. 9) described this as '*a kind of dish, or shallow basket of wicker work: ... of round form, and about six inches in diameter*' that had been placed '*by the side of the bones*'. In the third edition of his report (Williamson 1872, 15) the description of this vessel had changed. There was no mention of wicker work, it was now '*a kind of dish composed of pieces of bark, stitched together with strips of skin or animal sinew... the bottom was composed of a single flat piece of bark, round the edges of which the stitches used for holding the whole together can still be traced*'. It was also described as containing some decomposed material and, Williamson suggested, probably corresponded to the more frequently encountered ceramic 'Food Vessels'.

Unfortunately, this unique vessel has only survived in fragmentary form. The base, which is now split and distorted, a consequence of its drying out, is made of wood rather than bark, as a number of distorted fragments from the bark wall of the vessel. Nevertheless, modern scientific analysis provides an insight into the use of the vessel. Investigations into the '*food residue*' from the interior of the vessel suggest that this most likely represents a lining to waterproof it (Sheridan *et al.*, this volume), and the most recent investigation, using proteomics analysis, identifies the presence of bovine casein (Buckley *et al.*, 2013) on a sample of the stitching 'sinew'.

The animal bones
These were initially described by Williamson (1834, 14) as '*a few phalanges, about the size of a small dog*', but were soon afterwards identified by Professor William Buckland as those of a weasel (Williamson 1836, 14). The bones have been re-examined and have been identified as representing two species: fox (a single metatarsal) and pine marten (four complete phalanges and one incomplete phalanx). Their presence in the coffin '*amongst the decomposed skin, as though the foot of some animal had been buried with the body*' (Williamson 1834, 14) is now considered likely to be the result of fox and pine marten pelts being present in the coffin, or, as Williamson originally surmised, detached paws being used as amulets or charms.

The skeleton

The skeleton of Gristhorpe Man, though stained black, is both exceptionally complete and well preserved. This initially raised doubts about its integrity and whether some or all of it had been replaced at some stage in its history. Various analyses of Gristhorpe Man's cranial and post-cranial skeleton, the remarkably low lead content of his bones, his protein-rich childhood diet, and the radiocarbon dates for teeth and femur provide reassurance that the skeleton is of an Early Bronze Age, not Victorian, date. What could not be confirmed is whether the novel technique – immersion in animal glue – devised to conserve the 'rotten' skeleton ever took place. Was it just a figment of Williamson's mature imagination first documented nearly forty years after the fact, or indeed, an attempt to repudiate the originality of Professor Buckland's 'ingenious' idea (Montgomery and Gledhill this volume)? No trace of any sort of animal glue, whether derived from fish, cow, horse, or human collagen was found. If indeed it was treated in such a way, it has not left a recoverable trace in or on Gristhorpe Man's bones and does not appear to have affected either the radiocarbon dates or the stable isotope results. Whilst it is perhaps reassuring that such sustained exposure to gelatine-based glue, contrary to concerns at the start of the project, does not bear upon the results of scientific analyses, the inability to find it means Williamsn's 1872 account remains unverified. It is also, perhaps, a judicious reminder that despite the impressive suite of scientific instruments and novel techniques at our disposal, some of Gristhorpe Man's secrets remain unresolved, some 180 years after the burial's excavation. Whilst the trail-blazing members of the Scarborough Philosophical Society may have approved of our new discoveries, they could be forgiven a small, self-satisfied, smirk that some things have still eluded us and await the development of new methods or the application of a higher intellect to resolve.

The impact of the modern analyses of the Gristhorpe Man burial

In 1960, after describing the Gristhorpe burial, Paul Ashbee, the doyen of British Bronze Age barrow studies, commented: 'All this material is preserved in Scarborough Museum, but it is little known. The composite vessel, if still extant, is unique and the whole would amply repay study and definitive publication' (Ashbee 1960, 89). It has been over 50 years since Ashbee wrote those words and over 180 since the original excavation of the material. This volume follows his recommendation, but does so using methods and a synthetic treatment of human remains within their burial context that would not have been possible or even anticipated until very recently, such have been the advances made in archaeological science and bioarchaeology. In these concluding remarks, the editors place this unique discovery in the broader context of trends in the discipline and in research on the Bronze Age, in particular.

The ostentation of the Gristhorpe burial appears to have been matched by the physical attributes of the Man himself, features of which prompted Williamson and his 19th-century contemporaries to attribute high social standing to him (see Rowley-Conwy, this volume). His prominent stature and body mass suggest that he benefited from good nutrition and living conditions from birth. The absence of enamel hypoplastic lines in his teeth or other indicators of stressed growth support this assessment. The

high nitrogen isotope ratio obtained from his tooth and bone collagen indicates a substantial meat component to his diet that predisposed him to develop renal stones, a condition associated with older, well-fed males of higher socio-economic status today. It is likely that this pre-eminent social standing was built upon an active lifestyle that included strong lateralized use of his right upper limb, perhaps in raw material acquisition, manufacturing activities, and martial exploits that exposed him to several traumatic injuries in the form of healed fractures. In later life, he developed an intra-cranial tumour that may have caused physical and behavioural impairment, particularly of his dominant limb and those qualities that likely aided his rise to social prominence, such as the sophisticated use and comprehension of speech in social relations, physical strength and well co-ordinated, purposeful physical movements. The change he experienced in the later stages of his life course – from prowess and authority to aberrant behaviour and impairment – may have played a role in his elaborate burial, indicative of highly charged funerary rites, and in the retention of his memory in the succeeding generations.

References

Ashbee, P. (1960) The Bronze Age Round Barrow in Britain. London, Phoenix House Ltd.

Buckley, M. Melton, N. D. and Montgomery, J. (2013) Proteomics analysis of ancient food vessel stitching reveals >4,000–year-old milk protein. Rapid Communications in Mass Spectrometry 27, 1–8.

Elgee, H. W. and Elgee F. (1949) An Early Bronze Age burial in a boat-shaped wooden coffin from north-east Yorkshire. Proceedings of the Prehistoric Society 15, 87–106.

Gerloff, S. (1975) The Early Bronze Age daggers in Great Britain and a reconsideration of the Wessex Culure. Munich, Beck (Prähistorische Bronzefunde 6: 2).

Greenwell, W. (1890) Recent researches in barrows in Yorkshire, Wiltshire, Berkshire etc., Archaeologia 52, 1–72.

Hvass, L. (2000) Egtvedpigen. Viborg, Denmark, Sesam.

Jewitt, L. (1870) Grave-Mounds and their Contents: a Manual of Archæology. London, Groombridge.

Marsden, B. M. (1999) The Early Barrow Diggers. Stroud, Tempus.

O'Connor, S., Ali, E., Al-Sabah, S., Anwar, D., Bergström, E., Brown, K. A., Buckberry, J., Buckley, S., Collins, M., Denton, J., Dorling, K. M., Dowle, A., Duffey, P., Edwards, H. G. M., Faria, E. C., Gardner, P., Gledhill, A., Heaton, K., Heron, C., Janaway, R., Keely, B. J., King, D., Masinton, A., Penkman, K., Petzold, A., Pickering, M. D., Rumsby, M., Schutkowski, H., Shackleton, K. A., Thomas, J., Thomas-Oates, J., Usai, M.-R., Wilson, A. S. and O'Connor, T. (2011) Exceptional preservation of a prehistoric human brain from Heslington, Yorkshire, UK. Journal of Archaeological Science 38(7), 1641–1654.

Travis, W. (1836) *A Letter from William Travis, M. D., Scarborough, to Sir John V. B. Johnstone, Bart., M. P., President of the Scarborough Philosophical Society, communicating Discoveries made on the recent Opening of a British Tumulus in that Neighbourhood.* Scarborough, C.R. Todd.

Williamson, W. C. (1834) *Description of the Tumulus, lately opened at Gristhorpe, near Scarborough.* Scarborough, C.R. Todd.

Williamson, W. C. (1836) *Description of the Tumulus, lately lpened at Gristhorpe, near Scarborough,* second edition. Scarborough, C.R. Todd.

Williamson, W.C. (1872) *Description of the Tumulus opened at Gristhorpe, near Scarborough.* Scarborough. S.W. Theakston.

Williamson, W.C. (1896) *Reminiscences of a Yorkshire Naturalist.* London, George Redway.

INDEX